End-to-End Network Security
Defense-in-Depth

Omar Santos

Cisco Press

Cisco Press
800 East 96th Street
Indianapolis, Indiana 46240 USA

End-to-End Network Security Defense-in-Depth

Omar Santos

Copyright© 2008 Cisco Systems, Inc.

Published by:
Cisco Press
800 East 96th Street
Indianapolis, IN 46240 USA

All rights reserved. No part of this book may be reproduced or transmitted in any form or by any means, electronic or mechanical, including photocopying, recording, or by any information storage and retrieval system, without written permission from the publisher, except for the inclusion of brief quotations in a review.

Printed in the United States of America

First Printing   August 2007

Library of Congress Cataloging-in-Publication Data:

Santos, Omar.

  End-to-end network security : defense-in-depth / Omar Santos.

     p. cm.

  ISBN 978-1-58705-332-0 (pbk.)

  1. Computer networks—Security measures. I. Title.

  TK5105.59.S313 2007

  005.8—dc22

2007028287
ISBN-10: 1-58705-332-2
ISBN-13: 978-1-58705-332-0

Warning and Disclaimer

This book is designed to provide information about end-to-end network security. Every effort has been made to make this book as complete and as accurate as possible, but no warranty or fitness is implied.

The information is provided on an "as is" basis. The authors, Cisco Press, and Cisco Systems shall have neither liability nor responsibility to any person or entity with respect to any loss or damages arising from the information contained in this book or from the use of the discs or programs that may accompany it.

The opinions expressed in this book belong to the author and are not necessarily those of Cisco Systems.

Trademark Acknowledgments

All terms mentioned in this book that are known to be trademarks or service marks have been appropriately capitalized. Cisco Press or Cisco Systems, Inc. cannot attest to the accuracy of this information. Use of a term in this book should not be regarded as affecting the validity of any trademark or service mark.

Feedback Information

At Cisco Press, our goal is to create in-depth technical books of the highest quality and value. Each book is crafted with care and precision, undergoing rigorous development that involves the unique expertise of members from the professional technical community.

Readers' feedback is a natural continuation of this process. If you have any comments regarding how we could improve the quality of this book or otherwise alter it to better suit your needs, you can contact us through e-mail at feedback@ciscopress.com. Please make sure to include the book title and ISBN in your message.

We greatly appreciate your assistance.

Corporate and Government Sales

The publisher offers excellent discounts on this book when ordered in quantity for bulk purchases or special sales which may include electronic versions and/or custom covers and content particular to your business, training goals, marketing focus, and branding interests. For more information, please contact:

U.S. Corporate and Government Sales

1-800-382-3419

corpsales@pearsontechgroup.com

For sales outside the United States, please contact:

International Sales

international@pearsoned.com

Publisher	Paul Boger
Associate Publisher	Dave Dusthimer
Cisco Representative	Anthony Wolfenden
Cisco Press Program Manager	Jeff Brady
Executive Editor	Brett Bartow
Managing Editor	Patrick Kanouse
Development Editor	Betsey Henkels
Project Editor	Jennifer Gallant
Copy Editor	Karen A. Gill
Technical Editors	Pavan Reddy
	John Stuppi
Editorial Assistant	Vanessa Evans
Book and Cover Designer	Louisa Adair
Composition	ICC Macmillan Inc.
Indexer	Ken Johnson
Proofreader	Anne Poynter

Americas Headquarters	Asia Pacific Headquarters	Europe Headquarters
Cisco Systems, Inc.	Cisco Systems, Inc.	Cisco Systems International BV
170 West Tasman Drive	168 Robinson Road	Haarlerbergpark
San Jose, CA 95134-1706	#28-01 Capital Tower	Haarlerbergweg 13-19
USA	Singapore 068912	1101 CH Amsterdam
www.cisco.com	www.cisco.com	The Netherlands
Tel: 408 526-4000	Tel: +65 6317 7777	www-europe.cisco.com
800 553-NETS (6387)	Fax: +65 6317 7799	Tel: +31 0 800 020 0791
Fax: 408 527-0883		Fax: +31 0 20 357 1100

Cisco has more than 200 offices worldwide. Addresses, phone numbers, and fax numbers are listed on the Cisco Website at **www.cisco.com/go/offices.**

©2007 Cisco Systems, Inc. All rights reserved. CCVP, the Cisco logo, and the Cisco Square Bridge logo are trademarks of Cisco Systems, Inc.; Changing the Way We Work, Live, Play, and Learn is a service mark of Cisco Systems, Inc.; and Access Registrar, Aironet, BPX, Catalyst, CCDA, CCDP, CCIE, CCIP, CCNA, CCNP, CCSP, Cisco, the Cisco Certified Internetwork Expert logo, Cisco IOS, Cisco Press, Cisco Systems, Cisco Systems Capital, the Cisco Systems logo, Cisco Unity, Enterprise/Solver, EtherChannel, EtherFast, EtherSwitch, Fast Step, Follow Me Browsing, FormShare, GigaDrive, GigaStack, HomeLink, Internet Quotient, IOS, IP/TV, iQ Expertise, the iQ logo, iQ Net Readiness Scorecard, iQuick Study, LightStream, Linksys, MeetingPlace, MGX, Networking Academy, Network Registrar, Packet, PIX, ProConnect, RateMUX, ScriptShare, SlideCast, SMARTnet, StackWise, The Fastest Way to Increase Your Internet Quotient, and TransPath are registered trademarks of Cisco Systems, Inc. and/or its affiliates in the United States and certain other countries.

All other trademarks mentioned in this document or Website are the property of their respective owners. The use of the word partner does not imply a partnership relationship between Cisco and any other company. (0609R)

About the Author

Omar Santos is a senior network security engineer and Incident Manager within the Product Security Incident Response Team (PSIRT) at Cisco. Omar has designed, implemented, and supported numerous secure networks for Fortune 500 companies and the U.S. government, including the United States Marine Corps (USMC) and the U.S. Department of Defense (DoD). He is also the author of many Cisco online technical documents and configuration guidelines. Before his current role, Omar was a technical leader within the World Wide Security Practice and Cisco Technical Assistance Center (TAC), where he taught, led, and mentored many engineers within both organizations. He is an active member of the InfraGard organization. InfraGard is a cooperative undertaking that involves the Federal Bureau of Investigation and an association of businesses, academic institutions, state and local law enforcement agencies, and other participants. InfraGard is dedicated to increasing the security of the critical infrastructures of the United States of America.

Omar has also delivered numerous technical presentations to Cisco customers and partners, as well as executive presentations to CEOs, CIOs, and CSOs of many organizations. He is also the author of the Cisco Press books: *Cisco Network Admission Control,* Volume II: NAC Deployment and Troubleshooting, and *Cisco ASA: All-in-One Firewall, IPS, and VPN Adaptive Security Appliance.*

About the Technical Reviewers

Pavan Reddy, CCIE No. 4575, currently works as a consulting systems engineer for Cisco specializing ·
in network security. Pavan has been collaborating with customers and partners on the design and
implementation of large-scale enterprise and service provider security architectures for nearly ten years.
Before joining Cisco, Pavan worked as a network security engineer in the construction and financial
industries. Pavan also holds a bachelor of science degree in computer engineering from Carnegie Mellon.

John Stuppi, CCIE No. 11154, is a network consulting engineer for Cisco. John is responsible for
creating, testing, and communicating effective techniques using Cisco product capabilities to
provide identification and mitigation options to Cisco customers who are facing current or expected
security threats. John also advises Cisco customers on incident readiness and response methodologies
and assists them in DoS and worm mitigation and preparedness. John is a CCIE and a CISSP, and he
holds an Information Systems Security (INFOSEC) Professional Certification. In addition, John has a
BSEE from Lehigh University and an MBA from Rutgers University. John lives in Ocean Township,
New Jersey with his wife Diane and his two wonderful children, Thomas and Allison.

Dedications

I would like to dedicate this book to my lovely wife, Jeannette, and my two beautiful children, Hannah and Derek, who have inspired and supported me throughout the development of this book.

I also dedicate this book to my parents, Jose and Generosa. Without their knowledge, wisdom, and guidance, I would not have the goals that I strive to achieve today.

—Omar

Acknowledgments

I would like to acknowledge the technical editors, Pavan Reddy and John Stuppi. Their superb technical skills and input are what make this manuscript a success. Pavan has been a technical leader and advisor within Cisco for several years. He has led many projects for Fortune 500 enterprises and service providers. He was one of the key developers of the Cisco Operational Process Model (COPM). John has also led many implementations and designs for Cisco customers. His experience in worldwide threat intelligence provides a unique breadth of knowledge and value added.

Many thanks to my management team, who have always supported me during the development of this book.

I am extremely thankful to the Cisco Press team, especially Brett Bartow, Andrew Cupp, Betsey Henkels, and Jennifer Gallant for their patience and continuous support.

Finally, I would like to acknowledge the great minds within the Cisco Security Technology Group (STG), Advanced Services, and Technical Support organizations.

This Book Is Safari Enabled

The Safari® Enabled icon on the cover of your favorite technology book means the book is available through Safari Bookshelf. When you buy this book, you get free access to the online edition for 45 days.

Safari Bookshelf is an electronic reference library that lets you easily search thousands of technical books, find code samples, download chapters, and access technical information whenever and wherever you need it.

To gain 45-day Safari Enabled access to this book

- Go to http://www.ciscopress.com/safarienabled.
- Complete the brief registration form.
- Enter the coupon code UWF5-THKG-8X8Q-YHGK-QDVZ.

If you have difficulty registering on Safari Bookshelf or accessing the online edition, please e-mail customer-service@safaribooksonline.com.

Contents at a Glance

Contents

Command Syntax Conventions

The conventions used to present command syntax in this book are the same conventions used in the *IOS Command Reference*. The *Command Reference* describes these conventions as follows:

- **Boldface** indicates commands and keywords that are entered literally as shown. In actual configuration examples and output (not general command syntax), boldface indicates commands that are manually input by the user (such as a **show** command).

- *Italics* indicate arguments for which you supply actual values.

- Vertical bars (|) separate alternative, mutually exclusive elements.

- Square brackets [ ] indicate optional elements.

- Braces { } indicate a required choice.

- Braces within brackets [{ }] indicate a required choice within an optional element.

Foreword

Defense-in-Depth is a phrase that is often used and equally misunderstood. This book gives an excellent overview of what this really means and, more importantly, how to apply certain principles to develop appropriate risk mitigation strategies.

After you have assimilated the content of this book, you will have a solid understanding of several aspects of security. The author begins with an overview of the basics then provides comprehensive methodologies for preparing for and reacting to security incidents and, finally, illustrates a unique framework for managing through the lifecycle of security known as SAVE. Also provided are various Defense-in-Depth strategies covering the most current advanced technologies utilized for protecting information assets today. Equally as important are the case studies which provide the reader with real-world examples of how to put these tools, processes, methodologies, and frameworks to use.

Many reference documents and lengthy periodicals delve into the world of information security. However, few can capture the essence of this discipline and also provide a high-level, demystified understanding of information security and the technical underpinning required to achieve success.

Within these pages, you will find many practical tools both process related and technology related that you can draw on to improve your risk mitigation strategies. The most effective security programs combine attention to both deeply technical issues and business process issues. The author clearly demonstrates that he grasps the inherent challenges posed by combining these disparate approaches, and he conveys them in an approachable style. You will find yourself not only gaining valuable insight from *End-to-End Network Security,* but also returning to its pages to ensure you are on target in your endeavors.

We have seen dramatic increases in the type and nature of threats to our information assets. The challenge we face is to fully understand the compensating controls and techniques that can be deployed to offset these threats and do so in a way that is consistent with the business processes and growth strategies of the businesses and government we are trying to protect. This book strikes that delicate balance, and you will find it an invaluable element of your protection initiatives far into the future.

Bruce Murphy
Vice President
World Wide Security Practice
Cisco

Introduction

The network security lifecycle requires specialized support and a commitment to best practice standards. In this book, you will learn best practices that draw upon disciplined processes, frameworks, expert advice, and proven technologies that will help you protect your infrastructure and organization. You will learn end-to-end security best practices, from strategy development to operations and optimization.

This book covers the six-step methodology of incident readiness and response. You must take a proactive approach to security; an approach that starts with assessment to identify and categorize your risks. In addition, you need to understand the network security technical details in relation to security policy and incident response procedures. This book covers numerous best practices that will help you orchestrate a long-term strategy for your organization.

Who Should Read This Book?

The answer to this question is simple—everyone. The principles and best practices covered in this book apply to every organization. Anyone interested in network security should become familiar with the information included in this book—from network and security engineers to management and executives. This book covers not only numerous technical topics and scenarios, but also covers a wide range of operational best practices in addition to risk analysis and threat modeling.

How This Book Is Organized

Part I of this book includes Chapter 1 which covers an introduction to security technologies and products. In Part II, which encompasses Chapters 2 through 7, you will learn the six-step methodology of incident readiness and response. Part III includes Chapters 8 through 11 which cover strategies used to protect wireless networks, IP telephony implementations, data centers, and IPv6 networks. Real-life case studies are covered in Part IV which contains Chapter 12.

The following is a chapter-by-chapter summary of the contents of the book.

Part I, "Introduction to Network Security Solutions," includes:

- **Chapter 1, "Overview of Network Security Technologies."** This chapter covers an introduction to security technologies and products. It starts with an overview of how to place firewalls to provide perimeter security and network segmentation while enforcing configured policies. It then dives into virtual private network (VPN) technologies and protocols—including IP Security (IPsec) and Secure Socket Layer (SSL). In addition, this chapter covers different technologies such as intrusion detection systems (IDS), intrusion protection systems (IPS), anomaly detection systems, and network telemetry features that can help you identify and classify security threats. Authentication, authorization, and accounting (AAA) offers different solutions that provide access control to network resources. This chapter introduces AAA and identity management concepts. Furthermore, it includes an overview of the Cisco Network Admission Control solutions that are used to enforce security policy compliance on all devices that are designed to access network computing resources, thereby limiting damage from emerging security threats. Routing techniques can be used as security tools. This chapter provides examples of different routing techniques, such as Remotely Triggered Black Hole (RTBH) routing and sinkholes that are used to increase the security of the network and to react to new threats.

Part II, "Security Lifecycle: Frameworks and Methodologies," includes:

- **Chapter 2, "Preparation Phase."** This chapter covers numerous best practices on how to better prepare your network infrastructure, security policies, procedures, and organization as a whole against security threats and vulnerabilities. This is one of the most important chapters of this book. It starts by teaching you risk analysis and threat modeling techniques. You will also learn guidelines on how to create strong security policies and how to create Computer Security Incident Response Teams (CSIRT). Topics such as security intelligence and social engineering are also covered in this chapter. You will learn numerous tips on how to increase the security of your network infrastructure devices using several best practices to protect the control, management, and data plane. Guidelines on how to better secure end-user systems and servers are also covered in this chapter.

- **Chapter 3, "Identifying and Classifying Security Threats."** This chapter covers the next two phases of the six-step methodology for incident response—identification and classification of security threats. You will learn how important it is to have complete network visibility and control to successfully identify and classify security threats in a timely fashion. This chapter covers different technologies and tools such as Cisco NetFlow, SYSLOG, SNMP, and others which can be used to obtain information from your network and detect anomalies that might be malicious activity. You will also learn how to use event correlation tools such as CS-MARS and open source monitoring systems in conjunction with NetFlow to allow you to gain better visibility into your network. In addition, this chapter covers details about anomaly detection, IDS, and IPS solutions by providing tips on IPS/IDS tuning and the new anomaly detection features supported by Cisco IPS.

- **Chapter 4, "Traceback."** Tracing back the source of attacks, infected hosts in worm outbreaks, or any other security incident can be overwhelming for many network administrators and security professionals. Attackers can use hundreds or thousands of botnets or zombies that can greatly complicate traceback and hinder mitigation once traceback succeeds. This chapter covers several techniques that can help you successfully trace back the sources of such threats. It covers techniques used by service providers and enterprises.

- **Chapter 5, "Reacting to Security Incidents."** This chapter covers several techniques that you can use when reacting to security incidents. It is extremely important for organizations to have adequate incident handling policies and procedures in place. This chapter shows you several tips on how to make sure that your policies and procedures are adequate to successfully respond to security incidents. You will also learn general information about different laws and practices to use when investigating security incidents and computer crimes. In addition, this chapter includes details about different tools you can use to mitigate attacks and other security incidents with your network infrastructure components including several basic computer forensics topics.

- **Chapter 6, "Postmortem and Improvement."** It is highly recommended that you complete a postmortem after responding to security incidents. This postmortem should identify the strengths and weaknesses of the incident response effort. With this analysis, you can identify weaknesses in systems, infrastructure defenses, or policies that allowed the incident to take place. In addition, a postmortem helps you identify problems with communication channels, interfaces, and procedures that hampered the efficient resolution of the reported problem. This chapter covers several tips on creating postmortems and executing post-incident tasks. It includes guidelines for collecting post-incident data, documenting lessons learned during the incident, and building action plans to close gaps that are identified.

- **Chapter 7, "Proactive Security Framework."** This chapter covers the Security Assessment, Validation, and Execution (SAVE) framework. SAVE, formerly known as the Cisco Operational Process Model (COPM), is a framework initially developed for service providers, but its practices are applied to enterprises and organizations. This chapter provides examples of techniques and practices that can allow you to gain and maintain visibility and control over the network during normal operations or during the course of a security incident or an anomaly in the network.

Part III, "Defense-In-Depth Applied," includes:

- **Chapter 8, "Wireless Security."** When designing and deploying wireless networks, it is important to consider the unique security challenges that can be inherited. This chapter includes best practices to use when deploying wireless networks. You will learn different types of authentication mechanisms, including 802.1x, which is used to enhance the security of wireless networks. In addition, this chapter includes an overview of the Lightweight Access Point Protocol (LWAPP), Cisco Location Services, Management Frame Protection (MFP), and other wireless features to consider when designing security within your wireless infrastructure. The chapter concludes with step-by-step configuration examples of the integration of IPS and the Cisco NAC Appliance on the Cisco Unified Wireless Network solution.

- **Chapter 9, "IP Telephony Security."** IP Telephony solutions are being deployed at a fast rate in many organizations. The cost savings introduced with Voice over IP (VoIP) solutions are significant. On the other hand, these benefits can be heavily impacted if you do not have the appropriate security mechanisms in place. In this chapter, you will learn several techniques used to increase the security of IP Telephony networks. This chapter covers how to secure different IP telephony components such as the Cisco Unified CallManager, Cisco Unified CME, Cisco Unity, Cisco Unity Express, and Cisco Unified Personal Assistant. In addition, it covers several ways to protect against voice eavesdropping attacks.

- **Chapter 10, "Data Center Security."** In this chapter, you will learn the security strategies, technologies, and products designed to protect against attacks on your data center from both inside and outside the enterprise. Integrated security technologies, including secure connectivity, threat defense, and trust and identity management systems, create a Defense-in-Depth strategy to protect each application and server environment across the consolidated IP, storage, and interconnect data center networking infrastructure. Configuration examples of different solutions such as the Firewall Services Module (FWSM), the Intrusion Detection/Prevention System Module (IDSM), and the Application Control Engine (ACE) module for the Catalyst 6500 series switches are covered in detail. This chapter also covers the use of Layer 2 to Layer 7 security features in infrastructure components to successfully identify, classify, and mitigate security threats within the data center.

- **Chapter 11, "IPv6 Security."** This chapter covers an introduction to security topics in Internet Protocol Version 6 (IPv6) implementations. Although it is assumed that you already have a rudimentary understanding of IPv6, this chapter covers basic IPv6 topics. This chapter details the most common IPv6 security threats and the best practices that many organizations adopt to protect their IPv6 infrastructure. IPsec in IPv6 is also covered, with guidelines on how to configure Cisco IOS routers to terminate IPsec in IPv6 networks.

Part IV, "Case Studies," includes:

- **Chapter 12, "Case Studies."** This chapter covers several case studies representing small, medium-sized, and large-scale enterprises. Detailed example configurations and implementation strategies of best practices learned in earlier chapters are covered to enhance learning.

Introduction to Network Security Solutions

This chapter covers the following topics:

- Firewalls
- Virtual Private Networks (VPN)
- Intrusion Detection Systems (IDS) and Intrusion Prevention Systems (IPS)
- Anomaly Detection Systems
- Authentication, Authorization, and Accounting (AAA) and Identity Management
- Network Admission Control
- Routing Mechanisms as Security Tools

CHAPTER 1

Overview of Network Security Technologies

Technology can be considered your best friend. Nowadays, you can do almost everything over networked systems or the Internet—from simple tasks, such as booking a flight reservation, to a multibillion dollar wire transfer between two large financial organizations. You cannot take security for granted! An attacker can steal credit card information from your online travel reservation or launch a denial of service (DoS) attack to disrupt a wire transfer. It is extremely important to learn new techniques and methodologies to combat electronic penetrations, data thefts, and cyberattacks on critical information systems.

Organizations and individuals must educate themselves to be able to select the appropriate security technologies, tools, and methodologies to prevent and mitigate any security threats before they impact the business. This chapter describes the most common and widely used security products and technologies. These products and technologies include the following:

- Firewalls
- Virtual private networks (VPN)
- Intrusion detection systems (IDS) and intrusion prevention systems (IPS)
- Anomaly detection systems
- Authentication, authorization, and accounting (AAA) and identity management
- Network admission control

NOTE   This chapter introduces a range of security technologies and products. Becoming familiar with these topics will help you understand the methodologies and solutions presented in the rest of this book.

Firewalls

If you are a network administrator, security engineer, manager, or simply an end user, you have probably heard of, used, or configured a firewall. Historically, firewalls have been used as barriers to keep intruders and destructive forces away from your network. Today, firewalls and security appliances have many robust and sophisticated features beyond the traditional access control rules and policies. As you read through this section, you will learn more about the different types of firewalls and how they work, the threats they can protect you from, and their limitations.

TIP A detailed understanding of how firewalls and their related technologies work is extremely important for all network security professionals. This knowledge will help them to configure and manage the security of their networks accurately and effectively.

Several network firewall solutions offer user and application policy enforcement that provides multivector attack protection for different types of security threats. They often provide logging capabilities that allow the security administrators to identify, investigate, validate, and mitigate such threats. In addition, several software applications can run on a system to protect only that host. These types of applications are known as personal firewalls. This section includes an overview of both network and personal firewalls and their related technologies.

Network Firewalls

Network firewalls come in many flavors and colors. They range from simple packet filters to sophisticated solutions that include stateful and deep-packet inspection features. For example, you can configure simple access control lists (ACL) on a router to prevent an attacker from accessing corporate resources. Figure 1-1 illustrates how to configure a router to block access from unauthorized hosts and users on the Internet.

Figure 1-1 *Basic Packet Filter—Router with Basic ACLs*

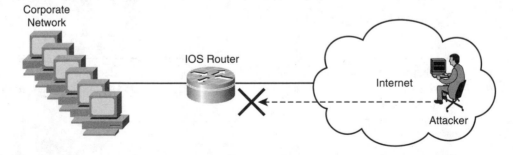

In Figure 1-1, the router is configured to deny all incoming traffic from Internet hosts to its protected network (the corporate network). In this example, an attacker tries to scan the protected network from the Internet, and the router drops all traffic.

NOTE   The use and configuration of different types of ACLs is covered in Chapter 2, "Preparation Phase."

The purpose of packet filters is to control access to specific network segments by defining which traffic can pass through to them. Packet filters usually inspect incoming traffic at the transport layer of the Open Systems Interconnection (OSI) model. For example, packet filters can analyze TCP or UDP packets and judge them against a set of predetermined rules called ACLs. They inspect the following elements within a packet:

- Source address
- Destination address
- Source port
- Destination port
- Protocol

Basic packet filters commonly do not inspect additional Layer 3 and Layer 4 fields such as sequence numbers, TCP control flags, and TCP acknowledgement (ACK) fields.

NOTE   The previous example illustrates a router configured with only a basic ACL. The Cisco IOS firewall solution provides enterprises and small/medium businesses sophisticated features beyond the traditional packet filters.

Network Address Translation (NAT)

Firewalls can also provide Network Address Translation (NAT) services. They can translate the IP addresses of protected hosts to a publicly routable address.

NOTE   Firewalls often use NAT; however, other devices such as routers and wireless access points provide support for NAT.

Figure 1-2 shows how a firewall translates the IP address of an internal host (192.168.1.100) to a public IP address (209.165.200.225) when the host attempts to access Cisco.com.

Figure 1-2 *Basic NAT*

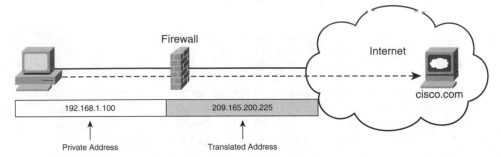

NAT enables organizations to use any IP address space as the internal network. A best practice is to use the address spaces that are reserved for private use (see RFC 1918, "Address Allocation for Private Internets"). Table 1-1 lists the private address ranges specified in RFC 1918.

Table 1-1 *Private Address Ranges Specified in RFC 1918*

IP Address Range	Network Mask
10.0.0.0 to 10.255.255.255	10.0.0.0/8
172.16.0.0 to 172.31.255.255	172.16.0.0/12
192.168.0.0 to 192.168.255.255	192.168.0.0/16

NAT techniques come in various types. The most common are Port Address Translation (PAT) and Static NAT. PAT allows many devices on a network segment to be translated to one IP address by inspecting the Layer 4 information on the packet. Figure 1-3 illustrates how three different machines on the corporate network are translated to a single public address.

In Figure 1-3, the host with IP address 192.168.1.100 attempts to access the web server with IP address 209.165.200.230. The firewall translates the internal address to 209.165.200.226 using the source TCP port 1024 and mapping it to TCP port 1234. Notice that the destination port remains the same (port 80) .

Figure 1-3   *PAT*

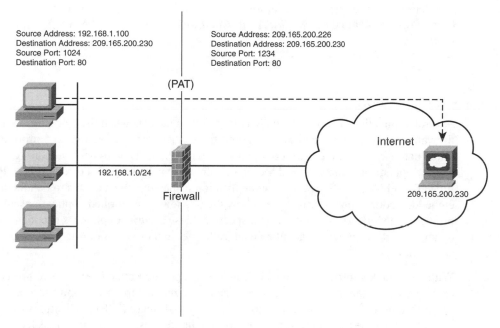

Source Address: 192.168.1.100
Destination Address: 209.165.200.230
Source Port: 1024
Destination Port: 80

Source Address: 209.165.200.226
Destination Address: 209.165.200.230
Source Port: 1234
Destination Port: 80

(PAT)

Internet

192.168.1.0/24

Firewall

209.165.200.230

Stateful Firewalls

Stateful inspection firewalls track every connection passing through their interfaces by examining not only the packet header contents but also the application layer information within the payload. This is done to find out more about the transaction than just the source and destination addresses and ports. Typically, a stateful firewall monitors the state of the connection and maintains a table with the Layer 3 and Layer 4 information. More sophisticated firewalls perform upper-layer protocol analysis, also known as *deep-packet inspection*, which is discussed later in this chapter. The state of the connection details whether such connection has been established, closed, reset, or is being negotiated. These mechanisms offer protection for different types of network attacks.

Cisco IOS firewall, Cisco Adaptive Security Appliances (ASA), Cisco PIX firewalls, and the Cisco Firewall Services Module (FWSM) for the Cisco Catalyst 6500 series switches are examples of stateful firewalls. They also have other rich features such as deep packet inspection.

NOTE For detailed deployment, configuration, and troubleshooting information, see the Cisco Press book titled *Cisco ASA: All-in-One Firewall, IPS, and VPN Adaptive Security Appliance*.

Deep Packet Inspection

Several applications require special handling of data packets when they pass through firewalls. These include applications and protocols that embed IP addressing information in the data payload of the packet or open secondary channels on dynamically assigned ports. Sophisticated firewalls and security appliances such as the Cisco ASA, Cisco PIX firewall, and Cisco IOS firewall offer application inspection mechanisms to handle the embedded addressing information to allow the previously mentioned applications and protocols to work. Using application inspection, these security appliances can identify the dynamic port assignments and allow data exchange on these ports during a specific connection.

With deep packet inspection, firewalls can look at specific Layer 7 payloads to protect against security threats. For example, you can configure a Cisco ASA or a Cisco PIX firewall running version 7.0 or later to not allow peer-to-peer (P2P) applications to be transferred over HTTP tunnels. You can also configure these devices to deny specific FTP commands, HTTP content types, and other application protocols.

NOTE The Cisco ASA and Cisco PIX firewall running version 7.0 or later provide a Modular Policy Framework (MPF) that allows a consistent and flexible way to configure application inspection and other features in a manner similar to the Cisco IOS Software Modular quality of service (QoS) command-line interface (CLI).

Demilitarized Zones

Numerous firewalls can configure network segments (or zones), usually called *demilitarized zones* (DMZ). These zones provide security to the systems that reside within them with different security levels and policies between them. DMZs have a couple of purposes: as segments on which a web server farm resides or as extranet connections to a business partner. Figure 1-4 shows a firewall (a Cisco ASA in this case) with two DMZs.

Figure 1-4   *DMZ Example*

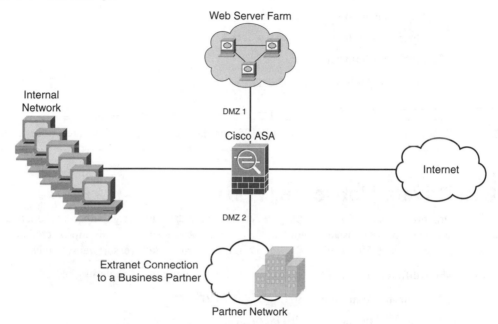

In Figure 1-4, DMZ 1 hosts web servers that are accessible by internal and Internet hosts. The Cisco ASA controls access from an extranet business partner connection on DMZ 2.

NOTE   In large organizations, you can deploy multiple firewalls in different segments and DMZs.

Personal Firewalls

Personal firewalls are popular software applications that you can install on end-user machines or servers to protect them from external security threats and intrusions. The term *personal firewall typically* applies to basic software that can control Layer 3 and Layer 4 access to client machines. Today, sophisticated software is available that not only provides basic personal firewall features but also protects the system based on the behavior of the applications installed on such systems. An example of this type of software is the Cisco Security Agent (CSA). CSA provides several features that offer more robust security than a traditional personal firewall. The following are CSA-rich security features:

- Host intrusion prevention
- Protection against spyware
- Protection against buffer overflow attacks

- Distributed host firewall features
- Malicious mobile code protection
- Operating system integrity assurance
- Application inventory
- Extensive audit and logging capabilities

NOTE   Host intrusion prevention systems (HIPS) are detailed and described later in this chapter.

Virtual Private Networks (VPN)

Organizations of all sizes deploy VPNs to provide data integrity, authentication, and data encryption to assure confidentiality of the packets sent over an unprotected network or the Internet. VPNs are designed to avoid the cost of unnecessary leased lines.

Many different protocols are used for VPN implementations, including these:

- Point-to-Point Tunneling Protocol (PPTP)
- Layer 2 Forwarding (L2F) Protocol
- Layer 2 Tunneling Protocol (L2TP)
- Generic Routing Encapsulation (GRE) Protocol
- Multiprotocol Label Switching (MPLS) VPN
- Internet Protocol Security (IPsec)
- Secure Socket Layer (SSL)

NOTE   PPTP, L2F, L2TP, GRE, and MPLS VPNs do not provide data integrity, authentication, and data encryption. On the other hand, you can combine L2TP, GRE, and MPLS with IPsec to provide these benefits. Many organizations use IPsec as their preferred protocol because it supports all three features described earlier (data integrity, authentication, and data encryption).

VPN implementations can be categorized into two distinct groups:

- **Site-to-site VPNs:** Allow organizations to establish VPN tunnels between two or more sites so that they can communicate over a shared medium such as the Internet. Many organizations use IPsec, GRE, and MPLS VPN as site-to-site VPN protocols.

- **Remote-access VPNs:** Allow users to work from remote locations such as their homes, hotels, and other premises as if they were directly connected to their corporate network.

Figure 1-5 illustrates a site-to-site IPsec tunnel between two sites (corporate headquarters and a branch office), as well as a remote access VPN from a telecommuter working from home.

Figure 1-5   *Site-to-Site and Remote Access VPN Example*

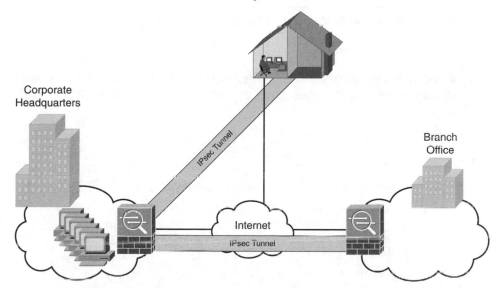

Cisco ASAs are used in the example shown in Figure 1-5. The Cisco ASA integrates many IPsec and SSL VPN features with firewall capabilities. Other Cisco products that support VPN features are as follows:

- Cisco VPN 3000 series concentrators
- Cisco IOS routers
- Cisco PIX firewalls
- Cisco Catalyst 6500 switches and Cisco 7600 series routers WebVPN services module
- Cisco 7600 series/Catalyst 6500 series IPsec VPN shared port adapter

---

NOTE   The use and deployment of these devices are described in Chapter 2. You can also find information about these devices at the Cisco website at cisco.com/go/security.

Technical Overview of IPsec

IPsec uses the Internet Key Exchange (IKE) Protocol to negotiate and establish secured site-to-site or remote access VPN tunnels. IKE is a framework provided by the Internet Security Association and Key Management Protocol (ISAKMP) and parts of two other key management protocols, namely Oakley and Secure Key Exchange Mechanism (SKEME).

NOTE	IKE is defined in RFC 2409, "The Internet Key Exchange."

ISAKMP has two phases. Phase 1 is used to create a secure bidirectional communication channel between the IPsec peers. This channel is known as the ISAKMP Security Association (SA).

Phase 1

Within Phase 1 negotiation, several attributes are exchanged, including the following:

- Encryption algorithms
- Hashing algorithms
- Diffie-Hellman groups
- Authentication method
- Vendor-specific attributes

The following are the typical encryption algorithms:

- **Data Encryption Standard (DES):** 64 bits long
- **Triple DES (3DES):** 168 bits long
- **Advanced Encryption Standard (AES):** 128 bits long
- **AES 192:** 192 bits long
- **AES 256:** 256 bits long

Hashing algorithms include these:

- Secure Hash Algorithm (SHA)
- Message digest algorithm 5 (MD5)

The common authentication methods are preshared keys (where the peers agree on a shared secret) and digital certificates with the use of Public Key Infrastructure (PKI).

NOTE   Typically, small and medium-sized organizations use preshared keys as their authentication mechanism. Several large organizations use digital certificates for scalability, for centralized management, and for the use of additional security mechanisms.

You can establish a Phase 1 SA in two ways:

- Main mode
- Aggressive mode

In main mode, the IPsec peers complete a six-packet exchange in three round-trips to negotiate the ISAKMP SA, whereas aggressive mode completes the SA negotiation in three packet exchanges. Main mode provides identity protection if preshared keys are used. Aggressive mode only provides identity protection if digital certificates are used.

NOTE   Cisco products that support IPsec typically use main mode for site-to-site tunnels and aggressive mode for remote-access VPN tunnels. This is the default behavior when preshared keys are used as the authentication method.

Figure 1-6 illustrates the six-packet exchange in main mode negotiation.

Figure 1-6 *Main Mode Negotiation*

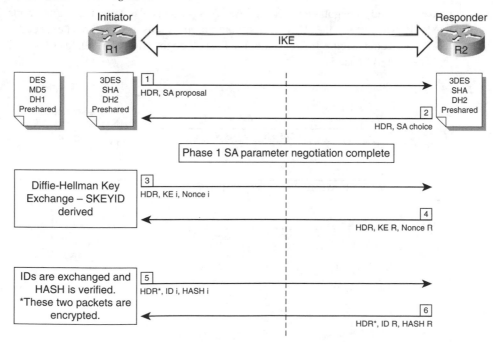

In Figure 1-6, two Cisco IOS Software routers are configured to terminate a site-to-site VPN tunnel between them. The router labeled as R1 is the initiator, and R2 is the responder. The following are the steps illustrated in Figure 1-6.

Step 1 R1 (the initiator) has two ISAKMP proposals configured. In the first packet, R1 sends its configured proposals to R2.

Step 2 R2 evaluates the received proposal. Because it has a proposal that matches the offer of the initiator, R2 sends the accepted proposal back to R1 in the second packet.

Step 3 Diffie-Hellman exchange and calculation is started. R1 sends the Key Exchange (KE) payload and a randomly generated value called a *nonce*.

Step 4 R2 receives the information and reverses the equation using the proposed Diffie-Hellman group/exchange to generate the SKEYID.

Step 5 R1 sends its identity information. The fifth packet is encrypted with the keying material derived from the SKEYID. The asterisk in Figure 1-6 is used to illustrate that this packet is encrypted.

Step 6 R2 validates the identity of R1, and R2 sends the identity information of R1. This packet is also encrypted.

Phase 2

Phase 2 is used to negotiate the IPsec SAs. This phase is also known as quick mode. The ISAKMP SA protects the IPsec SAs, because all payloads are encrypted except the ISAKMP header. Figure 1-7 illustrates the Phase 2 negotiation between the two routers that just completed Phase 1.

Figure 1-7 *Phase 2 Negotiation*

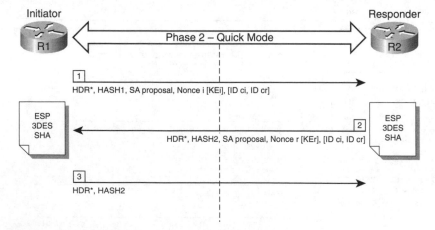

The following are the steps illustrated in Figure 1-7.

Step 1 R1 sends the identity information, IPsec SA proposal, nonce payload, and (optional) KE payload if Perfect Forward Secrecy (PFS) is used. PFS is used to provide additional Diffie-Hellman calculations.

Step 2 R2 evaluates the received proposal against its configured proposal and sends the accepted proposal back to R1 along with its identity information, nonce payload, and the optional KE payload.

Step 3 R1 evaluates the R2 proposal and sends a confirmation that the IPsec SAs have been successfully negotiated. This starts the data encryption process.

IPsec uses two different protocols to encapsulate the data over a VPN tunnel:

- **Encapsulation Security Payload (ESP):** IP Protocol 50
- **Authentication Header (AH):** IP Protocol 51

NOTE   ESP is defined in RFC 2406, "IP Encapsulating Security Payload (ESP)," and AH is defined in RFC 2402, "IP Authentication Header."

IPsec can use two modes with either AH or ESP:

- **Transport mode:** Protects upper-layer protocols, such as User Datagram Protocol (UDP) and TCP
- **Tunnel mode:** Protects the entire IP packet

Transport mode is used to encrypt and authenticate the data packets between the peers. A typical example of this is the use of GRE over an IPsec tunnel. Tunnel mode is used to encrypt and authenticate the IP packets when they are originated by the hosts connected behind the VPN device. Tunnel mode adds an additional IP header to the packet, as illustrated in Figure 1-8.

Figure 1-8 demonstrates the major difference between transport and tunnel mode. It includes an example of an IP packet encapsulated in GRE and the difference when it is encrypted in transport mode and tunnel mode.

NOTE   Tunnel mode is the default mode in Cisco IPsec devices.

Figure 1-8 *Tunnel and Transport Mode Example*

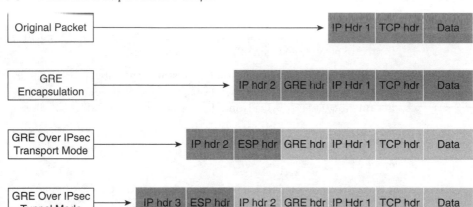

SSL VPNs

SSL-based VPNs are in high demand today. SSL is a matured protocol that has been in existence since the early 1990s. SSL is also referred to as Transport Layer Security (TLS). The Internet Engineering Task Force (IETF) created TLS to consolidate the different SSL vendor versions into a common and open standard.

One of the most popular features of SSL VPN is the ability to launch a browser like Microsoft Internet Explorer and Firefox and simply connect to the address of the VPN device. In most implementations, a clientless solution is possible. Users can access corporate intranet sites, portals, and e-mail from almost anywhere (even from an airport kiosk). Because most people allow SSL (TCP port 443) over their firewalls, it is unnecessary to open additional ports.

For more elaborate access to corporate resources, a lite-SSL client can be installed on a user machine. Cisco supports both clientless SSL VPN (WebVPN) and a lite-client. The SSL VPN Client (SVC) gives remote users the benefits of an IPsec VPN client without the need for network administrators to install and configure IPsec VPN clients on remote computers. The SVC uses the SSL encryption that is already present on the remote computer to authenticate to the VPN device. Cisco supports SSL VPN on the following products:

- Cisco ASA
- Cisco VPN 3000 series concentrators
- Cisco IOS routers
- Cisco WebVPN Services Module

Intrusion Detection Systems (IDS) and Intrusion Prevention Systems (IPS)

This section includes an overview of intrusion detection systems (IDS) and intrusion prevention systems (IPS). IDSs are devices that detect (in promiscuous mode) attempts from an attacker to gain unauthorized access to a network or a host to create performance degradation or to steal information. They also detect distributed denial of service (DDoS) attacks, worms, and virus outbreaks. IPS devices are capable of detecting all these security threats; however, they are also able to drop noncompliant packets inline. Packets that do not comply with security policies will not pass to the protected network. This is the major difference between IDS and IPS systems. Figure 1-9 shows how an IDS device is configured to promiscuously detect security threats.

Figure 1-9   *IDS Example*

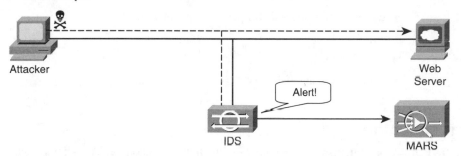

In Figure 1-9, an attacker sends a malicious packet to a web server. The IDS device analyzes the packet and sends an alert to a monitoring system (CS-MARS in this example). The malicious packet makes it to the web server. In contrast, Figure 1-10 shows how an IPS device is placed inline and drops the noncompliant packet, while sending an alert to the monitoring system.

Figure 1-10   *IPS Example*

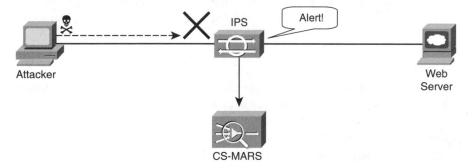

Two different types of IPS exist:

- Network-based (NIPS)
- Host-based (HIPS)

NOTE   Examples of NIPSs are the Cisco IPS 4200 sensors, the Catalyst 6500 IPS Module, and the Cisco ASA with the Advanced Inspection and Prevention Security Services Module (AIP-SSM). An example of a host-based IPS is CSA. More details and recommendation on how to protect your network with IPS devices are covered in Chapter 2.

Network-based IDS and IPS use several detection methodologies, such as the following:

- Pattern matching and stateful pattern-matching recognition
- Protocol analysis
- Heuristic-based analysis
- Anomaly-based analysis

Pattern Matching

Pattern matching is a methodology in which the intrusion detection device searches for a fixed sequence of bytes within the packets traversing the network. Generally, the pattern is aligned with a packet that is related to a respective service or, in particular, associated with a source and destination port. This approach reduces the amount of inspection made on every packet. However, it is limited to services and protocols that are associated with well-defined ports. Protocols that do not use Layer 4 port information are not categorized. This tactic uses the concept of signatures. A *signature* is a set of conditions that point out some type of intrusion occurrence. For example, if a specific TCP packet has a destination port of 1234, and its payload contains the string "ff11ff22," an alert is triggered to detect such a string. Alternatively, the signature might include an explicit starting point and endpoint for inspection within the specific packet.

TIP   One of the main disadvantages of pattern matching is that it can lead to a considerably high rate of false positives. False positives are alerts that do not represent a genuine malicious activity. In contrast, any alterations to the attack can lead to overlooked events of real attacks, which are normally referred to as false negatives.

A more refined method was created to address some of these limitations. This methodology is called *stateful pattern-matching recognition*, which dictates that systems performing this type of signature analysis must consider the chronological order of packets in a TCP stream. In particular, they should judge and maintain a stateful inspection of such packets and flows.

Protocol Analysis

Protocol analysis (or protocol decode-base signatures) is referred to as the extension to stateful pattern recognition. A network-based IDS accomplishes protocol analysis by decoding all protocol or client-server conversations. The NIDS identifies the elements of the protocol and analyzes them while looking for an infringement. Some intrusion detection systems look at explicit protocol fields within the inspected packets. Others require more sophisticated techniques, such as examination of the length of a field within the protocol or the number of arguments. For example, in Simple Mail Transfer Protocol (SMTP), the device may look at specific commands and fields such as **HELO, MAIL, RCPT, DATA, RSET, NOOP,** and **QUIT**. This technique diminishes the possibility of encountering false positives if the protocol being analyzed is properly defined and enforced. On the other hand, the system can alert numerous false positives if the protocol definition is ambiguous or tolerates flexibility in its implementation.

Heuristic-Based Analysis

A different approach to network intrusion detection is to perform *heuristic-based analysis*. Heuristic scanning uses algorithmic logic from statistical analysis of the traffic passing through the network. Its tasks are CPU and resource intensive. This is an important consideration while planning your deployment. Heuristic-based algorithms may require fine tuning to adapt to network traffic and minimize the possibility of false positives. For example, a system signature can generate an alarm if a range of ports is scanned on a particular host or network. The signature can also be orchestrated to restrict itself from specific types of packets (for example, TCP SYN packets).

Anomaly-Based Analysis

A different practice keeps track of network traffic that diverges from "normal" behavioral patterns. This practice is called *anomaly-based analysis*. You must define what is considered to be normal behavior. Systems and applications whose behavior can be easily considered normal could be classified as heuristic-based systems. However, sometimes it is challenging to classify a specific behavior as normal or abnormal based on different factors. These factors include negotiated protocols and ports, specific application changes, and changes in the architecture of the network.

A variation of this type of analysis is *profile-based detection*. This allows systems to orchestrate their alarms on alterations in the way that other systems or end users interrelate on the network.

Another kind of anomaly-based detection is protocol-based detection. This scheme is related to, but not to be confused with, the protocol-decode method. The protocol-based detection technique depends on well-defined protocols because it detects as an anomaly any unpredicted value or configuration within a field in the respective protocol.

More sophisticated anomaly detection techniques exist. These are described in the next section.

Anomaly Detection Systems

IDS and IPS provide excellent application layer attack-detection capabilities. However, they do have a weakness—they cannot detect DDoS attacks using valid packets. IDS and IPS devices are optimized for signature-based application layer attack detection. Most of them do not provide day-zero protection.

NOTE	Although some IPS devices do offer anomaly-based capabilities, which are required to detect such attacks, they require extensive manual tuning by experts and do not identify the specific attack flows. Cisco IPS Software Version 6.x and later support more sophisticated anomaly detection techniques. More information can be obtained at http://www.cisco.com/go/ips.

You can use anomaly-based detection systems to mitigate DDoS attacks and day-zero outbreaks. Typically, an anomaly detection system monitors network traffic and alerts or reacts to any sudden increase in traffic and any other anomalies. Cisco delivers a complete DDoS protection solution based on the principles of detection, diversion, verification, and forwarding to help ensure total protection. Examples of sophisticated anomaly detection systems are the Cisco Traffic Anomaly Detectors and the Cisco Guard DDoS Mitigation Appliances.

You can also use NetFlow as an anomaly detection tool. NetFlow is a Cisco technology that supports monitoring of network traffic. The beauty of NetFlow is that it is free with any licensed Cisco IOS image.

NOTE	Refer to the Cisco feature navigator to find out in what Cisco IOS image NetFlow is supported. You can access this tool at http://tools.cisco.com/ITDIT/CFN/jsp/index.jsp.

NetFlow uses a UDP-based protocol to periodically report on flows seen by the Cisco IOS device. A *flow* is a Layer 7 concept that consists of session setup, data transfer, and session teardown. You can also integrate NetFlow with Cisco Secure Monitoring and Response System (CS-MARS). When NetFlow is integrated with CS-MARS, you can take advantage of anomaly detection using statistical profiling, which can pinpoint day-zero attacks such as worm outbreaks.

NOTE	Chapter 3, "Identifying and Classifying Security Threats," provides more information on how to identify security threats using anomaly detection systems.

Authentication, Authorization, and Accounting (AAA) and Identity Management

AAA offers different solutions that provide access control to network resources. This section introduces AAA and identity management concepts.

Authentication is the process of validating users based on their identity and predetermined credentials, such as passwords and other mechanisms like digital certificates. Authentication is widely used in many different applications, from a user attempting to log in to the network, web server, and wireless access point to an administrator logging in to a firewall, router, or any other network device to successfully configure the former.

The authentication concept is simple. Before you can withdraw money from your favorite bank, the teller asks for your credentials (driver's license, account number, and so on). Similarly, networking devices, servers, and other systems can ask you for credentials such as passwords and digital certificates for you to obtain access to the network or any other resources.

Authorization is the method by which a network device assembles a set of attributes that regulates what tasks the user is authorized to perform. These attributes are measured against a user database. The results are returned to the network device to determine the user qualifications and restrictions.

Accounting is the process of gathering and sending user information to an AAA server used to track login times (when the user logged in and logged off) and the services that users access. This information can be used for billing, auditing, and reporting purposes.

Two common AAA protocols are used in networking today:

- Remote Authentication Dial-in User Service (RADIUS)
- Terminal Access Controller Access Control System Plus (TACACS+)

RADIUS

RADIUS is a widely implemented authentication standard protocol that is defined in RFC 2865. RADIUS operates in a client/server model. A RADIUS client is usually referred to as a *network access server* (NAS). A NAS is responsible for passing user information to the RADIUS server. Network devices such as routers, firewalls, and switches can act as a NAS and authenticate users based on the RADIUS server response.

Cisco develops and sells a RADIUS and TACACS+ server called Cisco Secure Access Control Server (ACS). Cisco Secure ACS supports a rich set of AAA features and applications. These advanced features include the following:

- Lightweight Directory Access Protocol (LDAP) and Open Database Connectivity (ODBC) user authentication support

- Flexible 802.1X authentication type support, including Extensible Authentication Protocol Transport Layer Security (EAP-TLS), Protected EAP (PEAP), EAP Flexible Authentication via Secure Tunneling (EAP-FAST), and EAP-Message Digest Algorithm 5 (EAP-MD5) and other protocols
- Timed-based access
- Downloadable for any Layer 3 device, including Cisco routers, Cisco PIX firewalls, Cisco ASA, and Cisco VPNs
- Device command authorization
- Advanced database synchronization and replication features
- Network access restrictions
- Detailed reporting and accounting capabilities
- User and device group profiles

NOTE   For more information about Cisco Secure ACS, go to http://www.cisco.com/go/acs.

Figure 1-11 illustrates the basic RADIUS authentication process.

Figure 1-11 *RADIUS Authentication Process*

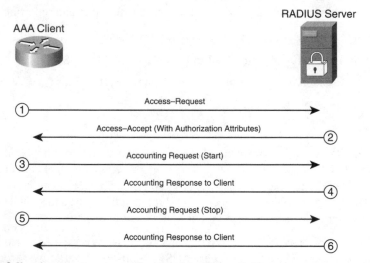

The following are the steps illustrated in Figure 1-11.

Step 1   An access-request is sent from the AAA client (a router in this example) to the RADIUS server.

Step 2   If the user is successfully authenticated, an access-accept is sent from the RADIUS server to the AAA client. This access-accept packet can contain authorization attributes if authorization is enabled. If the user is not successfully authenticated, an access-reject is sent instead.

Step 3   An accounting request (start) message is sent from the AAA client (if configured to do accounting) to the RADIUS server.

Step 4   If the RADIUS server is configured for accounting, it replies with an acknowledgement.

Step 5   At the end of the user session, an accounting request (stop) message is sent from the AAA client (if configured to do accounting) to the RADIUS server.

Step 6   If the RADIUS server is configured for accounting, it replies with an acknowledgement.

This exchange is done over UDP. Older implementations of RADIUS use UDP port 1645 for authentication and UDP port 1646 for accounting. The newer implementations use UDP port 1812 for authentication and UDP port 1813 for accounting.

NOTE   A RADIUS server can also send IETF or vendor-specific attributes to the AAA client depending on the implementation and services used. These attributes can contain information such as an IP address to assign the client and authorization information. RADIUS servers combine authentication and authorization phases into a single request and response communication cycle.

TACACS+

TACACS+ is an AAA security protocol developed by Cisco that provides centralized validation of users who are attempting to gain access to network access devices. The TACACS+ protocol offers support for separate and modular AAA facilities. The primary goal of the TACACS+ protocol is to supply complete AAA support for managing multiple network devices. Unlike RADIUS, TACACS+ uses TCP port 49 by default instead of UDP for its communications. However, it can allow vendors to use UDP. Cisco products use the TCP version for their TACACS+ implementation. The TACACS+ authentication concept is similar to RADIUS. The NAS sends an authentication request to the TACACS+ server, which in turn sends any of the following messages back to the NAS:

- **ACCEPT:** The user has been successfully authenticated and the requested service will be allowed. If authorization is required, the authorization process will begin at this point.

- **REJECT:** User authentication was denied. The user may be prompted to retry authentication depending on the TACACS+ server and NAS.

- **ERROR:** An error took place during authentication. This can be happen because of network connectivity problems or a configuration error.

- **CONTINUE:** The user is prompted to provide further authentication information.

After the authentication process is complete, if authorization is required, the TACACS+ server proceeds with the authorization phase. The user must first successfully be authenticated before proceeding to TACACS+ authorization.

As an industry standard, RADIUS is a more widely deployed protocol than TACACS+.

Identity Management Concepts

Many identity management solutions and systems automatically manage user access privileges within an organization. Today, enterprises are under great pressure to increase security and meet regulatory and governance requirements, resulting in greater urgency to deploy identity management solutions. Role-based authentication is a key concept of identity management. It helps to answer the critical compliance questions of "Who has access to what, when, how, and why?" For example, with role-based authentication, a contractor logging in to the network can access only the resources he should have access to. Based on his role and authorization parameters, he can be restricted from accessing critical financial information.

IEEE 802.1X is a standard that defines the encapsulation methodologies for the transport of EAP over any PPP or Ethernet media. 802.1X allows you to enforce port-based network access control when devices attempt to access the network. The 802.1x standard has three components:

- Supplicant
- Authenticator
- Authentication server

The *supplicant* is the software that resides on the end-user machine. The *authenticator* (typically a switch or wireless access point) relays the EAP information from the supplicant to an *authentication server* via the RADIUS protocol.

Cisco has a comprehensive identity management solution based on 802.1x called Identity-Based Networking Services (IBNS). IBNS is an integrated solution that uses Cisco products which offer authentication, access control, and user policies to secure network connectivity and resources. These products include the following:

- Cisco Catalyst family of switches
- Wireless LAN access points and controllers
- Cisco Secure ACS
- Cisco Secure Services Client

Additional and optional components include X.509 public key infrastructure (PKI) certificate architecture.

| NOTE | You can find detailed IBNS information including configuration and deployment guidelines at http://www.cisco.com/go/ibns. |

Information on how the IBNS and 802.1x solution is integrated into Cisco NAC is covered in the following section.

Network Admission Control

Network Admission Control is a multipart solution that validates the security posture of an endpoint system before entering the network. With NAC, you can also define what resources the endpoint has access to, based on the results of its security posture. NAC is a key part of the Cisco Self-Defending Network Initiative (SDNI). The SDNI mission is to dramatically improve the ability of the network to identify, prevent, and adapt to threats. NAC comes in two flavors:

- **NAC Appliance:** Based on the Cisco Clean Access (CCA)
- **NAC Framework:** A Cisco-sponsored industry wide initiative

NAC Appliance

NAC Appliance or Cisco Clean Access (CCA) enables an organization to enforce security policies by blocking, quarantining, and performing remediation of noncompliant systems. Remediation occurs at the discretion of the administrator. The policies and requirements enforced by NAC Appliance include checks for latest antivirus software, operating system (OS) patches and security patches. NAC Appliance can also perform vulnerability scanning on the end-user machine in addition to role-based authentication on users attempting to connect to the network. The NAC Appliance solution can restrict what resources these users can access, based on their role. All these policies and configurations are done in the Clean Access Manager (CAM).

The Cisco NAC Appliance has three major components:

- **Clean Access Server (CAS):** Acts as a network control device
- **Clean Access Manager (CAM):** Manages one or more servers
- **Clean Access Agent (optional):** Serves as an end-point lightweight client for device-based registry scans in unmanaged environments

The CAM can manage up to 40 CASs depending on the license and is licensed based on the number of CASs it supports. The CAS supports up to 1500 users depending on the license that is installed. The CAS license is based on the concurrent number of clients/users it supports.

NOTE For more information about the NAC Appliance licensing, visit http://www.cisco.com/en/US/products/ps6128/prod_pre_installation_guide09186a0080731366.html.

CAS can be deployed in in-band (IB) or out-of-band (OOB) modes. CASs can pass traffic in one of two ways:

- **Bridged mode:** Typically called Virtual Gateway mode
- **Routed mode:** In Real IP Gateway or NAT Gateway configurations

NOTE   You can configure the CASs in either mode, but only in one mode at a time. For example, if you configure a CAS in Virtual Gateway configuration, you cannot also configure it as a Real IP Gateway. This is because the mode selection affects the logical traffic path.

Figure 1-12 illustrates a CAS configured in Virtual Gateway mode. In this example, the unprotected (untrusted) segment is VLAN 110 and the protected (trusted) network is VLAN 10.

Figure 1-12 *CAS in Virtual Gateway Mode*

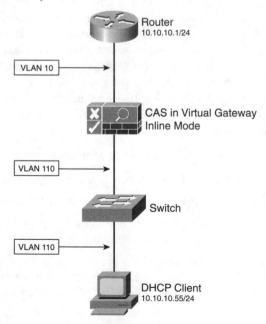

The client workstation has an IP address on the same subnet/range of the trusted network (10.10.10.0/24). In Virtual Gateway mode, the CAS acts as a bridge. DHCP client routes point directly to network devices on the protected network.

Figure 1-13 shows a CAS configured in Real IP mode.

Figure 1-13 *CAS in Real IP Mode*

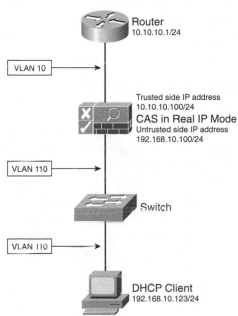

In Real IP mode, the CAS acts as a Layer 3 router. In this example, the CAS trusted and untrusted interfaces are in different subnets. The trusted subnet is 10.10.10.0/24, and the untrusted subnet is 192.168.10.0/24. In Real IP mode, DHCP clients usually point to the CAS to obtain their IP addresses and other DHCP information. It is a best practice to assign a 30-bit address to the DHCP clients. This enables you to isolate machines that can be infected with a virus and block them from infecting other machines in the network.

NOTE   The CAS can optionally be configured to translate the trusted network.

In summary, the NAC Appliance can operate in in-band (IB) or out-of-band (OOB) modes:

- **IB Virtual Gateway (L2 transparent bridge mode):** Acts as a bridge between the untrusted and trusted networks.

- **IB Real-IP Gateway:** Operates as the default gateway for the untrusted network.

- **IB NAT Gateway (used for testing only):** Acts as an IP router/default gateway and translates (NAT) the untrusted network.

- **OOB Virtual Gateway (L2 transparent bridge mode):** Initially acts as a virtual gateway during authentication and certification, before the user is switched out-of-band.

- **OOB Real-IP Gateway:** Initially acts as a Real-IP gateway during authentication and certification, before the user is switched out-of-band. (That is, the user is connected directly to the access network.)

- **OOB NAT Gateway (used for testing only):** Acts as a NAT gateway during authentication and certification, before the user is switched out-of-band.

You can deploy CASs in three physical deployment modes:

- Edge deployment
- Centralized deployment
- Centralized edge deployment

NOTE   The physical deployment method does not affect whether a CAS is in Layer 2 (bridged), Layer 3 (routed), IB, or OOB mode.

Figure 1-14 illustrates a NAC Appliance edge deployment. In this example, the untrusted interface is connected to VLAN 110, and the trusted interface is connected to VLAN 10. The CAM resides on the management segment (VLAN 123). In this example, the CAS is configured in Virtual Gateway mode and is mapping VLAN 10 with VLAN 110.

Figure 1-14 *NAC Appliance Edge Deployment*

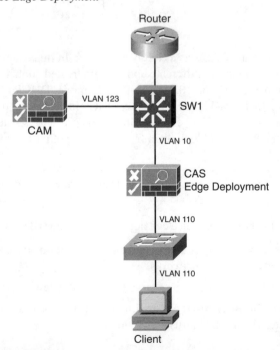

Figure 1-15 illustrates a NAC Appliance centralized deployment. In this example, both the CAS trusted and untrusted interfaces are physically connected to the central switch (SW1). The switch is configured with several VLANs. The untrusted VLAN is VLAN 110, the trusted VLAN is VLAN 10, and the management VLAN is VLAN 123.

Figure 1-15 *NAC Appliance Centralized Deployment*

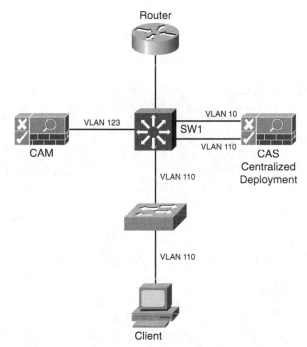

The NAC Appliance centralized deployments are the most common deployment option, because they are better suited for scalability in medium-to-large environments. In this example, the CAS is logically, not physically, in-line.

The NAC Appliance solution supports failover for high-availability. You can deploy the CAM and CAS in failover pairs, as illustrated in Figure 1-16.

The example shown in Figure 1-16 includes two CAMs (CAM-1 and CAM-2). CAM-1 is the primary (active) manager, and CAM-2 is configured in standby mode. If CAM-1 fails, CAM-2 takes over. In Figure 1-16, a total of four CASs are deployed: two active and two in standby. For scalability reasons, CAS-1 is performing posture validation for clients on the first three untrusted VLANs (VLAN 110, 111, and 112). The CAS-2 is enforcing posture validation on the last three untrusted VLANs (VLAN 113, 114, and 115). If CAS-1 fails, CAS-3 will take over, and if CAS-2 fails, CAS-4 will take over.

Figure 1-16 *NAC Appliance High Availability*

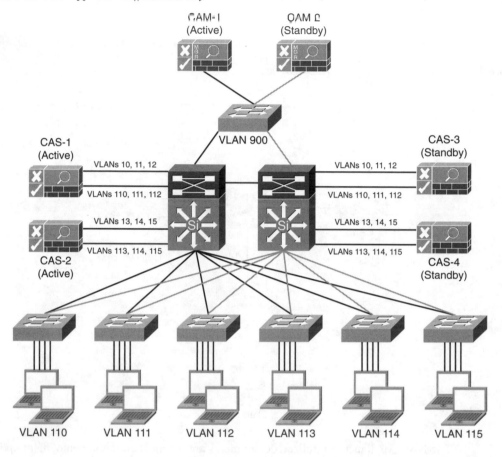

NOTE   Active-active failover configuration is not currently supported.

In most scenarios, a combination of different CAS deployment strategies are used. These are examples of the most common deployment types:

- Layer 2 IB for wireless environments
- Layer 3 or Layer 2 IB for remote access VPN
- Layer 2 OOB for campus LAN deployments

NOTE	This chapter introduces the basics of the NAC Appliance solution. For information about the configuration and troubleshooting of NAC Appliance, go to http://www.cisco.com/go/cca. Chapter 2 demonstrates how to deploy NAC Appliance to provide posture validations while preparing your network and infrastructure to self-protect against security threats.

NAC Framework

NAC Framework is a Cisco-led industry initiative to provide posture validation using embedded software in Cisco network access devices (NAD) such as routers, switches, VPN concentrators, Cisco ASA, wireless access points, and others. Many vendors are part of the Cisco NAC program. These Cisco partners include antivirus software vendors, remediation and patch management companies, identity software manufacturers, and others.

NOTE	To obtain the latest list of NAC program vendors/partners, go to http://www.cisco.com/go/nac and click on NAC program.

Similar to NAC Appliance, NAC Framework has three basic components:

- NAC Agent
- NAD
- Policy Server (Cisco Secure ACS or NAC Manager)

Optionally, you can use other vendor products such as external policy servers, remediation servers, and audit servers to provide more comprehensive admission control features. The NADs enforce policies configured in a centralized manager, while relaying the security credentials/information presented by the end-host NAC Agent. NAC Framework supports four different mechanisms when performing security posture validation on end-host machines:

- **NAC Layer 3 IP:** Uses EAP over UDP (EoU) and is typically deployed in Cisco IOS routers, Cisco ASA, and VPN 3000 concentrators.
- **NAC Layer 2 IP:** Uses EoU and is typically deployed in Cisco Catalyst switches. Address Resolution Protocol (ARP) and DHCP are the trigger mechanisms.
- **NAC Layer 2 802.1x:** Combines the traditional IBNS identity features and services with in-depth security posture validation.

The basic diagram shown in Figure 1-17 illustrates the NAC Framework from a high-level view.

Figure 1-17 *NAC Framework High-Level Overview*

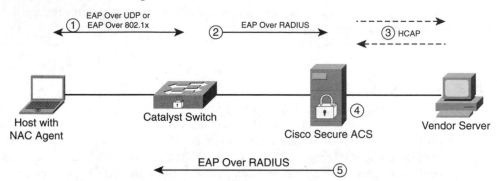

The following steps are illustrated in Figure 1-17:

Step 1 The NAD (a switch in this example) challenges the end-host to present its credentials. This is done via EoU or EAP over 802.1x.

Step 2 The NAD forwards the end-host credentials to the NAC Manager (Cisco Secure ACS server in this example) using the EAP protocol over RADIUS.

Step 3 Optionally, the Cisco Secure ACS forwards user or machine credentials to an external vendor server. This server can be an antivirus vendor server, authentication server, or any other external policy server. The vendor server replies to the Cisco Secure ACS with a token, based on the posture results for the end-host that is attempting to connect to the network.

Step 4 The Cisco Secure ACS receives the token or checks its internal policies.

Step 5 The Cisco Secure ACS sends the posture information to the NAD. Subsequently, the NAD enforces policies based on the posture of the end-host device.

NOTE   The NAD periodically polls the end-hosts to determine if a change has been made in their posture. The NAC Agent alerts the NAD of any changes on the client machine. The NAD uses this information to issue full revalidation and posture assessment. This mechanism prevents hosts from being validated but not checked if their security posture has changed after they have been granted access to the network.

NAC Agentless Hosts (NAH) are devices on which the Cisco NAC Agent has not been installed. These devices can be printers, IP Phones, scanners, and other systems such as contractor and guest workstations. If a device does not have the NAC Agent, it cannot respond to the EoU or 802.1x request from the NAD. Separate policies can be configured on the NAD to exclude the NAH MAC or IP address, or a range of addresses. In addition, a global policy can be configured on Cisco Secure ACS.

Cisco developed a protocol called Generic Authorization Message Exchange (GAME). Third-party audit servers use this protocol to communicate with Cisco Secure ACS when performing elaborate scans and audits on NAC nonresponsive hosts. An example of an audit server vendor is *Qualys*. Cisco Secure ACS is responsible for triggering the audit process for nonresponsive hosts with the audit server. Audit servers can scan the nonresponsive device for known threats and vulnerabilities to further determine their security posture.

NOTE   For more information about the Cisco-Qualys NAC solution, go to http://www.cisco.com/web/partners/downloads/partner/WWChannels/programs/nac_qualys_sol_guide.pdf or to the Qualys website at http://www.qualys.com/products/qgent/integrations/nac/.

It is recommended that you use an event correlation and reporting system, such as CS-MARS, in conjunction with NAC. The process of collecting, correlating, troubleshooting, and trending NAC event information enables you to make necessary real-time corrections and ongoing improvements to the security posture of your end-host devices. This subsequently decreases the risk of known and unknown security threats in your organization.

NOTE This chapter introduces the basics of the NAC Framework solution. For information about the detailed deployment, configuration, and troubleshooting, refer to the Cisco Press books titled *Cisco Network Admission Control, Volume I: NAC Framework Architecture and Design* and *Cisco Network Admission Control, Volume II: NAC Deployment and Troubleshooting*.

Chapter 2 demonstrates how to deploy NAC Framework to provide posture validations while preparing your network and infrastructure to self-protect against security threats.

Routing Mechanisms as Security Tools

Many people do not realize that routing is one of the most powerful security tools available. Several routing techniques help identify, classify, and mitigate security threats. Examples include remotely triggered black holes (RTBH) and sinkholes.

RTBH is a filtering technique that provides the ability to drop malicious traffic before it penetrates your network. Historically, RTBH has been a tool that many service providers have used to mitigate DDoS attacks. Many other organizations are now adopting RTBH.

In technical terms, a typical RTBH deployment requires running internal Border Gateway Protocol (iBGP) at the access and choke points and configuring a separate router strategically placed in the network to act as a trigger. This triggering router injects iBGP updates to the edge, causing the specified traffic to be sent to a null0 interface and subsequently be dropped. RTBH is highly scalable; therefore, it is primarily designed to mitigate against DDoS and worm outbreaks.

NOTE Chapter 2 describes RTBH benefits, operational gains, deployment considerations, and sample router configurations.

A sinkhole, in some cases, is just a router used to redirect malicious traffic to a single IP address where it can be scrutinized in greater detail. In other cases, it is just a segment (place or interface) within the network where this traffic is sent. Service providers initially implemented this technique to identify hosts where an attack or worm traffic was being generated. As with RTBH, enterprises now apply sinkholes. Initially, configuring a sinkhole router assisted in detecting infected devices or attackers when network intrusion detection or prevention systems were not available or when there were other architectural constraints. Today, IDSs are being integrated with sinkholes to better identify and classify these threats, consequently increasing infrastructure protection.

How do sinkhole routers work? A sinkhole router advertises IP addresses/networks not yet allocated by the Internet Assigned Numbers Authority (IANA). These addresses are referred to as *bogon* and *dark IP addresses.*

NOTE   You can find detailed information about bogon addresses at http://www.iana.org.

Some worms and attackers accidentally attempt to exploit these bogon addresses, which are advertised only locally. When the sinkhole router receives this traffic, it can log and discard it. These logs provide a list of infected hosts or attackers.

TIP   In enterprise environments, it is important to monitor dark IP address space instead of only bogon address space. In the future, you may see worms coded to ignore bogon addresses to avoid detection.

Figure 1-18 shows how to deploy a sinkhole router within an enterprise network.

In Figure 1-18, the host on the left is infected with a worm and is attacking and attempting to compromise the user machines. The traffic destined for both bogon addresses and the dark IP address space are inspected by the sinkhole alerting the administrator of this anomaly. You can integrate elaborate tools with sinkholes to easily detect these types of threats.

NOTE   Chapter 2 details the use of sinkholes as part of the preparation phase of the six-step methodology of incident readiness and response.

Figure 1-18 *Sinkhole Deployment Example*

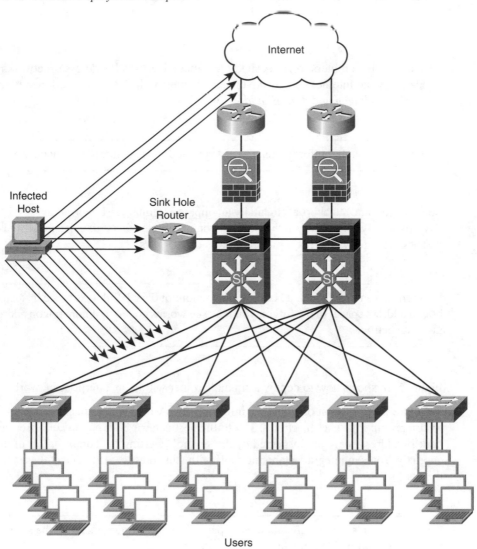

Summary

This chapter introduced a range of security technologies and products to help you understand the best practices and methodologies you will learn in later chapters. It presented an overview of how to place firewalls to provide perimeter security and network segmentation while enforcing configured policies. This chapter also gave an overview of VPN technologies and protocols. It covered IPsec and its related protocols in detail to enhance the learning. It also presented an overview of SSL VPNs and their uses.

IDS and IPS systems can aid in identifying and classifying security threats within your network. This chapter covered an overview and the differences between IDS and IPS technologies. Beyond IDS and IPS, anomaly detection systems help you react to day-zero outbreaks. This chapter also helps you understand the concept and technologies of anomaly detection systems.

AAA offers different solutions that provide access control to network resources. This chapter introduced AAA and identity management concepts. It included an overview of the Cisco Network Admission Control solutions used to enforce security policy compliance on all devices seeking to access network computing resources, thereby limiting damage from emerging security threats.

You can use routing techniques as security tools. This chapter gave you an example of different routing techniques such as RTBH and sinkholes that you can use to increase the security of the network and to react to new threats.

Security Lifestyle: Frameworks and Methodologies

This chapter covers the following topics:

- Risk Analysis
- Social Engineering
- Security Intelligence
- Creating a Computer Security Incident Response Team (CSIRT)
- Building Strong Security Policies
- Infrastructure Protection
- Endpoint Security
- Network Admission Control

Preparation Phase

While computer networks and sophisticated applications have allowed individuals to be more productive, the need to prepare for security threats has increased dramatically. Guarding against security threats includes preparing the infrastructure to protect not only against worms, viruses, and external denial of service (DoS) attacks, but also from internal threats such as theft of information and corporate espionage.

A six-step methodology on security incident handling has been adopted by many organizations, including service providers, enterprises, and government organizations. This methodology is composed of the following steps:

- Preparation
- Identification
- Classification
- Traceback
- Reaction
- Postmortem

This chapter covers the first and most crucial step in this methodology—the preparation phase.

Risk Analysis

Risk analysis is crucial. You need to know what you are protecting and how you are protecting it. What are your critical systems and assets? What constitutes your organization today? These are some initial questions you should ask yourself when starting any risk analysis process. You must know the difference between threats and vulnerabilities. *Threats* are occurrences that can affect a system or an organization as a whole. Examples of threats include fraud, theft of information, and physical theft. *Vulnerabilities* are flaws that make a system, an individual, or an organization exposed and susceptible to a threat or an attack.

On several occasions, when you ask security engineers, managers, architects, and executives to list or describe the critical systems of their organization their answers are contradictory. One of the main goals that members of an organization should have is to understand their environment and what they are trying to protect and what risks are most imminent.

Several methods of risk analysis have been published in books, websites, magazines, and blogs. Some take the quantitative approach; some take the qualitative approach; and others measure impact versus probability. This chapter does not favor one method over another but instead presents several best practices when analyzing security risks.

Threat Modeling

The primary goal of any threat modeling technique is to develop a formal process while identifying, documenting, and mitigating security threats. This process has a huge impact on any organization because it is basically a methodology used to understand how attacks can take place and how they will impact the network, systems, and users.

Organizations have adopted several threat modeling techniques. For example, Microsoft uses the DREAD model. The DREAD acronym defines five key areas:

- Damage potential
- Reproducibility
- Exploitability
- Affected users
- Discoverability

In the DREAD model, the first step is to quantify or estimate the damage potential of a specific threat. This estimate can include monetary and productivity costs followed by a probability study on the reproducibility and exploitability of the vulnerability at hand. In addition, the first step should identify which users and systems will be affected and how easily the threat can be discovered and identified.

NOTE   You can find more information about Microsoft threat modeling at http://msdn2.microsoft.com/en-us/security/aa570411.aspx.

Microsoft also has a threat modeling tool at http://msdn.microsoft.com/msdnmag/issues/03/11/resourcefile/default.aspx.

Another threat modeling technique is to create *attack trees*. Bruce Schneier, the chief technology officer of Counterpane Internet Security and the inventor of the Blowfish and Two-fish encryption algorithms, initially introduced this method. Attack trees represent attacks against a system or network in a hierarchical tree structure. The root node describes a goal, and the leaf nodes are various ways of reaching such a goal.

For example, the main goal of a specific attack may be to interrupt the services of an e-commerce web server farm. This goal will be the root of the tree. Each subsequent "tree branch or leaf" describes the methods used to take down that web server farm (that is, sending millions of spoofed TCP packets, compromising zombies on the Internet to launch DDoS attacks, and so on).

NOTE   A detailed white paper on attack tress by Bruce Schneier is posted at http://www.schneier.com/paper-attacktrees-ddj-ft.html.

Several other threat modeling techniques suggest the use and understanding of system and device roles. Identify what the network devices do and how they are used and placed within the infrastructure. Document and identify their functionality in the context of the organization as a whole; furthermore, configure them according to their role. For example, the same configuration of Internet-edge routers is not suitable for data center devices. Create easy-to-understand architecture diagrams that describe the composition and structure of your infrastructure and its devices. Elaborate the diagram by adding details about the trust boundaries, authentication, and authorization mechanisms.

Cisco has developed a methodology that goes beyond typical threat modeling techniques. This methodology or framework is called the Cisco Operational Process Model (COPM). COPM is a process model that was initially designed for service providers but has recently been adopted by many other organizations. This threat-mitigation practice goes beyond a single product or technology. The COPM framework helps you to prepare and anticipate the lack of operational security expertise by minimizing threats that cannot be completely controlled while controlling those that can be.

NOTE   Chapter 7, "Proactive Security Framework," describes COPM in detail.

COPM focuses on both business and technology groups throughout an organization, while also focusing on the availability and reliability of the infrastructure and its systems.

Total network visibility and complete control of elements is crucial to maintain services and business continuity. COPM is designed to introduce flexibility while improving security without relying on a single technology or product. Multiple technologies and features are used throughout the network to obtain visibility into network behavior and to maintain control during abnormal behavior.

How good is your network if you cannot manage it when an outbreak or attack is underway? Visibility is twofold. Network administrators should always have complete visibility of networking devices and the traffic within their infrastructure. At the same time, intruders must not have visibility to unnecessary services or vulnerable systems that can be exploited within an organization. The following section describes how you can perform periodic security penetration tests and audits to assess and evaluate the visibility of vulnerable systems within the organization. The "Infrastructure Protection" section later in this chapter describes several techniques that you can use to maintain the visibility of devices and systems within your infrastructure.

Penetration Testing

Penetration testing is often referred to as *ethical hacking*. Using this procedure, a trusted third party or a security engineer of an organization attempts to compromise or break into the network and its devices by scanning, simulating live attacks, and exploiting vulnerable machines to measure the overall security posture. Penetration testing techniques are of three common types:

- Black-box
- White-box
- Gray or Crystal-box

In the black-box technique, the tester has no prior knowledge of the network of the organization. Typically, the organization only gives the tester information about a specific system or domain for the "externally attempted" hack. In the white-box technique, the tester has been given more information (that is, network diagrams, list of devices, and so on) prior to starting the tests. The crystal-box test occurs when the tester is provided with an account on the internal network and standard access to the network.

NOTE   This section describes and lists several tools that you can use to assess the security posture of an organization. However, it is strongly recommended that you do not use any of these if you are unsure of the complications and side effects they may have in your organization. On many occasions, it is better to hire a third-party company to perform such tests.

Numerous security tools are designed to automate and ease the penetration testing process. These tools can be a combination of commercial vulnerability assessment tools and free open-source tools. Professional ethical hackers also develop their own tools to automate the test or to specifically test for new vulnerabilities. Commercial tools work by using sets of thousands of preset configurations or vulnerability tags (vuln-tags). Some of these commercial tools are focused on different areas (for example, web security, wireless security, and so on). Examples of commercial tools are Qualys Guard (http://www.qualys.com), and e-Eye Retina (http://www.eeye.com/html/index.html).

Hundreds of open-source tools exist, ranging from meticulously developed and supported tools to small scripts developed to perform a specific task. Table 2-1 lists some of the most commonly used open-source tools.

Table 2-1   *Common Open-Source Security Tools*

Tool	Description	Website
Metasploit	Comprehensive set of penetration testing and vulnerability assessment tools	http://metasploit.org
Nmap	Scanner	http://insecure.org/nmap
Cain and Abel	Password cracking	http://www.oxid.it/cain.html
John the Ripper	Password cracking	http://www.openwall.com/john/
AirCrack	WEP/WPA cracking tool	http://www.aircrack-ng.org/doku.php
AirSnort	802.11 WEP encryption cracking tool	http://airsnort.shmoo.com/
Nessus	(Now commercial) network scanner	http://www.nessus.org
Rainbow Crack	Password cracker	http://www.antsight.com/zsl/rainbowcrack/
Sara	Vulnerability assessment tool	http://www-arc.com/sara
HPing2	Packet crafter	http://www.hping.org
Kismet	Wireless sniffer	http://www.kismetwireless.net
NetStumbler	Windows-based wireless sniffer	http://www.stumbler.net
KisMAC	MAC-based wireless sniffer	http://kismac.de
Nikto	Web scanner	http://www.cirt.net/code/nikto.shtml
Paros Proxy	Web vulnerability assessment proxy	http://www.parosproxy.org

You can combine penetration testing with infrastructure device configuration audits to provide a comprehensive study of the security posture of an organization. For instance, on completion of the penetration test, you have an understanding of the current vulnerable systems within your organization. Even more, you have determined how visible these systems are to a potential attacker. You can combine this information with an analysis of the configuration of your infrastructure components, such as routers and firewalls.

NOTE   Some commercial tools are designed to perform device configuration and firewall rule analysis. Examples of those tools are the Cisco Configuration Assurance Solution (CCAS) (http://www.cisco.com/en/US/products/ps6364/prod_bulletin0900aecd802c8487.html), the AlgoSec Firewall Analyzer (http://www.algosec.com), and Security Risk Auditor from Redseal Systems (http://www.redseal.net).

CCAS automatically completes systematic audits of the production network configuration to detect device misconfigurations, policy violations, inefficiencies, and security gaps.

Cisco Advanced Services for Network Security group also provides comprehensive security posture assessment services, including detailed network security architectural reviews. For more information, go to http://www.cisco.com/en/US/products/svcs/ps2961/ps2952/serv_group_home.html.

The manual analysis of complex firewall policies is almost impossible because it is very time-consuming. As a result, it is difficult to detect many risks. The use of automated tools or professional services is a must.

TIP   Conduct penetration tests and network security architectural reviews periodically, because new threats and vulnerabilities are introduced on a daily basis. Doing so allows you to measure the effectiveness of the methods used to improve the overall security after the initial tests and architectural review.

You need to understand the confidentiality requirements and risks of these types of tests. To ensure unbiased results, executives often hire third-party security professionals to perform high-level audits within the network and infrastructure readiness tests without telling their own security engineers and managers. The results of such tests are often kept a secret until a contingency plan has been built. You also need to understand the ethics and laws governing these types of activities. If you are a security professional hired by an organization to perform these types of tests and reviews, going outside your contractual boundaries is not only unethical, but also illegal.

NOTE   The Cisco Press book titled *Penetration Testing and Network Defense* by Andrew Whitaker and Daniel P. Newman covers all the best practices of penetration testing in detail.

Social Engineering

Social engineering is one of the most dangerous risks that exist today. It goes beyond the most rigid and sophisticated security products and infrastructure components. How good is it to have the most expensive and elaborate authentication system in the world if your employee is going to give an outsider the password to access your network? The social engineering problem can only be solved with one of the most fundamental tools—education.

Some people say that social engineering comes in two types: technology based and human based. An example of technology-based social engineering is the use of technical tools to fool users into providing sensitive information. Human-based social engineering is the most dangerous of the two types. It can be accomplished through a simple phone call or by listening to a conversation in a break room within your organization. The attacker can use human psychology to obtain sensitive information. For example, someone can call one of your employees and try to obtain chunks of information that can be put together for further intrusion. An attacker can call one of your employees identifying himself as a security engineer who is performing a routine maintenance check on your system and ask for such sensitive information as IP addresses, gateways, and even passwords. *Phishing* is one of the most common types of social engineering today. The most common targets are financial institutions and online service companies. Phishing itself is not new, but its frequency has increased over the past few years. The typical phishing e-mail is the one claiming that your financial account information with a specific financial institution needs updating. The e-mail includes a link that sends you to a fake website where you are instructed to enter your password to update your information.

You need to be aware of another not-so-sophisticated social engineering technique. This one may include just a smile. Yes, a smile. Your organization may include the most colorful and elaborate badges for all employees, locked doors, and even security guards. However, employees tend to hold doors open for those who follow them into the building, especially if they are smiling and look confident. When they let others in, employees seldom check the photos of their IDs or whether they have an ID.

Education is one of the most fundamental safeguards and the most crucial in these types of scenarios and threats. Developing a good security awareness program is necessary for an organization of any size. You can use several techniques to educate your users (from flyers and periodic e-mails to web-based training and video-on-demand that your employees can view from anywhere anytime). This type of training should be mandatory.

NOTE   More information on end-user security awareness is covered in the section titled "Building Strong Security Policies" later in this chapter.

Security Intelligence

Always keep up to-date by analyzing intelligence reports about current vulnerabilities and threats. In addition, try to educate yourself on advanced security topics to help you better protect your network and reduce organizational risks. You can obtain security intelligence reports and information about new threats from numerous sites, such as http://hackerwatch.org, http://www.cert.org, and http://first.org.

Cisco has a free website where you can obtain the latest information on security vulnerabilities, worms, viruses, and other threats. This website is called the Cisco Security Center, and you can access it at http://tools.cisco.com/security/center/home.x. The Cisco Security Center includes not only a comprehensive list of threats, but also information on how you can use your existing infrastructure to reduce exposure to such threats. In addition, it includes information about the latest intrusion detection system/intrusion prevention system (IDS/IPS) signatures to detect and protect your network from the threats.

Several educational institutions also collaborate with large corporations like Cisco on many research activities. An example is the Internet Motion Sensor (IMS) created by the University of Michigan. IMS is a large cluster of systems configured to monitor blocks of routable unused IP addresses. Its website is http://ims.eecs.umich.edu, and it contains detailed information on the measurement and identification of the latest security threats and anomalies. Examples of other research initiatives and organizations are as follows:

- **CAIDA Network Telescope:** http://www.caida.org/analysis/security
- **The iSink:** http://wail.cs.wisc.edu
- **Common Vulnerability and Exposures:** http://cve.mitre.org
- **Team CYMRU Darknet Project:** http://www.cymru.com/darknet
- **The Honeynet Project:** http://honeynet.org

When obtaining security intelligence information, you must determine the level of risk of these vulnerabilities and the impact they may have in your organization. A good way to calculate this risk is by using the emerging standard in vulnerability scoring called the Common Vulnerability Scoring System (CVSS).

Common Vulnerability Scoring System

The National Infrastructure Advisory Council (NIAC) commissioned the development of CVSS as a combined effort by many industry leaders including Cisco. The CVSS standard is now maintained by the Forum for Incident Response and Security Teams (FIRST).

NOTE   For more information about FIRST, go to http://www.first.org.

CVSS metrics are divided into three major components:

- Base metrics
- Temporal metrics
- Environmental metrics

Cisco has an online tool where you can calculate your CVSS score at http://tools.cisco.com/security/center/cvssCalculator.x.

Base Metrics

Seven categories are used to calculate a "base score." These categories are the most elementary qualities of a specific vulnerability.

1 **Access vector:** Measures whether a vulnerability is exploitable locally, remotely, or both.

2 **Access complexity:** Appraises the complexity and level of effort required to exploit a specific vulnerability.

3 **Authentication:** Determines whether an attacker must be authenticated to exploit the vulnerability.

4 **Confidentiality impact:** Gauges the impact on confidentiality of a successful exploitation.

5 **Integrity impact:** Gauges the impact on confidentiality of a successful exploitation.

6 **Availability impact:** Describes the impact on availability of a successful exploitation of the vulnerability on the target system.

7 **Impact bias:** Allows you to prioritize one of the three impact metrics over the other two.

Temporal Metrics

CVSS has three different temporal metrics:

1 **Exploitability:** Describes the complexity required to exploit the vulnerability (unproven, proof-of-concept, functional, or highly exploitable).

2 **Remediation level:** Includes the level of an available workaround or solution. Describes whether there is an official fix, a temporary fix, a workaround, or no available solution.

3 **Report confidence:** Measures the credibility and confidence of the reported vulnerability (unconfirmed, uncorroborated, or confirmed).

Environmental Metrics

The environmental metrics are not scored in the Cisco Security Center website however, you can use them to represent the impact of a vulnerability based on your specific environment. Two metrics are used to calculate this impact:

1 **Collateral damage potential:** The likelihood for a loss of data, physical equipment, or property damage.

2 **Target distribution:** The relative size of the systems susceptible to such vulnerability.

— **None:** When no target systems exist

— **Low:** Typically when the vulnerability affects 1 to 15 percent of the systems within the organization

— **Medium:** Typically when the vulnerability affects 16 to 49 percent of the systems within the organization

— **High:** Typically when the vulnerability affects 50 percent or more of the systems within the organization

NOTE   Detailed information about the CVSS formulas is documented in a white paper published by NIAC at http://www.first.org/cvss/cvss-dhs-12-02-04.pdf.

Creating a Computer Security Incident Response Team (CSIRT)

It is unfortunate when large Fortune 500 companies do not have a Computer Security Incident Response Team (CSIRT). In some occasions, their CSIRT consists of one part-time employee. This is why it is extremely important to have management support when creating CSIRTs. It is difficult and problematic to create a CSIRT without management approval and support. Also, the support needed goes beyond budget and money. It includes executives, managers, and their staffs committing time to participate in the planning and improvement processes. Furthermore, it is equally crucial to get management commitment to award empowerment to the CSIRT. How good is a CSIRT if it does not have the authority to make an emergency change within the infrastructure if the organization is under attack or a victim of an outbreak?

NOTE   CSIRTs operate differently depending on the organization, its staff, their expertise, and budget resources. On the other hand, the best practices described in this chapter apply, generally, to any organization.

Who Should Be Part of the CSIRT?

Finding and retaining qualified security professionals is challenging. It can be also a struggle for organizations to justify additional headcount, especially for network security. Traditionally, information technology (IT) expenses are justified based on return on investment (ROI) and productivity metrics. On the other hand, security has been historically viewed as an additional cost. The opinion of many executives is changing, as organizations discover that better network security makes business transactions safer and reduces a big ticket item—liability.

In some cases, additional headcount is needed to create a formal CSIRT within an organization. However, on many occasions, the CSIRT can comprise staff from different departments within an organization. For example, an organization can have representatives from IT, Information Security (InfoSec), and engineering to be part of the CSIRT. The decision of whether to hire new staff or develop an in-house team depends on your organizational needs and budget. Clearly identify who needs to be involved at each level of the CSIRT planning, implementation, and operation. For instance, one of the most challenging tasks is the process of identifying the staff that will be performing security incident response functions.

In addition, identify which internal and external organizations will interface with the CSIRT. Evangelize and communicate the CSIRT responsibilities accordingly.

A question that many engineers, managers, and executives commonly ask is this: what skills should the CSIRT staff possess? The answer certainly goes beyond the in-depth technical expertise that the CSIRT contributor must have. Communication skills—both written and oral—are a plus. The CSIRT personnel must be able to communicate effectively to ensure that they obtain and supply the necessary and appropriate information. This leads to other critical qualities: the ability to respect confidentiality and integrity. This is obvious: integrity and confidentiality are crucial. Other key skills include:

- Handling stressful situations competently
- Managing time
- Problem solving/troubleshooting skills
- Working with teams effectively
- Handling situations diplomatically

NOTE   CERT has a section within its website dedicated to information about CSIRTs (http://www.cert.org/csirts).

Incident Response Collaborative Teams

Several virtual teams and collaborative efforts exist between large corporations and government organizations to exchange incident information and intelligence. The Cisco Critical Infrastructure Assurance Group (CIAG) has formed two groups that provide guidance and exchange ideas and information with many other large organizations. These groups are the Information Sharing and Analysis Centers (ISAC) and the Cisco Incident Response Communication Arena (CIRCA). CIRCA, specifically, exchanges information with several excellent sources, such as:

- Worldwide ISAC
- Telecom ISAC
- Information Technology ISAC
- Product Security Incident Response Team (PSIRT)

NOTE   You can obtain more information about these organizations at http://www.cisco.com/web/about/security/security_services/ciag/incident_response_support/index.html.

Tasks and Responsibilities of the CSIRT

You must develop and document roles and responsibilities for all CSIRT members and identify areas where authority may be ambiguous or overlapping. In addition, you may want to create a diagram or flowchart defining the CSIRT processes. You must develop policies and corresponding procedures. The following section details the importance of building strong security policies and procedures.

Building Strong Security Policies

What good does a firewall, IPS sensor, encryption device, and your favorite security product and tool do if you do not have guidelines, policies, and best practices on how to effectively configure and use them? Building strong security policies is crucial for any organization. These policies should be strong, yet realistically flexible to accommodate ever-changing requirements.

Policies communicate not only a standard but also an agreement on what should be the best practice for a specific situation (in this case, related to security). Policies must be detailed yet easy to understand and must also balance enforcement and productivity. A security policy is useless if it impedes productivity.

During the security policy design stages, you should define the reasons why such policy is needed. Also define the stakeholders, contacts, and their responsibilities. In addition, you should discuss how to handle violations to such a policy.

Depending on the size and goals of your organization, you may document the security policies in one large document or several small ones.

TIP

In most cases, smaller documents are easier to maintain and update. Occasionally, certain policies are appropriate for every site within your organization; others may be specific to specific environments.

An organization can have many different policies depending on its applications and systems. Some policies are implemented because of regulatory compliance to standards like Sarbanes-Oxley and the Health Insurance Portability and Accountability Act (HIPAA) of 1996. The following are some of the most common policies in every organization:

- Physical security policies
- Information protection
- Perimeter security
- Device security
- Acceptable use of specific applications and systems
- Remote access
- Wireless security policies
- Data center security policies
- Extranets and demilitarized zones (DMZ)
- Patch management

The following are examples of other elaborate policies:

- Lab security
- Acceptable encryption protocols
- Network admission control policies
- Identity management policies

Trust is the main subject in many policies. Many say that policies will not be written if you trust everyone to do the right thing. Ideally, you want to trust all resources, but that is unrealistic. Even defects in software and hardware are risks that you do not want to take by trusting everything that is not human. Different types of people (like your staff, guests, and contractors) should be trusted at different levels. Ensure that the level of access is commensurate with the level of trust.

TIP

SANS has several security policy templates that you can download at
http://www.sans.org/resources/policies/#template

Cisco has a Security Policy Builder tool at http://www.ciscowebtools.com/spb/.

Some people think of security policies as long documents that merely define what level
of access systems and people have. However, policies include all of the previously
mentioned items and topics, such as:

- Baseline router configuration parameters
- Guidelines for forwarding e-mails to external addresses
- Configuration management procedures and change control

Configuration management procedures and change control is a hot topic when planning
incident response procedures. *Security changes* are defined as changes to network
equipment that might impact the overall security of the network. Remember that these
policies have to be flexible enough to accommodate the changes that staff members make
to respond to security incidents and outbreaks. All security teams (such as InfoSec,
CSIRTs, and so on) should review the list of business and technical requirements to identify
specific network configuration or design issues to meet security needs.

Patch management is also a hot topic today. Always ensure that the current software
revision levels of network equipment, desktop machines, and servers are up-to-date with
security patches and hotfixes.

Update security policies regularly, or as needed. At a minimum, schedule an annual review
to ensure that security policies do not become obsolete because of technology changes and
demands. Also, include a provision for ad-hoc updates when higher-priority changes are
needed.

It is recommended that you engage subject matter experts (SME) when reviewing existing
policies because you should consider several factors in addition to those included during
the initial development. SMEs can provide valuable input into changes in technology and
best practices that may need to be incorporated in the specific policy. Security violations,
deviations, and relevant audit information should also be reviewed when considering an
existing policy.

You can use various techniques when planning, developing, and updating security
policies. Always take the following basic idea into consideration: the policy must
primarily reflect what is good for the security of the organization as a whole without
limiting productivity.

Infrastructure Protection

A typical network infrastructure is built with routers, switches, and other equipment that provide indispensable services designed to increase the productivity of your organization. Each day results in new security threats, including DoS attacks and worm and virus outbreaks deliberately created to directly or indirectly disrupt the services that your network infrastructure attempts to provide. That is why it is critical to understand how to protect your organizational infrastructure by using security tools and best practices to protect each system in your network. You need to know not only how to protect the infrastructure, but also how infrastructure components can help you identify, classify, and protect against these security threats.

You need to understand the different router planes and their architecture to better protect your infrastructure devices.

RFC 3654 defines two planes:

- Control plane
- Forwarding plane

ITU X805 defines three planes:

- Control plane
- Management plane
- End-user plane

Finally, Cisco defines three planes:

- Control plane
- Management plane
- Data plane

NOTE   The techniques you will learn in this chapter apply to all the techniques and processes previously described. The Cisco definitions are used.

The control plane traffic includes routing protocol traffic—that is, Border Gateway Protocol (BGP), Open Shortest Path First (OSPF), and Enhanced Interior Gateway Routing Protocol (EIGRP) updates. The management plane traffic is basically all management communications, such as Secure Shell (SSH), Telnet, Simple Network Management Protocol (SNMP), RADIUS, and TACACS+. The data plane traffic (as derived from its name) includes all transit traffic not destined to the router. Figure 2-1 illustrates the difference between the three planes.

Figure 2-1 *Router Planes*

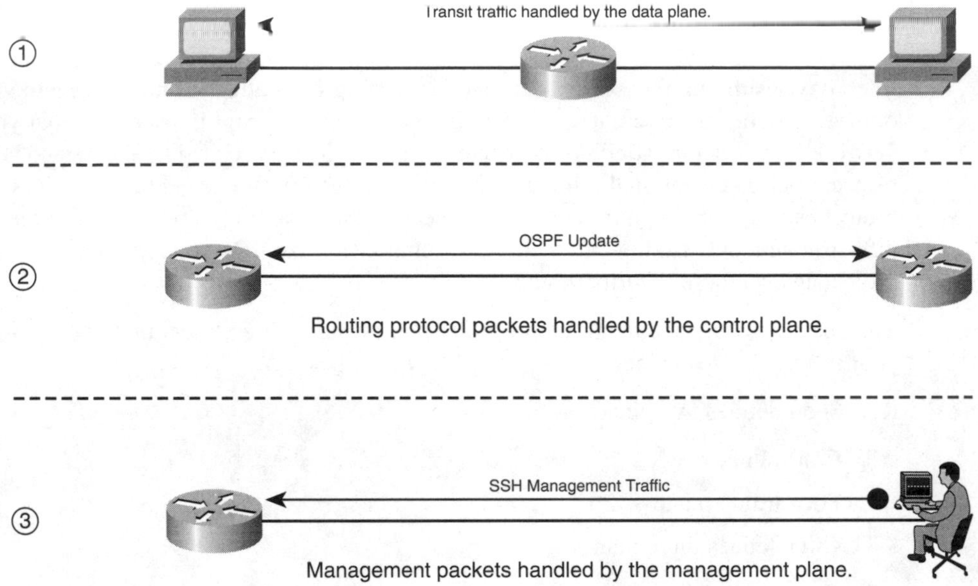

In the first (1) part of Figure 2-1, two workstations are sending traffic to each other, and the traffic is routed via an intermediary router. The data plane handles all this traffic. In the second (2) part of Figure 2-1, two routers are exchanging OSPF updates. The control plane handles this traffic. The third (3) and last part of Figure 2-1 illustrates a network administrator managing the router using the SSH protocol. The management plane handles this traffic.

The control and management plane traffic is always destined to the router. The processor in software platforms handles this traffic (traffic is Cisco Express Forwarding (CEF) switched in interrupt level.) In contrast, in high-end platforms such as the Catalyst 6500 or the Cisco 12000 series routers, control and management plane traffic is sent to hardware modules like the MFSC/SUP720 and then sent to the process level for processing. In some cases, data plane traffic may also reach the control plane. For instance, packets with IP options are process-switched (handled by the processor). Another example is when a router receives a packet that cannot be routed, the packet is sent to the control plane; subsequently, the router generates an Internet Control Message Protocol (ICMP) unreachable message.

From the many techniques you can use to better prepare and protect your infrastructure, these are the most crucial and frequently implemented:

- Strong device access control
- Securing of routing protocols
- Disabling of unnecessary services on network components

- Locking down of unused ports on network access devices
- Control of resource exhaustion
- Policy enforcement
- Telemetry and logging

Strong Device Access Control

Strong device access control implies establishing the appropriate mechanisms to prevent unauthorized access to networking devices such as routers and switches. You can spend millions of dollars on the most sophisticated network devices, but these devices can be the worst investment you have ever made if they can be easily "owned" by the enemy (attackers). This is why it is critical to become familiar with what access mechanisms are available on each infrastructure device. You need to know how they work, which ones are "on by default," and how others can be "turned on." It is also useful to know how to secure/restrict these mechanisms as necessary so you can better protect the infrastructure as a whole.

Many access mechanisms are supported by different network access devices. Following are some examples:

- Console access
- Asynchronous connections
- Telnet
- rlogin
- SSH
- HTTP and HTTPs access via web-based GUIs

NOTE   Several of these access mechanisms are enabled by default in infrastructure devices. For example, console and modem access are enabled by default in Cisco routers, while other mechanisms need to be enabled manually.

Cisco and other organizations recommend several best practices to help secure access to network devices. The following sections include those most commonly recommended.

SSH Versus Telnet

SSH is a protocol that provides strong authentication and encryption. This is why it is recommended over insecure protocols like rlogin and Telnet. SSH comes in Version 1 and Version 2. The second version of SSH is recommended and should be used whenever it is supported, because it fixes a series of security issues found in the previous version. SSH supports the most common encryption ciphers:

- Advanced Encryption Standard (AES)
- Data Encryption Standard (DES)
- Triple DES (3DES)
- International Data Encryption Algorithm (IDEA)
- RC4-128

SSH can also tunnel TCP connections that allow file transfers with secure copy (SCP).

Four basic steps are required to enable SSH on a Cisco IOS Software device:

Step 1   Configure a hostname and domain name. The hostname "myrouter" and the domain name "cisco.com" are used in this example.

```
Router(config)# hostname myrouter
myrouter(config)# ip domain-name cisco.com
```

Step 2   Generate a Rivest, Shamir, and Adleman (RSA) protocol key pair. This automatically enables SSH.

```
myrouter(config)#crypto key generate rsa
The name for the keys will be: myrouter.cisco.com
Choose the size of the key modulus in the range of 360 to 2048 for your
   General Purpose Keys. Choosing a key modulus greater than 512 may take
   a few minutes.
How many bits in the modulus [512]: 2048
% Generating 1024 bit RSA keys, keys will be non-exportable...[OK]
myrouter(config)#
*Dec 14 02:40:23.093: %SSH-5-ENABLED: SSH 2.0 has been enabled
```

Step 3   (Optional) Configure time-out and number of authentication retries. These values depend on your environment; however, the 60-second timeout is appropriate in most cases.

```
myrouter(config)# ip ssh time-out 60
myrouter(config)# ip ssh authentication-retries 2
```

Step 4   Optionally, but highly recommended, configure VTYs to only accept SSH.

```
myrouter(config)# line vty 0 4
myrouter(config-line)# transport input ssh
```

The following steps demonstrate how to enable SSH on a PIX security appliance or a Cisco Adaptive Security Appliance (ASA):

Step 1   Configure the hostname and domain name in the security appliance.

```
ciscoasa(config)#hostname ciscoasa1
ciscoasa1(config)#domain-name cisco.com
```

Step 2   Configure a username and password, and use authentication, authorization, and accounting (AAA) authentication. In this example, local authentication is used. The username is **user1**, and the password is **cisco123**.

```
ciscoasa1(config)#username user1 password cisco123
ciscoasa1(config)#aaa authentication ssh console LOCAL
```

Step 3   Generate the RSA key pair for the security appliance (similarly to IOS). In this example, the modulus size is 2048.

```
ciscoasa1(config)#crypto key generate rsa modulus 2048
```

Step 4   Define the hosts/networks allowed to connect to the specific interfaces of the security appliance. In this example, only machines in the 10.10.10.0/24 network can connect via SSH on the inside interface.

```
ciscoasa1 (config)#ssh 10.10.10.0 255.255.255.0 inside
```

Step 5   Optionally, you can specify the version of SSH allowed on the PIX/ASA. By default, both SSH Version 1 and Version 2 are allowed. In this example, only clients that support SSH Version 2 are allowed to connect to the appliance.

```
ciscoasa1(config)# ssh version 2
```

Local Password Management

TACACS+ and RADIUS servers provide the best options for authentication of management access to networking devices. They provide numerous functions that ease the management of user accounts while providing higher security mechanisms. Local authentication is more susceptible to being broken than authentication using remote TACACS+ or RADIUS servers. That is why it is recommended to do the following:

- Encrypt any passwords shown in the configuration files. In IOS devices, you can encrypt the passwords in their configuration file by using the **service password-encryption** global command.

- Change default passwords.

- Limit the authentication failure rate. It is recommended, as a best practice, to configure a maximum threshold of three consecutive unsuccessful login attempts and to enable the generation of log messages when this limit is reached by using the **security authentication failure rate 3 log** command in IOS devices. This locks access to the router for a period of 15 seconds after three unsuccessful login attempts to protect against dictionary attacks. Dictionary attacks are an old trick. An attacker uses a script that tries thousands of words stored in a file using them as the password. A dictionary attack can be successful if a weak password is used or if you do not protect against it by limiting the authentication failure rate.

Configuring Authentication Banners

Sometimes people overestimate the benefits of configuring authentication banners. Banners with detailed warnings often make it easier to prosecute attackers who break into your systems. In some cases, you may be forbidden to monitor the activities of unauthorized users unless you have taken steps to notify them of your intent to do so.

Typically, authentication banners include the following information:

- A warning that the system you are trying to access should be used only by authorized personnel
- A detailed explanation that the unauthorized use of such a device is illegal, and individuals who attempt to break in are subject to prosecution
- A notice that the use of such a device may be monitored
- Specific notices required by certain local authorities

Interactive Access Control

You have already learned that you can access network devices via several interactive methods such as Telnet, rlogin, SSH, and local asynchronous, even modem connections for out-of-band access. On Cisco IOS devices, these interactive access methods have two basic types of lines (or sessions). The first type is the use of standard lines used by console and dialup modem connections. The first type of these connections are known as TTYs. TTY stands for "Text Telephone." The "Y" has a historical value referenced to the first text telephones. Now the term TTY refers to a serial connection to a computerized device. The second type of standard lines is the virtual TTYs (VTYs). VTYs are used by remote connections such as Telnet and SSH. This section shows the best way to protect interactive access.

One of the most common practices in Cisco IOS devices is to disable interactive logins on lines that will not need them. You can use the **login** and **no password** commands at the line configuration level. Another good practice is to restrict access to allow only the specific protocols (that is, SSH). In Cisco IOS devices, you can do this with the **transport input** command (for example, **transport input ssh**).

Always restrict the IP addresses or networks from which access will be granted to network access devices. In Cisco IOS, you can achieve this by using the **access-class** command in conjunction with an ACL. In the following example, an access list is configured to allow devices only on the 10.10.10.0/24 network to access the router via SSH.

```
Myrouter#configure terminal
myrouter(config)#access-list 10 permit 10.10.10.0 0.0.0.255
myrouter(config)#line vty 0 4
myrouter(config-line)#access-class 10 in
myrouter(config-line)#transport input ssh
```

On the Cisco ASA and PIX, you can restrict administrative access in a similar fashion by using the **ssh**, **telnet**, **http**, and **asdm location** commands. The **ssh** command restricts SSH connections to the security appliance. The **telnet** command restricts Telnet connections. The **http** and **asdm location** commands restrict HTTPS access via the Adaptive Security Device Manager (ASDM). In the following example, the only host allowed to access and manage the Cisco ASA via SSH and ASDM is 172.18.85.123.

```
ciscoasa# configure terminal
ciscoasa(config)# ssh 172.18.85.123 255.255.255.255 inside
ciscoasa(config)# http 172.18.85.123 255.255.255.255 inside
ciscoasa(config)# asdm location 172.18.85.123 255.255.255.255 inside
```

As with the Cisco ASA/PIX, in Cisco IOS, you can enable HTTP authentication with the **ip http authentication** command. The following example shows a configuration listing for HTTP authentication using RADIUS.

```
myrouter(config)#aaa new-model
myrouter(config)#aaa authentication login default group radius
myrouter(config)#aaa authorization exec default group radius
myrouter(config)#ip http server
myrouter(config)#ip http authentication aaa
myrouter(config)#tacacs-server host 172.18.85.181
myrouter(config)#tacacs-server key cisco123
```

You can also restrict who can administer the IOS device via HTTP by using the **ip http access-class** command. The following example shows how 10.10.10.123 is the only host allowed to connect via HTTP to the router.

```
mrouter(config)# access-list 9 permit host 10.10.10.123
mrouter(config)# ip http access-class 9
myrouter(config)# ip http max-connections 3
```

In this example, the router is configured to limit the maximum number of concurrent connections to three with the **ip http max-connections** command.

You can also configure timeouts to avoid idle sessions from consuming an administrative session indefinitely. In Cisco IOS, you can modify the idle timeout with the **exec-timeout** command, as shown in the following example. In this example, the **exec-timeout** is configured for 5 minutes.

```
myrouter(config)#line vty 0 4
myrouter(config-line)#exec-timeout 5
```

On the Cisco ASA, you can do the same by configuring the **ssh timeout** or **telnet timeout** commands as follows.

```
ciscoasa(config)# ssh timeout 5
ciscoasa(config)# telnet timeout 5
```

Another trick on Cisco IOS devices is to enable TCP keepalives on incoming sessions with the **service tcp-keepalives-in** command. The use of this command protects against malicious orphan connections.

Several IOS login enhancements have occurred since Cisco IOS Software Release 12.3(4)T. The **login delay** command was introduced to allow a delay between login attempts, making dictionary attacks harder to exploit.

NOTE   Dictionary attacks were defined earlier in this chapter.

The **login block-for** command allows you to limit the frequency of failed login attempts in Cisco IOS routers. The frequency is limited by defining a maximum number of failed attempts within a specified period. When this number is reached, the Cisco IOS router does not accept additional connections for a "quiet period." You can also create an ACL to include trusted systems and networks from which legitimate connections are expected. This is called an exception ACL, and it is configured in conjunction with the **login quiet-mode access-class** global command.

In the example that follows, the Cisco IOS router will enter a 60-second quiet period if 15 failed login attempts are exceeded within 60 seconds. The access list included next will make an exception for the authorized system with IP address 10.10.10.123. In addition, logging messages will be generated for every 10th failed login and every 15th successful login.

```
myrouter(config)# access-list 99 permit host 10.10.10.123
myrouter(config)# login block-for 60 attempts 15 within 60
myrouter(config)# login quiet-mode access-class 99
myrouter(config)# login on-failure log every 10
myrouter(config)# login on-success log every 15
```

Role-Based Command-Line Interface (CLI) Access in Cisco IOS

Role-based command-line interface (CLI) access is often referred to as CLI views. This is a feature introduced in Cisco IOS Software Release 12.3(7)T. The purpose of this feature is to explicitly control the commands that are accepted and the configuration information that is visible to different groups of users depending on their role. For instance, certain users from your network operations group could have limited access to EXEC and configuration commands and no access to security configuration commands. In contrast, you may want to allow the users in your security group to invoke security configuration commands such as crypto commands and others.

The three basic views or levels of access are as follows:

- **Root view:** The highest administrative view, this is equivalent to a user with level 15 privileges. To create new CLI views, you need to be in "root view" access.

- **Superview:** Do not include commands; in fact, you can only configure commands in CLI views. However, users logged into a superview account can access all the commands that are configured for any of the CLI views that are part of the superview.

- **Lawful intercept view:** This view is only available in Cisco IOS devices that support the lawful intercept subsystem. The purpose of this view is to restrict access to lawful intercept commands and configuration information.

NOTE   There is one root view, by default. You can define a total of 15 CLI views and superviews and only 1 lawful intercept view. For you to create a view, an "enable" password must exist. In addition, AAA must be enabled with the **aaa new-model** command, and the administrator must have level 15 privileges to access the root view. You must enable authorization with the **aaa authorization** command.

Follow these steps to create CLI views in Cisco IOS routers.

Step 1   Use the **enable view** command to access the root view, as shown in the following example:

```
myrouter# enable view
Password: (enter enable or enable secret password)
*Dec 25 00:03:28.123: %PARSER-6-VIEW_SWITCH: successfully set to view
'root'
```

Step 2   After entering in root view mode, you can create a new view with the **parser view** command. In the following example, a view called **myADMIN** is created with the password **1qaz@WSX**.

```
myouter# configure terminal
myrouter(config)# parser view myADMIN
^Dec 25 01:08:51.123: %PARSER-6-VIEW_CREATED: view 'Admin123'
  successfully created.
myrouter(config-view)# password 5 1qaz@WSX
```

Step 3   You can permit or exclude commands within the view with the commands sub-command, as follows:

```
myrouter(config-view)# commands exec include show interfaces
myrouter(config-view)# commands exec include all
myrouter(config-view)# commands configure include-exclusive crypto
```

Step 4   You can assign a user or a group to a CLI view in two ways. The first method is with the use of a AAA local user database. The second (and preferred method) is to use an external AAA server. You can associate local users to a CLI view with the **username** command, as shown here:

```
myrouter(config)# username operator1 view Operators password 1qaz@WSX
myrouter(config)# username sec_op1 view SecOps password xsw2ZAQ!
```

In this example, two users are created. The user **operator1** is associated with a view called **Operators**. The second user, **sec_op1**, is associated with a view called **SecOps**.

TIP   When you use an external AAA server, you must use the attribute "cli-view-name" to assign a user to a specific CLI view.

Controlling SNMP Access

SNMP is a network management protocol that many organizations use. Administrators use SNMP not only to manage infrastructure devices but also to manage servers and other systems within their organization. SNMP is a powerful tool, because administrators can reach numerous devices within a large network, push and download configurations, and obtain system statistics. SNMP is considered a "double-edged sword" by many people, because an attacker can do the same thing when SNMP is not secured properly.

SNMP has three versions:

- Version 1
- Version 2 (commonly referred to as 2c)
- Version 3

Version 1 and Version 2c are weak in security functions and existing vulnerabilities. However, they are the most commonly deployed. In Version 1 and 2c, access to MIB objects is controlled by the use of community strings. However, these versions do not provide authentication or encryption mechanisms. Not having basic security capabilities such as authentication or encryption on a management protocol is like leaving your car unlocked and with the windows down in the worst neighborhood. SNMP Version 3 incorporates security features such as authentication, identity, and access control. Version 3 has multiple authentication options, including username, message digest algorithm 5 (MD5), and Secure Hash Algorithm (SHA) authentication. This version also provides privacy with DES encryption, and authorization and access controls based on views. Of course, the recommendation is for you to use SNMP Version 3 over the other two versions. On the other hand, this may not be possible because you may have devices (or SNMP applications) that do not support SNMP Version 3. In this case, you can improve security by doing the following:

- Changing any default or standard community strings such as "private" or "public"
- Defining nontrivial community strings
- Setting SNMP to send a trap on community-name authentication failures
- Defining access control rules on networking devices to only allow SNMP communication from trusted management hosts; of course, the management host should also be secured. You will learn how to secure management hosts and other systems in the "Endpoint Security" section.

Securing Routing Protocols

Routing protocols play a crucial role in the infrastructure of any organization. They use algorithms to select the best paths for datagrams within a network or set of networks. Understanding how to configure and use routing protocols is a must for any network administrator. On the same note, understanding how to secure these protocols is vital.

This book assumes that you are already familiar with routing protocols. However, here is a quick refresh. Routing protocols are divided into two major categories:

- Interior Gateway Protocols (IGP)
- Exterior Gateway Protocols (EGP)

IGPs handle routing within an autonomous system. In other words, typically IGPs route traffic between the routers within an enterprise. These protocols keep track of how to get from one destination to the other inside a network or set of networks that you administer. In most cases, all the networks you manage combined are just one autonomous system. Some large organizations use more complex techniques, including several autonomous systems. IGPs are also divided into two categories:

- **Distance vector protocols:** Use a distance calculation plus an outgoing network interface (a vector) to choose the best path to a destination network. Routing Information Protocol (RIP) and Interior Gateway Routing Protocol (IGRP) are examples of distance vector protocols.

- **Link state protocols:** These track the status and connection type of each link and produce a calculated metric based on these and other factors, including some set by the network administrator. Link state protocols know whether a link is up or down and how fast it is. Using this information, link state protocols calculate the "cost" of routing the datagrams within a network. For example, link state protocols may take a path that has more hops but uses a faster medium in preference to a path using a slower medium with fewer hops. Open Shortest Path First (OSPF) is the most widely used link state protocol.

EGPs control routing outside an autonomous system. Internet service providers (ISP) typically use EGPs to route traffic between separate organizations. The most common exterior gateway routing protocol is BGP.

You can use many different techniques to attack routing protocols. The most common are the injection of illegitimate routing updates and DoS attacks specifically against routing.

Several tools you can use are already built into BGP, Intermediate System-to-Intermediate System (IS-IS), OSPF, EIGRP, and RIPv2 that help secure your infrastructure routing. The most common tools/techniques are as followed:

- Configuring static routing peers
- Authentication
- Route filtering
- Time-to-live (TTL) security checks

Configuring Static Routing Peers

Several routing protocols include different mechanisms that dynamically discover routing peers. Unfortunately, the same mechanisms can be easily used to insert bogus routers into the routing infrastructure. You can statically configure a list of trusted neighbors to avoid this problem. However, this technique causes controversy among administrators because, in large organizations, it can mean hundreds of configuration lines. For this reason, many prefer to use authentication mechanisms.

Authentication

Authentication is now available on most routing protocols. You can configure routing devices with a predefined shared secret key that is used to validate each routing update. Most routing protocols support two types of neighbor authentication: plaintext and MD5. With plaintext authentication, a secret key is included inside each routing update message. This does not provide much security because an attacker can easily read keys. MD5 authentication works by processing each routing update with an MD5 hash function and by including the resulting signature (digest) as part of the routing update message. When you are using MD5, the shared secret key is never sent over the network only the hashing information or digest.

Figure 2-2 illustrates a topology in which four Cisco IOS routers and a Cisco ASA are configured with OSPF and with MD5 authentication.

Figure 2-2 *OSPF Authentication*

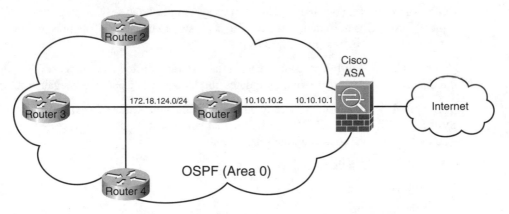

All routers and the Cisco ASA belong to the OSPF area 0. The following example shows the configuration of OSPF MD5 neighbor authentication on the router labeled Router 1.

```
router ospf 10
  network 172.18.124.0 0.0.0.255 area 0
  network 10.10.10.0 0.0.0.255 area 0
  area 0 authentication message-digest
```

```
!
interface Ethernet1
  ip address 10.10.10.2 255.255.255.0
  ip ospf authentication message-digest
  ip ospf message-digest-key 10 md5 1qaz@WSX
```

The first highlighted line shows how MD5 authentication is enabled for area 0. The second and third highlighted lines show how OSPF MD5 authentication is enabled on Ethernet 1. The shared key on this example is **1qaz@WSX**.

The following example shows the configuration of the Cisco ASA. The commands are almost identical to the Cisco IOS router.

```
router ospf 5
  network 10.10.10.0 0.0.0.255 area 0
  area 0 authentication message-digest
!
interface GigabitEthernet0/1
  ip address 10.10.10.1 255.255.255.0
  ospf authentication message-digest
  ospf message-digest-key 10 md5 1qaz@WSX
```

Notice that the Cisco ASA OSPF authentication configuration is similar to the Cisco IOS router. The actual code was ported from IOS. One of the differences is that OSPF interface subcommands are not preceded by the word "ip."

NOTE For more information about neighbor authentication in Cisco IOS, refer to http://www.cisco.com/univercd/cc/td/doc/product/software/ios124/124cg/hsec_c/part25/schroutr.htm.

For more about routing authentication in Cisco ASA, refer to http://www.cisco.com/univercd/cc/td/doc/product/multisec/asa_sw/v_7_2/conf_gd/general/ip.htm.

Route Filtering

You can use route filtering to prevent specific routes from being propagated throughout the network. You can use route filtering as a security mechanism, because filters can help ensure that only legitimate networks are advertised and that networks that are not supposed to be propagated are never advertised. For example, you can filter RFC-1918 private addresses.

NOTE For more information about routing security, see http://www.cisco.com/en/US/netsol/ns744/networking_solutions_program_home.html.

Time-to-Live (TTL) Security Check

TTL Security Check is a security feature implemented in BGP. It helps protect BGP peers from multihop attacks. This feature is based on the Generalized TTL Security Mechanism (GTSM) defined in RFC 3682 and applies only to external BGP (eBGP).

NOTE	Several organizations are working to implement this feature for other routing protocols, such as OSPF and EIGRP.

You can configure a minimum acceptable TTL value for the packets exchanged between two eBGP peers when you use the TTL Security Check feature in Cisco IOS. After you enable TTL Security Check, both BGP peers send all their updates with a TTL of 255. In addition, routers establish a peering session only if the other eBGP peer sends packets with a TTL equal to or greater than the TTL value configured for the peering session. By default, eBGP uses a TTL value of 1; the only exception is when eBGP multihop is used.

NOTE	If a router receives a packet with TTL values less than the calculated value, it silently discards it.

You can enable the TTL security check by using the **neighbor <ip address> ttl-security** command as shown in the following example:

```
Router(config)# router bgp 123
Router(config-router)# neighbor 209.165.200.226 ttl-security hops 3
```

In this example, TTL security check is enabled for the 209.165.200.226 eBGP neighbor which is three hops away. This router then accepts only BGP packets with a TTL value of 252 or greater.

NOTE	For more information about TTL security check, go to http://www.cisco.com/en/US/ products/ps6350/products_configuration_guide_chapter09186a0080455621.html.

Disabling Unnecessary Services on Network Components

Infrastructure devices in some cases come with a list of services turned on by default that are considered appropriate for most network environments. However, it is always a good idea to disable unnecessary services because some services present a vulnerability that could be used maliciously to gain unauthorized access or disrupt service.

NOTE   Not all environments have the same requirements but, on many occasions, disabling these unnecessary services not only enhances security but also helps preserve system resources.

The following is the list of Cisco IOS services that Cisco recommends you disable because they have the possibility of being used for malicious purposes:

- Cisco Discovery Protocol (CDP)
- Finger
- Directed Broadcast
- Maintenance Operations Protocol (MOP)
- BOOTP Server
- ICMP redirects
- IP source routing
- PAD
- Proxy ARP
- IDENT
- TCP and User Datagram Protocol (UDP) small servers
- IPv6

Cisco Discovery Protocol (CDP)

CDP is a protocol that allows you to obtain information about other devices within the network. This information can include the platform, model, software version, and IP addresses of network devices adjacent to the Cisco IOS routers.

NOTE   CDP is a Cisco proprietary Layer 2 protocol that is enabled by default.

CDP is a useful tool in the hands of an administrator, but it is a tool to be feared in the hands of an attacker. You can disable CDP globally when the service is not used or per interface when CDP is still required. As a rule of thumb, you should disable CDP on interfaces facing nontrusted networks such as the Internet. To disable CDP globally, use the **no cdp run** command. If you want to disable CDP on a specific interface, you can use the **no cdp enable** interface subcommand. For example:

```
myrouter(config)# interface Ethernet1
myrouter(config-if)# no cdp enable
```

TIP	You should always check for features that depend on CDP before disabling it. Features that depend on CDP are On-Demand Routing (ODR) and Cisco IP Telephony solutions.

Finger

The Finger protocol is used to obtain information about users logged into systems within the network. If you are running Cisco IOS Software versions prior to 12.1(5) and 12.1(5)T, Finger is on by default. Attackers can use Finger in reconnaissance attacks because it does not reveal much sensitive information. However, attackers can use chunks of information to obtain a better understanding of your environment. Always disable Finger whenever possible. You can do this with the **no service finger** command. In Versions 12.1(5) or 12.1(5)T and later, the Finger service is disabled by default; however, if for some reason it was turned on, you can disable it with the **no ip finger** command.

Directed Broadcast

Cisco IOS software versions prior to 11.2 have IP Directed Broadcast enabled by default. You are probably not running a version of IOS this old. However, because directed broadcasts have been used for DoS attacks (that is, SMURF), it is always recommended that you keep IP Directed Broadcast disabled. If for some reason the IP Directed Broadcast feature was enabled, you can disable it with the **no ip directed-broadcast** interface subcommand, as shown in the following example:

```
myrouter(config)# interface Ethernet1
myrouter(config-if)# no ip directed-broadcast
```

Maintenance Operations Protocol (MOP)

MOP was designed for remote communications between hosts and servers. Cisco IOS routers can use MOP to gather configuration information when communicating with DECnet networks.

NOTE	By default, MOP is enabled on all Ethernet interfaces and disabled on all other type of interfaces.

It is recommended that you disable the MOP service whenever possible, because this service has several vulnerabilities. To disable MOP, use the **no mop enabled** interface subcommand, as shown in the following:

```
myrouter(config)# interface Ethernet1
myrouter(config-if)# no mop enabled
```

BOOTP Server

The Bootstrap protocol allows a system to configure itself at boot time by dynamically obtaining the following information:

- An IP address
- The IP address of the BOOTP server
- A configuration file

BOOTP is defined in RFC 951. Cisco IOS routers can act as BOOTP servers. This service is turned on by default and is used by features such as AutoInstall. If not needed, this service should be disabled with the **no ip bootp server** global configuration command.

ICMP Redirects

Cisco IOS routers send ICMP redirect messages when ICMP redirects a packet through the same interface on which it was received. Attackers can sniff these packets and use them to discover network topology information. Disable ICMP redirects whenever possible with the **no ip redirects** interface subcommand, as shown here:

```
myrouter(config)# interface Ethernet1
myrouter(config-if)# no ip redirects
```

IP Source Routing

IP source routing enables a device to control the route that the datagram will take toward its destination. This feature is rarely used because it is not practical in environments today. Attackers can take advantage of older IP implementations that do not process source-routed packets properly and may be able to crash machines running these implementations by sending altered packets with source routing options. It is recommended that you disable IP source routing whenever possible with the **no ip source-route** command.

Packet Assembler/Disassembler (PAD)

Packet Assembler/Disassembler (PAD) allows some devices such as character-mode terminals to connect to legacy X.25 networks. PAD is enabled on Cisco IOS routers. In some cases, PAD can be used to gain unauthorized access, because its security is weak. Disable PAD whenever possible with the **no service pad** global command.

Proxy Address Resolution Protocol (ARP)

Proxy Address Resolution Protocol (ARP) is used to reach devices on a remote subnet without configuring specific routes to a network device. When you are performing proxy ARP, a network device answers all ARP requests on the local subnet on behalf of systems some hops away. Attackers can also use proxy ARP to obtain information about hosts behind routers in attempting to figure out the topology of your network.

NOTE   Proxy ARP is defined in RFC 1027.

It is recommended that you disable Proxy ARP on interfaces that connect to untrusted networks. On Cisco IOS, you can disable Proxy ARP with the **no ip proxy-arp** interface subcommand, as shown in the following example:

```
myrouter(config)# interface Ethernet1
myrouter(config-if)# no ip proxy-arp
```

IDENT

The TCP Client Identity Protocol (IDENT) allows a system to query the identity of a user initiating a TCP connection or a host responding to a TCP connection. The IDENT protocol enables you to obtain identity information by connecting to a TCP port on a system and issuing a simple text string requesting information.

NOTE   IDENT is defined in RFC 1413.

Attackers can use IDENT as another reconnaissance tool. Always disable IDENT whenever possible with the **no ip identd** global configuration command.

TCP and User Datagram Protocol (UDP) Small Servers

TCP and UDP small servers are daemons that typically run on UNIX systems and that were designed for diagnostic purposes. Cisco IOS Software also provides an implementation of UDP and TCP small servers that enables echo, chargen, daytime, and discard services. Unless strictly necessary, these services should be disabled because a potential attacker can use them to gather information or even to redirect traffic.

TCP and UDP small services are disabled by default on Cisco IOS Software Versions 11.3 and later. However, if for some reason they have been enabled, you can disable them by using the **no service tcp-small-servers** and **no service udp-small-servers** global configuration commands.

IP Version 6 (IPv6)

Historically, Cisco IOS–affected systems running IPv6 have had a couple of vulnerabilities. The execution of these vulnerabilities could lead to a system crash or the execution of arbitrary code. Only devices that were explicitly configured to process IPv6 traffic have been affected. That is why it is recommended that you disable IPv6 when not required, subsequently eliminating the potential exposure to vulnerabilities like those previously mentioned.

You can disable IPv6 on a per-interface basis using the **no ipv6 enable** and **no ipv6 address** interface subcommands, as shown here:

```
myrouter(config)# interface Ethernet1
myrouter(config-if)# no ipv6 enable
myrouter(config-if)# no ipv6 address
```

NOTE Chapter 11, "IPv6 Security," details how to secure IPv6 implementations.

Locking Down Unused Ports on Network Access Devices

This is a best practice that may be common sense for you but many network administrators overlook it. Several network devices have their ports and interfaces enabled by default. For instance, all Ethernet ports on Cisco Catalyst Switches running CatOS are enabled by default. Leaving unused ports enabled opens the chance for unauthorized access. It is always recommended that you keep all unused ports disabled. You can disable a port/interface on a Cisco Catalyst switch running CatOS with the **set port disable** command, as shown in the following example:

```
Console> (enable) set port disable 2/4
Port 2/4 disabled.
Console> (enable)
```

In this example, Ethernet port 2/4 is disabled on a Cisco Catalyst switch.

On devices running Cisco IOS, all interfaces are disabled by default; however, if an interface has been enabled and it is not in use, you should disable it with the shutdown interface subcommand as shown next:

```
myrouter(config)# interface Ethernet1
myrouter(config-if)# shutdown
```

Control Resource Exhaustion

Today, a growing number of DDoS attacks are being designed to specifically target key infrastructure devices. These types of attacks typically try to consume CPU resources, input queues, and memory. Worms and viruses that are generally designed to target end hosts generate large volumes of traffic that quite often exhaust most of the resources available in infrastructure equipment. You can implement several best practices by controlling the utilization of the limited resources in a device.

- Resource thresholding notification
- CPU protection
- Receive access control lists (rACLs)
- Control Plane Policing (CoPP)
- Scheduler Allocate/Interval

Resource Thresholding Notification

Always monitor the resource usage of infrastructure devices for unusual sustained high levels of CPU utilization, low free memory, and large volumes of dropped packets. These practices ease the detection and classification of attacks and outbreaks.

NOTE   Chapter 3, "Identifying and Classifying Security Threats," details numerous techniques to successfully identify and classify network attacks and outbreaks.

Several Cisco platforms provide automatic notification mechanisms that are generally based on SNMP or syslog. These mechanisms generate alarms when unusual levels of CPU or memory are detected. It is recommended that you use the Cisco IOS CPU thresholding notification and memory thresholding notification.

NOTE   The CPU thresholding notification was introduced in Cisco IOS Software Version 12.0(26)S.

You can configure two types of thresholds:

- **Rising CPU threshold:** Specifies the percentage of CPU utilization that will trigger a notification.
- **Falling CPU threshold:** Specifies the percentage of CPU resources that triggers a CPU threshold notification when CPU usage falls below this level for a configured period.

The following are the steps required to configure CPU threshold notification.

Step 1   Enable CPU threshold violation notification as traps and inform requests with the **snmp-server enable traps cpu threshold** command as follows:

```
myrouter(config)# snmp-server enable traps cpu threshold
```

Step 2   Configure the router to send CPU traps to a trusted SNMP server
(10.10.10.123 in this example).

```
myrouter(config)# snmp-server host 10.10.10.123 traps
mycommunitystring cpu
```

Step 3   Configure the threshold notification parameters. In the following
example, the CPU utilization threshold is set to 80 percent for a rising
threshold notification and 20 percent for a falling threshold notification
with a 5-second polling interval.

```
myrouter(config)# process cpu threshold type total rising 80 interval 5
falling 20 interval 5
```

You can also configure memory threshold notifications. You can configure the router to send
notifications to a trusted SNMP server to indicate that free memory has fallen below a
configured threshold. In addition, you can reserve memory to ensure that sufficient memory
is available to issue critical notifications.

NOTE   Memory threshold notifications were introduced in Cisco IOS Software Version 12.2(18)S.

You can configure processor memory or input/output memory thresholds. To configure a
processor memory threshold, use the **memory free low-watermark processor threshold**
global command. You can specify input/output memory thresholds with the **memory free
low-watermark io threshold** command.

In addition, you can mitigate low-memory conditions by reserving a region of memory for
the router to use for the issuing of critical notifications. Reserving a block of memory for
these functions is useful because when a router is overloaded by processes the amount of
available memory might fall to levels insufficient for it to issue critical notifications. Use
the **memory reserve critical kilobytes** command to accomplish this.

NOTE   You can obtain more information about Cisco IOS memory thresholding notification at
http://www.cisco.com/en/US/products/sw/iosswrel/ps1838/
products_feature_guide09186a00801b1bee.html.

CPU Protection

Attackers already know that targeting CPUs and network processors can affect more than
just one server within an organization. Worms and DDoS can bring network infrastructure
devices onto their knees costing thousands of dollars. Attackers typically follow two
strategies when targeting a CPU. The first tactic that attackers employ is generating large

volumes of traffic to the CPU or network processor because CPUs always have a finite capacity for processing packets. All processors have a limit regardless of the size or technology used. For this reason, some security experts say, It does not matter how much traffic a device can pass; what's important is how much traffic a device can drop.

The second tactic that attackers employ is making the network device generate large volumes of packets. They do this by sending traffic to the network device, to the location on the device where the CPU is expected to process and generate certain responses to specific requests. An example is sending malformed packets and making the network device send ICMP unreachable messages.

To counteract these two strategies be sure to take advantage of the following best practices:

- **Filtering of traffic sent to the CPU:** This is a key best practice. You should always make sure that only the expected protocols are used with the network device. When building these filters consider that, under normal circumstances, most traffic handled by infrastructure equipment is in transit over the forwarding path. Only a small portion of the traffic needs to be sent to the CPU for further analysis over the receive path. The traffic destined to the infrastructure equipment typically includes routing protocols, remote access protocols such as SSH and Telnet, or SNMP.

NOTE   Remember the rules you learned earlier in this chapter for protecting SNMP communications. Receive ACLs (or rACLs) are an example of a filtering technique.

- **Rate limit traffic sent to the CPU:** The filters discussed in the previous bullet should be combined with rate limiting techniques whenever possible. Another best practice is to implement a feature available on Cisco IOS routers called Control Plane Policing (CoPP). CoPP combines filtering with rate limiting to ensure that permitted traffic never reaches levels that could overwhelm the CPU. This feature is covered later on in this chapter (in the "Control Plane Policing (CoPP)" section).

- **Traffic requiring CPU packet generation:** Always control traffic that requires the CPU to generate packets. An example is using the **ip icmp rate-limit** command on Cisco IOS routers to prevent ICMP unreachable attacks.

- **Processor versus interrupt time:** Each time a Cisco router or switch (depending on the platform and feature implemented) receives a packet, it needs to interrupt other tasks to find out what to do with the packet. You can implement the **scheduler allocate** command or feature to tell the router to stop processing interrupts and to handle other tasks at regular intervals. This helps reduce the effects of fast packet floods.

Receive Access Control Lists (rACLs)

Receive access control lists (rACLs) are used to protect the Route Processor (RP) on high-end routers from malicious or unwanted traffic that could degrade performance.

NOTE   From the time this rACLs feature was originally introduced in 12.0 (22S for the Cisco 12000 series routers), numerous service providers have taken advantage of it. However, it is now available on other high-end routing platforms including the Cisco 7500 Series Routers and the Cisco 10000 Series Routers.

An rACL is just a standard or an extended ACL that controls the traffic sent by the various line cards to the RP. Because these high-end routers are designed in a distributed architecture, this type of ACL only affects the traffic destined to the RP and does not affect the transit traffic (traffic passing through the router).

rACLs comprise mainly permit statements that allow the protocols and specific sources that are expected to send traffic to the RP. These ACLs may also include deny statements to block specific unwanted traffic.

NOTE   All ACLs have an implicit deny statement at the end.

The following is an example of an rACL. The rACL number is 123. It can be any number, however, all the access control entries (ACE) must use the same number. In the following example, the router IP address is 209.165.200.225. Only BGP and OSPF are permitted from the 192.168.10.0/24 network; all other traffic is denied.

```
!The following ACEs allow BGP traffic to the RP (209.165.200.225)
access-list 123 permit tcp 192.168.10.0 0.0.0.255 host 209.165.200.225 eq bgp
access-list 123 permit tcp 192.168.10.0 0.0.0.255 eq bgp host 209.165.200.225
!
!The following ACEs allow OSPF traffic to the RP (notice that the OSPF multicast
  address is
!used instead of 209.165.200.225)
access-list 123 permit ospf 192.168.10.0 0.0.0.255 host 224.0.0.5
```

Optionally, you can deny specific traffic to protocols like UDP, TCP, and ICMP for tracking purposes. To do so, you can add the following lines to the ACL.

```
access-list 123 deny udp any any
access-list 123 deny tcp any any
access-list 123 deny icmp any any
access-list 123 deny ip any any
ip receive access-list 123
```

NOTE   Do not forget to always apply the rACL with the **ip receive access-list <num>** command, as shown in the last line in the previous example. rACLs are created on the RP and then pushed to the line card processors. All received packets are first sent to the line card CPU; however, any packets requiring processing by the RP are then compared against the rACL before they are sent to the RP.

rACLs increase security by protecting the RP from direct attacks. However, because they are just filters, they do not provide rate limiting benefits that could control large volumes of traffic that may match the permitted sources and protocols. CoPP offers rate limiting techniques that replace the need for rACLs.

TIP   When deploying the rACLs, always remember to start slowly. In other words, gradually improve security over time because, if you start too aggressively, your chance of dropping legitimate traffic increases.

Control Plane Policing (CoPP)

You can configure Quality of Service (QoS) policies to rate limit the traffic sent to the RP that is protecting the control plane from reconnaissance and DDoS attacks. With the Modular QoS Command-line (MQC) policies, you can permit, block, or rate limit traffic to the RP. You can use MQC to define traffic into separate classes and to apply distinct QoS policies based on different criteria.

NOTE   CoPP was introduced initially in 12.2(18)S for Cisco 7200, Cisco 7300, and Cisco 7500 series routers, and it is now available on most IOS-based platforms.

The following example includes the definition of two classes: one for OSPF traffic, and one for SSH used for remote management.

```
!ACL classifying OSPF traffic sourced from 192.168.10.0/24
ip access-list extended ospf-traffic-acl
 remark OSPF traffic class
permit ospf 192.168.10.0 0.0.0.255 host 244.0.0.4
!
!ACL classifying SSH traffic sourced from a management network (192.168.20.0/24)
ip access-list extended mgmt-traffic-acl
 remark CoPP remote management traffic
permit tcp 192.168.20.0 0.0.0.255 host 209.165.200.225 eq 22
!
!Once the ACLs are configured, they are applied to each access class
class-map match-all ospf-class
  match access-group name ospf-traffic-acl
!
class-map match-all ssh-class
  match access-group name mgmt-traffic-acl
!
!Apply the specific class to the actual policy (policy-map)
policy-map copp-policy
 class ospf-class
!SSH traffic is limited to a rate of 15,000 bps; if traffic
!exceeds that rate, it is dropped
  class ssh-class
```

```
      police 15000 1500 1500 conform-action transmit exceed-action drop
!
!Finally, apply the policy to the control plane
control-plane
  service-policy input copp-policy
```

NOTE   You can obtain an informative white paper on how to deploy CoPP from
http://www.cisco.com/en/US/products/sw/iosswrel/ps1838/
products_white_paper0900aecd802b8f21.shtml.

Scheduler Allocate/Interval

You can use the **scheduler interval** command to control the CPU time spent on processes
versus interrupts. This is helpful when you are under attack or during a worm outbreak.
When the router is handling thousands of packets per second, the console or Telnet/SSH
access may be slow and it may be almost impossible do anything.

In the following example, process-level tasks will be handled no less frequently than every
500 milliseconds.

```
myrouter(config)# scheduler interval 500
```

In newer platforms, the **scheduler allocate** command is used instead of **scheduler interval**.
The **scheduler allocate** command is used to configure two intervals:

* Interval with interrupts enabled
* Interval with interrupts masked

The following example includes the **scheduler allocate** command with the values included
in AutoSecure (a Cisco IOS feature explained later in this chapter in the "Cisco IOS
AutoSecure" section).

```
myrouter(config)# scheduler allocate 4000 1000
```

Cisco recommends these values for most environments.

NOTE   The **scheduler interval** and **scheduler allocate** commands should not cause negative
effects. It is recommended that these two commands be part of your standard router
configuration, unless you have a specific reason to avoid using them.

Policy Enforcement

An entire book could be devoted to a discussion of policy enforcement. Also, you must
design the enforcement of security policies according to your organization goals.
Therefore, this section cannot fully cover policy enforcement or provide recommendations

specific to your own business organization. It can, however, outline some common strategies that you can use when configuring network infrastructure devices to make sure that access to the areas of your network and its devices is granted only when needed by authorized sources.

The most common security policy enforcement mechanism is the use of packet filters at the various edges of the network. For example, you can configure firewalls or ACLs on routers to act as the first line of protection against external threats. Again, you should configure security policies based on the area in which your infrastructure components reside. For example, you will not configure the same policies for your Internet edge devices as the policies configured for your datacenter, core, and so on. Many engineers call this "configuration per device role." The roles of your device should develop your configuration templates. You can take several best practices into consideration when developing such configuration templates:

- Always make sure that external authorized sources can only communicate with internal devices via the expected protocols and ports.

- RFC 3330 describes the special use of IP addresses that may require filtering from sources of external devices. You should always filter packets with RFC 1918 private IP addresses that are not expected to be routed on the Internet.

- Follow the basic antispoofing services defined in RFC 2827.

The common technique used to accomplish these tasks is called Infrastructure Protection ACLs (iACLs). You can also configure Unicast Reverse Path Forwarding (Unicast RPF) for antispoofing.

Infrastructure Protection Access Control Lists (iACLs)

Using iACLs is a technique that was developed by ISPs, however, it is now a common practice by enterprises and other organizations. Employing iACLs involves the use of ACLs that prevent direct attacks to infrastructure devices. You configure these ACLs to specifically allow only authorized traffic to the infrastructure equipment while allowing transit traffic. Cisco recommends that you configure iACLs into four different sections or modules:

1 On the Internet edge, deny packets from illegal sources (RFC 1918 and RFC 3330 addresses). In addition, deny traffic with source addresses belonging within your address space entering from an external source. For example, if your address space is 209.165.201.0/24, you should configure an iACL to deny traffic from any external source by using an address from this space. The following example includes iACL entries (part of ACL number 123) used to deny RFC 3330 special-use addresses.

```
access-list 123 deny ip host 0.0.0.0 any
access-list 123 deny ip 127.0.0.0 0.255.255.255 any
access-list 123 deny ip 192.0.2.0 0.0.0.255 any
access-list 123 deny ip 224.0.0.0 31.255.255.255 any
```

The following entries deny RFC 1918 traffic.

```
access-list 123 deny ip 10.0.0.0 0.255.255.255 any
access-list 123 deny ip 172.16.0.0 0.15.255.255 any
access-list 123 deny ip 192.168.0.0 0.0.255.255 any
```

2 Configure iACL entries providing explicit permission for traffic from trusted external sources destined to your infrastructure address space.

3 Deny all other traffic from external sources destined to infrastructure components addresses as shown in the following example.

```
access-list 123 deny ip any 209.165.201.0 0.0.0.255
```

4 Unlike ISPs, enterprises are the destination for traffic. The last section of the iACL permits all other normal backbone traffic destined to noninfrastructure destinations for only specific protocols and ports. For example, you can allow HTTP for a web server bank with IP address space 209.165.200.0/24, as follows:

```
access-list 123 permit tcp any 209.165.200.0 0.0.0.255 eq http
```

ISPs allow all transit traffic at the end of the iACL using a **permit ip any any** ACL entry.

Unicast Reverse Path Forwarding (Unicast RPF)

Unicast Reverse Path Forwarding (Unicast RPF) is a feature that can replace the use of RFC 2827 ingress traffic filtering techniques. Unicast RPF is configured and enabled on a per-interface basis. The main purpose of Unicast RPF is to verify that all packets received from a specific interface have a source address that is reachable via that same interface. The router drops all packets that do not comply.

NOTE   You must turn on Cisco Express Forwarding (CEF) for Unicast RPF to work.

Two Unicast RPF modes are available:

- **Strict mode:** Requires that the source IP address of an incoming packet has a reverse path to the same interface from which it has arrived.

- **Loose mode:** Requires that the source IP address of an incoming packet has a reverse path to any interface on the device (except null0). In many cases, an enterprise may have dual connections to the Internet; therefore, Unicast RPF strict mode is not feasible. Only use Unicast RPF strict mode in deployments where the reverse path entries match the traffic paths, otherwise you risk discarding legitimate traffic.

The following example demonstrates how to enable Unicast RPF strict mode on an interface (FastEthernet 1/0 in this case).

```
Router(config)# interface FastEthernet 1/0
Router(config-if)# ip verify unicast source reachable-via rx
```

The following example demonstrates how to enable Unicast RPF loose mode on an interface (Serial2 in this case).

```
Router(config)# interface Serial2
Router(config-if)# ip verify unicast source reachable-via any
```

Automated Security Tools Within Cisco IOS

The feature within Cisco IOS called AutoSecure enables you to lock down your routers by enhancing the security of the management and the forwarding planes. Similarly, you can perform automatic audit and self-configuration options with Cisco Security Device Manager (SDM).

Cisco IOS AutoSecure

Cisco AutoSecure disables the unnecessary global services previously discussed in this chapter. It also enables certain services that help further secure global services that are often necessary. In addition, Cisco AutoSecure hardens administrative access by enabling appropriate security-related logging features. It is recommended in most environments because it implements a range of best practices that help secure any organization. It also reduces the time required to configure each item by hand.

NOTE Cisco AutoSecure was introduced in Cisco IOS Software Version 12.3 and in subsequent 12.3T releases for the Cisco 800, 1700, 2600, 3600, 3700, 7200, and 7500 Series Routers.

Cisco AutoSecure has two modes of operation:

- **Interactive:** Users select their own options for services and other security-related features.
- **Noninteractive:** This mode automatically enables a set of Cisco recommended security features and disables unnecessary services.

TIP The Interactive mode enables you to have more control over the router security features that you want to enable. However, if you need to quickly secure a router without much human intervention, the noninteractive mode is appropriate.

You can also specify what part of the AutoSecure suite of commands and features you would like to configure. The following example shows the options of the **auto secure** command.

```
myrouter#auto secure ?
  firewall        AutoSecure Firewall
  forwarding      Secure Forwarding Plane
  full            Interactive full session of AutoSecure
  login           AutoSecure Login
  management      Secure Management Plane
  no-interact     Non-interactive session of AutoSecure
  ntp             AutoSecure NTP
  ssh             AutoSecure SSH
  tcp-intercept   AutoSecure TCP Intercept
  <cr>
```

In the next example, the **auto secure** command is invoked with no options; therefore, the complete suite of configuration options is presented to the user.

```
myrouter#auto secure
                --- AutoSecure Configuration ---
*** AutoSecure configuration enhances the security of
the router, but it will not make it absolutely resistant
to all security attacks ***
AutoSecure will modify the configuration of your device.
All configuration changes will be shown. For a detailed
explanation of how the configuration changes enhance security
and any possible side effects, please refer to Cisco.com for
AutoSecure documentation.
At any prompt you may enter '?' for help.
Use ctrl-c to abort this session at any prompt.
Gathering information about the router for AutoSecure
Is this router connected to internet? [no]: yes
Enter the number of interfaces facing the internet [1]: 1
Interface                IP-Address       OK? Method Status                  Protocol
FastEthernet0/0          unassigned       YES NVRAM  administratively down down
FastEthernet0/1          unassigned       YES NVRAM  administratively down down
Enter the interface name that is facing the internet: FastEthernet0/0
Securing Management plane services...
Disabling service finger
Disabling service pad
Disabling udp & tcp small servers
Enabling service password encryption
Enabling service tcp-keepalives-in
Enabling service tcp-keepalives-out
Disabling the cdp protocol
Disabling the bootp server
Disabling the http server
Disabling the finger service
Disabling source routing
Disabling gratuitous arp
Here is a sample Security Banner to be shown
at every access to device. Modify it to suit your
enterprise requirements.
Authorized Access only
  This system is the property of So-&-So-Enterprise.
  UNAUTHORIZED ACCESS TO THIS DEVICE IS PROHIBITED.
  You must have explicit permission to access this
  device. All activities performed on this device
  are logged. Any violations of access policy will result
  in disciplinary action.
Enter the security banner {Put the banner between
k and k, where k is any character}:
~  UNAUTHORIZED ACCESS TO THIS DEVICE IS PROHIBITED.
   You must have explicit permission to access this
   device. All activities performed on this device
   are logged. Any violations of access policy will result
   in disciplinary action.
```

```
~
Enable secret is either not configured or
 is the same as enable password
Enter the new enable secret:1qaz@WSX
Confirm the enable secret :1qaz@WSX
Enter the new enable password:2wsx!QAZ
Confirm the enable password:2wsx!QAZ
Configuration of local user database
Enter the username: admin
Enter the password:1qaz@WSX
Confirm the password:1qaz@WSX
Configuring AAA local authentication
Configuring Console, Aux and VTY lines for
local authentication, exec-timeout, and transport
Securing device against Login Attacks
Configure the following parameters
Blocking Period when Login Attack detected: 15
Maximum Login failures with the device: 3
Maximum time period for crossing the failed login attempts: 60
Configure SSH server? [yes]: yes
Enter the domain-name: cisco.com
Configuring interface specific AutoSecure services
Disabling the following ip services on all interfaces:
 no ip redirects
 no ip proxy-arp
 no ip unreachables
 no ip directed-broadcast
 no ip mask-reply
Disabling mop on Ethernet interfaces
Securing Forwarding plane services...
Enabling CEF (This might impact the memory requirements for your platform)
Enabling unicast rpf on all interfaces connected
to internet
Configure CBAC Firewall feature? [yes/no]: yes
This is the configuration generated:
no service finger
no service pad
no service udp-small-servers
no service tcp-small-servers
service password-encryption
service tcp-keepalives-in
service tcp-keepalives-out
no cdp run
no ip bootp server
no ip http server
no ip finger
no ip source-route
no ip gratuitous-arps
no ip identd
banner motd ^C  UNAUTHORIZED ACCESS TO THIS DEVICE IS PROHIBITED.
  You must have explicit permission to access this
  device. All activities performed on this device
  are logged. Any violations of access policy will result
  in disciplinary action.
^C
security passwords min-length 6
security authentication failure rate 10 log
enable secret 5 $1$gGZi$aoXeicM9JVVMfi0K6lF150
enable password 7 14141B180F0B7B79777C66
username admin password 7 030752180500701E1D
aaa new-model
aaa authentication login local_auth local
line con 0
```

```
   login authentication local_auth
   exec-timeout 5 0
   transport output telnet
line aux 0
   login authentication local_auth
   exec-timeout 10 0
   transport output telnet
line vty 0 4
   login authentication local_auth
   transport input telnet
line tty 1
   login authentication local_auth
   exec-timeout 15 0
line tty 192
   login authentication local_auth
   exec-timeout 15 0
login block-for 15 attempts 3 within 60
ip domain-name cisco.com
crypto key generate rsa general-keys modulus 1024
ip ssh time-out 60
ip ssh authentication-retries 2
line vty 0 4
   transport input ssh telnet
service timestamps debug datetime msec localtime show-timezone
service timestamps log datetime msec localtime show-timezone
logging facility local2
logging trap debugging
service sequence-numbers
logging console critical
logging buffered
interface FastEthernet0/0
 no ip redirects
 no ip proxy-arp
 no ip unreachables
 no ip directed-broadcast
 no ip mask-reply
 no mop enabled
interface FastEthernet0/1
 no ip redirects
 no ip proxy-arp
 no ip unreachables
 no ip directed-broadcast
 no ip mask-reply
 no mop enabled
ip cef
access-list 100 permit udp any any eq bootpc
interface FastEthernet0/0
 ip verify unicast source reachable-via rx allow-default 100
ip inspect audit-trail
ip inspect dns-timeout 7
ip inspect tcp idle-time 14400
ip inspect udp idle-time 1800
ip inspect name autosec_inspect cuseeme timeout 3600
ip inspect name autosec_inspect ftp timeout 3600
ip inspect name autosec_inspect http timeout 3600
ip inspect name autosec_inspect rcmd timeout 3600
ip inspect name autosec_inspect realaudio timeout 3600
ip inspect name autosec_inspect smtp timeout 3600
ip inspect name autosec_inspect tftp timeout 30
ip inspect name autosec_inspect udp timeout 15
ip inspect name autosec_inspect tcp timeout 3600
ip access-list extended autosec_firewall_acl
 permit udp any any eq bootpc
 deny ip any any
```

```
interface FastEthernet0/0
 ip inspect autosec inspect out
 ip access-group autosec_firewall_acl in
!
end
Apply this configuration to running-config? [yes]:yes
```

In the previous example, the router has the interface (FastEthernet0/0) that is connected to the Internet. The AutoSecure utility applies predefined commands based on best practices for Internet-edge routers. The router then guides the user on enabling other features, such as defining a banner, configuring passwords and administrative accounts, and enabling Cisco IOS Firewall set or Context-Based Access Control (CBAC).

Cisco Secure Device Manager (SDM)

SDM is an intuitive web-based tool designed for configuring LAN, WAN, and security features on a router. SDM includes a feature called Security Audit that is used to verify your existing router configuration and make sure that it includes the recommended security mechanisms suited for most environments. The SDM Security Audit is based on the Cisco IOS AutoSecure feature.

NOTE SDM does not support all AutoSecure features. For a complete list of the functions that Security Audit checks for, and for a list of the few AutoSecure features unsupported by Security Audit, go to http://www.cisco.com/en/US/products/sw/secursw/ps5318/ products_user_guide_chapter09186a0080656061.html#wp1061799.

Complete the following steps to have SDM perform a security audit, and then fix the configuration deficiencies it finds.

Step 1 Log in to SDM via HTTPS. For example, if your router IP address is 192.168.10.1, you can access SDM by typing **https://192.168.10.1**.

Step 2 After you have logged in, select **Security Audit** from the left frame or navigation panel.

Step 3 Click **Perform Security Audit**. The Welcome page of the Security Audit Wizard appears.

Step 4 Click **Next**. The Security Audit Interface Configuration screen is shown.

Step 5 You have to tell SDM which of your router interfaces connect to the Internet (or outside networks) and which connect to your protected (or inside) networks. Select either the **Inside** or **Outside** check box to indicate where each interface connects and click **Next**.

Step 6   SDM verifies your router configuration and identifies any security deficiencies. A window pops-up displays listing the configuration options being audited and whether the current router configuration passes such tests. Optionally, you can save the audit report to a file by clicking **Save Report**.

Step 7   Click **Close**.

Step 8   The list of possible security problems is displayed. Check the **Fix it** boxes next to any problems that you want SDM to fix. You can view a description of each problem and a list of the Cisco IOS commands that will be added to your configuration by clicking **Problem Description**.

Step 9   Click **Next**. SDM may display one or more screens requiring you to enter information to fix certain problems. Enter the information as required and click **Next** for each of those screens.

Step 10   A summary page listing all the configuration changes that SDM will make is displayed. To send those changes to the router, click **Finish**.

NOTE   You can also use the One-Step Lockdown feature in SDM to test your router configuration for any potential security problems and fix them automatically.

Telemetry

The automated measurement and transmission of data for analysis is what many people call *telemetry*. Cisco routers and switches have different mechanisms that offer a form of telemetry. An example is NetFlow. You can use NetFlow to obtain statistical information that can help you identify and classify attacks. This information can be collected from the CLI or can be exported to monitoring tools such as Cisco Secure Monitoring, Analysis, and Response System (CS-MARS) and Arbor Peakflow. The use of monitoring and event correlation tools is recommended because it can save you numerous hours of your busy schedule trying to digest information from logs, NetFlow, and other sources.

NOTE   Detailed information about how to identify and classify attacks is covered in Chapter 3. However, this section includes several telemetry best practices that help you better prepare and protect your infrastructure.

You must accurately synchronize the time and date with network telemetry. This is why it is crucial to enable Network Time Protocol (NTP) in network devices. Imagine trying to analyze and correlate network events if all your routers, switches, firewalls, and other network devices have different times and dates. For instance, if you were analyzing firewall logs and correlating them to NetFlow data, and the time was not synchronized, this task could be impossible.

NOTE   You can obtain information about NTP at http://www.ntp.org or at http://www.cisco.com/en/US/tech/tk648/tk362/tk461/tsd_technology_support_sub-protocol_home.html.

Another best practice is to send network telemetry information over out-of-band (OOB) mechanisms because this minimizes the chance for disruption of the information that provides network visibility, which is critical to successfully operating and defending the network. This is why it is always recommended that you have a management VLAN or section of the network where an interface of each network device can communicate with management stations and systems.

NetFlow data helps you identify DDoS attacks, network worms, and other forms of undesirable traffic. In addition, it is a key auditing and forensics tool. For instance, you can collect NetFlow data and map Network Address Translations (NAT) and ensure that your policy enforcement measures are working as expected.

NOTE   Chapter 3 includes several NetFlow configuration examples. It also shows how you can identify and classify security events using event correlation tools, such as CS-MARS.

Endpoint Security

This section includes several best practices and tips that you can use when implementing techniques and tools to increase the security of your endpoints (workstations, servers, and so on). You need to perform two major tasks when you are preparing your organization to enhance endpoint security. The first is patch management and keeping the endpoint systems (servers and workstations specifically) up-to-date. The second is using security software like the Cisco Security Agent (CSA) on servers and user desktop machines to protect them against known and unknown security threats.

Patch Management

A solid patch management strategy is crucial with the rise of widespread worms and malicious code that targets known vulnerabilities on unpatched systems. This is why the increasing governance and regulatory compliance enforcement by organizations like

HIPAA and Sarbanes-Oxley has pressed organizations hard to gain better control and oversight of their information assets.

The main objective of a patch management program is to create a consistently configured environment that is secure against known vulnerabilities in operating system and application software. Patch management solutions vary in design and implementation. Regardless, several technology-neutral best practices are listed in this section and can be followed no matter what patch management software or solution you use.

A good practice is to designate a point person or a team that is responsible for keeping up-to-date on newly released patches and security threats that affect the systems and applications deployed within your organization. Have a complete and accurate asset inventory to determine whether all existing systems are accounted for when preparing and deploying patches and updates.

Also, prioritize and schedule the necessary application patches/updates. A patch update cycle must exist to facilitate the application of standard patch releases and updates. You can perform the cycle in a scheduled time fashion or based on events. You can implement the time-based scheduled cycle weekly, biweekly, or monthly, depending on the organization policies. In contrast, you can coordinate the scheduling cycle with critical security patches and updates. This plan should help you deal with the prioritization and scheduling of updates that must be deployed in a more immediate fashion.

Preferably, you should test patches and updates before deploying them to your systems. In critical situations when a security patch is needed because of a worm or a security outbreak, detailed testing may not be possible or feasible. The initial phases of production rollout can be considered an additional component of the testing process. Rollouts are often implemented in tiers with the initial tiers often involving less critical systems. Based on the performance of these stages of the patch deployment process, the entire environment will be updated, and the testing process can be considered finished with the completion of final acceptance testing.

Regular audits and assessment help gauge the success and extent of patch management efforts. You should always determine what systems you need to patch for any given vulnerability or a bug. In addition, you should always verify that the systems that are supposed to be updated have been patched.

Patch management software packages are available from many vendors. The following are some of the most popular ones:

- IBM Tivoli
- Unicenter
- Microsoft SMS
- PatchLink
- Altiris

The major requirement for any patch management system is the ability to accurately track deployed hardware and software throughout the enterprise, including remote users and office locations.

Cisco Security Agent (CSA)

CSA provides several more robust security features than a traditional antivirus or a personal firewall solution. The rich security features of CSA include:

- Host intrusion prevention
- Protection against spyware
- Protection against buffer overflow attacks
- Distributed host firewall features
- Malicious mobile code protection
- Operating system integrity assurance
- Application inventory
- Extensive audit and logging capabilities
- Protection against file modification or deletion

The CSA solution has two major components:

- **Cisco Security Agent Management Center (CSA-MC):** The management console where all groups, policies, and agent kits are configured
- **Cisco Security Agent:** The agent installed on end-user machines

The CSA-MC is the central management system that allows you to define and distribute policies, provide software updates, and maintain communications to the CSAs installed in end-user machines and servers. CSA-MC comes with a list of predefined groups you can use to meet initial needs. A group is the only element required to build an agent kit. The use of groups eases the management of large numbers of agents. When using groups, you can consistently apply the same policy to numerous hosts.

Agent kits are the configuration and installation packages of the agent software to be deployed to end-user machines. You must associate agent kits with configured groups. Agents installed on end-user hosts are automatically placed into their assigned group or groups when they register with CSA-MC. The agents enforce the associated policies of each group.

NOTE   Chapter 12, "Case Studies," includes a case study showing the deployment of CSA. You can get more information and documentation at http://www.cisco.com/en/US/products/sw/secursw/ps5057/index.html.

It is recommended that you place the CSAMC server on your management network (management VLAN). When doing this, you need to understand how the agents communicate with CSAMC and vice versa. The agents communicate with CSAMC over TCP port 5401, with a fallback to TCP port 443 (if TCP port 5401 communication is not possible). By default, CSA Profiler uses TCP port 5402 to communicate with CSAMC; however, this is configurable. Make sure that any firewalls or filtering devices allow this communication. CSAMC should be reached by all systems that are running the agent.

Another important factor is that the hardware running CSAMC must be sized appropriately. The current version of CSAMC is capable of managing up to 100,000 agents. However, it is recommended that you install and strategically deploy additional CSAMC servers depending on your network topology and geographical needs.

NOTE   For a list of hardware requirements, refer to the release notes on the Cisco website at http://www.cisco.com/en/US/products/sw/secursw/ps5057/index.html.

During the lab test and pilot phases, it is recommended that you start by using the default CSA policies (depending on the type of system where the agent is installed). The default CSA policies provide a good level of protection to the end hosts. Tuning of these is recommended; however, these default policies are known for stopping new and unknown threats.

Always select at least one host per each distinct application environment during the initial testing phase. During the pilot, the test hosts should be a mirror sample of the production systems. In addition, you may want to use a test machine per each server type to ensure no negative impact from CSA agent software installation. It is also recommended that you create a group for each type of application environment that needs to be protected.

Building and tuning of CSA policies is a continuous task; therefore, you must have the proper staff and procedures to minimize the administrative burden. The security staff is not only responsible for maintaining the CSAMC policies, but also for creating and organizing exception rules appropriately, and for monitoring user activity. You can organize the exception rules as follows:

- Create a global exception policy to allow legitimate traffic and application behavior that is required on all the systems within the organization. Subsequently, add these global exception rules to this exception policy.
- Create one exception policy for each group.
- Apply these policies to their respective groups, and collect all necessary data to complete any additional tuning.

When you start the deployment of the agent kits throughout the organization, always start by deploying the agents in test mode throughout your organization. It is a best practice to collect and analyze results and start policy tuning (as needed). After the initial tuning is done, enable protection mode.

NOTE   Make sure that your security, operations, and engineering staff members are trained to support your deployment.

Network Admission Control

In Chapter 1, "Overview of Network Security Technologies," you learned the concepts of Network Admission Control (NAC) and the differences between the appliance-based approach and the architecture-based framework solution. The architecture-based framework solution is intended to use a collection of both Cisco networking and security technologies, as well as existing deployments of security and management solutions from other vendors. This section includes several best practices when implementing NAC within your environment. These best practices can be followed when preparing, designing, or implementing any of the NAC solutions (Framework or Appliance).

NOTE   Chapter 12 includes a case study where NAC is deployed. The configuration of NAC appliance and NAC Framework components is also in that chapter.

Phased Approach

To achieve a successful enterprise-wide deployment of the Cisco NAC solutions, it is first necessary to have a solid background in the operational, management, and support functions required by such a deployment. Create a clear and detailed test and implementation plan to overcome challenges and follow a phased approached. For instance, it is always strongly recommended that you test any new technology or product in a lab environment first. Subsequently, you should complete and carefully evaluate a pilot within a limited production environment. If at all possible, this environment should include a sample of the systems available within the rest of the production network. This allows your network and security staff to quantify the effects of the new NAC solution on the organization without actually affecting the production network. This may not be easy to do in many smaller environments; however, it is still recommended. Your security and network staff members will gain valuable training and experience with the new technologies being deployed and understand their interaction with the existing infrastructure.

The following are the key points and phases when planning, designing, testing, and deploying NAC throughout your organization:

- **Readiness assessment:** Complete a readiness assessment of your current infrastructure. Assuming that the organization has a corporate security policy, complete a gap analysis determining what NAC policies to develop.

- **Stakeholders:** Identify who will be the stakeholders during the initial tests and the rest of the deployment.

- **Initial lab testing:** Build an initial lab environment.

- **Test plans:** Create a detailed test plan for lab and limited-production pilot.

- **Initial tuning:** Complete any initial tuning of policies, configurations, and procedures on the test network.

- **Final deployment strategy:** Start the deployment in the production environment in accordance with the deployment model devised from the pilot environment. Monitor the deployment stages and tune accordingly.

Testing and validation are critical best practices. Proper lab testing can significantly reduce production downtime, help your network and security support staff to become familiar with the NAC solution, and assist in streamlining the implementation processes. To be effective, however, the organization must allocate the necessary resources to build and maintain the appropriate lab environment, apply necessary resources to perform the correct tests, and use a recommended testing methodology that includes measurement collection. Without giving each of these areas detailed attention, the testing and validation process may not meet the expectations of an organization.

Many organizations do not take the time to build the recommended test lab environment. Consequently, they have deployed solutions incorrectly and have experienced network failures that could have been isolated in a lab environment. In some environments, this is acceptable because the cost of downtime does not offset the cost of a sophisticated lab environment. Many organizations, however, cannot tolerate downtime. These organizations are strongly urged to develop the recommended test labs, test types, and test methodologies to improve production network quality.

Identify a section of the network where you can successfully test the new NAC features and devices you may be implementing. This helps to minimize potential exposure and to more safely identify any production issues. For example, in the previous chapter, you learned how to successfully deploy Layer 2, Layer 3, wireless, and remote access VPN NAC features on different sites within an organization. During the pilot selection phase, you may identify an area or branch office where you can test the specific features to be deployed.

Pilot selection identifies where and how the pilot will be completed. The limited-production pilot may start with one device in a low-impact area and extend to multiple devices in a higher-impact area. You should perform a risk analysis to identify what areas and users can deal with some possible production impacts. You can also use the "monitor-mode" approach. In other words, you can configure the Cisco Secure ACS policies for Healthy,

Quarantine, and Transition. You should, however, still allow users to access the network. This way you can quantify the impact of enforcing the configured policies and determine what and why machines are being quarantined or placed into any other state.

Base the duration of this pilot on the time it takes to sufficiently test and evaluate all the software, hardware, and third-party features and their dependencies. During the pilot phase, monitor and document results in a manner similar to that used in the initial lab testing. This can include user surveys, pilot data collection, and problem identification.

Administrative Tasks

You need to recognize the administrative tasks that are involved in maintaining all the NAC policies. Some of the most common administrative tasks include:

- **Keeping the operating system (OS) policies up-to-date:** Update your NAC policies in ACS every time a new OS critical patch comes out. If you fail to update, the host will be allowed to the network without having this update installed. This can be an administrative headache. That is why it is important that you have clear procedures and the correct staff in place to be able to support these tasks.

- **Keeping your antivirus policies up-to-date:** In the NAC Appliance solution, you can configure the Clean Access Manager (CAM) to automatically download information from Cisco about the latest antivirus patches. In contrast, in NAC framework solution, you have to configure Cisco Secure ACS to work in concert with antivirus vendor software (such as Trend Micro OfficeScan policy server) to validate endpoint antivirus credentials. In this case, you also have to keep up with the latest signatures in the antivirus server. Commonly, this is done by automatic mechanisms helping the administrative overhead of such tasks.

- **Maintaining remediation servers and third-party software:** Remediation servers need to be up-to-date so that you can successfully remediate machines that are put into quarantine for not having the latest version of the required software dictated in the configured NAC policies. What good is an expensive car if you do not have the fuel to run it? The same principle applies here. You can have the most elaborate remediation servers and mechanisms; however, if you do not keep them up-to-date, they might not be useful when you try to fix machines that have been put into quarantine because of the discovery of security deficiencies. You can obtain the most current list of third-party remediation partners from http://www.cisco.com/en/US/netsol/ns466/networking_solutions_package.html.

Staff and Support

Prepare your networking and security staff members to support the common administrative tasks discussed in the previous section. In addition, establish a clear technical support structure and a well-structured call routing process to provide end users the correct resources as quickly as possible. Most NAC-related support calls to your help desk will involve users who are not able to access the network (or are granted limited access) because their machines do not meet the standards that the security policy is enforcing. Consequently, these calls will most likely be high severity/priority calls. This is a worthy consideration when you are planning the deployment of the NAC solution and evaluating the impact on your support staff.

Educating users on setting the severity of the service request accurately, based on the impact to the organization, allows you to allocate the appropriate resources to resolve problems more efficiently. Using online resources and education material will also help alleviate the support process. The "life expectancy" of these calls will depend on why the user cannot access the network. For instance, a user may open a service request because his machine has been placed into quarantine and has failed to install an OS patch or antivirus signature update. In another instance, a user workstation may be infected and require more detailed work.

Have clearly defined escalation procedures. Having solid escalation procedures prevents service requests from being escalated prematurely. During the troubleshooting process, the engineer assigned to assist the user may determine that an onsite engineer is required to resolve the issue. Have a clear process in place for the engineer to contact a resource onsite.

Summary

This chapter is one of the most vital chapters of this book. It covered the fundamentals of how to better prepare yourself, your network, and your organization as a whole against security threats and vulnerabilities. It presented risk analysis and threat modeling techniques and discussed the process of creating strong security policies. This chapter also described how necessary CSIRTs are for your organization and provided the most common techniques when forming and managing a CSIRT.

Topics such as security intelligence and social engineering were covered in this chapter. Securing your infrastructure is one of the most challenging tasks. This chapter gave you detailed information on how to protect your infrastructure against many different vulnerabilities and threats.

You learned how to better secure end-user systems and servers (endpoint security) in this chapter. In addition, you read a summary of how identity management and Network Admission Control (NAC) can help you protect against viruses, worm outbreaks, and other vulnerabilities. The best practices outlined in this chapter are crucial for any organization.

This chapter covers the following topics:

- Network Visibility
- Telemetry and Anomaly Detection
- Intrusion Detection and Intrusion Prevention Systems (IDS/IPS)

CHAPTER 3

Identifying and Classifying Security Threats

Worms and denial of service (DoS) attacks are used maliciously to consume the resources of your hosts and network that would otherwise be used to serve legitimate users. In some cases, misconfigured hosts and servers can send traffic that consumes network resources unnecessarily. Having the necessary tools and mechanisms to identify and classify security threats and anomalies in the network is crucial. This chapter presents several best practices and methodologies you can use to successfully and quickly identify and classify such threats.

Most people classify security attacks into two separate categories: *logic attacks* and *resource attacks*. Logic attacks exploit existing software deficiencies and vulnerabilities to cause systems to crash, to substantially degrade their performance, or to enable attackers to gain access to a system. An example of this type of attack is the exploit of the Microsoft PnP MS05-039 Overflow Vulnerability, in which the attacker exploits a stack overflow in the Windows "plug and play" (PnP) service. You can exploit this vulnerability on Windows 2000 without a valid user account. Another example is the famous and old *ping-of-death*, whereby an attacker sends the system Internet Control Message Protocol (ICMP) packets that exceed the maximum legal length (65535 octets). You can prevent most of these attacks by either upgrading the vulnerable software or by filtering particular packet sequences.

The second category of attacks is referred to as resource attacks. The goal with these types of attacks is to overwhelm the victim system/network resources, such as CPU and memory. In most cases, this is done by sending numerous IP packets or forged requests. An attacker can build up a more powerful attack with a more sophisticated and effective method of compromising multiple hosts and installing small attack daemon(s). This is what many call *zombies* or *bot* hosts/nets. Subsequently, an attacker can launch a coordinated attack from thousands of zombies onto a single victim. This daemon typically contains both the code for sourcing a variety of attacks and some basic communications infrastructure to allow for remote control. A zombie attack is illustrated in Figure 3-1.

Figure 3-1 *Zombies and Bots*

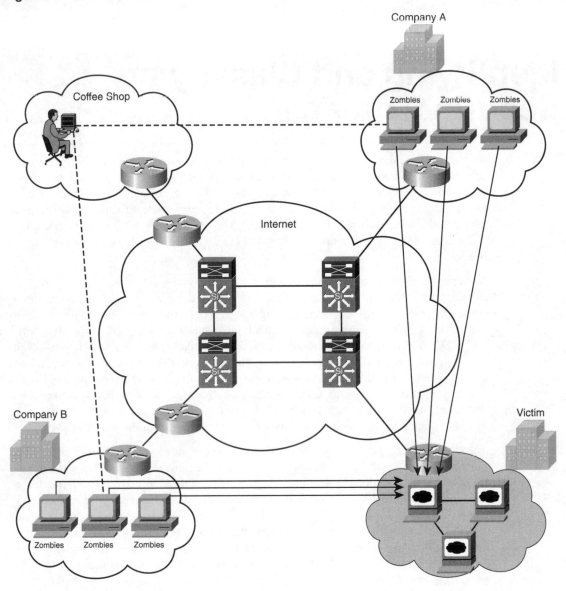

In Figure 3-1, an attacker controls compromised hosts in Company A and Company B to attack a web server farm in another organization.

You can use different mechanisms and methodologies to successfully identify and classify these threats/attacks depending on their type. In other words, depending on the threat, you can use specific techniques to identify and classify them accordingly. Following are the most common methodologies:

- The use of anomaly detection tools
- Network telemetry using flow-based analysis
- The use of intrusion detection and intrusion prevention systems (IDS/IPS)
- Analyzing network component logs (that is, SYSLOG from different network devices, accounting records, application logs, Simple Network Management Protocol (SNMP), and so on)

Complete visibility is one of the key requirements when identifying and classifying security threats. The following sections explain best practices for achieving complete network visibility and the use of the previously mentioned tools and mechanisms.

Network Visibility

The first step in the process of preparing your network and staff to successfully identify security threats is achieving complete network visibility. You cannot protect against or mitigate what you cannot view/detect. You can achieve this level of network visibility through existing features on network devices you already have and on devices whose potential you do not even realize. In addition, you should create strategic network diagrams to clearly illustrate your packet flows and where, within the network, you may enable security mechanisms to identify, classify, and mitigate the threat. Remember that network security is a constant war. When defending against the enemy, you must know your own territory and implement defense mechanisms in place. Figure 3-2 illustrates a fairly simple high-level enterprise diagram.

Figure 3-2 *High-Level Enterprise Diagram*

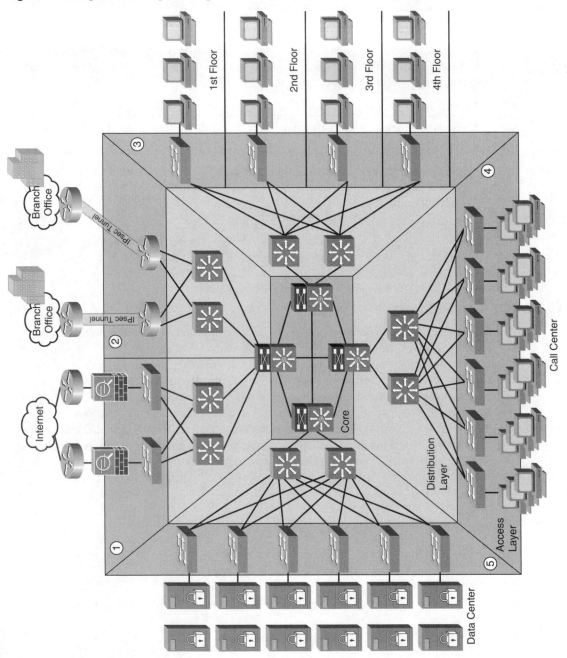

In Figure 3-2, the following sections are numbered:

1 **The Internet edge:** In this example, the enterprise headquarters is connected to the Internet via redundant links. Two Cisco Adaptive Security Appliances (ASA) are configured to protect the infrastructure.

2 **Site-to-Site VPN:** The headquarters office is connected to two branches via IPsec site-to-site VPN tunnels terminated on two Cisco IOS routers.

3 **End users:** The headquarters building has its sales, finance, engineering, and marketing departments on four separate floors.

4 **Call center:** There is a call center with more than 100 agents on the 5th floor.

5 **Data center:** The data center includes e-commerce, e-mail, database, and other application servers.

You can create this type of diagram not only to understand the architecture of your organization but also to strategically identify places within the infrastructure where you can implement telemetry mechanisms like NetFlow and identify choke points where you can mitigate an incident. Notice that the access, distribution, and core layers/boundaries are clearly defined.

Look at the example illustrated in Figure 3-3. A workstation at the call center usually communicates over TCP port 80 (HTTP) to a server in the data center. This traffic is allowed within the access control lists because it is legitimate traffic to the server. However, the traffic from this specific workstation increased more than 400 percent over normal. Subsequently, performance on the server is degraded, and the infrastructure is congested with unnecessary packets.

In this case, NetFlow was configured at the distribution layer switch, and the administrator was able to detect the anomaly. The administrator then configures a host-specific ACL to deny the traffic from the call center workstation, as shown in Figure 3-4. In more sophisticated environments, you can even implement remotely triggered black hole (RTBH) routing to mitigate this incident.

In the example illustrated in Figure 3-4, the problem was a defect within the call center workstation application. The administrator was able to perform detailed analysis and patch the machine while preventing disruption of service.

Figure 3-3 *NetFlow at the Distribution Switch*

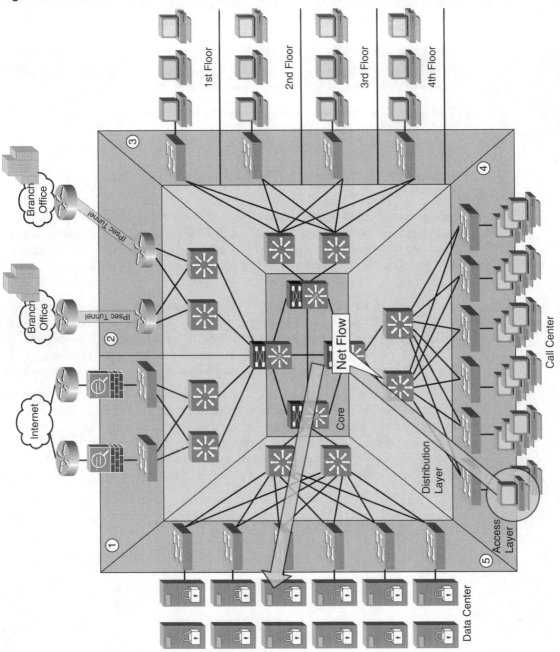

Figure 3-4 *Abnormal Traffic Stopped*

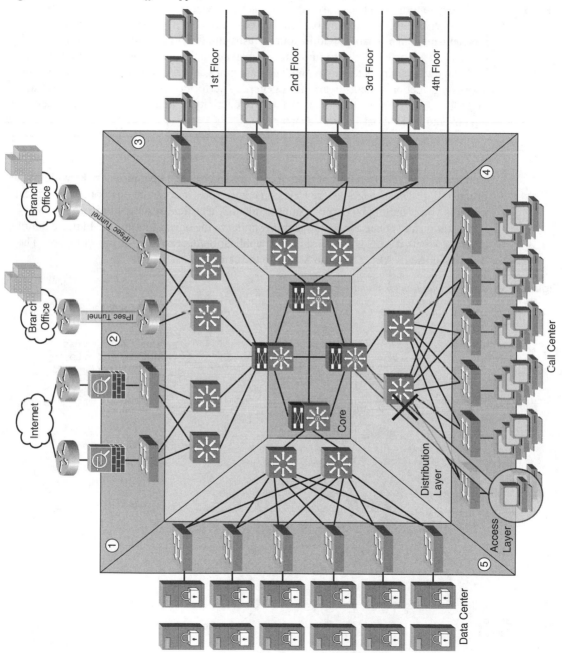

TIP   To detect abnormal and possibly malicious activity, you must first establish a baseline of normal network activity, traffic patterns, and other factors. NetFlow, as well as other mechanisms, can be enabled within your infrastructure to successfully identify and classify threats and anomalies. Prior to implementing an anomaly-detection system, you should perform traffic analysis to gain an understanding of general traffic rates and patterns. In anomaly detection systems, learning is generally performed over a significant interval, including both the peaks and valleys of network activity. Anomaly detection and telemetry are covered in detail later in this chapter.

You can also develop a different type of diagram to visualize operational risks within your organization. These diagrams are based on device roles and can be developed for critical systems you want to protect. For example, identify a critical system within your organization and create a layered diagram similar to the one in Figure 3-5. In this example, a database called ABC is the most critical application/data source for this company. The diagram presents ABC Database Server in the center.

Figure 3-5   *Layered Diagram for Visualizing Risk*

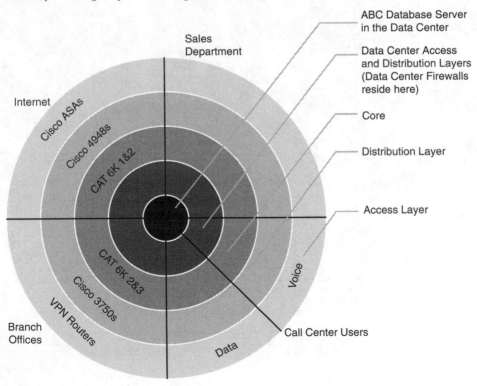

You can use this type of diagram to audit device roles and the type of services they should be running. For example, you can decide in what devices you can run services like Cisco NetFlow or where to enforce security policies. In addition, you can see the life of a packet within your infrastructure depending on the source and destination. An example is illustrated in Figure 3-6.

Figure 3-6   *Illustrating a Packet Flow*

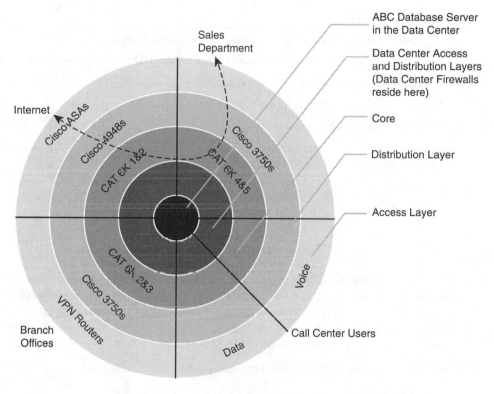

Figure 3-6 shows the packet flow that occurs when a user from the sales department accesses an Internet site. You know exactly where the packet is going based on your architecture and your security and routing policies. This is a simple example; however, you can use this concept to visualize risks and to prepare your isolation policies.

NOTE   Additional examples and techniques are covered in Chapter 7, "Proactive Security Framework."

Telemetry and Anomaly Detection

Anomaly detection systems passively monitor network traffic, looking for any deviation from "normal" or "baseline" behavior that may indicate a security threat or a misconfiguration. You can use several commercial tools and even open source tools to successfully identify security threats within your network. These tools include the following:

- Cisco NetFlow
- Cisco Security Monitoring, Analysis and Response System (CS-MARS)
- Cisco Traffic Anomaly Detectors and Cisco Guard DDoS Mitigation Appliances
- Cisco IPS sensors (Version 6.x and later)
- Cisco Network Analysis Module (NAM)
- Open Source Monitoring tools

The following are other technologies and tools you can use to achieve complete visibility of what is happening within your network:

- Syslog
- SNMP

NetFlow

Cisco NetFlow was initially introduced as a packet accounting system for network administration and, in some cases, for billing. However, today you can use NetFlow to listen to the network itself, thereby gaining valuable insight into the overall security state of the network. This is why it is classified as a form of telemetry that provides information about traffic passing through or directly to each router or switch.

NetFlow is supported in the following Cisco platforms:

- Cisco 1700
- Cisco 1800
- Cisco 2800
- Cisco 3800
- Cisco 4500
- Cisco 7200
- Cisco 7300
- Cisco 7500

- Cisco 7600/6500 (hybrid and native configurations)
- Cisco 10000
- Cisco 12000

NOTE	Indicated models have platform-specific considerations. Please refer to http://www.cisco.com/go/netflow for more compatibility information.

The word *netflow* is a combination of *net* (or network) and *flow*. What is a *flow*? An individual flow comprises, at a minimum, the following elements:

- Source IP address.
- Destination IP address.
- Protocol.
- Source port number. (With certain protocols, this can be a type/code or any other construct—for example, ICMP.)
- Destination port number. (With certain protocols, this can be a type/code or any other construct—for example, ICMP.)

NetFlow also can give you information about network traffic. This information varies somewhat depending on what version of NetFlow Data Export (NDE) you run. The most commonly deployed versions are Versions 5 and 9. Following is some of the additional information you can obtain from a flow in NetFlow Version 5:

- Start time of the flow.
- End time of the flow.
- Number of packets in the flow.
- Amount of data transferred in the flow.
- Type of Service (ToS) bits present in the flow or Differentiated Services Code Point (DSCP) type.
- Logical OR of all TCP flags present in TCP-based flows (platform-specific caveats apply).
- Input interface ifIndex.
- Output interface ifIndex.
- Origin-AS or destination-AS information, if Border Gateway Protocol (BGP) is enabled on the routers/Layer 3 switches in question. (The selection of origin- or destination-AS reporting is made during the configuration of NetFlow on each device.)

- BGP next-hop information, if BGP is enabled on the routers/Layer 3 switches in question.

- Fragmentation information (known as *fragmentation bit*).

All this information can be exported to monitoring systems for further analysis. NetFlow Version 9 supports the same reporting capabilities as NetFlow Version 5 with some additional information. One of the biggest advantages of NetFlow Version 9 is its ability to be configured by the use of templates to use various features to export additional or different information to external systems. In NetFlow Version 5 and earlier, you can export the flow data over UDP. NetFlow Version 9 supports NDE via TCP and SCTP, as well as the classic UDP mode.

NOTE   All new NetFlow development is based on NetFlow Version 9.

In NetFlow Version 9, you can use a template describing the NDE fields within the flow information. This template information is contained in the first NetFlow Version 9 NDE packets sent to the NDE destination (monitoring system) after NDE is enabled on the router or switch. This information is also periodically retransmitted. When the configuration of NDE fields is changed on the router or switch, the updated template is immediately transmitted.

The IETF Internet Protocol Flow Information eXport (IPFIX) working group (WG) has been tasked with developing a common standard for IP-based flow export. This working group has selected Cisco NetFlow Version 9 as the technology of choice.

NOTE   The IPFIX requirements are defined in RFC 3917. RFC 3954 explains the evaluation of NetFlow Version 9 in IPFIX. The actual outcome and the criteria for the selection of NetFlow Version 9 as the basis for the IPFIX standard are defined in RFC 3955.

It is recommended that you use an isolated out-of-band (OOB) management network to allow you to access and control NetFlow-enabled devices over the network, even when you are under attack or during any security incident or network malfunction. When you transmit network telemetry over the OOB network, you reduce the chance for disruption of the information that provides insightful network visibility.

Enabling NetFlow

Typically, enabling NetFlow on software-based platforms consists of one or two steps:

- Enabling NetFlow on the relevant physical and logical interfaces
- (Optional) Enabling the device (NDE) to export the flow information from the device to an external monitoring system

When you configure NetFlow, you must decide between ingress or egress NetFlow for each device. This decision depends on the use and the topology. You can also enable NetFlow for both ingress and egress.

NOTE   Egress NetFlow is dependent on the version of Cisco IOS you are running. For more information, go to http://www.cisco.com/go/fn.

The following example shows how you can enable *ingress* NetFlow on a particular interface (GigabitEthernet0/0 in this case):

```
myrouter#configure terminal
myrouter(config)#interface GigabitEthernet0/0
myrouter(config-if)#ip flow ingress
```

To enable egress NetFlow, use the **ip flow egress** interface subcommand as follows:

```
myrouter(config)#interface GigabitEthernet0/0
myrouter(config-if)#ip flow egress
```

NOTE   Ingress NetFlow is the most commonly used method. Egress NetFlow is more commonly used with MPLS VPN. The MPLS Egress NetFlow Accounting feature allows you to capture IP flow information for packets undergoing MPLS label disposition. In other words, it captures packets that arrive on a router as MPLS packets and are transmitted as IP packets. Egress NetFlow accounting might adversely affect network performance because of the additional accounting-related computations that occur in the traffic-forwarding path of the router.

The following example shows how to configure the NetFlow-enabled device to export the flow data to a monitoring system:

```
myrouter(config)#ip flow-export version 5
myrouter(config)#ip flow-export source loopback 0
myrouter(config)#ip flow-export destination 172.18.85.190 2055
```

In this example, NDE Version 5 is used. All NetFlow export packets are sourced from a loopback interface configured in the router (loopback 0). The destination is a Cisco Secure Monitoring and Response System (CS-MARS) box with the IP address 172.18.85.190 and the destination UDP port 2055.

It is recommended that you alter the setting of the active flow timeout parameter from its default of 30 minutes to the minimum value of one minute. This helps you achieve an environment that is closer to real time. You can do this with the **ip flow-cache timeout active** command, as shown here:

```
myrouter(config)#ip flow-cache timeout active 1
```

NOTE   The default value for the number of minutes that an active flow remains in the cache before it times out is 30.

The default value for the number of seconds that an inactive flow remains in the cache before it times out is 15.

Collecting NetFlow Statistics from the CLI

To view the basic NetFlow information from the CLI, you can use the **show ip cache flow** command, as shown in Example 3-1:

Example 3-1   *Output of the* **show ip cache flow** *Command*

```
myrouter#show ip cache flow
IP packet size distribution (9257M total packets):
   1-32   64   96  128  160  192  224  256  288  320  352  384  416  448  480
   .088 .314 .011 .011 .027 .001 .007 .001 .013 .016 .002 .002 .000 .001 .000

    512  544  576 1024 1536 2048 2560 3072 3584 4096 4608
   .000 .001 .002 .043 .452 .000 .000 .000 .000 .000 .000

IP Flow Switching Cache, 4456704 bytes
  43 active, 65493 inactive, 884110623 added
  3341579080 ager polls, 0 flow alloc failures
  Active flows timeout in 30 minutes
  Inactive flows timeout in 15 seconds
  last clearing of statistics never
Protocol         Total    Flows   Packets Bytes  Packets Active(Sec) Idle(Sec)
--------         Flows     /Sec    /Flow  /Pkt    /Sec    /Flow      /Flow
TCP-Telnet     1072696      0.2       17   578     4.4      9.8       15.3
TCP-FTP          33386      0.0     2392    57    18.6    697.2        7.6
```

Example 3-1 *Output of the* **show ip cache flow** *Command (Continued)*

```
TCP-FTPD          2967       0.0     2869  1049     1.9      4.3     15.2
TCP-WWW        9091735       2.1      222   904   470.3      6.0      5.6
TCP-SMTP        538619       0.1        1    59     0.2      6.9     15.9
TCP-X             3246       0.0       44   909     0.0      0.1     13.4
TCP-BGP         280550       0.0        2    44     0.1      7.2     15.8
TCP-NNTP          2306       0.0        1    46     0.0      0.0     18.1
TCP-Frag             7       0.0       19   152     0.0      8.8     15.4
TCP-other     48037166      11.1      115   887  1289.2      4.5      6.2
UDP-DNS        1043579       0.2        2    74     0.4      3.9     15.9
UDP-NTP         891663       0.2        1    79     0.2      0.0     15.5
UDP-TFTP        138376       0.0        7    55     0.2     21.2     15.5
UDP-Frag          9736       0.0      182  1366     0.4     22.1     15.4
UDP-other    816395802     190.0        1   109   316.9      0.1     18.8
ICMP           6533952       1.5       13    95    20.5      8.3     15.5
GRE                239       0.0       41    97     0.0     66.9     15.2
IP-other         34558       0.0     3907   156    31.4     66.1     15.0
Total:       884110583     205.8       10   750  2155.4      0.5     17.9
SrcIf         SrcIPaddress     DstIf        DstIPaddress     Pr SrcP DstP   Pkts
Fa1/1         14.38.1.9        Null         255.255.255.255  11 0044 0043      1
Fa1/1         0.0.0.0          Null         255.255.255.255  11 0044 0043    209
Fa0/0         172.18.173.68    Fa1/0        14.36.1.208      06 05BC 01BB    452
Fa0/0         172.18.173.68    Fa1/0        14.36.1.186      06 0631 01BB    388
Fa1/0         14.36.1.120      Null         14.36.255.255    11 008A 008A      3
Fa0/0         14.36.1.120      Null         14.36.255.255    11 008A 008A      3
Fa0/0         172.18.124.223   Fa1/0        14.36.197.213    06 8107 2323   1547
Fa0/0         172.18.124.66    Null         14.36.1.184      06 EC83 01BB      1
Fa1/0         14.36.8.48       Fa0/0        172.18.124.154   06 15FE 0FA5      1
Fa1/0         14.36.8.48       Fa0/0        172.18.124.154   06 15FF 0FA5      1
Fa1/0         14.36.8.48       Fa0/0        172.18.124.154   06 15FD 0FA5      1
Fa1/0         14.36.1.3        Fa0/0        172.18.123.69    01 0000 0303      3
Fa1/0         14.36.8.36       Fa0/0        172.18.124.66    11 0202 0202      4
Fa1/0         14.36.99.77      Fa0/0        172.18.124.225   06 01BB 137C     85
Fa1/0         14.36.197.213    Fa0/0        172.18.124.223   06 2323 8107    780
Fa0/0         172.18.124.223   Fa1/0        14.36.1.203      06 8105 2323 19992167
Fa0/0         172.18.85.169    Local        14.36.1.1        06 8E5E 0017     97
Fa0/0         172.18.124.225   Fa1/0        14.36.99.77      06 137C 01BB     85
Fa0/0         172.18.124.128   Fa1/0        14.36.1.128      06 916E 2323    138
Fa0/0         172.18.124.128   Fa1/0        14.36.1.128      06 916D 2323     54
Fa1/0         14.36.1.208      Fa0/0        172.18.173.68    06 01BB 05BC    678
```

In the highlighted line, you can see that a host (172.18.124.223 is sending 19,992,167 packets to 14.36.1.203. This may be abnormal behavior or an infected machine. The protocol is 06 (TCP), the source port is 33029 (Hex 8105), and the destination port is 8995 (Hex 2323).

You can also obtain export flow information using the **show ip flow export** command, as shown in Example 3-2:

Example 3-2   *Output of the* **show ip flow export** *Command*

```
myrouter#show ip flow export
 Flow export v5 is enabled for main cache
   Exporting flows to 172.18.85.190 (2055)
   Exporting using source IP address 172.18.124.47
   Version 5 flow records
   884111088 flows exported in 31352026 udp datagrams
   0 flows failed due to lack of export packet
   4 export packets were sent up to process level
   0 export packets were dropped due to no fib
   0 export packets were dropped due to adjacency issues
   0 export packets were dropped due to fragmentation failures
   0 export packets were dropped due to encapsulation fixup failures
```

In Example 3-2, you can see that the router is exporting the NetFlow information to the 172.18.85.190 device (a CS-MARS in this case) over UDP port 2055. The source IP address is 172.18.124.47. A total of 884,111,088 flows have been exported in 31,352,026 UDP datagrams. Please note that all protocol numbers, source ports, and TCP/UDP destination ports are shown in hexadecimal. ICMP packets are represented with the source port field set to 0000, the first two bytes of the destination field set to the ICMP type, and the second two bytes to the ICMP code. If you are using features such as policy-based routing (PBR), Web Cache Communications Protocol (WCCP), Network Address Translation (NAT), or Unicast Reverse Path Forwarding (uRPF) ACLs, you will see a (DstIf) value of *Null*. To see packet drops caused by ACLs, uRPF, PBR, or null routes, use the **show ip cache flow** with the **include Null** option, as shown in Example 3-3:

Example 3-3   *Output of the* **show ip cache flow | include Null** *Command*

```
myrouter#show ip cache flow | include Null
 Fa1/0        14.36.1.8        Null        255.255.255.255 11 0044 0043      1
 Fa1/1        0.0.0.0          Null        255.255.255.255 11 0044 0043    891
 Fa0/0        172.18.124.66    Null        14.36.1.184     06 80AC 01BB      3
 Fa0/0        14.1.17.111      Null        14.38.201.1     06 51CD 00B3      2
 Fa1/0        172.18.124.11    Null        172.18.124.255  11 0089 0089     18
 Fa1/0        172.18.124.153   Null        172.18.124.255  11 008A 008A      3
```

To see flows that contain thousands or millions of packets, you can use **show ip cache flow | include K** or **show ip cache flow | include M** commands, respectively.

The Cisco Catalyst 6500 switches and Cisco 7600 router obtain NetFlow information via the Multilayer Switching (MLS) cache. In addition, the amount and type of data recorded in the table must be selected. The **mls flow ip interface-full** command provides the most useful information and can be configured as follows:

```
CAT6k(config)# mls flow ip interface-full
CAT6k(config)# mls nde interface
```

TIP	If your NetFlow table has too many entries, you can try to reduce the MLS aging time. For PFC2, set the aging time high enough to keep the number of entries within the 32,000 flow range of the PFC2. For PFC3, set the aging time high enough to keep the number of entries within the 64,000 flow range of the PFC3.
	Make sure you set the aging time to 1 second when using bridged-flow statistics with a Supervisor Engine 2 (SUP2). If some protocols have fewer packets per flow running, reduce the MLS fast aging time.
	The following site includes detailed configuration and design information for NetFlow on Catalyst 6500 switches:
	http://www.cisco.com/en/US/partner/products/hw/switches/ps708/products_configuration_guide_chapter09186a0080207758.html

SYSLOG

System logs or SYSLOG provide you with information for monitoring and troubleshooting devices within your infrastructure. In addition, they give you excellent visibility into what is happening within your network. You can enable SYSLOG on network devices such as routers, switches, firewalls, VPN devices, and others. This section covers how to enable SYSLOG on routers, switches, the Cisco ASA, and Cisco PIX security appliances.

Enabling Logging (SYSLOG) on Cisco IOS Routers and Switches

The logging facility on Cisco IOS routers and switches allows you to save SYSLOG messages locally or to a remote host. By default, routers send logging messages to a logging process. The logging process controls the delivery of logging messages to various destinations, such as the logging buffer, terminal lines, a SYSLOG server, or a monitoring event correlation system such as CS-MARS. You can set the severity level of the messages to control the type of messages displayed, in addition to a time stamp to successfully track the reported information.

TIP	It is extremely important that your SYSLOG and other messages are time-stamped with the correct date and time. This is why the use of NTP is strongly recommended (*see the NTP example in Chapter 2, "Preparation Phase"*).

The following example shows the commands necessary to configure SYSLOG on Cisco IOS devices:

```
myrouter#configure terminal
myrouter(config)#logging on
myrouter(config)#logging host 172.18.85.190
```

In this example, the router is configured to send the SYSLOG messages to a host with IP address 172.18.85.190. (This is the CS-MARS used in the examples of the previous sections.)

On Cisco IOS routers, the log messages are not time-stamped by default. To enable time stamping of log messages, use the **service timestamps log datetime** command. The following example shows the different options of this command:

```
myrouter(config)#service timestamps log datetime ?
   localtime      Use local time zone for timestamps
   msec           Include milliseconds in timestamp
   show-timezone  Add time zone information to timestamp
   year           Include year in timestamp
```

You can specify the severity level of the SYSLOG messages. The following are the different levels you can configure:

- **Level 0:** Emergencies
- **Level 1:** Alerts
- **Level 2:** Critical
- **Level 3:** Errors
- **Level 4:** Warnings
- **Level 5:** Notifications
- **Level 6:** Informational
- **Level 7:** Debugging

To set the severity level of log messages sent to a SYSLOG server, use the **logging trap** command. The following example shows the options of this command:

```
myrouter(config)#logging trap ?
   <0-7>          Logging severity level
   alerts         Immediate action needed         (severity=1)
   critical       Critical conditions             (severity=2)
   debugging      Debugging messages              (severity=7)
   emergencies    System is unusable              (severity=0)
   errors         Error conditions                (severity=3)
   informational  Informational messages          (severity=6)
   notifications  Normal but significant conditions (severity=5)
   warnings       Warning conditions              (severity=4)
```

It is recommended that you send SYSLOG messages over a separate management segment, just as you learned to do earlier in this chapter in the "NetFlow" section.

Enabling Logging Cisco Catalyst Switches Running CATOS

To enable the logging of system messages to a SYSLOG server on Cisco Catalyst switches running Catalyst Operating System (CATOS), use the following commands:

```
set logging server enable
set logging server syslog server 172.18.85.190
set logging timestamp enable
set logging server severity 4
```

In this example, the switch is configured to send the SYSLOG messages to the host with IP address 172.18.85.190. Time stamp is enabled, and the severity level of the messages sent to the external server is set to 4 or warnings. Setting logging to the debugging level can cause performance problems. A good rule of thumb is to set the logging severity to 4 or warnings.

NOTE   A good whitepaper describing best practices when managing Cisco Catalyst switches running CATOS is located at http://www.cisco.com/en/US/products/hw/switches/ps663/products_tech_note09186a0080094713.shtml.

Enabling Logging on Cisco ASA and Cisco PIX Security Appliances

The commands used to enable logging and to send SYSLOG messages to a SYSLOG server are the same on the Cisco ASA and the Cisco PIX security appliances. To enable logging, use the **logging on** command. To configure the ASA or PIX to send logs to a SYSLOG server, use the **logging host** command, and to change the log severity level, use the **logging trap** command. The following example demonstrates the use of these commands.

```
ciscoasa(config)# logging on
ciscoasa(config)# logging host inside 172.18.85.190
ciscoasa(config)# logging trap informational
```

In this example, the Cisco ASA is configured to send its logs to the host with IP address 172.18.85.190, and the severity level is set to informational.

On the Cisco ASA and Cisco PIX security appliances, all SYSLOG messages begin with a percent sign (%) and are designed as follows:

```
%PIX|ASA  Level Message_number: Message_text
```

The following is an example of a SYSLOG message.

```
Apr 09 2007 07:35:56: %ASA-6-302021: Teardown ICMP connection for faddr
192.168.202.22/0 gaddr 192.168.202.40/0 laddr 192.168.202.40/0
```

- **PIX|ASA:** A static value indicating that the log message is generated by a Cisco ASA or Cisco PIX.

- **Level:** The severity level (1–7). For most environments, it is recommended that you set the severity level to 4 to avoid performance issues. You may want to temporally increase it to a higher value when troubleshooting a specific problem.

- **Message number:** A unique 6-digit number that identifies the SYSLOG message.

- **Message text:** The description of the log message. It sometimes includes IP addresses, port numbers, or usernames.

You can filter SYSLOG messages on the Cisco ASA, Cisco PIX, and Cisco FWSM to send only specific events to a particular output destination. In other words, you can configure the device to send all SYSLOG messages to one output destination and also to send a subset of those SYSLOG messages to a different output destination. You can also configure the Cisco ASA, Cisco PIX, and Cisco FWSM to send SYSLOG messages based on specific criteria, such as the following:

- Message ID number (range of 104024 to 105999)

- Severity level

- Message class

For example, you can use the **logging class <message_class>** command to specify the specific class.

TIP   All Cisco ASA and Cisco PIX messages are defined in detail at http://www.cisco.com/univercd/cc/td/doc/product/multisec/asa_sw/v_7_2/syslog/logmsgs.htm.

This site also includes the different SYSLOG message classes and associated message ID numbers.

SNMP

SNMP is one of the most basic forms of getting information from your network. It is a Layer 7 protocol designed to obtain information from network devices. This information includes but is not limited to the following:

- Device health statistics (CPU, memory, and so on)

- Device errors

- Network traffic statistics

- Packet rates

- Packet errors

The SNMP solution has three components:

- **An SNMP manager:** The system used to control and monitor the activities of network hosts using SNMP.

- **An SNMP agent:** The software component within the managed device that maintains the data for the device and reports this data, as needed, to managing systems.

- **A Management Information Base (MIB):** An information storage medium that contains a collection of managed objects (MIB modules) within each device. MIB modules are written in the SNMP MIB module language, as defined in STD 58, RFC 2578, RFC 2579, and RFC 2580.

In Chapter 2, you learned about the three versions of SNMP and the security implications of each version. That chapter also showed you how to protect SNMP environments. This section covers the basic commands on how to enable SNMP on Cisco IOS and the Cisco ASA and Cisco PIX security appliances.

Enabling SNMP on Cisco IOS Devices

As a best practice, you should set the system contact, location, and serial number of the SNMP agent so that your management servers can obtain these descriptions. This information is useful when responding to incidents. The following example shows how to enter the contact information on the Cisco IOS device:

```
myrouter#configure terminal
myrouter(config)#snmp-server contact John Route
myrouter(config)#snmp-server location 1st Floor NY Office
myrouter(config)#snmp-server chassis-id ABC12345
```

In the previous example, the name of the administrator is John Route, the device is located on the 1st floor of an office in New York, and the chassis identification number is ABC12345.

The following example shows how you can configure SNMP Version 3 on a Cisco IOS device:

```
myrouter(config)#snmp-server group mygroup v3 auth
```

SNMP Version 3 supports authentication. In the previous example, an SNMP group named mygroup is configured for SNMP Version 3. Authentication is also enabled with the **auth** keyword. When you configure the **snmp-server group** command, there are no default values for authentication. To specify authentication user parameters, use the **snmp-server user** command, as shown in the following example:

```
myrouter(config)#snmp-server user admin1 mygroup v3 auth md5 zxasqw12
*Feb  8 15:45:04.902: Configuring snmpv3 USM user, persisting snmpEngineBoots.
Please Wait...
```

In the previous example, a user (*admin1*) is configured and mapped to the SNMP group *mygroup*. Authentication is done with MD5, and the password is *zxasqw12*. After you invoke this command, the preceding warning message is displayed. You should match all this information in your SNMP management server.

To verify the configuration, you can invoke the **show snmp user** command as follows:

```
myrouter#show snmp user
User name: admin1
Engine ID: 8000000903000013C4EC5528
storage-type: nonvolatile        active
Authentication Protocol: MD5
Privacy Protocol: DES
Group-name: mygroup
```

To view SNMP group information, invoke the **show snmp group** command, as shown in Example 3-4.

Example 3-4 *Output of the* **show snmp group** *Command*

```
myrouter#show snmp group
groupname: ILMI                          security model:v1
readview : *ilmi                         writeview: *ilmi
notifyview: <no notifyview specified>
row status: active
groupname: ILMI                          security model:v2c
readview : *ilmi                         writeview: *ilmi
notifyview: <no notifyview specified>
row status: active
groupname: mygroup                       security model:v3 auth
readview : v1default                     writeview: <no writeview specified>
notifyview: <no notifyview specified>
row status: active
```

The configured group (mygroup) is shown in the highlighted line.

NOTE   The following site includes detailed information on how to configure SNMP Version 1 and 2:

http://www.cisco.com/univercd/cc/td/doc/product/software/ios124/124tcg/tnm_c/snmp/confsnmp.htm#wp1032846

This document also includes the following information:

- Configuring the router as an SNMP manager

- Enabling the SNMP Agent Shutdown mechanism

- Defining the maximum SNMP Agent packet size

- Disabling the SNMP Agent

- Limiting the number of Trivial File Transfer Protocol (TFTP) servers used via SNMP

- Configuring SNMP notifications
- Configuring interface index display and interface indexes and configuring long name support
- Configuring SNMP support for VPNs
- Configuring MIB persistence

Enabling SNMP on Cisco ASA and Cisco PIX Security Appliances

The Cisco ASA and the Cisco PIX security appliances support only SNMP Versions 1 and 2c. They both support traps and SNMP read access; however, SNMP write access is not supported. The following example shows how to configure an ASA to receive SNMP Version 2c requests from host 172.18.85.190 on the inside interface:

```
ciscoasa(config)# snmp-server host inside 172.18.85.190 Version 2c
ciscoasa(config)# snmp-server location Raleigh NC Branch
ciscoasa(config)# snmp-server contact Jeff Firewall
ciscoasa(config)# snmp-server community th1s1sacommstrng
```

The ASA in this example is located in a branch office in Raleigh, North Carolina. The point of contact is Jeff Firewall, and the community string is <th1s1sacommstrng>. You can use the **snmp deny version** command to deny SNMP packets from other SNMP versions. The following example shows the available options:

```
ciscoasa(config)# snmp deny version ?
configure mode commands/options:
  1    SNMP version 1
  2    SNMP version 2 (party based)
  2c   SNMP version 2c (community based)
  3    SNMP version 3
```

NOTE   You can obtain the MIBs for any Cisco device at http://www.cisco.com/public/sw-center/netmgmt/cmtk/mibs.shtml.

Cisco Security Monitoring, Analysis and Response System (CS-MARS)

CS-MARS enables you to identify, classify, validate, and mitigate security threats. In the previous sections in this chapter, you learned different mechanisms that give you visibility of the network and its devices, such as NetFlow, SYSLOGs, and SNMP. The analysis and manipulation of the data provided by these features can be a time-consuming process and, in some environments, may even be impossible because of the staff requirements.

CS-MARS supports the correlation of events from numerous networking devices from different vendors. The supported devices include:

- Cisco IOS routers and switches
- Cisco ASA
- Cisco PIX
- NetFlow
- Cisco Security Agent
- Cisco Secure ACS
- Cisco IDS/IPS
- Third-party firewalls such as Checkpoint and Netscreen
- Third-party antivirus software
- Third-party IDS/IPS systems such as snort
- Operating system (Windows and UNIX/Linux) events
- Application-specific events

NOTE   A complete of list of supported devices can be found at http://www.cisco.com/en/US/ products/ps6241/products_device_support_tables_list.html.

For a complete list of available CS-MARS models, go to http://www.cisco.com/go/mars.

CS-MARS provides a powerful and interactive dashboard with several key items. It includes a topology map that comprises real-time hotspots, incidents, attack paths, and detailed investigation with full incident disclosure, allowing immediate verification of valid threats. Figure 3-7 shows the CS-MARS main dashboard.

Note that the system has processed more than 22,000,000 NetFlow events (or flows) over a period of 24 hours, and more than 44,000,000 security and network events. This automated process is accomplished by analyzing device logs such as firewalls and by using intrusion prevention applications, third-party vulnerability assessment data, and Cisco Security MARS endpoint scans to eliminate false positives. Users can quickly fine-tune the system to further reduce false positives. This will be impossible to successfully analyze without the use of a system such as CS-MARS.

Figure 3-8 shows the bottom part of the CS-MARS main dashboard. There you can see a topology map of devices within the network, an attack diagram, and event statistics and graphs.

Figure 3-7 *CS-MARS Main Dashboard*

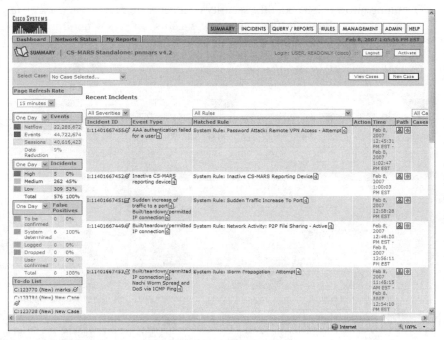

Figure 3-8 *CS-MARS Topology Map, Attack Diagram, and Event Statistics*

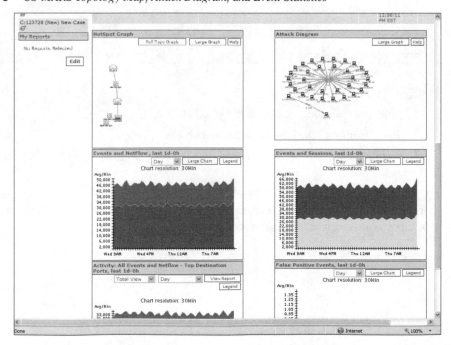

You can view the topology map and attack diagram in full view, as shown in Figure 3-9. Obtaining information about the security incident is simple. If you click on any of the arrows representing the traffic flow, a new window displays with information about the specific incident or session.

Figure 3-9 *CS-MARS Attack Diagram Full View*

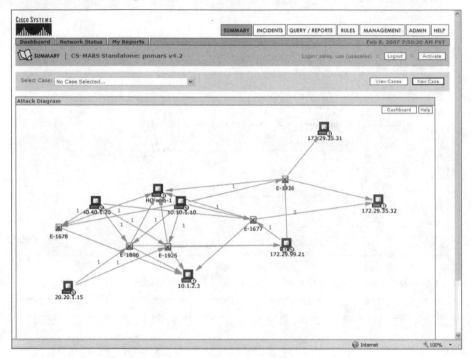

The hosts are color-coded:

- Brown means that the host is the attacker.
- Red means that the host is being attacked.
- Purple means that the host is being attacked and is attacking other hosts in the network.

CS-MARS can do a reverse DNS lookup to give you exact information on the specific hosts and devices. You can run numerous reports in CS-MARS. Figure 3-10 shows an example of reports and graphics you can obtain in CS-MARS.

Figure 3-10 *CS-MARS Detailed Graphics and Reports*

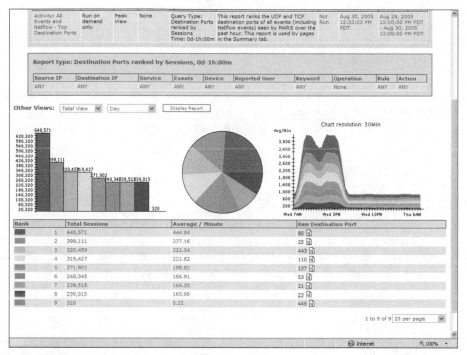

In Figure 3-10, you can see a summary of the most used ports and protocols within a given period. These graphics are based on NetFlow information. The graphic on the right shows the traffic trend. Notice that the traffic starts increasing during normal business hours of 8:00 a.m. to around 5:00 p.m. (0800 to 1700). These types of graphics can help you to create a baseline of what is normal within your network. Then you can identify anomalies and possible security incidents.

NOTE   Chapter 12, "Case Studies," includes a case study in which CS-MARS is used to successfully identify, classify, and mitigate an attack. It also includes examples of how to add monitored devices into CS-MARS.

Cisco Network Analysis Module (NAM)

The Cisco Network Analysis Module (NAM) is designed to analyze and monitor traffic in the Catalyst 6500 series switches and Cisco 7600 series Internet routers. It uses remote monitoring (RMON), RMON extensions for switched networks (SMON), and SNMP MIBs to obtain information from the device. The NAM can also collect and analyze NetFlow information on remote devices.

To use the NAM to collect NetFlow data from a remote device, you must configure the remote device to export NDE packets to UDP port 3000 on the NAM. By default, the local supervisor engine of the switch is always available as an NDE device. Optionally, SNMP community strings are used to upload convenient textual strings for interfaces on the remote devices that are monitored in NetFlow records.

NOTE   A complete NAM installation and configuration guide is located at http://www.cisco.com/en/US/products/sw/cscowork/ps5401/products_installation_and_configuration_guides_list.html.

Open Source Monitoring Tools

You can use several open source monitoring tools in conjunction with NetFlow. If your organization is small, or if you do not have the budget for more sophisticated monitoring tools, you can take advantage of any of these open source tools that are freely available. Table 3-1 includes the most commonly used open source monitoring tools.

Table 3-1   *Open Source Monitoring Tools*

Tool Name	Website
Caida's Cflowd Analysis Software	http://www.caida.org/tools/measurement/cflowd
My Netflow Reporting System by Dynamic Networks	http://www.dynamicnetworks.us/netflow/index.html
OSU Flow-tools	http://www.splintered.net/sw/flow-tools
Flow Viewer	http://ensight.eos.nasa.gov/FlowViewer
Flowd	http://www.mindrot.org/projects/flowd
NetFlow Monitor (NF)	http://netflow.cesnet.cz
Ntop	http://ntop.ethereal.com/ntop.html
Panoptis	http://panoptis.sourceforge.net
Plixer's Scrutinizer	http://www.plixer.com/products/free-netflow.php
Stager	http://software.uninett.no/stager

Most of these tools are designed to run in common *NIX-type operating systems, including Linux, FreeBSD, Mac OS/X, and Solaris. Some of these tools support the storage of data in databases such as MySQL and Oracle. Despite the fact that these open source tools are free, they are extremely useful for collecting NetFlow from routers and storing the raw flows for auditing and forensic purposes. The most commonly used tool is the OSU flow-tool, which is typically used in conjunction with other packages that provide detailed graphs, charts, and on-demand queries. Visit each of the websites listed in Table 3-1 to learn more about which tool is most suitable for your environment.

Cisco Traffic Anomaly Detectors and Cisco Guard DDoS Mitigation Appliances

The Cisco traffic anomaly detectors and DDoS mitigation appliances provide a new approach that not only detects increasingly complex and unrepresentative denial of service attacks but also mitigates their effect to ensure business continuity and resource availability. The Cisco DDos solution has two distinct appliances:

- Cisco Traffic Anomaly Detector (TAD) XT
- Cisco Guard XT

This solution is also available in the form of two individual modules for the Catalyst 6500 series switches and the Cisco 7600 Internet routers:

- Catalyst 6500/Cisco 7600 Router Anomaly Guard Module
- Catalyst 6500/Cisco 7600 Router Traffic Anomaly Detector Module

The detectors (whether the appliances or the modules) are designed to promiscuously monitor network traffic while looking for any variation from what is "normal," which may indicate a DDoS attack or a worm outbreak. The Cisco TAD XT alerts the Cisco Guard XT when it detects an anomaly by providing detailed reports and specific alerts.

This solution uses a Multiverification Process (MVP) architecture integrating different verification, analysis, and enforcement techniques. The MVP has five components:

- Static and dynamic DDoS filters
- Active verification (anti-spoofing) implementing source-authentication mechanisms that help ensure proper identification of legitimate traffic
- Anomaly recognition
- Protocol analysis designed to identify Layer 7 attacks, such as HTTP error attacks
- Rate limiting that prevents flows from overwhelming the target while more detailed monitoring is taking place

Figure 3-11 illustrates how the Cisco TAD XT and the Cisco Guard XT work.

Figure 3-11 *Cisco TAD XT Detects an Anomaly and Updates the Guard XT*

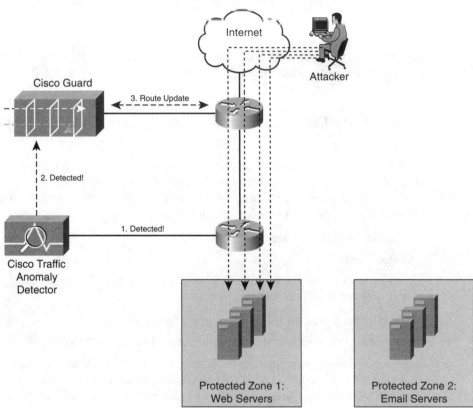

In Figure 3-11, two zones are protected by the Cisco TAD XT: a web server farm and an e-mail server farm. The Cisco Guard is placed at the Internet edge, and the Cisco TAD XT resides a couple of hops in the inside of the corporate network. The following are the steps illustrated in Figure 3-11.

Step 1   An attacker starts a DDoS from the Internet, and the Cisco TAD XT detects the anomaly (spike of traffic).

Step 2   The Cisco TAD XT updates the Cisco Guard XT. The Cisco Guard XT can be triggered in several ways:

— Through direct use of the web-based device manager

— Via the CLI

— Through automatic use of the "protect by packet" feature (illustrated in this example)

Step 3   After the Cisco Guard XT is activated, the Cisco Guard XT performs additional screening, and then the traffic destined to the zone under attack is diverted to the Cisco Guard XT in any of the following ways:

— The Cisco Guard XT can issue a BGP route update telling the router to divert the traffic to the Cisco Guard TX.

— If you are using the Catalyst 6500/7600 modules, the Route Health Injection (RHI) feature can trigger the packet diversion.

— A route is injected externally into the network.

Step 4   The attack traffic is redirected to the Cisco Guard XT, and legitimate traffic is allowed to the protected zone, as illustrated in Figure 3-12.

Figure 3-12   *Attack Traffic Redirected*

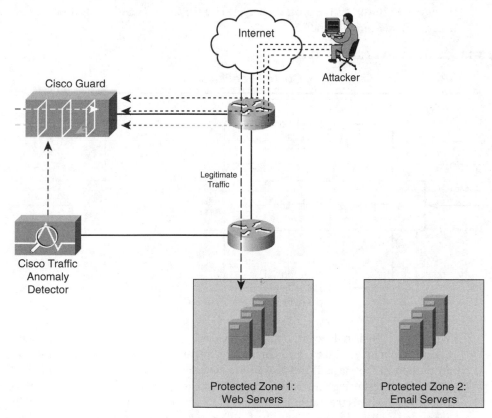

The Cisco Guard can also be deployed with other anomaly detection systems. Examples of this include Arbor's Peakflow SP and Peakflow X. Arbor's Peakflow SP is designed for service providers, and Peakflow X is designed for enterprises. Typically, enterprises deploy the Cisco Guard XT at their Internet edge, or they co-locate it at their Internet service provider network to avoid the unnecessary traffic consuming their bandwidth. Because of this, numerous service providers offer managed network DDoS protection, hosting DDoS protection, peering point DDoS protection, and infrastructure protection services. This is based on a solution that Cisco makes available to service providers called "clean pipes."

NOTE   For more information about clean pipes, go to http://www.cisco.com/go/cleanpipes.

Figure 3-13 illustrates the protection cycle that the Cisco Guard XT follows to analyze, filter, and rate-limit the traffic.

Figure 3-13 *Cisco Guard XT Protection Cycle*

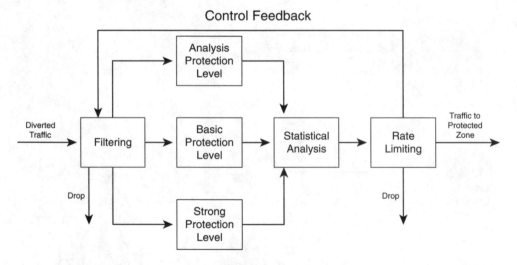

When the traffic is redirected to the Cisco Guard XT, it first filters the traffic using several filtering techniques. If the Cisco Guard XT determines that the packets are malicious, it drops them at this stage. If the packets are not malicious, the packets are sent to different protection levels using several types of authentication methods. Subsequently, the Cisco Guard XT analyzes the traffic flow, drops the traffic that exceeds the defined rate that the zone can handle, and then injects the legitimate traffic back to the zone. A closed-loop feedback cycle dynamically adjusts its protection policies.

NOTE	For more detailed information on how to configure the Cisco Guard XT and the Cisco TAD XT, go to http://www.cisco.com/en/US/products/ps5888/ products_installation_and_configuration_guides_list.html.

Intrusion Detection and Intrusion Prevention Systems (IDS/IPS)

In Chapter 1, "Overview of Network Security Technologies," you learned the basics about IDS and IPS systems. IDSs are devices that in promiscuous mode detect malicious activity within the network. IPS devices are capable of detecting all these security threats; however, they are also able to drop noncompliant packets inline. Traditionally, IDS systems have provided excellent application layer attack-detection capabilities; however, they were not able to protect against day-zero attacks using valid packets. The problem is that most attacks today use valid packets. On the other hand, now IPS systems such as the Cisco IPS software Version 6.x and later offer anomaly-based capabilities that help you detect such attacks. This is a big advantage, since it makes the IPS devices less dependent on signature updates for protection against DDoS, worms, and any day-zero threats. Just like any other anomaly detection systems, the sensors need to learn what is "normal." In other words, they need to create a baseline of legitimate behavior.

The Importance of Signatures Updates

Traditionally, IPS and IDS systems depend on signatures to operate. Because of this, it is extremely important to tune the IPS/IDS device accordingly and to develop policies and procedures to continuously update the signatures. The Cisco IPS software allows you to automatically download signatures from a management station. Signature updates are posted to Cisco.com almost on a weekly basis. In Chapter 2, you learned about the Cisco Security Center (historically named mySDN or my Self Defending Network). This is an excellent resource to obtain information about the latest IPS signatures and other security intelligence information.

NOTE	The Cisco Security Center site is http://www.cisco.com/security.
	The Cisco Security Center provides up-to-date security intelligence data, in addition to detailed IDS/IPS signature information.
	Although the IPS sensors can work without a license key, you must have a license key to obtain signature updates from Cisco.com. To obtain a license key, you must have a Cisco Service for IPS service contract. For more information, go to http://www.cisco.com/go/ license.

The Cisco IPS Device Manager (IDM) is a web-based configuration utility used to manage individual IPS sensors, Catalyst 6500 IPS modules, and the Advanced Inspection and Prevention Security Services Module (AIP SSM) for the Cisco ASA. You can configure the IPS device via IDM to automatically obtain and install signatures from an FTP or SCP server.

NOTE   You cannot automatically download service pack and signature updates from Cisco.com. You need to download service packs and signatures updates from Cisco.com to an FTP or SCP server. Then you can configure your IPS device to access the files on your server. You can also use the Cisco Security Manager IPS Manager Console (IPSMC) to manage your IPS devices. You can configure IPSMC to automatically download the signature updates and service packs from Cisco.com and then install them in your IPS devices. For more information about IPSMC, go to http://www.cisco.com/go/security.

Complete the following steps to configure IDM to automatically download signatures from your FTP or SCP server.

Step 1   Log in to IDM with an administrator account and navigate to **Configuration > Auto Update**.

Step 2   Select the **Enable Auto Update** check box.

Step 3   Enter the IP address of the remote server where the signature update or service packs are saved.

Step 4   Select either **FTP** or **SCP** for your transport mechanism/server type.

Step 5   Enter the path to the directory on the remote server where the updates are located in the **Directory Path**.

Step 6   Enter the username and password of the account in your FTP or SCP server.

Step 7   You can configure the IPS device to check for updates hourly or on a weekly basis. If you want your IPS device to check for updates hourly, check the **Hourly** check box. Then enter the time you want the updates to start and the hour interval at which you want the IPS device to contact your remote server for updates. The IPS sensor checks the directory you specified for new files in your server. Only one update is installed per cycle even if there are multiple available files.

Step 8   Check the **Daily** check box if you want the IPS device to automatically check for updates on a daily basis. Then enter the time you want the updates to start and check the days you want the IPS device to check for updates in your SCP or FTP server.

Step 9   To save and apply your configuration, click **Apply**.

The Importance of Tuning

Chapter 1 showed you the important factors to consider when tuning your IPS/IDS devices. Each IPS/IDS device comes with a preset number of signatures enabled. These signatures are suitable in most cases; however, it is important that you tune your IPS/IDS devices when you first deploy them and then tune them again periodically. You could receive numerous false positive events (false alarms), which could cause you to overlook real security incidents. The initial tuning will probably take more time than any subsequent tuning. The initial tuning process is hard to perform manually, especially in large environments where several IPS/IDS devices are deployed and hundreds of events are generated in short periods. This is why it is important to use event correlation systems to alleviate this process and save numerous hours. CS-MARS is used in the following example to perform initial tuning and event analysis.

In this example, several IPS devices are sending their events to a CS-MARS. The administrator completes the following steps to perform initial tuning:

Step 1 Log in to the CS-MARS via the web interface.

Step 2 Click **Query/Reports** tab.

Step 3 Select the **Activity: All–Top Event Types (Peak View)** option from the second pull-down menu under the **Load Report as On-Demand Query with Filter** section, as shown in Figure 3-14.

Figure 3-14 *CS-MARS Query/Reports*

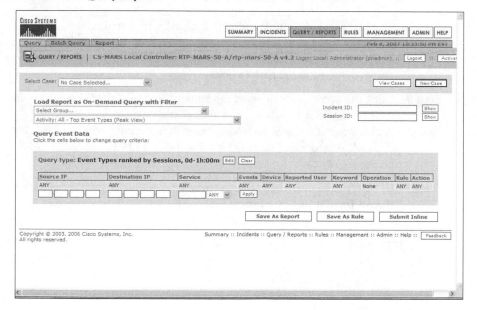

Step 4 Click the **Edit** button to select the time interval for the query and enter **1** day under the **Filter by time** section to trigger the CS-MARS to display the top event types in the past 24 hours, as shown in Figure 3-15.

Figure 3-15 *Selecting the Query Time Interval*

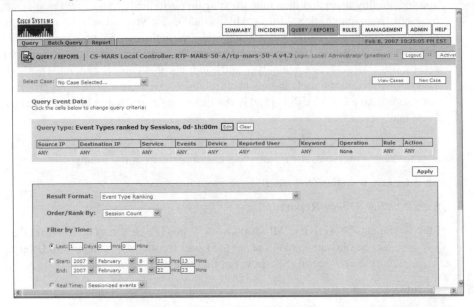

Step 5 Click **Apply** and **Submit Inline** in the next screen to obtain the report. The report in Figure 3-16 is shown. In this report, the administrator notices that there have been more than 480 ARP Reply-to-Broadcast events detected in the past 24 hours.

Step 6 Click the event to obtain more information and read the following from the CS-MARS details screen: "This signature detects an ARP Reply packet where the destination MAC address in the ARP payload is a layer 2 broadcast address. This is not normal traffic and can indicate an ARP poisoning attack."

Step 7 Click **q** by the event and select **Source IP Address Ranking** under the **Result format** section to investigate the source, as shown in Figure 3-17.

Figure 3-16 *Top Event Types*

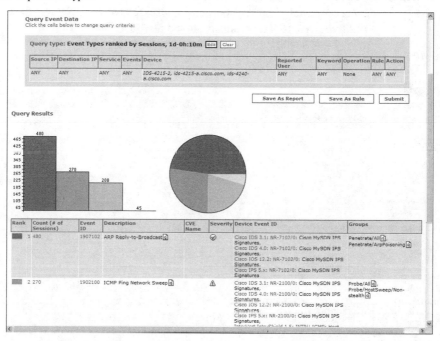

Figure 3-17 *Verifying Sources*

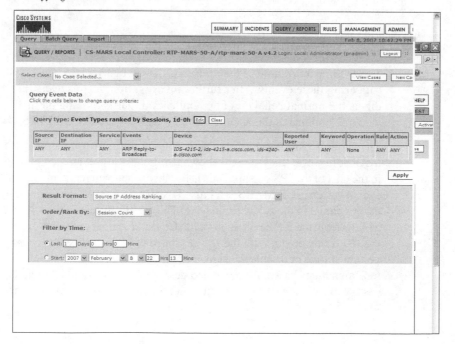

Step 8 Click **Apply** and **Submit Inline** in the following screen to obtain the new report, including the source IP addresses for the *ARP Reply to Broadcast* events. The report is shown as illustrated in Figure 3-18.

Figure 3-18 *IP Sources Report*

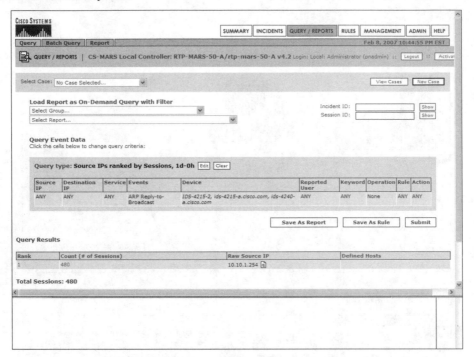

The administrator notices that only one device (10.10.1.254) is triggering these events. After further investigation, he discovers that this is the normal behavior of an application that is running on that machine and marks this incident as a **False Positive** in CS-MARS.

The administrator notices that these events are not shown anymore in CS-MARS; however, they are still shown using the **show events** command in the CLI of the IPS sensors. This is because when you mark an incident/event/session in CS-MARS as a **False Positive**, it does not disable or tune this signature in the actual IPS device. The events are still sent to the CS-MARS from the IPS devices; however, CS-MARS does not process these events. If you do not want the IPS sensor to send or process the events, you must tune or disable the signature on the IPS device. You can tune signatures based on source and destination. For example, in this case, you can tune the IPS signature not to alert you if the host with the

IP address 10.10.1.254 sends this type of packet. However, you can configure the IPS signature to alert you if any other device generates this type of traffic.

Anomaly Detection Within Cisco IPS Devices

When you configure a Cisco IPS device running Versions 6.x and later with anomaly detection services, the IPS device initially goes through a learning process. This is done to configure a set of policy thresholds based on the normal behavior of your network. Three different modes of operation take place when an IPS device is configured with anomaly detection:

- Learning mode
- Detect mode
- Inactive mode

The initial learning mode is performed over a period of 24 hours, by default. The initial baseline is referred to as the knowledge base (KB) of your traffic.

TIP   The IPS sensor does not detect attacks during the initial learning phase. If you experience an attack during this period, your results will not reflect a baseline of normal network behavior. This is an important point to take into consideration. Depending on your environment, you may want to have the IPS device in learning mode longer than the default 24 hours because this is a configurable value. Do not initially enable your IPS device with anomaly detection over a weekend if your organization operates mostly during normal business hours and days. This is a huge mistake that many people make.

To configure the IPS sensor using IDM to start the learning mode, go to **Configuration > Policies > Anomaly Detections > ad0 > Learning Accept Mode** and select the **Automatically accept learning knowledge base** check box. In that section, you can also specify the learning period length.

After the learning process, a KB is created that replaces the initial KB. The IPS device then automatically goes into detect mode. Any traffic flows that violate thresholds in the KB trigger the IPS device to generate alerts. The IPS device also keeps track of gradual changes to the KB that do not violate the thresholds and adjusts its configuration.

You can turn off the anomaly detection functionality on your IPS device. This is called being in *inactive mode*. In certain circumstances, this is needed. An example is when you have an asymmetric environment and the IPS device gets traffic from different directions, causing it to operate incorrectly.

NOTE	The traffic anomaly engine in Cisco IPS devices uses nine anomaly detection signatures covering TCP, UDP, and other protocols. Each signature has two subsignatures: one for the scanner and the other for the worm-infected host. All of these signatures are enabled by default, and they are in the 13000 range.

Similarly to the Cisco TAD XT, the anomaly detection feature in Cisco IPS devices uses zones. The purpose of configuring zones is to make sure that you do not have false positives and false negatives. A *zone* is a set of destination IP addresses. Three different zones exist:

- **Internal:** You configure this zone with the IP address range of your internal network.
- **Illegal:** You configure this zone with IP address ranges that should never be seen in normal traffic. Here you should use unallocated IP addresses or bogon IP addresses.
- **External:** This is the default zone. By default, it has the Internet range of 0.0.0.0-255.255.255.255.

To configure the Internal zone in your IPS device using IDM, complete the following steps:

Step 1 Navigate to **Configuration > Policies > Anomaly Detections > ad0 > Internal Zone**. The Internal Zone tab appears.

Step 2 Click the **General** tab.

Step 3 Select the **Enable the Internal Zone** check box.

Step 4 Enter your internal subnets/IP address range in the **Service Subnets** field. IDM also allows you to configure protocol and other specific thresholds.

NOTE	For more information on how to configure other thresholds and anomaly detection functionality, refer to the Cisco IPS configuration guides located at http://www.cisco.com/univercd/cc/td/doc/product/iaabu/csids/csids13/idmguide/index.htm.

Summary

Identification and classification of security threats mainly concerns visibility. In this chapter, you learned how important it is to have complete network visibility and control to successfully identify and classify security threats in a timely fashion. This chapter also covered different technologies and tools that can be used to obtain information from your network and detect anomalies that can be malicious activity. This chapter provided overviews of Cisco NetFlow, SYSLOG, and SNMP. You also learned about robust event correlation systems, such as CS-MARS and open source monitoring systems that can be used in conjunction with NetFlow to allow you to gain better visibility in your network.

This chapter also provided an overview of anomaly detection solutions, in addition to tips on IPS/IDS tuning and the new anomaly detection features that Cisco IPS software supports.

This chapter covers the following topics:

- Traceback in the Service Provider Environment
- Traceback in the Enterprise

CHAPTER 4

Traceback

For many years, enterprises, service providers, the government, and many other organizations have tried to develop tools and techniques to aid in the traceback of attacks. This chapter covers several lessons learned and techniques developed over the past to successfully trace back attacks or prepare the infrastructure to make this process easier. The techniques to track individual packets in a network must be done in an efficient, scalable fashion. The main goal of the traceback process is to find the source of attack or malignant traffic. By analyzing the packet contents of the attack traffic, you can determine information that may lead you to the source.

The traceback level of effort and methodologies may not be the same in all organizations. For instance, Internet service providers may use different techniques than those used in enterprises.

In the past, it was sometimes difficult to trace back attacks because of the use of spoofed packets. In addition, the packet stream may have been transmitted though many network devices that performed NAT, making it difficult for some enterprises and service providers to trace the original source IP address of the packet. Service providers and enterprises are now implementing antispoofing techniques that make it more difficult for spoofed attacks to succeed. For this reason, most attacks today are not sourced from spoofed IP addresses. Antispoofing techniques include the following:

- Source address validation described in RFC 2827/BCP38 and RFC 3704/BCP84
- Denial of your address space from external sources
- Denial of RFC 1918 private address space in your Internet edge routers
- Denial of multicast source addresses
- Filtering for RFC 3330 special use IPv4 addresses
- Use of Unicast Reverse Path Forwarding (uRPF)
- Cable source verification—Enhancements within Cisco cable modem termination system (CMTS) products that protect against spoofed attacks in Data-over-Cable Service Interface Specifications (DOCSIS) cable systems

NOTE   In Chapter 2, "Preparation Phase," you learned these techniques and how to protect your infrastructure against spoofed packets. See Chapter 2 to learn how to implement these types of infrastructure protection mechanisms.

Traceback in the Service Provider Environment

For the implementation of traceback techniques to be successful, they must meet the following requirements:

- Do not violate current protocol semantics and can be successful without changes in the core routing structure

- Are difficult for the attacker to detect and can function in a passive mode, without requiring much intervention

- Are useful in asymmetric environments

- Work through multiple hops, across jurisdictions

- Allow you to generate a good postmortem after an attack has mitigated

In some cases, it is difficult for the implementation of traceback techniques to meet all the requirements previously listed, and it is especially difficult for service providers. This is why it is extremely important for service providers to cooperate with each other to successfully trace back attacks. This is especially true because attackers are aware of many traceback schemes.

TIP   Major cooperative efforts exist between service providers and several organizations that promote these efforts. An example is the North American Network Operators Group (NANOG), which has excellent resources and information at http://www.nanog.org.

Another example is the Forum for Incident Response and Security Teams (FIRST), which has excellent resources and best practice guides at http://www.first.org/resources/guides.

When there are large numbers of sources or when sources are well distributed, traceback solutions often become extremely complex and expensive. Speed is a significant limitation of hop-by-hop traceback; therefore, hop-by-hop traceback can be difficult. It also requires substantial collaboration. For example, Figure 4-1 illustrates an old method being used by an individual who is attacking a victim who is numerous hops away from different service providers.

Figure 4-1   *Hop-by-Hop Traceback*

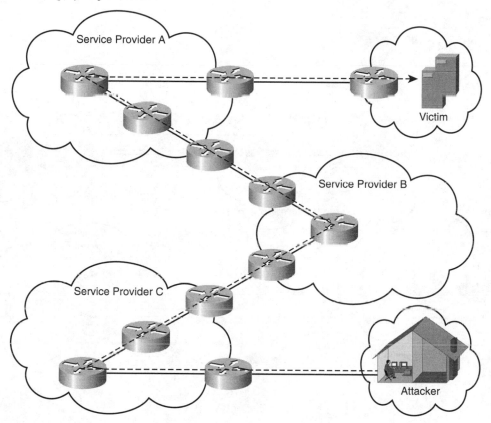

In this case, collaboration between service providers may be needed, and hop-by-hop traceback may take longer than expected. However, this is not what we typically see today. Figure 4-2 illustrates a more interesting scenario.

Figure 4-2 *Hop-by-Hop Traceback with Botnets or Zombies*

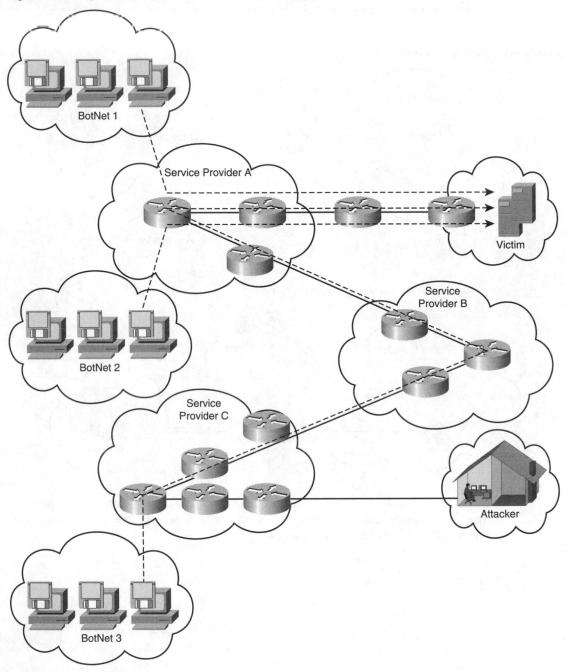

In Figure 4-2, the attacker controls three different botnets or groups of zombies. In this case, hop-by-hop traceback can be time consuming and ineffective. Botnets can consist of several hundred compromised machines. Even a relatively small botnet with only a couple of hundred bots can cause significant damage. The IP distribution of these bots makes the implementation of ingress filters (or filtering) difficult, especially because separate organizations are involved. In most cases, botnets are used to infect or spread malware to other machines. In numerous cases, botnets are controlled by the attacker who is using encrypted tunnels to protect his own communication channel.

Botnets come in hundreds of different types, some of which include:

- Agobot/Phatbot/Forbot/XtremBot
- SDBot/RBot/UrBot/UrXBot
- mIRC-based bots
- DSNX bots
- Q8 bots
- kaiten.cPerl-based bots

TIP   Shadowserver.com is an excellent website that reports botnet activity on the Internet on a daily basis. Many organizations use this information to become familiar with current trends. This site provides detailed graphics and metrics.

You can also obtain technical information about different types of bots at http://www.cert.org or at http://packetstormsecurity.nl.

Attackers who launch DDoS attacks can gain a major advantage by using reflectors to complicate the traceback process; this is known as *attack obfuscation*. Instead of the victim being able to trace back the attack traffic from himself directly to the slave, he must induce the operator of one of the reflector sites to do so on his behalf which can be administratively cumbersome or difficult.

Tracking botnets is a dilemma for many service providers and other organizations. To successfully perform traceback, you need to gather a significant amount of data about existing botnets, in many cases by analyzing captured malware. Many organizations are engaged in research to learn more about botnets and new techniques to combat them. An example of this is the Honeynet Project (http://honeynet.org). Honeynets are a collection of purposefully insecure machines (or honeypots) that are placed on the Internet for attackers to compromise. Researchers can then investigate and learn more about current threats. At the minimum, honeynets collect the following information to learn more about botnets:

- DNS name or IP address of the Internet relay chat (IRC) server and port number
- In some cases, passwords to connect to the IRC server (when applicable)
- Nickname of bot and ident (identification) structure
- IRC channel to join and channel password

Many researchers have observed that updates on the botnet malware are performed frequently. To understand this process more fully, consider an old worm whose propagation started in several botnets, Zotob.x. Zotob was created by Farid Essebar (known by his handle as Diabl0). He was a small-time adware/spyware installer, using Mytob (a mass mailing worm) to infect machines and install adware for money. On August 25, 2005, Essebar was arrested in Morocco. The FBI stated that it holds evidence that Essebar was paid by Atilla Ekici (known as coder), who used stolen credit card numbers to build Mytob variants, as well as Zotob. Many service providers and other organizations spent numerous hours investigating this incident. One of the methods used was the *backscatter technique*. Backscatter is a system that Chris Morrow and Brian Gemberling created while they were working at a major service provider in the United States. This method addresses the need of finding the entry point of a spoofed attack. It combines sinkhole routers and remotely triggered black hole (RTBH) filtering to create a traceback system that provides a result within minutes.

You can use Border Gateway Protocol (BGP)-enabled routers to set specific prefixes to a known and individually handled "next-hop" and see interesting effects when you set the "next-hop" in BGP for a host that is under attack to a single address that will be routed locally. Typically, you set a static route to Null0 so that the attack traffic is advertised with the new "next-hop." An Internet Control Message Protocol (ICMP) unreachable message is transmitted by a network device when it receives packets whose destination is unreachable (Null0). This "unreachable noise" is called a *backscatter*.

NOTE   Backscatter has been advocated by many people, but many also question its benefits. You can find more details about the backscatter technique at http://www.secsup.org/Tracking. Another good presentation on backscatter, which is by Barry Greene, a senior Cisco SP expert, is located at http://www.nanog.org/mtg-0110/ppt/greene.ppt.

Furthermore, if that traceback is then performed using a scheme that relies on observing a high volume of spoofed traffic, such as ITRACE or probabilistic packet marking, the attacker can undermine the traceback by spreading the trigger traffic of each slave across many reflectors. Doing this greatly increases the amount of time required by the traceback scheme to gather sufficient traffic to analyze. These methodologies have been suggested due to research initiatives by several organizations (mainly educational institutions). However, the initiatives, in most cases, are considered "science projects."

Many others have attempted IP traceback techniques such as probabilistic packet marking and deterministic packet markings; these attempts, however, have also been considered science projects.

NOTE   Wikipedia has a good, high-level description of probabilistic packet marking and deterministic packet markings at http://en.wikipedia.org/wiki/IP_Traceback.

Traceback in the Enterprise

The ability to track where attacks are coming from and the techniques that are used within an enterprise depend on the type of attack. If the attacks are coming from external sources, such as the Internet, the enterprises often depend on their providers to be able to track down sources of attack. Additionally, the network telemetry techniques and features discussed in Chapter 3, "Identifying and Classifying Security Threats," are extremely helpful for tracking where attack traffic is being generated.

One of the most powerful tools is NetFlow because it can give macroanalytical information on the traffic traversing your network. Traceback goes hand in hand with the identification and classification phases of incident response. NetFlow, SYSLOGs, DNS, and other telemetry mechanisms in conjunction with event correlation tools such as Cisco Secure Monitoring and Response System (CS-MARS) and Arbor Peakflow X are particularly helpful to trace back security incidents.

Just from a router command line (CLI), you can use NetFlow to collect valuable information. For example, if you notice a sudden increase in traffic over TCP port 445, you can use the **show ip cache flow** command with the **include** option to see the hosts that are sending this type of traffic, as shown in the following example:

```
myrouter>show ip cache flow | include 01BD
 Fa1/0          10.36.1.66      Fa0/0           172.18.85.178   06 C5BC 01BD    93123135
```

Because NetFlow uses hexadecimal numbers for the protocol, source, and destination ports, 01BD is used in the include statement (01BD hexadecimal = 445 decimal). As you can see from the output, the router has received 93123135 TCP port 445 packets on its FastEthernet 1/0 interface from a host with the IP address 10.36.1.66, which is destined to a host with the IP address 172.18.85.178 residing on the FastEthernet0/0 interface.

In the following example, CS-MARS is used in combination with NetFlow and a Cisco IPS sensor. In Figure 4-3, the CS-MARS alerts the administrator about a host spreading the Nachi worm and doing a DoS via ICMP ping. The incident ID is I:155164925.

Figure 4-3   *Worm Incident in CS-MARS*

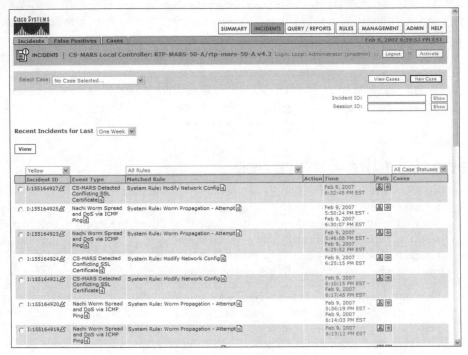

When the administrator clicks the **Attack Path** icon on the right, a new screen with the attack topology is displayed, as shown in Figure 4-4.

In Figure 4-4, you can see that the infected host is 172.19.124.35, and it is attacking a host with the IP address 172.18.124.67. This is a simple topology; however, CS-MARS is able to show you each hop based on the information imported and its configuration. Graphical representation like this one can save you many hours of investigation.

An additional example is shown in Figure 4-5.

Figure 4-4 *Attack Path*

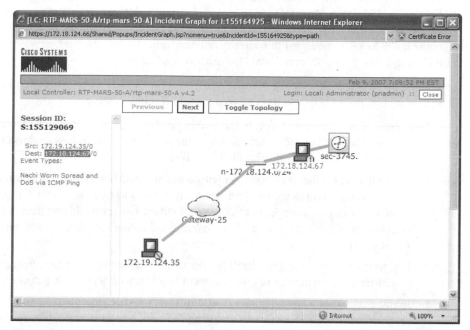

Figure 4-5 *Dot-Dot Attack*

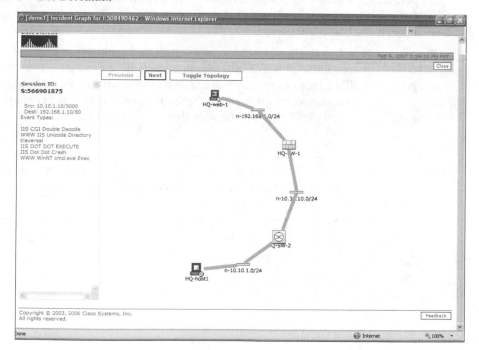

In Figure 4-5, a host with the IP address 10.10.1.10 (HQ-host1) is attempting to crash an IIS server (192.168.1.10 or HQ-web-1) by performing a dot-dot crash and running an attack. Notice that each hop in between is clearly represented, making the traceback process simple. CS-MARS correlated this information analyzing events from a Cisco IPS sensor and from firewall logs from a Cisco PIX security appliance.

Tracing botnet controllers and determining if you are a victim can be difficult. The following tips might help you or your organization if it has zombies:

- If you see a good deal of IRC traffic within your organization, it may be worth investigating further. IRC traffic is not common in most enterprises, and most of the botnets are organized and controlled over IRC.

- You can look for the most commonly used default IRC port (6667). In addition, you will want to expand to the full port range (from 6660 to 6669 or 7000). On the other hand, many botnet controllers can use nonstandard IRC ports. If you have a firewall within your organization, take a look at outbound connection attempts on any suspicious ports.

- IRC traffic usually manifests itself in cleartext, so sensors can be built to sniff particular IRC commands or other protocol keywords on a network gateway.

- If you notice that a large quantity of systems within your organization are trying to resolve the same DNS names or accessing the same server at once, you should immediately investigate further because those systems may be zombies. Also, periodically check your DNS caches. Many command and control tools will use a DNS domain that the herder (botnet administrator) can easily change as needed to relocate the botnet infrastructure.

- You can look for other obvious symptoms of being a victim. For example, if you see much port-scan traffic, it is a definite sign that machines are infected. You can use proper IDS/IPS signatures to find these and then investigate the source. In addition, if you see a lot of unexpected outbound SMTP traffic, you are likely to be hosting spam bots. You can use NetFlow to get statistics about these type of attacks.

NOTE   Chapter 12, "Case Studies," includes case studies with examples of how different types of organizations identify, classify, trace, and react to security incidents. Common traceback mechanisms are used in those examples.

Summary

Tracing back the source of attacks, infected hosts in worm outbreaks, or any other security incident can be overwhelming for many network administrators and security professionals. Attackers can use hundreds or thousands of botnets or zombies that can greatly complicate traceback and hinder mitigation after traceback succeeds. This chapter covered several techniques that can help you successfully trace back the sources of such threats; covering both service provider and enterprise techniques. Remember, traceback mainly involves the packet source. Using network telemetry tools like NetFlow, syslog, DNS, and others in conjunction with event correlation systems can save you hundreds of work hours and, consequently, save you money.

This chapter covers the following topics:

- Adequate Incident-Handling Policies and Procedures
- Laws and Computer Crimes
- Security Incident Mitigation Tools
- Forensics

CHAPTER 5

Reacting to Security Incidents

Reacting to security incidents can be an overwhelming and difficult task if you are not prepared. This chapter covers several best practices, techniques, and tips for use when reacting to security incidents. In the previous chapters, you learned how to identify, classify, and trace security incidents. Without successful identification, classification, and traceback, you will never be able to effectively react to any security event. Therefore, it is important that you understand the topics covered in previous chapters before reading this one.

Adequate Incident-Handling Policies and Procedures

The steps you take when reacting to security incidents depend on the type of threat you are mitigating. For example, if you are mitigating a distributed denial-of-service (DDoS) attack, you will probably not take the same steps as when reacting to a theft of information where the attacker does not make that much noise on the network. However, when reacting to any security incident, time is one of the most critical factors.

It is extremely important to have well-defined incident handling policies in place. In Chapter 2, "Preparation Phase," you learned that without defined policies and procedures for mitigation, you can put yourself in a difficult position when a security outbreak or event occurs. Following these policies or procedures is important.

These policies may be in the form of standalone documentation, or they may be incorporated into other documentation such as company security policies or disaster recovery plans. You may consider developing different procedures and response mechanisms when responding to a direct DDoS attack versus a worm outbreak, or when information has been stolen. Not all security incidents are the same, and you should make sure that the appropriate response procedures are in place.

You should try to create a security policy and be serious about covering all facets of security. Ideally, you should develop security policies in the preparation phase.

Collaboration between support teams within your organization may be necessary when responding to security incidents. After you have successfully identified a security incident, classified it, and tracked it, you must notify the appropriate personnel. For example, if you are a member of the Information Security (InfoSec) or Security Operations (OpSec) team, you may need to involve administrators from separate parts of your organization. You may not have access to the affected device or may not be an expert on a specific application. This is why collaboration is so important.

The reason for setting up collaboration between support teams is to establish lines of communication and ensure that personnel understand the areas of responsibility and capability for each partner. In addition, you should provide a detailed description of the incidents technical aspects to your collaborative teams. This will aid in prompt acknowledgment and understanding of the problem. However, great care should be taken, because you do not want to distribute sensitive information unnecessarily.

You should also have adequate emergency procedures in place. In some cases, you may need to discuss issues and tasks within external teams. For example, suppose that you are a member of the OpSec group and you are trying to get information about a specific system that an external team controls. After several attempts, you have received no response. With the correct escalation procedures in place, the task of getting the right people involved becomes easier. Similarly, you should have emergency procedures when other teams try to engage your staff. The main goal of incident response is to restore control of the network and its systems and to limit the impact and damage. Many people say that, in some cases, shutting down affected systems or disconnecting the system from the network may the only practical solution. However, if you have the necessary tools in place, you may be able to quarantine and remediate such systems without unplugging them from the network. For example, you can use routing as a security mechanism and isolate systems within your network. You can use mechanisms such as remotely triggered blackholes (discussed later in this chapter) and in other cases put systems in quarantine segments so that you can patch them accordingly when security outbreaks occur.

Having a systematic approach for patch management is crucial. For instance, if you have a good system in place to provide security operating system and application patches as soon as they become available, your systems are far less likely to fall prey to major attacks. An updated security management system is not a top priority for many companies; however, attackers, worms, and malware do not wait for you to patch every system manually. More importantly, in the case of worm outbreaks, having a distributed patch management system can save you and your staff considerable time thereby saving your organization money.

It is important to create checklists of procedures to be followed during an incident. Documenting events as they happen is important. On most occasions, you may feel as if you do not have time to completely document events in detail during the incident. However, during the identification, classification, and traceback phases, you should gather as much information about the incident as possible. Attempt to answer the following questions:

- What type of incident are you experiencing?
- When did the attack occur (date and time)?
- Where did the attack occur?
- What systems were affected and compromised?

NOTE   Chapter 6, "Postmortem and Improvement," includes examples of these checklists and incident response reports.

These are some of the most fundamental questions that need to be answered. You may develop more specific questions on a case-by-case basis.

Another procedure that you must document is when to involve law enforcement. Incident response is probably one of the disciplines most affected by legal considerations because many incidents involve some sort of crime. Consequently, your organization might want to prosecute the attacker, and in this case, it must consider the legal implications of the incident. If legal implications are present, you must assist law enforcement in all aspects of their investigation. Different laws and regulations are covered in the next section.

Laws and Computer Crimes

In most cases, United States and international laws might affect or impact the incident response process. If you want to prosecute an attacker, you might merely have to contact local authorities. In some cases, however, you will need to contact the Federal Bureau of Investigation or equivalent organizations in other countries, especially when dealing with attacks that involve international boundaries. International and inter-jurisdictional cooperation is difficult. What is illegal in one country may not be in another.

Typically, you have three different options. The first option is to mitigate the problem and move on. The second is to prosecute the attacker in his own country (assuming that the security event you experienced is illegal in that country). The third option is to apply for extradition and prosecute the offender in the country where the incident happened. If you opt for the second or third option, you should seek assistance from your local authorities.

NOTE   The procedures and circumstances for engaging law enforcement depend on your local laws. International laws may also apply.

The U.S. laws distinguish between crimes *against* computers and crimes *involving* computers. For example, a DDoS or a person gaining unauthorized access to a computer or network is classified as a crime "against a computer." On the other hand, if a person commits an assault against someone else or any other felony in which a computer was only the tool used to commit the crime, this is classified as a crime "involving a computer."

The "Computer Fraud and Abuse Act" is the standard statute covering computer crimes in the United States. This was initially introduced in 1986 and updated ten years later in 1996. Title 18, Section 1030, covers crimes against computers.

NOTE   You can access Title 18, Section 1030 at the Cornell University Law School website at http://www4.law.cornell.edu/uscode/html/uscode18/usc_sec_18_00001030----000-.html.

The U.S. Department of Justice has a website where you can obtain specific information on who to contact when reporting a security incident. You can access the website at http://www.cybercrime.gov/reporting.htm.

An excellent document titled "Searching and Seizing Computers and Obtaining Electronic Evidence in Criminal Investigations" can be accessed at http://www.cybercrime.gov/s&smanual2002.htm.

Another initiative by the U.S. government is the Internet Crime Complaint Center (IC3). IC3 is a partnership between the Federal Bureau of Investigation (FBI) and the National White Collar Crime Center (NW3C). The website is http://www.ic3.gov.

TIP   *Infragard* is an organization that is the product of a collaborative effort between the FBI, local enforcement agencies, and private organizations. It has created Special Interest Groups (SIGs), which are resources dedicated to the safeguarding of specific critical infrastructures of both private industry and government through information-sharing networks and a private secure portal of communication. You can obtain more information about Infragard and local chapters at http://www.infragard.net

---

If you work in the health care industry, you should be aware of several new regulations, such as the Health Industry Portability and Accountability Act (HIPAA). The act requires all persons with access to this information to take reasonable care to protect the integrity and confidentiality of patient data. Not only hospitals and health care facilities, but also insurers are now implementing security safeguards and completing risk assessments to ensure the privacy of patients.

Security Incident Mitigation Tools

This section includes several tools and techniques that you can use when mitigating security incidents, such as DDoS and worm outbreaks.

TIP   The mitigation technique and enforcement depends on your network architecture and design. This section covers the most common techniques. As a rule of thumb, you want to base your mitigation operations as close as possible to the source of the attack.

Access Control Lists (ACL)

When you react to a DDoS or to a worm outbreak, one of the most important matters is how fast you can quarantine and isolate the problem. *Quarantining* is the process of identifying all infected machines and blocking them from the network to prevent them from infecting other systems (in case of a worm outbreak). The easiest way to quarantine or block systems is by using router and firewall access control lists (ACL) and VLAN ACLs (or VACL) on Cisco switches. VACLs allow port-level filtering on a VLAN basis. In most cases, VACLs are more feasible when blocking an infected machine. VACLs are applied directly on the switch port, thereby enabling you to do per-host filtering.

It is extremely important that you be familiar with your network topology and understand how all the VLANs are configured. It is a best practice to document the devices (or at least the device types) that reside within each VLAN. This will be extremely helpful to you when you are in the mitigating phase of your reaction to attacks and worm outbreaks.

Another best practice is to prioritize your network resources and critical systems. During the reaction phase, you should protect the most critical systems first.

For more information on tools that can be used for asset management and asset classification, see Chapter 7, "Proactive Security Framework."

TIP   The Cisco Catalyst 6000 series of switches has a switching engine known as a Policy Feature Card (PFC) that contains specialized application-specific integrated circuits (ASIC) that enable the blocking of traffic to occur at close to wire speed on the switch.

One of the major problems with ACLs and VACLs is that you must apply them throughout the network quickly. You can use tools such as the Cisco Security Manager (CSM) to deploy ACLs quickly in your network. You can also use commercial tools such as OpsWare, and SolSoft.

Many security administrators allocate a range of extended ACL numbers that can be dynamically used when mitigating security incidents. For instance, you can assign 190 to 199 for security reaction ACLs, if this range is not in use anywhere else in your network. Some people recommend configuring, on each network, a dummy list device which is well documented with a detailed description so that staff will know that this ACL is reserved and will know its purpose. If you have NetConfig, you can create templates to ease the deployment.

Private VLANs

Private VLANs can be used to achieve Layer 2 isolation of hosts within a VLAN. Some people use private VLANs in their data center to isolate servers in case they are compromised or infected. However, private VLANs do not provide perfect isolation. For example, you can insert a Layer 3 device to a promiscuous port and hop from one system to another using the destination IP address with the Layer 3 device MAC address. This type of attack and others are explained extensively in the whitepaper at http://www.cisco.com/en/US/netsol/ns340/ns394/ns171/ns128/networking_solutions_white_paper09186a008014870f.shtml#wp1002364.

Remotely Triggered Black Hole Routing

Remotely triggered black hole (RTHB) routing is a technique that can be used to drop all attack traffic based on either destination or attack source addresses. Source and destination-based RTBH filter undesirable traffic by forwarding it to the Null0 interface (a pseudointerface that is always up and can never forward or receive traffic). Performance is not a significant challenge with RTBH because it occurs directly in the forwarding path or Cisco Express Forwarding (CEF).

NOTE   This section assumes that you have a basic understanding of Border Gateway Protocol (BGP). If you need to review BGP, refer to http://www.cisco.com/en/US/tech/tk365/tk80/tsd_technology_support_sub-protocol_home.html which includes a comprehensive list of BGP-related FAQs, configuration guidelines, and troubleshooting tips.

Destination-based RTBH works by filtering traffic destined to the hosts being attacked or by filtering an infected host (in worm outbreaks) at the boundary closest to the source. The trigger is typically a router that sends a routing update (iBGP in most cases) to other edge routers configured for black hole filtering. The trigger sends an update with the next-hop IP address defined in a static route pointing to Null0. This is illustrated in Figure 5-1.

Figure 5-1   *Destination-Based RTBH*

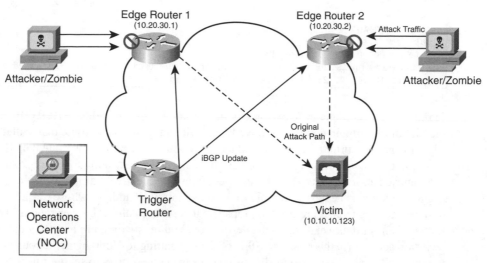

In Figure 5-1, two zombies are attacking a web server (10.10.10.123). The network administrator in the Network Operations Center (NOC) notices the attack and configures a static route on the trigger router with the destination host address (10.10.10.123), pointing it to Null0. This trigger router then sends an iBGP update to the two other routers causing it to drop the attack traffic. Example 5-1 is the trigger router configuration:

Example 5-1   *Trigger Router Configuration*

```
interface loopback0
 ip address 10.20.30.18 255.255.255.255
!
interface Null0
 no ip unreachables
!
router bgp 64555
 no synchronization
 no bgp client-to-client reflection
 bgp log-neighbor-changes
 redistribute static route-map rtbh-trigger

 neighbor rtbh-group peer-group
 neighbor rtbh-group remote-as 64555
 neighbor rtbh-group update-source loopback0
 neighbor rtbh-group route-reflector-client
 neighbor 10.20.30.1 peer-group rtbh-group
!
route-map rtbh-trigger permit 10
 match tag 666
 set ip next-hop 192.168.20.1
```

continues

Example 5-1 *Trigger Router Configuration (Continued)*

```
    set local-preference 200
    set origin igp
    set community no-export
route-map rtbh-trigger deny 20
! The following is the static route that drops the traffic from the infected machine
ip route 10.10.10.123 255.255.255.255 Null0 tag 666
```

In the previous configuration example, a static route for the IP address (10.10.10.123) of the victim is configured pointing to Null0 and with a tag of 666. A route map called rtbh-trigger is applied prior to redistributing the static route into BGP. This route map is configured to match on a tag value of 666. It also sets the next-hop to 192.168.20.1 which is an unused address space that you must configure to selectively drop the traffic. The trigger router sets the next-hop route for the destination IP address whose traffic will be dropped. Route updates are used to propagate this route to all iBGP peer routers. These routers then set their next-hop to the destination. You must configure a static route for the next-hop address (in this example, 192.168.20.1) pointing to Null0 in all the routers where you want the traffic to be dropped. This enables the edge routers to set their next-hops accordingly and forward all traffic for the black-holed destination IP address to Null0. In this example, the local preference is set to 200, and the origin is set to the remote Interior Gateway Protocol (IGP) system. The community is set to no-export, so these routes will not be advertised to external BGP (eBGP) peers.

NOTE   For RTBH to operate successfully, the trigger router must have an iBGP peering relationship with the other two routers. If you use BGP route reflectors, the trigger router must have an iBGP relationship with the route reflectors in every cluster.

If the attacker uses nonspoofed addresses for the attack, you can also do source-based RTBH just by adding a static route to the source or source network, as shown in the following example.

```
ip route 192.168.20.2 255.255.255.255 Null0 tag 666
```

In this example, the attacker is using the IP address 192.168.20.2. However, an attacker could target a legitimate IP address by spoofing it as the source of an attack and counting on you to black-hole the source using sourced-based RTBH filtering. This is why having antispoofing mechanisms in place is crucial for every network in any organization.

Forensics

Many people say that computer forensics is similar to a crime scene investigation, in most cases, the security event you are investigating may be an actual crime. You should determine which computer forensic methodology is most appropriate for your organization.

This investigation can be done by you or your own staff, by law enforcement, or by private sector computer forensic specialists. One of the most critical items to remember is the consequences of mishandling evidence. Forensics is a broad topic, and the laws and handling of evidence vary based on your locality. This chapter is intended to give you only some of the common tools and mechanisms that you can use to perform basic forensics after a security event.

NOTE   References to several whitepapers and tools are listed in the sections that follow.

Log Files

After a security incident, you can use log files to obtain clues on what happened. However, logs are useful only if they are actually read. Even in small networks, logs from servers, networking devices, end-host machines, and other systems can be large, and their analysis may be tedious and time consuming. That is why it is important to use event correlation systems and other tools to better analyze and study log entries. You can use robust systems such as CS-MARS or even simple tools and programs such as Swatch. *Swatch* stands for Simple Watcher. It is an open source tool written in Perl that is capable of searching a file for a list of strings and then performing specific actions when such a string is found. Swatch was designed to do real-time monitoring of server log files; however, you can also use it to handle a standalone file. It was also designed to analyze syslog archives, but you can use it on any file.

NOTE   The Swatch open source project is maintained on Source Forge at http://swatch. sourceforge.net.

Another excellent tool is Splunk. You can use this tool to conduct real-time searches of different types of event logs from different systems.

NOTE   For more information about Splunk, go to http://www.splunk.com. In addition, http://www.loganalysis.org includes information about numerous log parsers that can be used for forensic purposes.

Different systems have different log formats. If it is necessary to compare files, it can be challenging to match up fields. For example, logs from routers are not the same as logs from firewalls or other networking devices. Similarly, logs from Linux or UNIX servers are not the same as logs from Windows systems. CS-MARS can help you analyze all these different types of logs. Also, some open source tools can help you analyze system logs from UNIX/Linux and Windows machines. The following sections include the most commonly used tools.

Linux Forensics Tools

Two of the most commonly used Linux forensics tools are Autopsy and the Sleuth Kit. These programs are intuitive and are a compilation of the following:

- File system layer tools
- File system journal tools
- Meta data layer tools
- Disk image file tools

Despite the fact that Autopsy and the Sleuth Kit run on Linux, they support the NTFS, FAT, Ext2/3, and UFS1/2 file systems. You can download Autopsy and the Sleuth Kit free from http://www.sleuthkit.org.

Figure 5-2 is a screen shot of Autopsy.

Figure 5-2   *Autopsy Linux Forensics Tool*

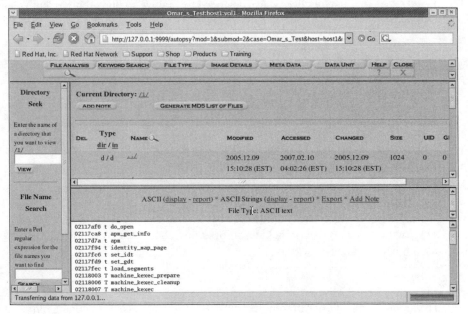

Figure 5-2 shows how you can use Autopsy to analyze the files and directories within a system. You can use this tool to see the names of deleted files. Autopsy can create timelines that contain entries for the "Modified, Access, and Change" times of both allocated and unallocated files. It also allows you to create a "case" to track each security incident.

When collecting information from a Linux or UNIX-based system, you can also use simple tools and commands such as **netstat** and **pstree**. You can use the **netstat -tap** command as shown in Figure 5-3 to obtain information about the active connections in a system.

Figure 5-3   **netstat** *Command Output*

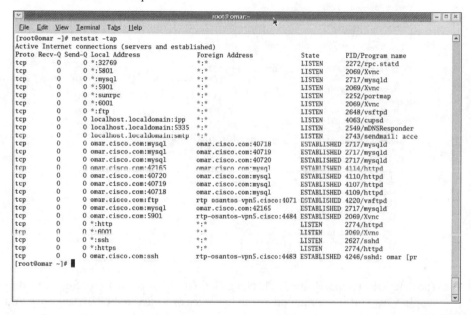

In Figure 5-3, you can see the output showing the different established connections on the system.

NOTE   On UNIX- and Linux-based systems (including Mac OS X), use the **man netstat** command to obtain detailed documentation on the available options of the **netstat** command.

You can also use the **pstree** utility on a Linux system to display the processes on the system in the form of a tree diagram. This allows you to have a better view of the processes running on the system that may be part of malicious software. Figure 5-4 includes a screen shot of the output of the **pstree -hp** command. The **-h** option is used to show the current process and its ancestors, and the **-p** option is used to display the process IDs (PID).

Figure 5-4 **pstree** *Command Output*

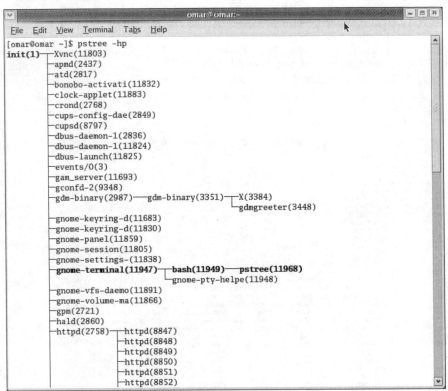

The detailed whitepaper titled "Checking UNIX/LINUX Systems for Signs of Compromise" supplies insightful information on the forensics of Linux and UNIX systems. You can download the whitepaper from http://www.ucl.ac.uk/cert/nix_intrusion.pdf.

Windows Forensics

The most commonly used toolkit for forensics in Windows-based systems is Systernals. *Systernals* is a compilation of several tools used for analysis, troubleshooting, and forensics of Windows machines. This toolkit was initially created by Mark Russinovich and Bryce Cogswell, and Microsoft acquired it in July 2006. Systernals toolkit includes the following:

- File and disk utilities
- Network statistical and analysis utilities
- Process illustration and analysis utilities
- Security configuration utilities
- System resource usage and configuration tools

| NOTE | Microsoft has an excellent whitepaper about Windows forensics best practices and methodologies at http://www.microsoft.com/technet/security/guidance/disasterrecovery/computer_investigation/default.mspx. |

Guidance Software also develops sophisticated forensics tools. Its EnCase product suite includes different integrated tools that facilitate seamless sharing of evidentiary data and solve the resource drain of encrypted data.

| NOTE | For more information about the EnCase suite of tools, go to http://www.guidancesoftware.com. |

It is important to remember that no matter the vendor, the forensics tool you select must give you flexibility when conducting investigations and should help mask complexity when forensics data is shared with untrained individuals.

Summary

In this chapter, you learned how important it is for any organization to have adequate incident handling policies and procedures. You also learned general information about the different laws and practices involved when you are investigating security incidents and computer crimes. This chapter also included detailed information about different tools you can use to mitigate attacks and other security incidents with your network infrastructure components. This chapter concluded with a discussion of basic computer forensics topics.

This chapter covers the following topics:

- Collected Incident Data
- Root-Cause Analysis and Lessons Learned
- Building an Action Plan

CHAPTER 6

Postmortem and Improvement

After any security incident, you should hold a postmortem. At this postmortem, you should look at the full chronology of events that took place during the incident. This chapter includes common best practices when documenting a security incident postmortem.

The postmortem is one of the most critical steps in incident management. The development of the postmortem should be based on analysis of the gaps that enabled a security incident to occur and resulting recommendations for improvements. These recommendations will impact your policies, processes, standards, and guidelines. They will also indirectly impact people—your staff and other personnel. Based on gap analysis, you should design and implement solutions as necessary.

Postmortems can also help you justify increases to your budget for technology solutions that can help you avoid damage that you experienced during the incident. This is why it is important that you identify all weaknesses and holes in systems, infrastructure defenses, or policies that allowed the incident to take place.

Collected Incident Data

The postmortem is one of the most important parts of incident response and is also the part that is most often omitted. As mentioned in the previous chapter, documenting events that occurred during the previous phases (identification, classification, traceback, and reaction) is important to effectively create a good postmortem following a security incident. The collection of this data is important because it can be used for future improvement in the process, policies, and device configuration. This data can also be used to calculate the cost and the total hours of involvement and may help you justify additional funding of the incident response team.

This also can help you to understand changes in new security threats and trends. You can use the data and lessons learned from the postmortem as input to improve security policies, processes, and system configurations. This is illustrated in Figure 6-1.

Figure 6-1   *Postmortem Looped Feedback*

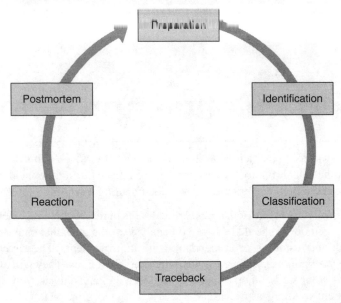

Try to address the "who, what, how, when, why" questions in your postmortem. Table 6-1 demonstrates this approach.

Table 6-1   *Typical Questions Answered in a Postmortem*

Type	Question
Who	Who was affected by this incident?
	Who reported the incident?
	Were the right people engaged?
	Were customers impacted?
	Were partners impacted?
	Was communication between staff and other teams appropriate?
What	What systems were affected by this incident?
	What processes were affected by this incident?
	What tools were used to identify, classify, trace back, and mitigate the incident?
	What worked well?
	What did not work well?
	What were the key lessons learned from the incident?
	What other contingency plans in the organization could be applied?

Table 6-1   *Typical Questions Answered in a Postmortem (Continued)*

Type	Question
How	How was the incident first identified?
	How could the recovery process have been shortened after a fix was identified?
	How effective was the incident diagnosis and response?
	How effective was the communication process?
When	When was the incident first identified?
	When was the incident first reported?
	When was the incident mitigated?
Why	Why did a procedure fail?
	Why was a procedure difficult to implement?
	Why was your methodology successful?

The answers to questions like those included in Table 6-1 should be collected in a collaborative effort between the team members who help on the identification, classification, traceback, and reaction phases. Keep in mind that if you ask questions that are too broad, you may have different perspectives within your staff. This is not necessarily a problem; however, you want to collect clear and concrete facts. If you ask questions that are too narrow, you may end up limiting the input and information that you can collect and analyze from your team experience during the incident. On the other hand, you should collect data that is clear and concrete, rather than collecting data simply because it is available and may be incorrect.

The analysis of the data collected in the postmortem will also help you to measure the success of the incident response team. However, the postmortem process will fail miserably if the problem review board is used as a forum to point fingers at specific staff members or organizational divisions. The most important thing is to understand that the data collected in the initial stage of the postmortem helps you organize a list of lessons learned during the incident.

Figure 6-2 shows the first part of a basic incident response report and postmortem. In this example, Joe Doe from a fictitious company called SecureMe is the author of the report.

Figure 6-2 *Incident Response Report and Postmortem Example*

SecureMe, Inc. Incident Response Report and Postmortem

Reported by: Joe Doe	Date: 07/05/2009
Phone: (555) 123-1234	Email: jdoe@somedomain.com
Date of Incident: 07/04/2009	Time of Incident: 9:30 a.m. EST
Incident ID (if applicable): CSIRT-987654321	External Service Request (If applicable): 601234569

Incident Summary:
Numerous ICMP packets were sent by an unauthorized system to a sales e-commerce web-server farm.

How was it discovered? Abnormal behavior was noticed from CS-MARS incident using Netflow data. An automatic e-mail notification from the system was received at 9:30 a.m.	What actions and technical mitigation have been taken? The source of attack was confirmed by using Netflow data and CS-MARS reports. An access control list was deployed at the Internet edge router to mitigate the attack.

Select the type of incident:

X	Denial of Service Attack	Unauthorized Application Access	Other
	Worm or Virus	Website Defacement	(please specify):
	Theft of information data	Identity Theft	

List all the systems that were affected: Sales e-Commerce web servers	List all departments or business units that were affected: Sales Department

Where any of the affected systems mission critical? [X] Yes [ ] No	Was the source of the attack/incident spoofed? [ ] Yes [x] No

What was the source?

X	External unauthorized user	Former employee	Other
	Internal employee (full time)	Internal guest	(please specify):
	Contractor	Unknown	

Was law enforcement contacted? [ ] Yes [x] No
If yes, what department (i.e., local enforcement, FBI, etc):

In Figure 6-2, a member of the SecureMe incident response team reports that numerous ICMP packets were sent to a web server farm that is part of an e-commerce solution that belongs to its sales department. The fields on the form include most of the questions listed in Table 6-1. Figure 6-2 is merely a basic example. You can expand this form by incorporating more detailed information that is appropriate for your environment and organization, such as the following:

- Total person-hours spent working on the incident
- Elapsed time from the beginning of the incident to its resolution
- Elapsed time for each stage of the incident handling process
- Total hours spent by the incident response team in responding to the initial report of the incident
- Estimated monetary damage from the incident

Root-Cause Analysis and Lessons Learned

Always remember that "lessons learned" is knowledge or understanding gained by experience (in this case, by the experience during the security incident). The Lessons Learned section in your postmortem should focus on identifying incremental and innovative improvements that will measurably improve the following areas of the organization:

- Processes and policies
- Technology and configurations

The postmortem should include both negative and positive experiences. You should highlight the recurrence of successful outcomes while helping to prevent the recurrence of unsuccessful outcomes.

The Lessons Learned section in the postmortem will also help you to improve your risk management processes. You can incorporate these lessons learned into several areas of risk management. One of the key inputs to risk identification is historical information. An input to both qualitative and quantitative risk analysis is identified risks, which can be obtained in your postmortem. Each incident response team should evolve to reflect new threats, improved technology, and lessons learned.

You should establish criteria for a lessons learned process. More importantly, you should turn "lessons learned" into "applied lessons." The following section gives you tips on how to build an action plan from the lessons learned during each phase of the incident response.

Figure 6-3 shows the Lessons Learned section of the SecureMe Incident Response Report and Postmortem.

Figure 6-3   *Lessons Learned Section of Report*

SecureMe, Inc. Incident Response Report and Postmortem Lessons Learned
Success stories (describe what good, repeatable practices and procedures took place):
How well did the incident response staff and management perform in dealing with the incident?
Were the documented procedures followed? Explain if they were adequate.
What information was needed sooner?
What should be done differently the next time a similar incident takes place?
What corrective actions can prevent similar incidents in the future?
What additionally tools or resources are needed?

The questions and information in the form outlined in Figure 6-3 are just examples of the items you can incorporate within your Lessons Learned section in your postmortem. In addition, you can build a rating system of different areas within your incident response ecosystem. For instance, you can list several areas under several major sections, such as the following:

- Tools and resources
- Incident response policies and processes
- Incident response team
- Timeliness of resolution
- Collaboration with other teams

Under each of these categories, you can list more detailed items or subcategories and then rate them. You can use a simple scale from 1 to 5, such as the following:

1 Poor

2 Needs improvement

3 Average

4 Good

5 Excellent

NOTE   The rating system outlined here is just an example. The numbering scheme should be based on the needs of your organization.

At the end of this phase, you can calculate an overall average and use metrics to rate the effectiveness of your incident response process and resources.

Building an Action Plan

After you have collected all necessary information and documented the different lessons learned, you should build a comprehensive action plan to address any deficiencies in processes, policies, or technology. Some underlying causes may remain unknown at the time of the initial post-incident meetings; however, you can capture these causes as open action items to be closed when you have completed your final research.

Prioritize the gaps identified to make sure that you address the most critical first. In addition, understand the root cause of gaps and problems identified. One aspect that sometimes gets lost in the incident postmortems is exploring the reasons for the problems identified. If you do not pay attention to underlying causes, you may fix specific problems and improve particular procedures; however, you will likely encounter different consequences of the same fundamental errors that caused those particular problems.

When you build an improvement plan based on the information collected in the lessons learned, each action item should have the following (at the very minimum):

- Clear description
- Person assigned
- Due date for follow-up
- Priority

This reduces risks that could develop if you fail to follow up on items that can present future threats. This concept is illustrated in Figure 6-4.

Figure 6-4   *Action Items*

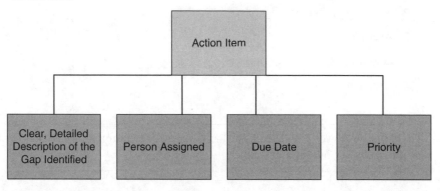

Summary

It is highly recommended that your Computer Security Incident Response Team (CSIRT) perform a postmortem after any security incident. This postmortem should identify the strengths and weaknesses of the incident response effort. With this analysis, you can identify weaknesses in systems, infrastructure defenses, or policies that allowed the incident to take place. In addition, the postmortem can help you identify problems with communication channels, interfaces, and procedures that hampered the efficient resolution of the reported problem.

This chapter offered you several tips on how to create effective postmortems and how to execute post-incident tasks. It included guidelines for collecting post-incident data, documenting lessons learned during the incident, and building action plans to close any gaps that are identified.

It is worth mentioning that many individuals claim to always conduct post-incident analysis; however, they rarely execute and close the gaps identified. Always make sure that you follow up an incident by addressing all the gaps and communicating the lessons learned to other members of the organization. Follow up by educating employees, especially the incident coordinators. Having a group of people who know all the processes and who can guide the various departments of the company to cooperate in response to an issue is important. Work with incident coordinators to fix processes or create new ones. Incident coordinators may also be able to help educate the rest of the company on these processes. You definitely want everyone in the organization to understand at least where to report a suspected problem or concern.

This chapter covers the following topics:

- SAVE Versus ITU-T X.805
- Identity and Trust
- Visibility
- Correlation
- Instrumentation and Management
- Isolation and Virtualization
- Policy Enforcement
- Visualization Techniques

CHAPTER 7

Proactive Security Framework

Many network security frameworks are in the marketplace and most of them have the common goal of providing a methodical and efficient approach to network security. No framework is perfect, you should choose an approach that can help reduce the time, cost, and resources needed to plan and deploy your security strategy. This chapter highlights best practices and benefits of different security frameworks.

A framework can help you establish a view of your entire security landscape, identify potential capability gaps, and prioritize initiatives for improvement.

The Security Assessment, Validation, and Execution (SAVE) framework, formerly known as the Cisco Operational Process Model (COPM), is a security framework that enables visibility and control for end-to-end security. Cisco initially designed SAVE for the Internet service provider (ISP) part of the Next-Generation Network (NGN) initiative. However, you can also apply its practices to enterprises.

Today, malicious traffic within ISPs is spreading faster than before because attack tools are becoming more sophisticated and easier to find. ISPs have witnessed a transformation in the community that engages in cybercrime activities for financial reward, otherwise known as the *miscreant economy*. The principles introduced by SAVE allow ISPs and other organizations to defend against these threats while maintaining control and visibility of their networks.

SAVE defines network security in six major categories or "pillars." Figure 7-1 illustrates the different categories within the SAVE framework.

The six pillars in SAVE are as follows:

- Identity and trust
- Visibility
- Correlation
- Instrumentation and management
- Isolation and virtualization
- Policy enforcement

Figure 7-1 *SAVE Categories Illustrated*

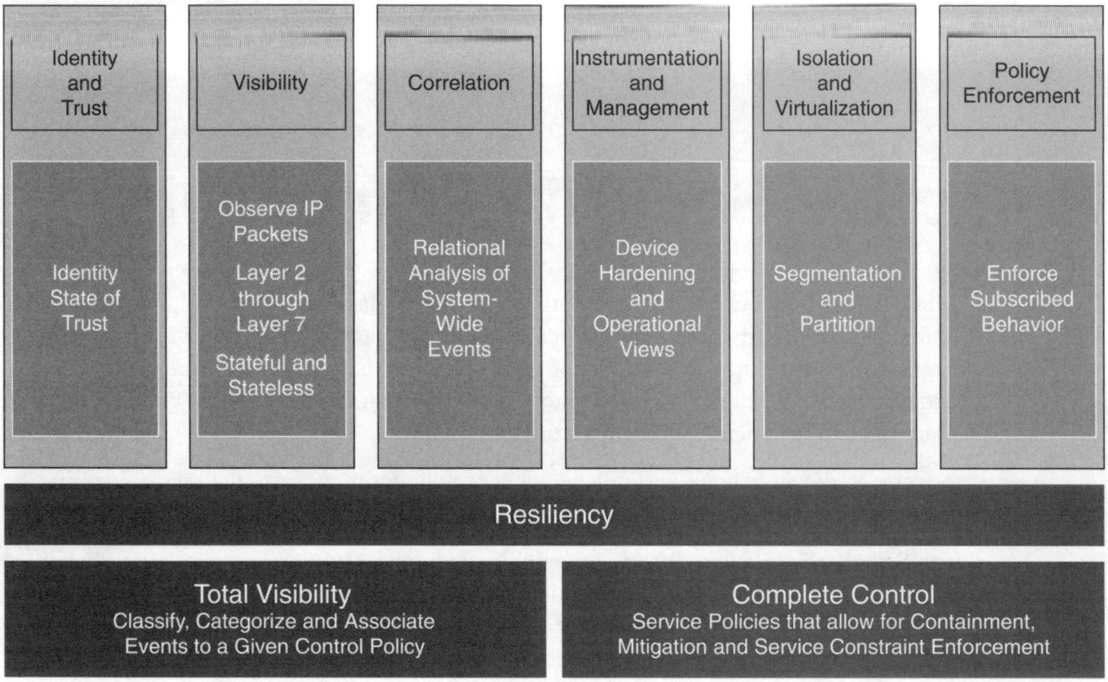

SAVE Versus ITU-T X.805

There is a security methodology created by the Lucent consulting practice called ITU-T X.805, "Security Architecture for Systems Providing End-to-End Communications." ITU-T X.805 defines a threat model that includes five categories:

- Destruction
- Corruption
- Removal
- Disclosure
- Interruption

ITU-T X.805 defines three security layers:

- Infrastructure layer
- Services layer
- Applications layer

Figure 7-2   *ITU-T X.805 Security Layers*

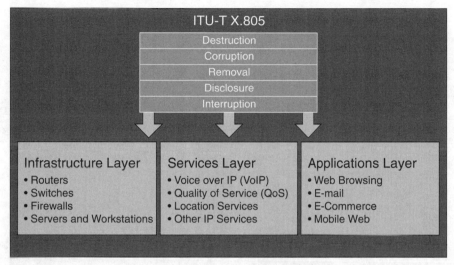

The ITU-T X.805 infrastructure layer includes all infrastructure devices, including:

- Routers
- Switches
- Firewalls
- Servers
- End-user workstations

The services layer includes services such as the following:

- Voice over IP (VoIP)
- Quality of service (QoS)
- Location services
- Other IP services

The applications layer includes all Layer 7 applications that run on the network infrastructure. Each layer has unique threats, vulnerabilities, and ways to mitigate them. X.805 also has three security planes:

- End-user plane
- Control/Signaling plane
- Management plane

These security planes are illustrated in Figure 7-3.

Figure 7-3   *ITU-T X.805 Planes*

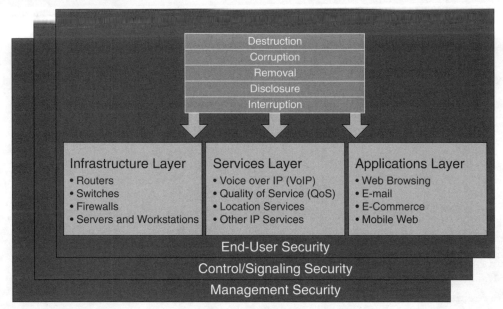

X.805 also includes eight security dimensions that apply to each security layer and plane. The following are these dimensions:

- **Access control:** Firewall policies and access control lists (ACL).

- **Authentication:** Public key infrastructure (PKI), shared secrets, and one-time-passwords.

- **Nonrepudiation:** Syslogs and digital signatures.

- **Data confidentiality:** This confidentiality occurs through the use of encryption.

- **Communication security:** Transport mechanisms such as IP Security (IPsec) and Secure Socket Layer (SSL) virtual private networks (VPN), in addition to Layer 2 Tunneling Protocol (L2TP) tunnels.

- **Data integrity:** Hashing with message digest algorithm 5 (MD5) and Secure Hash Algorithm (SHA).

- **Availability:** Examples include redundancy with Hot Standby Router Protocol (HSRP) or Virtual Router Redundancy Protocol (VRRP).

- **Privacy:** Encryption and Network Address Translation (NAT).

The eight security dimensions are illustrated in Figure 7-4.

Confused yet? X.805 is an overcomplicated approach. Cisco has tried to evolve it to make it more practical to use; however, X.805 is not a true end-to-end security framework and is even potentially harmful in the market and in standards.

Figure 7-4   *ITU-T X.805 Security Dimensions*

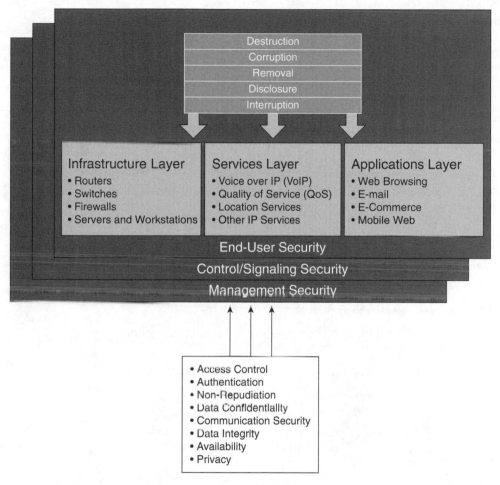

SAVE introduces a roles-based approach for security assessment in a simple manner. Each device on the network serves a purpose and has a role; subsequently, you should configure each device accordingly. SAVE defines five different planes:

- **Management plane:** Distributed and modular network management environment.

- **Control plane:** Includes routing control. This is often a target because the control plane depends on direct CPU cycles.

- **User/Data plane:** Receives, processes, and transmits network data among all network elements.

- **Services plane:** Layer 7 application flow built on the foundation of the other layers.

- **Policies:** The business requirements. Cisco calls policies the business glue for the network. Policies and procedures are part of this section, and they apply to all the planes in this list.

These planes are illustrated in Figure 7-5.

Figure 7-5 *Planes in SAVE*

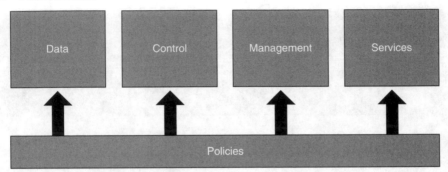

SAVE also presents security in two different perspectives:

* Operational (reactive) security
* Proactive security

This is illustrated in Figure 7-6.

Figure 7-6 *Operational and Proactive Security*

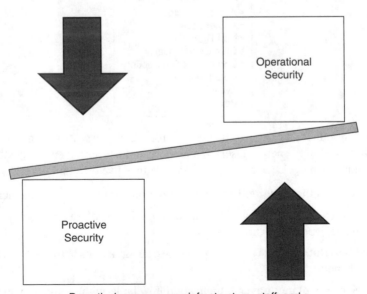

Improve your capabilities to react to security incidents.

Operational Security

Proactive Security

Proactively prepare your infrastructure, staff, and organization as a whole. Learn about new attack vectors and mitigate them with the appropriate hardware, software, and architecture solutions.

You should have a balance between proactive and reactive security approaches. Prepare your network, staff, and organization as a whole to better identify, classify, trace back, and react to security incidents. In addition, proactively protect your organization while learning about new attack vectors, and mitigate those vectors with the appropriate hardware, software, and architecture solutions. You can achieve this balance using what you learned in Chapter 2, "Preparation Phase." The best practices described there help you to proactively prepare and protect your network and organization as a whole.

Identity and Trust

Identity and trust is one of the SAVE pillars. You should consider deploying a complete trust and identity management solution for secure network access and admission at every point in the network. The following are the most common technologies that are part of the identity and trust pillar:

- Authentication, authorization, and accounting (AAA)
- Cisco Guard active verification
- DHCP snooping
- Digital certificates and PKI
- Internet Key Exchange (IKE) protocol
- IP Source Guard
- Network Admission Control and 802.1x
- Routing protocol authentication
- Strict Unicast Reverse Path Fowarding (Unicast RPF)

These technologies are illustrated in Figure 7-7.

AAA

In Chapter 1, "Overview of Network Security Technologies," you learned the basic concepts of AAA. In Chapter 2, "Preparation Phase," you learned best practices for enabling authentication on networking devices for infrastructure protection. In this chapter, AAA concepts are aligned to the identity and trust pillar. A lack of appropriate user management techniques creates numerous direct business risks, including lower productivity, duplicate and conflicting user information, lack of information security, and difficulty in evaluating regulatory compliance. AAA goes beyond the normal authentication and authorization when accessing network devices for management purposes. You should implement a combination of authentication, access control, and user policies to secure network connectivity and resources to which only specific users should be provided access. This access includes the authentication of databases, web servers, e-mail, and other applications, in addition to authentication of users when they attempt to access network segments and their resources.

Figure 7-7 *Identity and Trust*

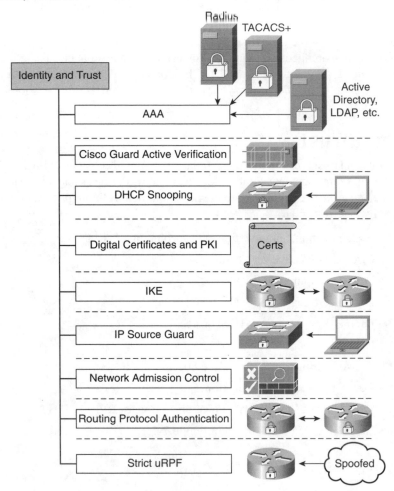

Other examples include authentication for remote access VPN and authentication of wireless users. The identity lifecycle consists of account setup, maintenance, and teardown. Account setup includes giving users the appropriate level of access to resources necessary to do their jobs. Account maintenance consists of keeping user identity information up-to-date and appropriately adjusting levels of access to resources needed to conduct business. Account teardown consists of deactivating the user account when the user is no longer affiliated with the company.

Stronger forms of authentication, such as PKI and one-time passwords (OTP), are increasingly used to control user access to corporate resources. Several solutions provide these kinds of services. You should always look for solutions that provide flexible authorization policies that are tied to the user identity, the network access type, and the security of the machine used to access the network. In addition, the ability to centrally track and monitor the connectivity of network users is of primary importance in isolating unwanted and excessive use of valuable network resources.

NOTE   Management, monitoring (correlation), and isolation are discussed later in this chapter, because they are separate SAVE categories or pillars.

As you learned in Chapter 1, TACACS+ and RADIUS are the most commonly used AAA protocols. Cisco Secure ACS supports both of these protocols and provides support for advanced authentication mechanisms, including the interoperability to external directory services, OTP servers, PKI, and other authentication solutions.

Cisco Secure ACS is an important component of the Cisco Identity-Based Networking Services (IBNS) architecture based on port-security standards such as 802.1x (an IEEE standard for port-based network access control). It is also the "brains" behind the Cisco Network Admission Control (NAC) Framework solution.

NOTE   Examples of the use of Cisco Secure ACS are discussed in the case studies included in Chapter 12, "Case Studies." The Cisco Secure ACS documentation is located at http://www.cisco.com/en/US/products/sw/secursw/ps2086/ tsd_products_support_maintain_and_operate.html.

A good white paper on how to place the Cisco ACS servers within your network is located at http://www.cisco.com/en/US/products/sw/secursw/ps2086/ products_white_paper09186a0080092567.shtml.

Cisco Guard Active Verification

The Cisco Guard provides multiple layers of defense to identify and block all types of attacks with extreme accuracy. It has integrated dynamic filtering capabilities and active verification technologies. These capabilities and technologies are implemented through the use of a patented Multiverification Process (MVP) architecture, which can process suspicious flows by applying numerous levels of analysis. The MVP enables malicious packets to be identified and removed, while allowing legitimate packets to flow freely.

NOTE   In Chapter 3, "Identifying and Classifying Security Threats," you learned how to use the Cisco Guard in conjunction with the Cisco Detector and other third-party solutions to identify and classify attacks.

DHCP Snooping

DHCP snooping is another technology or feature that can be considered part of identity and trust. It is a DHCP security feature that filters DHCP messages by building and maintaining a binding table. This table contains information that corresponds to the local untrusted interfaces of a switch, such as:

- MAC address of the device connected to the switch
- IP address of the device connected to the switch
- DHCP lease time
- DHCP binding type
- VLAN number
- Interface information

NOTE   The DHCP snooping table does not contain information regarding hosts interconnected with a trusted interface. An untrusted interface is an interface that is configured to receive packets from an untrusted network or device. A trusted interface is an interface that is configured to receive only messages from within the trusted network or device.

You can configure DHCP snooping for a single VLAN or a range of VLANs. The following example shows how to enable DHCP snooping on VLANs 10 through 50:

Example 7-1 *IP DHCP Snooping*

```
!enable DHCP snooping globally
!
ip dhcp snooping vlan 10 50
!apply DHCP snooping on VLANs 10 to 50
!
ip dhcp snooping information option
!
interface GigabitEthernet1/1
ip dhcp snooping limit rate 100
!this interface is classified as an untrusted interface, and the rate limit is
   configured.

!You may not want to configure untrusted rate limiting to more than 100 pps.
!Normally, the rate limit applies to untrusted interfaces.
!If you want to set up rate limiting for trusted interfaces, keep in mind that
   trusted
!interfaces aggregate all DHCP traffic in the switch, and you will need to adjust
   the rate
!limit to a higher value.
```

You can use the **show ip dhcp snooping** command to verify your configuration, as shown in the following example:

Example 7-2 *Ouput of the* **show ip dhcp snooping** *command*

```
myswitch#show ip dhcp snooping
Switch DHCP snooping is enabled
DHCP snooping is configured on following VLANs:
10,20,30,40,50
Insertion of option 82 is enabled
Option 82 on untrusted port is not allowed
Verification of hwaddr field is enabled
Interface                   Trusted      Rate limit (pps)
-----------------------     -------      ----------------
GigabitEthernet1/1          no           100
```

In the previous example, you can see that DHCP snooping is enabled on VLANs 10, 20, 30, 40, and 50 (which are VLANs enabled on this switch). The interface GigabitEthernet1/1 is an untrusted interface, and rate limit is applied to 100 packets per second (pps). To configure an interface as a trusted interface, you must use the **ip dhcp snooping trust** interface subcommand.

IP Source Guard

IP Source Guard is a Layer 2 feature that works in conjunction with DHCP snooping. When IP Source Guard is enabled, all IP traffic on the port is initially blocked, with the exception of DHCP packets that are processed by the DHCP snooping feature (if enabled). After the end host receives a valid IP address from the DHCP server, or when a user configures a static IP source binding, a Port Access Control List (PACL) is applied on the port to restrict the client IP traffic to specific source IP addresses that are configured in the binding configuration. The switch drops all IP traffic with a source IP address other than that in the IP source binding.

An important note to remember is that if you configure IP Source Guard on a trunk port with a large number of VLANs that have DHCP snooping enabled, you might run out of ACL hardware resources, and depending on your platform, some packets might be switched in software. You can configure two levels of IP traffic filtering with IP Source Guard:

- **Filtering source IP addresses:** Only IP traffic with a source IP address that matches the IP source binding entry is permitted.

- **Filtering on Source IP and MAC address:** This is based on source IP address and its associated MAC address.

To enable IP Source Guard, use the **ip verify source vlan dhcp-snooping interface** subcommand, as shown in the following example:

```
interface GigabitEthernet1/1
 ip verify source vlan dhcp-snooping
```

To verify the configuration, you can use the **show ip verify source interface gigabitEthernet 1/1** command, as shown in the following example:

```
myswitch#show ip verify source interface gigabitEthernet 1/1
Interface  Filter-type  Filter-mode  IP-address       Mac-address         Vlan
---------  -----------  -----------  ---------------  -----------------   ---------
Gi1/1      ip-mac       active       10.10.1.1                            10
Gi1/1      ip-mac       active       deny-all                             11-20
```

Digital Certificates and PKI

Digital certificates and PKI are also technologies that are used for trust and identity. Digital certificates bind an identity to a pair of electronic keys that can be used to encrypt and sign digital information. A digital certificate makes it possible to verify a claim that someone has the right to use a given key. This verification helps to prevent people from using phony keys to impersonate other users. Used in conjunction with encryption, digital certificates provide a more complete security solution than traditional username and password schemes. Digital certificates ensure the identity of all parties involved in a transaction.

The following are some of the most common uses of digital certificates:

- IPsec VPN tunnel authentication
- SSL transactions
- Code signing
- Application authentication (that is, e-mail, e-commerce, and so on)

IKE

IKE provides authentication mechanisms for IPsec VPN tunnels. This protocol is also an example of identity and trust technologies.

NOTE   Detailed information on IKE authentication mechanisms is covered in Chapter 1.

Network Admission Control (NAC)

NAC is also an example of a trust and identity technology. As you learned in Chapters 1 and 2, NAC appliance and framework provide a solution to evaluate whether end-host workstations are compliant with security policies before they enter the network. These policies can include antivirus, antispyware software, operating system updates, security patches, and other preconfigured options. In addition, the role-based authentication features provide more granular access to end hosts and users.

Routing Protocol Authentication

Another example of a trust and identity technique is the implementation of routing protocol authentication. Border Gateway Protocol (BGP), Enhanced Interior Gateway Routing Protocol (EIGRP), Open Shortest Path First (OSPF), Routing Information Protocol (RIP) and Intermediate System-to-Intermediate System Protocol (IS-IS) all support various forms of authentication mechanisms.

NOTE These authentication mechanisms are discussed in Chapter 2 in detail.

Strict Unicast RPF

Strict Unicast RPF is an antispoofing mechanism that verifies the source address of a packet received on a router interface by verifying the forwarding table of the router. If the source address is reachable through the same interface on which the packet was received, the router processes the packet; if not, the packet is dropped. You can also categorize Unicast RPF as a trust and identity mechanism.

NOTE Unicast RPF is discussed in Chapter 2.

Visibility

Network visibility is one of the most important pillars within the SAVE framework. In fact, two of the most important components of SAVE are visibility and control. The following are the most common technologies that can be used to obtain and maintain complete network visibility:

- Anomaly detection
- Intrusion detection system/intrusion prevention system (IDS/IPS) [IOS, Cisco Security Agent (CSA), network-based intrusion detection system/network-based intrusion prevention system (NIDS/NIPS)]
- Cisco Network Analysis Module (NAM)
- Layer 2 and Layer 3 information [Cisco Discovery Protocol (CDP), routing tables, Cisco Express Forwarding (CEF) tables]

These are illustrated in Figure 7-8.

Figure 7-8 *Technologies That Help to Achieve and Maintain Complete Network Visibility*

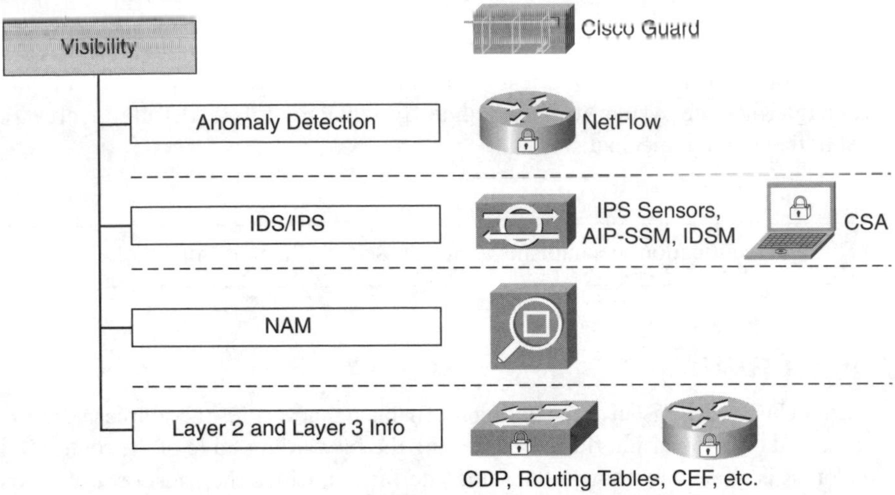

Anomaly Detection

Anomaly detection can be performed by various tools that provide insightful information on exactly what is happening within your network. These tools or technologies include the following:

- NetFlow
- Arbor Peakflow SP and Peakflow X
- Cisco Anomaly Detector XT

NOTE Anomaly detection technologies and solutions are discussed in Chapters 1 and 2.

IDS/IPS

IDSs and IPSs also provide visibility into what is happening on the network. Most of the network IDS and IPS systems rely on signatures for detection and protection. For this reason, it is extremely important to keep signatures up-to-date and to tune the IDS/IPS devices accordingly. Cisco IPS 6.0 now supports anomaly detection capabilities that allow you to detect day-zero vulnerabilities more easily.

NOTE   An introduction to network IDS and IPS systems is covered in Chapter 1. Chapter 3 teaches you how to use network IDS and IPS systems to successfully identify and classify security threats. The configuration of IPS systems is covered within the case studies included in Chapter 12.

Host-based intrusion prevention systems, such as the Cisco Security agent, also provide information about the behavior of end-host systems by extending the visibility to each end point (host or servers).

Cisco Network Analysis Module (NAM)

The Cisco NAM is an integrated network monitoring solution for the Cisco Catalyst 6500 series switches. Ciso NAM is designed to give you visibility into the network by showing you information about applications running on your network and the performance of these applications. The Cisco NAM solution includes a web-based traffic analyzer GUI that presents statistical information to the administrator. The Cisco NAM uses Management Information Bases (MIB) for Remote Monitoring II (RMON II), Differentiated Services Monitoring (DSMON), Switch Monitoring (SMON), and other mechanisms to analyze and store the collected data.

NOTE   The following link provides detailed information about NAM:
http://www.cisco.com/en/US/products/hw/modules/ps2706/ps5025/index.html.

The configuration guide is located at http://www.cisco.com/en/US/products/hw/switches/ps708/products_configuration_guide_book09186a00805e081e.html.

Layer 2 and Layer 3 Information (CDP, Routing Tables, CEF Tables)

Layer 2 and Layer 3 routing features can provide insightful information and increase visibility. Features such as CDP, CEF, and IP routing tables can give you topological information about the network. It is important to notice that in the hands of the enemy, tools like CDP can be destructive. Therefore, it is recommended that you enable CDP only on trusted interfaces.

NOTE   For more information on best practices to use when implementing CDP, refer to Chapter 2.

Correlation

In previous chapters, you learned the different aspects of event correlation. For example, you learned that the more complex the network and devices deployed, the more event messages, alarms, and alerts these devices will generate. In the end, far more data is generated than anyone can easily scan, and it is located in numerous places. In this chapter, you learn the importance of event correlation for maintaining good visibility of what is happening in the network. This chapter also describes tools and technologies you can deploy to successfully correlate events, while maintaining visibility and control of the network. Event correlation tools enable you to efficiently use your staff time and skills, and they prevent revenue loss resulting from downtime. The following are examples of correlation tools:

- Cisco Security Monitoring, Analysis, and Response System (CS-MARS)
- Arbor Peakflow SP and Peakflow X
- Cisco Security Agent Management Center (CSA-MC) basic event correlation

These tools are illustrated in Figure 7-9.

Figure 7-9   *Example of Tools That Help You Maintain Network Visibility*

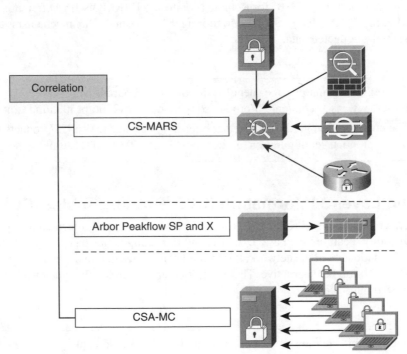

CS-MARS

CS-MARS supports events from routers, switches, firewalls, VPN devices, IPS/IDS solutions, operating system logs, application logs, and many other items. It supports both Cisco and non-Cisco devices.

NOTE   Chapter 3 teaches how you can use CS-MARS to successfully identify and classify security threats. The configuration of CS-MARS is covered within the case studies included in Chapter 12.

Arbor Peakflow SP and Peakflow X

Arbor Peakflow SP (for service providers) and Peakflow X (for enterprises) are excellent tools that allow you to obtain network visibility. Based on information collected from routers, such as interface statistics and NetFlow, Peakflow SP and Peakflow X can show you details of the traffic traversing throughout your network.

NOTE   For more information about these tools, go to http://www.arbor.net.

Arbor has excellent white papers about anomaly detection and combating day-zero threats at http://www.arbor.net/resources_researchers.php.

Cisco Security Agent Management Console (CSA-MC) Basic Event Correlation

CSA-MC can also provide you with basic host-based event correlation. You can gain visibility of what exactly is happening within each endpoint (user workstations and servers).

Instrumentation and Management

Instrumentation and management is also an important category within the SAVE framework. You should always implement protocols and mechanisms that achieve the management of every network device. Having good instrumentation and management mechanisms in place not only allows you to provision configurations to your network devices, but it also helps you to maintain control of your environment. Some examples of management and instrumentation tools are as follows:

- Cisco Security Manager (CSM)
- Configuration logger and configuration rollback

- Embedded device managers
- Cisco IOS XR XML interface
- Simple Network Management Protocol (SNMP) and remote monitoring (RMON)
- Syslog

These tools are illustrated in Figure 7-10.

Figure 7-10 *Example of Instrumentation and Management Tools*

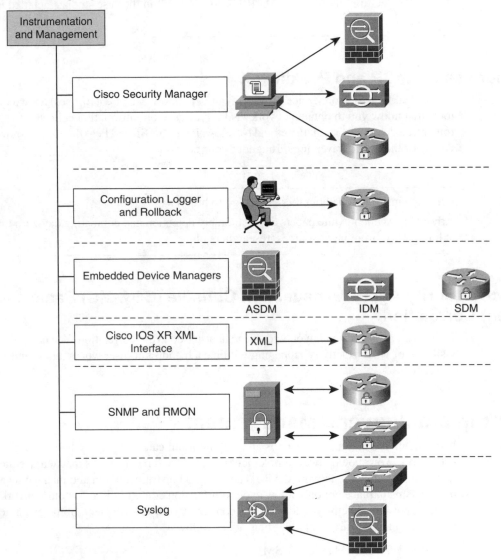

Cisco Security Manager

CSM helps you configure Cisco firewalls, IPS devices, and VPN tunnels easily. It not only saves you time in the provisioning phase, but it can also be used to update enforcement policies in firewalls and routers when needed. CSM achieves scalability through policy-based management techniques that are used to simplify administration.

Configuration Logger and Configuration Rollback

The Cisco IOS configuration logger logs all changes that are manually entered at the command-line prompt. In addition, it can notify registered clients about any changes to the log.

NOTE   The contents of the configuration log are stored in the run-time memory; the contents of the log are not persisted after reboots. The Configuration Logger Persistency feature allows you to keep the configuration commands entered by users after reloads. You can enable the Configuration Logger Persistency feature by using the **archive log config persistent save** command.

The Cisco IOS Software configuration rollback feature allows you to keep a journal file containing a log of the changes and discard them if needed. The purpose of this feature is to revert (or roll back) to a previous configuration. You can use the **configure replace** command to roll back to a previous configuration state.

NOTE   More information about the Cisco IOS configuration rollback feature is located at http://www.cisco.com/en/US/products/sw/iosswrel/ps5207/ products_feature_guide09186a0080356ea5.html#wp1066264.

Embedded Device Managers

In small environments, you can use embedded devices managers to configure and manage network access devices such as routers, switches, firewalls, IPS devices, and others. Numerous Cisco devices come with an embedded device manager. Examples include the following:

- **Cisco Adaptive Security Device Manager (ASDM):** Manages Cisco PIX and Cisco Adaptive Security Appliance (ASA) security appliances
- **Cisco IPS Device Manager (IDM):** Manages Cisco IPS sensors, in addition to Advanced Inspection and Prevention Security Services Module (AIP-SSM) for the Cisco ASA
- **Security Device Manager (SDM):** Manages Cisco IOS routers

Cisco IOS XR XML Interface

The Cisco IOS XR software supports an extensible markup language (XML) application programming interface (API) that helps you develop external management applications for routers that run Cisco IOS XR software.

NOTE   The following site has detailed information about the Cisco IOS XR XML interface:

http://www.cisco.com/en/US/products/ps5845/tsd_products_support_series_home.html

SNMP and RMON

SNMP allows you to exchange management information between network devices and central management servers. SNMP is the most commonly used network device management protocol.

NOTE   In Chapter 2, you learn the basics of SNMP and what is most important: how to secure it.

The RMON protocol provides you with freedom when selecting network-monitoring probes and consoles with features that not only provide ease of management, but also can be used for greater visibility and control of the network.

Syslog

In Chapters 2 and 3, you learn how syslog can provide you with details on what is happening in network devices, while also allowing you to achieve more control and visibility of the network. Firewalls, routers, switches, and other networking devices can send insightful information to administrators via syslog. The combination of syslog and event correlation systems gives you powerful capabilities.

Isolation and Virtualization

The fifth pillar in the SAVE framework addresses network isolation and virtualization. Several isolation and virtualization techniques and tools are available, including the following:

- Cisco IOS Role-Based CLI Access (CLI Views)
- Anomaly detection zones
- Network device virtualization

- Segmentation with VLANs
- Segmentation with firewalls
- Segmentation with VRF/VRF-Lite

These techniques and tools are illustrated in Figure 7-11.

Figure 7-11 *Examples of Isolation and Virtualization Techniques and Tools*

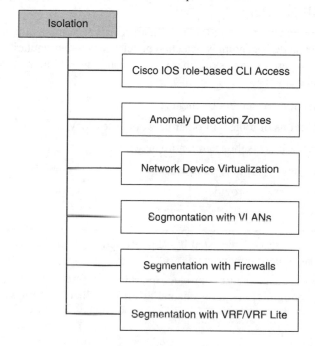

Another isolation technique is maintaining separation between the different network planes. For example, keep the data plane separate from the control and management planes, by also implementing the necessary policies to protect each of them.

Cisco IOS Role-Based CLI Access (CLI Views)

You can consider the Cisco IOS routers Role-Based CLI Access feature a form of virtualization. This feature, otherwise known as CLI Views, allows you to define a virtual set of operational commands and configuration capabilities that provide selective or partial access to Cisco IOS **exec** and **configuration** mode commands. A *view* is a framework of policies that defines which commands are accepted and which configuration information is visible to the user based on his role.

NOTE   The following site has detailed information about this feature.

http://www.cisco.com/en/US/products/ps6350/
products_configuration_guide_chapter09186a0080455b96.html#wp1027184

Anomaly Detection Zones

The Cisco Detector XT and the Cisco Guard XT allow you to configure zones to
categorize and define anomaly detection policies for more granularity and customization.
The following are examples of zones you can configure within the Cisco traffic
anomaly detectors:

- Collections of servers or clients
- Collections of routers or other network access devices
- Network links, subnets, or entire networks
- Single users or whole companies
- Internet service providers

NOTE   The following site provides step-by-step instructions on how to create zones in Cisco
Detector and Guard implementations:

http://www.cisco.com/en/US/products/ps5887/
products_configuration_guide_chapter09186a00804bee78.html#wp1043192

Network Device Virtualization

Several networking devices support virtualization. You can take advantage of device
virtualization to segment and apply different policies within your infrastructure, while
saving money in hardware. For example, you can partition a single hardware device into
multiple virtual devices. In most cases, each virtual device acts as an independent device.
The following devices support virtualization:

- Cisco PIX
- Cisco ASA
- Cisco Firewall Services Module (FWSM) for the Catalyst 6500 series switches
- Cisco IPS sensors running version 6.x or later
- The Cisco Application Control Engine (ACE) family for the Cisco Catalyst 6500
  series switches

The Cisco PIX, Cisco ASA, and FWSM can be configured in multiple context mode in
which each context has its own security policy, interfaces, and administrators. Having

multiple contexts is similar to having multiple standalone devices. Figure 7-12 illustrates how a Cisco FWSM is deployed with three contexts (admin, context-1, and context-2) to segment different servers in a data center).

Figure 7-12 *Security Contexts in FWSM*

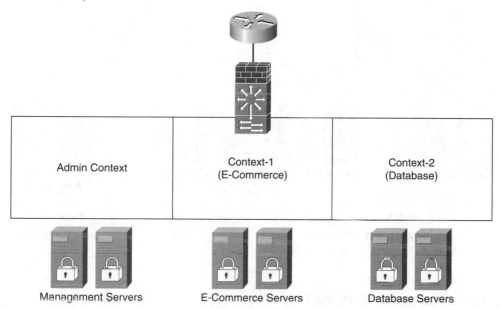

Many features are supported in Cisco ASA, Cisco PIX, and Cisco FWSM running in multiple-context mode; however, some features are not supported, including VPN and dynamic routing protocols.

NOTE   Chapter 10, "Data Center Security," includes sample configurations of Cisco FWSM virtualization to provide data center security. Chapter 12, "Case Studies," also has configuration examples of virtualization in Cisco PIX and Cisco ASA security appliances.

Segmentation with VLANs

You can achieve network segmentation and isolation in many ways. The use of VLANs is one of the most commonly used methods because of its simplicity and ease of deployment. Figure 7-13 illustrates how you can isolate/segment different types of devices just by using VLANs.

Figure 7-13 *Segmentation Using VLANs*

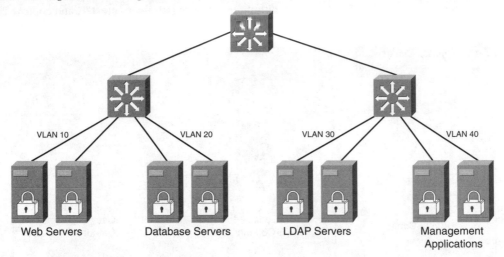

In Figure 7-13, a set of web, database, Lightweight Directory Access Protocol (LDAP), and management servers are isolated by simply configuring four separate VLANs (VLANs 10, 20, 30, and 40, respectively).

Segmentation with Firewalls

In many situations, you can simply segment or isolate parts of the network, servers, or users by placing firewalls. Firewalls also provide more granular policy enforcement mechanisms. Sometimes you can use firewalls with VLAN segmentation, as illustrated in Figure 7-14.

In Figure 7-14, the same servers and the four separate VLANs are configured. In addition, a pair of Cisco ASAs are placed to provide segmentation services while enforcing more granular security policies.

Segmentation with VRF/VRF-Lite

You can also use Multiprotocol Label Switching (MPLS) VPN routing and forwarding (VRF) or the MPLS VRF-Lite feature on Cisco IOS routers for network segmentation purposes. This concept is illustrated in Figure 7-15.

Figure 7-14 *Segmentation Using VLANs and Firewalls for Policy Enforcement*

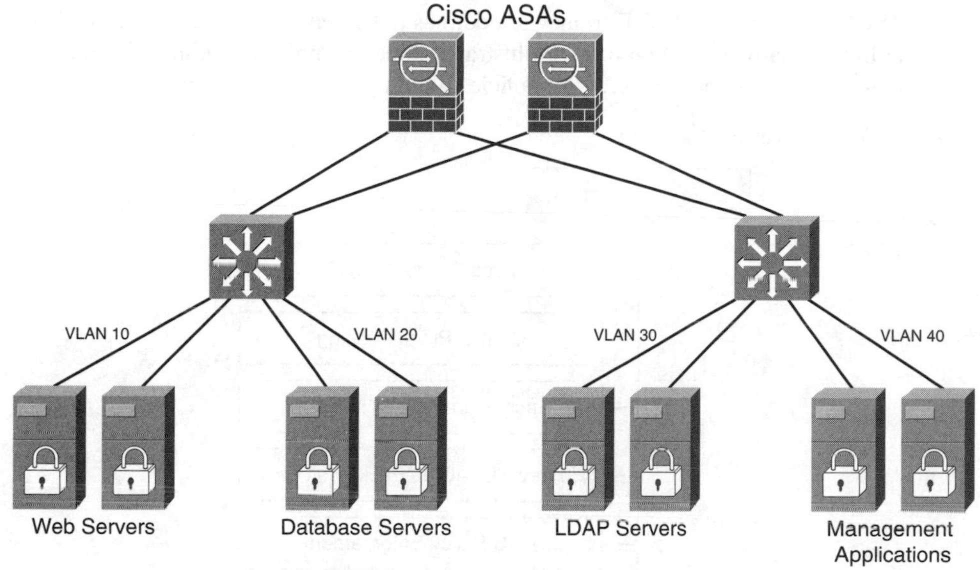

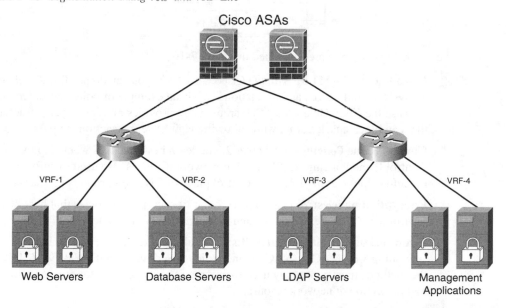

Figure 7-15 *Segmentation Using VRF and VRF-Lite*

The main challenge of implementing VRFs and VRF-Lite is that most enterprises do not run MPLS within their corporate network. More importantly, their staffs do not have the skills to implement MPLS because it is a complicated routing technology. This segmentation technique is mainly implemented by service providers.

Policy Enforcement

The last pillar in the SAVE framework defines policy enforcement. You can enforce policy in many ways. Figure 7-16 illustrates some examples of techniques and features that allow you to enforce security policies within your organization:

Figure 7-16 *Policy Enforcement*

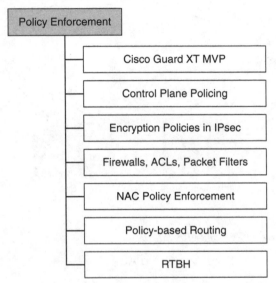

The following examples are illustrated in Figure 7-16.

- **Cisco Guard XT MVP:** With the Cisco Guard XT, you can do per-flow-level attack analysis, identification, and mitigation. This is an example of policy enforcement, because the Cisco Guard XT MVP architecture provides multiple layers of defense that can block attack traffic, while allowing legitimate transactions to pass.

- **Control Plane Policing:** In Chapter 2, you learn best practices when deploying Control Plane Policing (CoPP) in your network. CoPP is also used to enforce predefined policies to protect the control plane of Cisco IOS routers in your network.

- **Encryption policies:** You can enforce security encryption policies that best fit your environment in IPsec site-to-site and remote access VPN tunnels.

- **Firewalls, packet filters, and ACLs:** Firewalls, packet filters, and ACLs (including VLAN ACLs [VACLs] and policy-based ACLs in the Catalyst 6500) are the methods most commonly used to enforce security policies for segmentation and protection of network resources.

- **NAC policy enforcement:** You can configure NAC Appliance and NAC Framework policies to ensure that only compliant machines can enter the network. Based on your configured policies, you can quarantine and remediate noncompliant machines.

- **Policy-based routing (PBR):** You can also use PBR on routers and Layer 3 devices to define enforcement policies for traffic within your network.

- **Remotely triggered black holes (RTBH):** In previous chapters, you learn how you can block attack traffic or infected hosts using RTBH. RTBH is another example of how you can reactively enforce policies within your network.

Visualization Techniques

This section includes a few examples of how you can create topology maps and other diagrams to visualize your network resources and apply SAVE. These diagrams give you the basic idea so that you can then customize the diagrams to fit your organizational needs.

You can create circular diagrams like the one illustrated in Figure 7-17. Typically, these types of diagrams include resources that surround a critical system or area of the network you want to protect. In Figure 7-17, a cluster of database servers is illustrated in the center of the diagram. Several layers describe the devices in the topology in relation to different sections of the network.

Figure 7-17 *Topology Map Visualization*

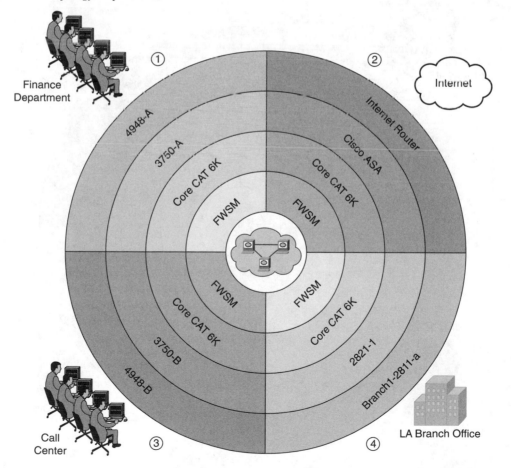

The illustration in Figure 7-17 helps you visualize and understand the different layers of protection you can apply within your network to protect the mission-critical systems. The diagram in Figure 7-17 has four major sections that portray the path from and to the protected system and the following sections of the network:

1 Finance department users

2 Internet

3 Call Center

4 Branch Office in Los Angeles, California (LA)

You can also visualize packet flows and understand how security policies can be applied to each network device to protect critical systems and the infrastructure as a whole. An example is illustrated in Figure 7-18.

Figure 7-18 *Traffic Flow Visualization*

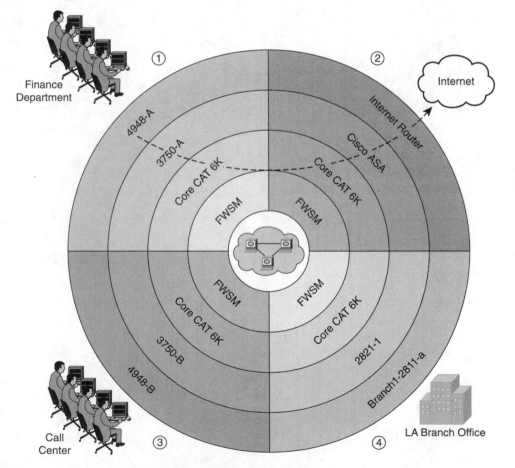

Figure 7-18 illustrates an example of the packet flow when a user from the finance department accesses the Internet. There you can see the devices that these packets touch and the relation to the critical systems.

You can identify where you can apply the technologies that belong to each SAVE pillar. For example, Figure 7-19 shows how you can apply technologies that enable you to gain and maintain visibility of what is happening in your network.

Figure 7-19 *Visibility Techniques Applied*

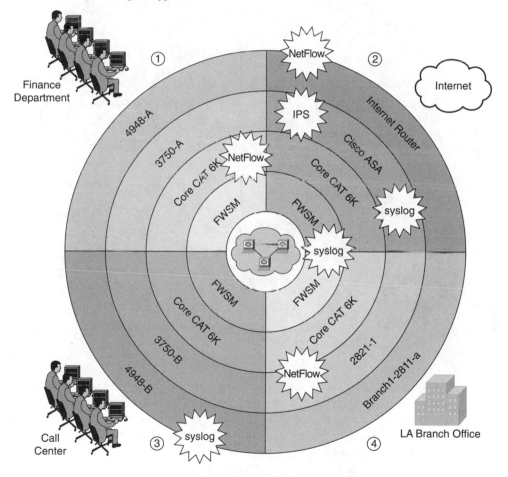

Figure 7-19 shows you how you can enable syslog on devices such as the switches, routers, FWSM for the Cisco Catalyst 6500 series switches, and Cisco ASA. It also shows you places where you want to enable NetFlow, IPS services, and other features.

Figure 7-20 shows where you can enforce policies to restrict access.

Figure 7-20 *Policy Enforcement Visualization*

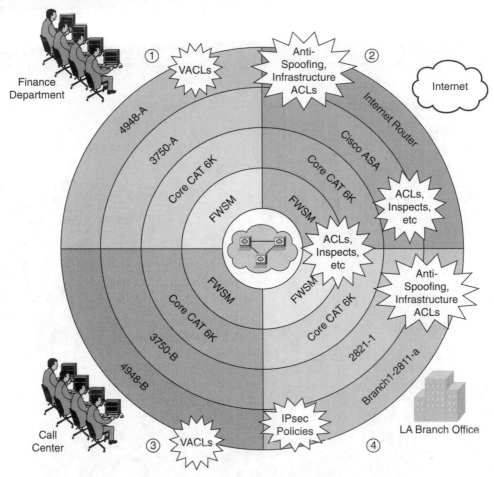

You can apply ACLs and IP inspection features on the Cisco ASA and the FWSM. In addition, you can apply VACLs on the access switches and antispoofing and infrastructure ACLs on the Internet router and other routers within the network. You can also enforce strict IPsec policies for the site-to-site connectivity between the main office and the branch office.

NOTE   Antispoofing and infrastructure ACLs are discussed in Chapter 2, "Preparation Phase." Chapter 12, "Case Studies," also provides some examples within the case studies it covers.

You can also create similar diagrams to visualize where you can apply the technologies and features described on each of the pillars in SAVE. SAVE advocates the understanding of device roles and their appropriate configuration. For example, the Internet edge routers do not have the same role as the other routers within the topology in the previous examples. Despite that, Internet edge routers can be the same model and run the same software versions as other routers, and their configuration should be modeled after their role.

NOTE   The types of diagrams shown in Figures 7-18, 7-19, and 7-20 are not limited to only these technologies, features, and applications. You can customize them to your specific needs.

Summary

SAVE is a framework that was initially developed for service providers, but you can apply its practices to any organization. This chapter covers SAVE in detail. Examples of technologies within the six SAVE main categories are discussed. Visibility and control are two of the most important topics and concepts within SAVE. This chapter provides examples of techniques and practices that can allow you to gain and maintain visibility and control over the network during normal operations or during the course of a security incident or an anomaly in the network.

Defense-In-Depth Applied

This chapter covers the following topics:

- Overview of Cisco Unified Wireless Network Architecture
- Authentication and Authorization of Wireless Users
- Lightweight Access Point Protocol (LWAPP)
- Wireless Intrusion Prevention System Integration
- Management Frame Protection (MFP)
- Precise Location Tracking
- Network Admission Control (NAC) in Wireless Networks

CHAPTER 8

Wireless Security

Wireless networks are becoming more and more popular. Not only can you take advantage of wireless networking at the office, home, a hotel, and coffee shops, but also at airports, train stations, and many other places. Wireless networks increase productivity. Your employees can save time by sending and receiving e-mail or accessing information on network servers from a conference room or any location within your organization that has wireless connectivity. You can also implement a voice over wireless LAN (WLAN) solution. With a WLAN, your employees can reach each other anywhere within your organization without having to rely on cellular coverage that can be spotty or nonexistent.

Now the bad news: wireless networks are a major target for attackers. One of the biggest challenges today is to make sure that the appropriate tools and mechanisms are used to protect data in transit across wireless networks. In addition, the wireless infrastructure needs to be protected against attacks targeted to the wireless networking devices. Stories abound of attackers gaining access to wireless networks not only to steal information but also to attack other networks.

After reading this chapter, you will become familiar with some of the technologies, tools, and mechanisms that are typically used to protect your wireless network. You will also learn best practices to use when securing the Cisco Unified Wireless Architecture.

The 802.11a, 802.11b, and 802.11g are the most widely deployed WLAN technologies today. Historically, 802.11 WLAN security includes the use of open or shared-key authentication and static wired equivalent privacy (WEP) keys. This combination offers a rudimentary level of access control and privacy but each element can be compromised.

The low cost of wireless deployments makes them popular (that is, you do not have to worry about expensive cabling solutions and portability issues). However, inexpensive equipment also makes it easier for attackers to gain unauthorized access. Rogue access points and unauthorized, poorly secured networks compound the odds of a security breach. The best practices you learned in previous chapters play a crucial role when protecting the infrastructure, analyzing risks, and building the most appropriate operational security program for your organization.

In this chapter, you will also learn the different authentication mechanisms in wireless networks. In addition, you will become familiar with advanced topics such as:

- Wireless intrusion detection and prevention services (IDS/IPS)

- Precise location tracking
- Network Admission Control (NAC) in wireless networks

Overview of Cisco Unified Wireless Network Architecture

The Cisco Unified Wireless Architecture is a multiservice solution designed for any type of organization. It can be deployed in your corporate offices, branches, retail stores, hospitals, manufacturing plants, warehouses, educational institutions, financial institutions, government agencies, and any other type of organization that needs wireless connectivity. Industry standards including the IEEE 802.11 and the draft IETF Control and Provisioning of Wireless Access Points (CAPWAP) are supported.

Because the Cisco Unified Wireless Network is a multiservice solution, it supports data, voice, and video applications. Some examples of data applications are as follows:

- E-mail
- Internet access
- Virtual private network (VPN) access
- Inventory management applications
- Asset tracking
- Mobile healthcare applications

You can also run Voice over IP (VoIP) over WLAN. The Cisco Unified Wireless Network Architecture also supports video, such as video surveillance applications, video streaming applications for e-learning, and others. The Cisco Unified Wireless solution provides interoperability with the Cisco Wireless IP Phones to provide comprehensive voice communications using Cisco Unified CallManager and Cisco Wi-Fi access points. The Cisco Compatible Extensions program gives third-party manufacturers the ability to design industry-standard and Cisco innovations into a wide variety of devices. Other advanced features such as wireless intrusion detection and prevention, precise location tracking, and Network Admission Control (NAC) are also supported.

You can implement wireless networks in all sizes. For example, you can have merely a couple of wireless access points or wireless routers within your organization, as illustrated in Figure 8-1.

In Figure 8-1, a wireless access point and a wireless router are accepting connections from end-user workstations, laptops, and wireless scanners. This approach is only appropriate for small environments. It is not feasible for medium and large organizations because it does not provide centralized management and ease of deployment. The Cisco Unified Wireless Network solution provides centralized management that allows you to easily deploy WLAN configurations with the same level of security, scalability, and reliability to all wireless networking devices within your organization. Figure 8-2 illustrates the main components of the Cisco Unified Wireless Network.

Figure 8-1   *Basic Wireless Network*

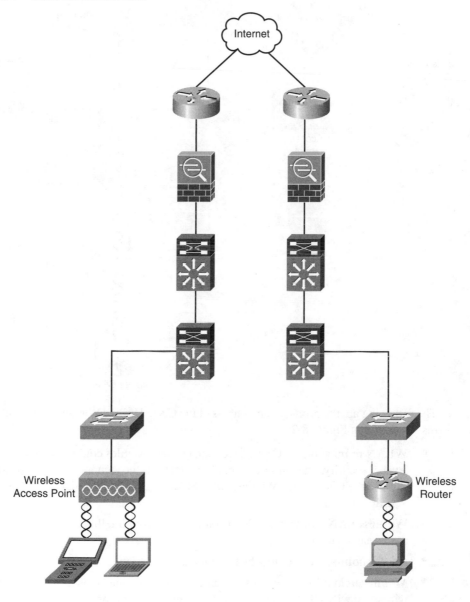

Figure 8-2 *The Cisco Unified Wireless Network Architecture*

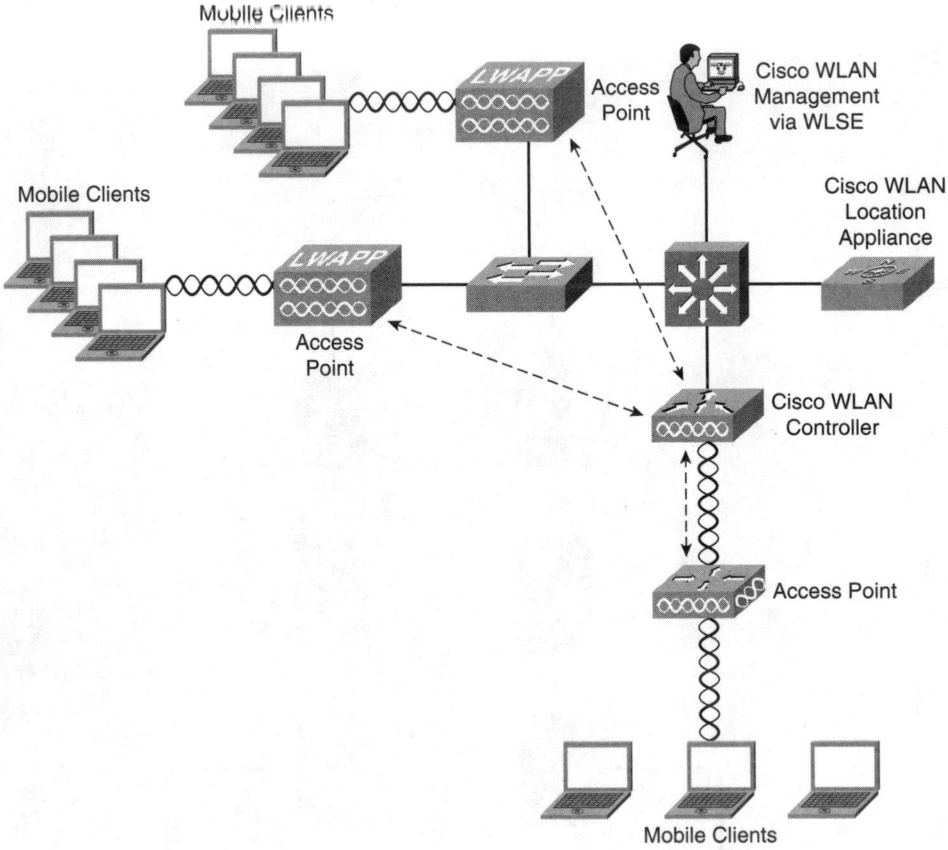

The following are the primary components of the Cisco Unified Wireless Network solution (as illustrated in Figure 8-2):

- **WLAN management:** Centralized management enables configuration of the same level of security, scalability, and reliability features throughout your organization. You can use the CiscoWorks Wireless LAN Solution Engine (WLSE) or the CiscoWorks WLSE express.

- **Wireless LAN controllers:** Provision of centralized intelligence for wireless access point management.

- **Access points:** Devices to which mobile devices connect.

- **Mobile clients:** End-user workstations, laptops, personal assistant (PDAs), and other wireless devices that ensure peak performance and interoperability.

- **Mobility services:** Services such as voice over wireless LAN, wireless intrusion detection and prevention, precise location tracking (Cisco WLAN Location Appliance), and others.

NOTE   For general information about the Cisco wireless devices, go to
http://www.cisco.com/go/wireless.

You can deploy wireless access points within your organization in two modes: unified mode
(as illustrated in Figure 8-2) and autonomous mode. In autonomous mode, a WLSE
network management appliance is deployed with autonomous access points. Some access
points act as domain controllers (WDS) for sets of access points communicating over the
wired network using the Wireless LAN Context Control Protocol (WLCCP). This is
illustrated in Figure 8-3.

Figure 8-3   *Autonomous Wireless Access Points*

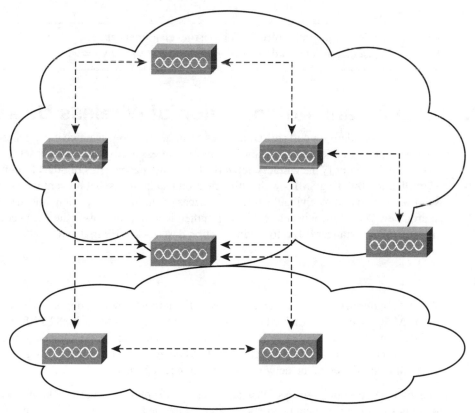

The main difference between the unified and autonomous modes is that in unified mode,
access points operate with the Lightweight Access Point Protocol (LWAPP) and work
in conjunction with Cisco wireless LAN controllers and the Cisco Wireless Control
System (WCS). When configured with LWAPP, the access points can automatically detect

the best-available Cisco wireless LAN controller and download appropriate policies and configuration information with no manual intervention. Autonomous access points are based on Cisco IOS software and may optionally operate with the Cisco WLSE. Autonomous access points, along with the Cisco WLSE, deliver a core set of features and may be field-upgraded to take advantage of the full benefits of the Cisco Unified Wireless Network as requirements evolve.

You can individually manage Cisco Aironet autonomous access points via the command-line interface (CLI), a web interface, the CiscoWorks WLSE, or CiscoWorks WLSE Express. On the other hand, Cisco recommends that you upgrade any existing Cisco Aironet access points operating autonomously to run LWAPP and operate them as lightweight access points to receive all the features, benefits, and mobility services of the Cisco Unified Wireless Network.

NOTE   Cisco provides free upgrade software for existing customers at http://tools.cisco.com/support/downloads/pub/MDFTree.x?butype=wireless.

Authentication and Authorization of Wireless Users

The 802.11 standard supports different types of authentication. The two most generic types are open and shared-key authentication. In most wireless networks, a service set ID (SSID) is specified to identify the wireless network. The basic mechanisms of 802.11 augment the identification by using SSIDs with authentication mechanisms that prevent the client from sending data to and receiving data from the access point unless the client has the correct shared key. One of the most basic wireless authentication protocols is the wired equivalent privacy (WEP) standard. The following section describes WEP in detail.

WEP

WEP, an optional encryption standard in 802.11 that most vendors support, is implemented in the MAC layer. WEP-enabled devices encrypt the payload of each 802.11 frame before transmission by using an RC4 stream cipher. The packets are then decrypted in the wireless access point. WEP encrypts only data between 802.11 stations. After the frame enters the wired side of the network, WEP no longer applies.

During the encryption process, WEP arranges a key schedule (otherwise known as a *seed*) by concatenating the shared secret key supplied by the user of the sending station with a random-generated 24-bit initialization vector (IV). The IV lengthens the life of the secret key because the station can change the IV for each frame transmission. WEP inputs the resulting seed into a pseudorandom number generator that produces a key-stream equal to the length of the frame payload plus a 32-bit integrity check value (ICV), as illustrated in Figure 8-4.

Figure 8-4 *WEP Process*

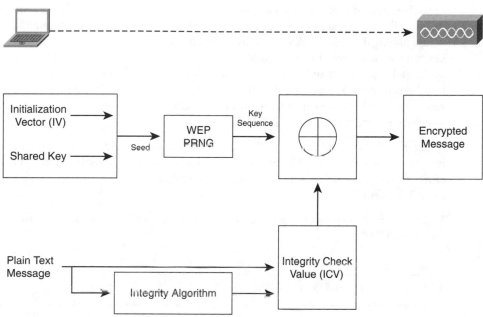

The following steps are illustrated in Figure 8-4:

1   The ICV is calculated using CRC-32 and concatenated to the plaintext message.

2   A random IV and the shared secret key are also concatenated producing the seed.

3   This seed is the input to the WEP Pseudorandom Number Generator (PRNG). WEP uses RC4 PRNG of RSA Data Security to produce a pseudorandom sequence.

4   The message is encrypted by using an XOR operation with the sequence generated in the previous step.

5   The encrypted message is sent to the other end.

The ICV is a check sum that the receiving station eventually recalculates and compares to the one sent by the sending station to determine whether the transmitted data underwent any form of tampering while in transient. If the receiving station calculates an ICV that does not match the one found in the frame, the receiving station can reject the frame or flag the user.

NOTE   WEP shared secrets use 40-bit, 64-bit, or 128-bit keys.

WEP has some limitations and has undergone extensive examination and criticism over the past years. In short, WEP is vulnerable because of its relatively short IVs and keys that remain static. For a large, busy network, this reoccurrence of IVs can happen within an hour or so. Because of this, you will have many frames or packets with similar key-streams. Technically, an attacker can gather frames based on the same IV to determine the shared values among the wireless devices. This information can be key-stream or the shared secret key. The static nature of the shared secret keys emphasizes this problem. In many cases, system administrators and users use the same keys for months or even years. This gives mischievous culprits plenty of time to monitor and attack the WEP-enabled networks. Now some vendors deploy dynamic key distribution solutions based on 802.1X, which definitely improves the security of wireless LANs.

Many now recommend the use of IP security (IPsec) to ensure data confidentiality, integrity, and authenticity. The only caveat is that when you deploy IPsec in a WLAN environment, you need to install an IPsec software client on every machine that connects to the wireless network.

WEP has several enhancements. The first one is the use of the Temporal Key Integrity Protocol (TKIP) .

NOTE   TKIP is often referred to as WEP Version 2.

The second enhancement is the use of the Advanced Encryption Standard (AES) encryption protocol instead of RC4, which is used in older WEP implementations.

The Wi-Fi Protected Access (WPA) standard uses TKIP to provide additional security features. WPA is discussed in the next section.

WPA

WPA (using TKIP) includes a per-packet keying (PPK) and message integrity check (MIC) and an extension of the initialization vector from 24 bits to 48 bits. WPA mitigates the WEP threat by implementing different keys on a per-packet basis. It does this by hashing the IV and WEP keys to produce a temporal key. This temporal key is then combined with the IV and fed to an XOR operation with the plaintext message.

Today WPA combines TKIP and user authentication via IEEE 802.1x and the EAP (Extensible Authentication Protocol). This combination mitigates vulnerabilities from several angles and represents a significant security upgrade over WEP.

NOTE	The following site includes a whitepaper with detailed information about WEP, WPA, and other authentication mechanisms:
	http://www.cisco.com/en/US/netsol/ns340/ns394/ns348/ns386/networking_solutions_white_paper09186a00800b469f.shtml

802.1x on Wireless Networks

In Chapter 1, "Technology Overview," you learned the basics of the 802.1X. As a refresher, 802.1x is a standard that defines the encapsulation methodologies for the transport of the Extensible Authentication Protocol (EAP) protocol.

NOTE	EAP was originally defined in RFC 2284, which is now obsolete due to RFC 3748.

The 802.1X standard allows you to enforce access control when wired and wireless devices attempt to access the network. Figure 8-5 illustrates the main components of 802.1x.

Figure 8-5   *802.1x in Wireless Networks*

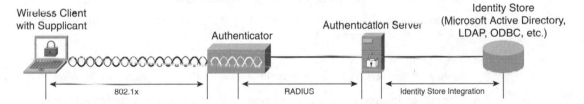

The following are the main components of 802.1x illustrated in Figure 8-5:

- **Supplicant:** Software running on the client workstation
- **Authenticator:** The wireless access point
- **Authentication Server:** RADIUS server such as the Cisco Secure Access Control Server (ACS)
- **External Database:** External database such as the Microsoft Active Directory, Lightweight Directory Access Protocol (LDAP), or any Open Database Connectivity (ODBC) repository.

NOTE	The Cisco comprehensive identity-based solution, which is based on 802.1x, is referred to as Identity Based Networking Services (IBNS).

The basic 802.1x authentication negotiation scheme is illustrated in Figure 8-6.

Figure 8-6 *802.1x Authentication Negotiation Basics*

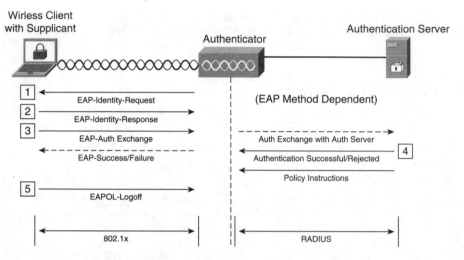

The following are the steps illustrated in Figure 8-6:

1 The client attempts to connect to the wireless network, and the wireless access point sends an EAP identity request to the client (supplicant).

2 The user enters his credentials, and the client machine sends the EAP identity reply to the wireless access point.

3 Depending on the EAP method, the client starts an authentication exchange to the authentication server. An EAP tunnel passes directly to the authentication server.

4 The authentication server accepts or rejects the user and sends further information/instructions based on the authentication and authorization of the user.

At the end of the session, the client sends an EAPOL Logout message.

The different types of EAP methods are categorized as follows:

- Challenge/response based
- Cryptographic based
- Tunneling methods
- Generic token and one-time-passwords

The challenge-response-based EAP methods are the following:

- EAP with Message Digest 5: Uses MD5 hashing for authentication exchange
- Cisco LEAP: Authentication based on usernames and passwords
- EAP using the Microsoft Challenge Handshake Authentication Protocol Version 2 (MSCHAPv2)

The cryptographic-based EAP method is as follows:

- EAP over Transport Layer Security (EAP-TLS): Uses x.509 digital certificates and TLS for authentication

The most common EAP tunneling methods are as follows:

- Protected EAP (PEAP)
- EAP Tunneling Transport Layer Security (EAP-TTLS)
- EAP Flexible Authentication via Secure Tunneling (EAP-FAST): Designed not to require certificates

The EAP Generic Token Card (EAP-GTC) is an EAP method used for generic token cards and one-time passwords.

NOTE   EAP-GTC is defined in RFC 3748. It does not protect the authentication data in any way.

The following sections describe each EAP method.

EAP with MD5

When you configure EAP-MD5, both the client and the authentication server must have a shared secret established out-of-band. This shared secret is typically a password associated with an identity/username. Figure 8-7 illustrates the primary steps within the EAP-MD5 authentication method.

Figure 8-7   *EAP-MD5*

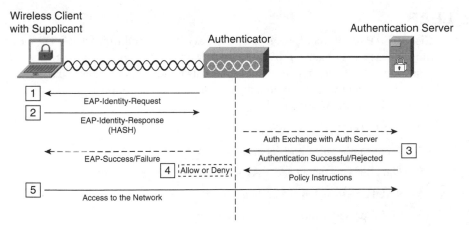

The following are the steps illustrated in Figure 8-7:

Step 1 A random challenge is sent to the supplicant from the wireless access point.

Step 2 The client sends its response containing the hash of the challenge created using the shared secret.

Step 3 The RADIUS authentication server verifies the hash and accepts or rejects the authentication.

Step 4 The wireless access point allows or disallows access based on the RADIUS authentication server decision.

Step 5 If the authentication is successful, the client gains access to the network.

Because EAP-MD5 is purely an authentication protocol, it does not provide encryption after the authentication process. Therefore, all the messages are transmitted in cleartext after authentication. In addition, because it is only a client authentication protocol, the server side is not authenticated. Subsequently, you cannot detect rogue wireless access points if you implement EAP-MD5. The use of mutual authentication provides a means of reducing the risk of users installing rogue access points within the infrastructure, because mutual authentication also requires the client to authenticate the server and, most definitely, rogue devices will not do this. Another way you can try to protect against rogue access points is to lock down your switches so that you can use only authorized MAC addresses on your wired network. This is explained later in this chapter.

TIP   EAP-MD5 is vulnerable to dictionary and brute-force attacks when used with Ethernet and wireless.

Cisco LEAP

Cisco LEAP was initially developed to address the vulnerabilities that WEP showed. At that time, it was an alternative protocol that allowed you to deploy wireless networks without requiring a certificate infrastructure for clients by leveraging authentication mechanisms that were already available within the infrastructure. The following are some of the benefits presented by using Cisco LEAP:

- 802.1x EAPOL messages are used within Cisco LEAP.
- Server authentication is achievable.
- The client username and password are sent over MS-CHAP.
- RADIUS is used as the authentication server.
- LEAP provides mechanisms for deriving and distributing encryption keys.

Many people are now migrating from Cisco LEAP to full 802.1x implementations.

EAP-TLS

EAP-TLS provides several features. For example, it supports mutual authentication providing an encrypted transport layer and the capability to change the keys dynamically. EAP-TLS requires the use of digital certificates. You need to keep this in mind when thinking about deploying EAP-TLS within your network.

NOTE	EAP-TLS is defined in RFC 2246.

During the TLS handshake phase, the client and wireless device establish a session exchanging symmetric session keys used to encrypt the transport during the data transfer phase. TLS has two layers:

- **Record layer:** Includes information about fragmentation, MAC, and encryption
- **Message layer:** Includes four different types of messages

The following are the four message types:

- **Change cipher spec:** This defines a change in the session context to be used by the record layer.
- **Alert message:** There are approximately 26 different alert message subtypes. (They include access denied, close notify, decryption failed, and certificate revoked.)
- **Handshake protocol:** During the handshake protocol, the client and the server exchange different hello messages; server authentication and key exchange messages; client authentication and key exchange messages; and the finalization message to close the session.
- **Application data:** This is the actual data that is transmitted over the TLS tunnel.

EAP-TLS does not use all parts of the TLS record protocol; however, it uses the TLS handshake for mutual authentication, for cipher suite negotiation, and for derivation of the session keys. EAP-TLS was initially designed for PPP connections; however, in wireless implementations, EAP-TLS is used as a strong and secure mechanism for mutual authentication and key establishment; then the native WEP mechanisms of the wireless device are used to encrypt the data.

PEAP

Many people refer to PEAP as the true EAP-TLS in wireless implementations. PEAP uses EAP-TLS functionality by securing the open exchanges, but it keeps things simple. For instance, PEAP requires only server-side certificates; however, it can still perform mutual authentication between the client and the server. It also uses TLS for the secure tunnel and lengthens the EAP-TLS exchange beyond the finished message to add client authentication and key exchange. One of the disadvantages of PEAP is that it is considered to be a chatty protocol. The PEAP protocol has two phases:

- **Phase 1:** Used to establish a secure tunnel using the EAP-TLS with server authentication
- **Phase 2:** Authenticates the client based on EAP methods, exchange of arbitrary information, and other PEAP-specific means using the information established during Phase 1

Many people use PEAP because it is simple to implement within a wireless infrastructure.

EAP Tunneled TLS Authentication Protocol (EAP-TTLS)

EAP-TTLS is basically the same as EAP-TLS; however, it extends the client authentication by the use of a method called *tunneled authentication*. With EAP-TTLS, the client does not need a digital certificate (only the authentication server requires one), thereby simplifying the client identity management.

NOTE   EAP-TTLS enables you to also use legacy authentication methods such as password-based methodologies.

EAP-FAST

EAP-FAST was initially known as the Tunneled EAP (TEAP) and as LEAP Version 2. EAP-FAST is classified by many as the most comprehensive and secure EAP type suitable for wireless implementations. It addresses the risks of man-in-the-middle and dictionary attacks. In addition, EAP-FAST reduces the hardware requirements, making it a flexible deployment model and more attractive to many people.

EAP-FAST authentication does not require the use of a specific encryption type. Instead, the WLAN encryption type to be used is determined by the client wireless network interface card capabilities.

If the client devices do not support WPA2 or WPA, you can deploy 802.1X authentication with dynamic WEP keys, but, because of the well-known exploits against WEP keys, this WLAN encryption mechanism is not recommended. If you must support WEP-only clients, it is recommended that you employ a session-timeout interval which requires that the clients derive a new WEP key on a frequent interval.

TIP	30 minutes is the recommended session interval for typical WLAN data rates.

Cisco has a comprehensive list of frequently asked questions about EAP-FAST at http://www.cisco.com/en/US/products/hw/wireless/ps4555/ products_qanda_item09186a00802030dc.shtml.

EAP-GTC

EAP-GTC enables you to use hardware token cards as one-time-passwords. An example of a hardware token card is the RSA SecurID solution.

NOTE	For more information about RSA SecurID, go to http://rsa.com.

You can use EAP-GTC inside the TLS tunnel created by PEAP. You can use this EAP method to implement a two-factor authentication solution to avoid common password compromises and combine it with your remote access VPN solution. For instance, a user can use the token card for both wireless and remote access VPN authentication. If you are just starting to deploy a WLAN, you must decide whether token deployment is cost effective. Many people justify the cost of token deployment by using this authentication mechanism with other network infrastructure authentication, such as remote access VPN.

In summary, the two EAP methods that most people implement today are EAP-FAST and PEAP. EAP-FAST provides more flexibility when deployed with 802.1x or NAC. EAP-FAST is easy to implement, and it is not Cisco proprietary. It supports Windows single-sign-on and provides support for login script operation with any user database such as Microsoft Active Directory, Lightweight Directory Access Protocol (LDAP), and one-time password (OTP). In addition, because EAP-FAST does not require certificates, you can configure it easily and distribute it for Cisco Aironet client devices with the Cisco Aironet Configuration Administration tool.

TIP	It is recommended that you employ either WPA2 (AES-CCM) or WPA (TKIP) encryption, which are both dependent on the NIC card capabilities in the specific deployment.

Configuring 802.1x with EAP-FAST in the Cisco Unified Wireless Solution

This section describes how to configure the wireless LAN context (WLC), the Cisco Secure Services Client (CSSC), and Cisco Secure Access Control Server (ACS) to perform 802.1x authentication using EAP-FAST. Figure 8-8 illustrates the topology used in this configuration example.

Figure 8-8 *Configuring 802.1x with EAP-FAST on the Cisco Unified Wireless Solution*

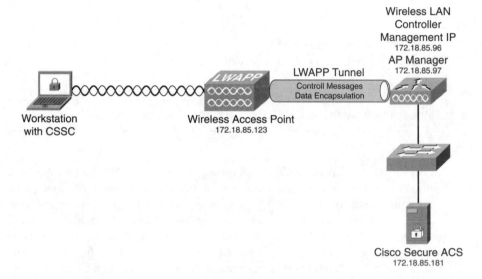

Figure 8-8 shows a workstation with the CSSC connecting to a Cisco wireless access point (with IP address 172.18.85.123) in a lightweight configuration controlled by a WLC. The management IP address of the WLC is 172.18.85.96, and the AP manager IP address is 172.18.85.97. The WLC forwards all authentication requests to a Cisco Secure ACS.

Configuring the WLC

Complete the following steps to configure the WLC to use the Cisco Secure ACS server for authentication. Cisco Secure ACS validates the user credentials using the Windows database. (The Cisco Secure ACS server configuration is covered in the next section.)

Step 1 Log in to the WLC as an administrator and click the **Security** tab; then click **New** to add a new RADIUS server, as illustrated in Figure 8-9. You will then see the screen shown in Figure 8-10.

Figure 8-9 *Adding a RADIUS Server to the WLC*

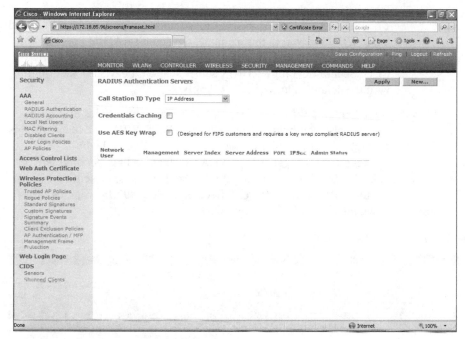

Figure 8-10 *RADIUS Server Configuration on the WLC*

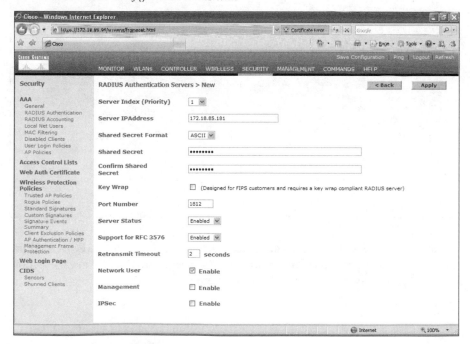

Step 2   In the screen shown in Figure 8-10, enter the RADIUS server information. In this case, the Cisco Secure ACS IP address is 172.18.85.181. Enter a shared key to mutually authenticate the WLC and the RADIUS server. In this example, the default RADIUS port UDP/**1812** is used. Ports UDP/1645 (legacy) and UDP/1812 are supported by Cisco Secure ACS for RADIUS authentication. Leave all other options with the default values and click **Apply**.

Step 3   By default, the WLC uses 802.1x for the security policies in WLANs. You can also combine 802.1x with static WEP, WPA, and others. In this example, 802.1x is used without WEP/WPA. To enable this configuration, navigate to the **WLANs** tab and edit the configured WLAN. (In this example, the WLAN SSID is named **ciscotest**.) Under **Security Policies** and **Layer 2 Security**, select **802.1x** from the drop-down menu, as shown in Figure 8-11.

Figure 8-11   *WLAN Layer 2 Security Policy*

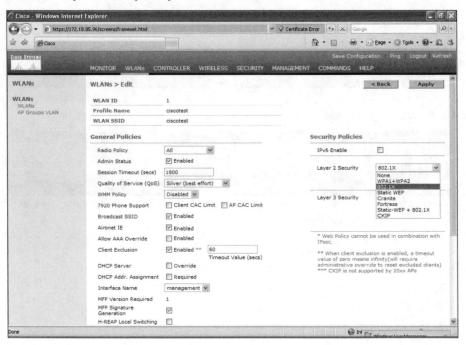

Step 4   Scroll down on the same screen and choose the configured Cisco Secure ACS server on the drop-down menu under the **RADIUS Servers** section, as shown in Figure 8-12. Click **Apply**.

Figure 8-12 *Selecting the Configured RADIUS Server*

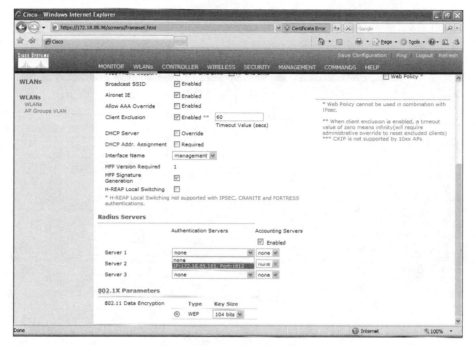

The next section shows you how to configure the Cisco Secure ACS server.

Configuring the Cisco Secure ACS Server for 802.1x and EAP-FAST

Complete the following steps to configure the Cisco Secure ACS server for 802.1x authentication using the EAP-FAST method. You first add the WLC as AAA client on the Cisco Secure ACS server.

To add the WLC as a AAA client on Cisco Secure ACS, click the **Network Configuration** radio button. You can create a network device group to maintain a collection of AAA clients and AAA servers, or you can use the default **Not Assigned** network device group. In this example, the WLC is added to the **Not Assigned** default group. Click the **Not Assigned** group.

Step 1   Click **Add Entry**. The screen shown in Figure 8-13 is displayed.

Step 2   Complete the form by entering the hostname and IP address of the **WLC**. (**WLC** is the hostname, and **172.18.85.96** is the management IP address of the WLC in this example.)

Figure 8-13 *Adding an AAA Client into Cisco Secure ACS*

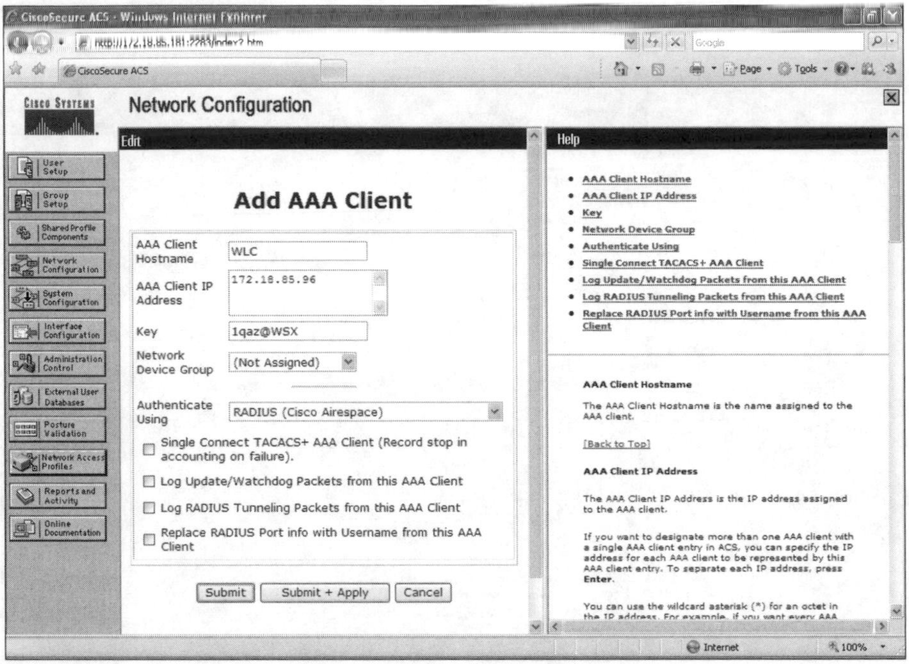

Step 3 Enter the shared secret to be used between the Cisco Secure ACS server and the WLC. (In this example, the key is **1qaz@WSX**.)

Step 4 Choose **RADIUS** (Cisco Airspace) under the drop-down menu in the Authenticate Using section.

Step 5 Click **Submit + Apply**.

Step 6 In this example, the Cisco Secure ACS server queries an external Windows 2003 server for authentication credentials. Navigate through the radio button sequence as follows. Click **External User Databases > Database Configuration > Windows Database > Configure**.

Step 7 Under the Windows EAP Settings, check the **Enable password change inside PEAP** or **EAP-FAST** checkbox, as illustrated in Figure 8-14.

Step 8 Click **Submit**.

Step 9 Navigate to **External User Databases > Unknown User Policy** and click the **Check the following external user databases** radio button.

Step 10 Click the **Windows Database** from **External Databases** to **Selected Databases**, as shown in Figure 8-15.

Step 11 Click **Submit**.

Figure 8-14 *Windows EAP Settings*

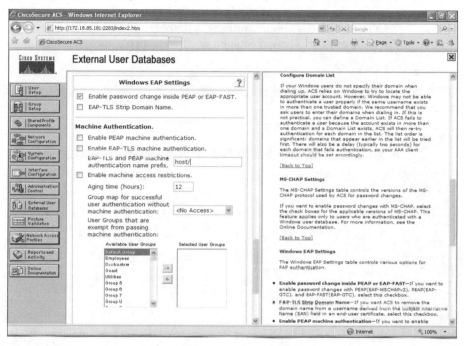

Figure 8-15 *Selecting the Windows Database on the Unknown User Policy*

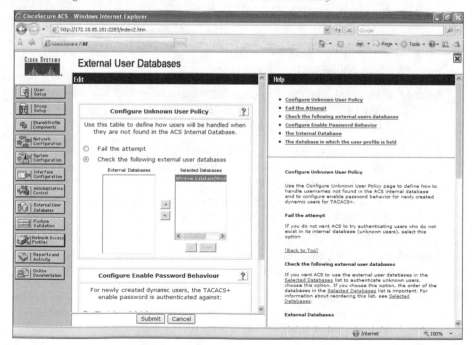

Step 12 Next, you have to enable EAP-FAST support on the Cisco Secure ACS
Server. To do this, navigate via the radio buttons to **System
Configuration > Global Authentication Setup > EAP-FAST
Configuration**. The screen in Figure 8-16 is displayed.

Figure 8-16 *Enabling EAP-FAST on Cisco Secure ACS*

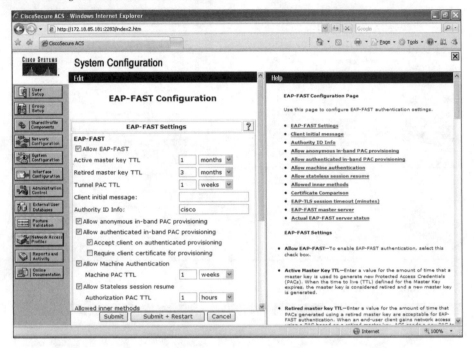

Step 13 Check **Allow EAP-FAST**.

Step 14 In this example, the recommended (default) values for **Active master
key TTL** (1 month), **Retired master key TTL** (3 months), and **Tunnel
PAC TTL** (1 week) are selected.

Step 15 The **Authority ID Info** text is shown on some EAP-FAST client
software; in this case, **cisco** is the text configured and displayed. This can
be anything you want. On the other hand, the CSSC (used in this
scenario) does not display this descriptive text for the PAC authority.
However, the word **cisco** will be displayed if any other client (802.1x
supplicant) is used.

Step 16 Check the **Allow anonymous in-band PAC provisioning** checkbox.
This enables Automatic PAC Provisioning for EAP-FAST-enabled clients.

Step 17 The CSSC supports EAP-FAST Version 1a, which uses MS-CHAPv2 for
authentication. Scroll down and check **EAP-MSCHAPv2** under the
Allowed inner methods section, as shown in Figure 8-17.

Figure 8-17 *EAP-MSCHAPv2 and EAP-FAST Master Server Configuration*

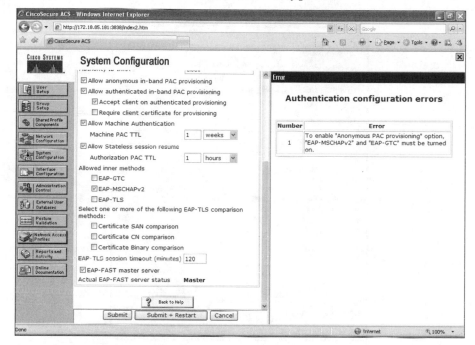

Step 18 Check the **EAP-FAST master server** check box to configure this Cisco Secure ACS server as the master. The Actual EAP-FAST Master server status line will say **Master**. Any other Cisco Secure ACS servers (if present in your organization) will use this server as the master PAC authority to avoid the need to provision unique keys for each Cisco Secure ACS in a network.

Step 19 Click **Submit + Restart**.

Configuring the CSSC

This section shows how to configure the CSSC to authenticate to the wireless network using EAP-FAST. Complete the following steps to configure the CSSC.

Step 1 Launch the CSSC and click **Create Network**.

Step 2 The Network Profile screen shown in Figure 8-18 is displayed. Under **Network Configuration Summary** and **Authentication**, click **Modify**.

Figure 8-18 *CSSC Network Profile Screen*

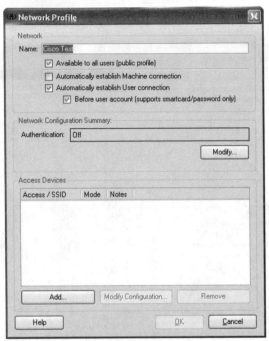

Step 3 The Network Authentication screen shown in Figure 8-19 is displayed. Turn on authentication by clicking the radio button labeled **Turn On** under the **Authentication Methods** section, as illustrated in Figure 8-19. In this example, the **Use Username as Identity** button is selected, because the user credentials are being used for authentication.

Step 4 Under the **Protocol** list, check **FAST** and click the **Configure** button.

Step 5 The Configure EAP Method screen shown in Figure 8-20 is displayed. Under the **Tunneled Method**, you can choose **Any Method** to allow the CSSC to use any EAP method offered by the wireless infrastructure. In this example, the **EAP-MSCHAPv2** method is selected, because we are doing external authentication to a Windows Active Directory user database. If, however, you choose the **Any Method** option, it will work, but in some cases, you may want to be selective to force the use of only one EAP method. (In this case, the method is **EAP-MSCHAPv2**.)

Step 6 Leave all other default values as they are, and click **OK**.

Step 7 Click **OK** in the **Network Authentication** screen.

Figure 8-19 *CSSC Network Authentication Screen*

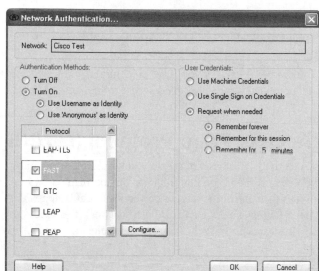

Figure 8-20 *CSSC Configure EAP Method Screen*

Step 8   Only wireless networks that have SSIDs enabled for broadcast are visible within the CSSC. In this example, the WLC is configured not to broadcast the SSID. Consequently, you must manually define the SSID in the CSSC. To define the SSID in CSSC, click the **Add** button under the **Access Devices** section of the **Network Profile** screen. The SSID used previously is **ciscotest**.

Step 9   Click **Add Access**.

Step 10 Click **OK**.

Step 11 The CSSC attempts to connect to your wireless network. If it does not automatically make this attempt, click **Connect** from the CSSC main screen.

Step 12 You are prompted for your user credentials, and if successfully authenticated, you are granted access to the network.

Lightweight Access Point Protocol (LWAPP)

In the Cisco Unified Wireless Architecture, a wireless LAN controller (WLC) is used to manage the wireless access point configuration and firmware creating an LWAPP tunnel. LWAP provides the control messaging protocol and data encapsulation. In other words, the wireless client data packets are encapsulated between the access point and the WLC. Figure 8-21 illustrates how a WLC controls a wireless access point over an LWAPP tunnel.

Figure 8-21 *LWAPP Tunnel*

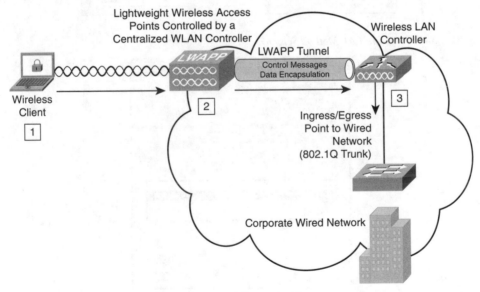

The following steps are illustrated in Figure 8-21:

1 The wireless client sends a packet to the wireless access point.

2 The wireless access point decrypts the packet and encapsulates it with an LWAPP header, forwarding it to the WLC.

3 The WLC removes the LWAPP header and forwards the packet to its destination in the corporate wired network.

NOTE   When a client on the corporate wired network sends replies to the wireless client, the packet first goes into the WLC where it is encapsulated with an LWAPP header and forwarded to the appropriate wireless access point. Subsequently, the access point removes the LWAPP header and encrypts the packet if necessary.

The LWAPP control messages are encrypted using the AES-CCM encryption method. The shared encryption key is derived and exchanged when the access point joins the WLC.

NOTE   The payload of the encapsulated LWAPP data is not encrypted. Therefore, you should follow infrastructure protection best practices to protect the wired network.

The following are the major steps or stages used in the LWAPP:

Step 1   **Discovery:** The wireless access point looks for a controller. The LWAPP Discovery Response from the controller contains the following important information from the WLC:

— Controller name (sysName)

— Controller type

— Controller capacity

— Current wireless access point load in the WLC

— Master controller status information used for redundancy

— Access point manager IP address and the number of access points joined to the manager

(a) When the AP is powered on, if a static IP address has not been previously configured, the AP issues a DHCP DISCOVER to get an IP address.

(b) If Layer 2 mode is supported, the AP attempts a Layer 2 LWAPP Discovery by sending an Ethernet broadcast message.

(c) If Layer 2 mode is not supported or the AP fails to find a WLC, the AP attempts a Layer 3 LWAPP Discovery.

(d) If a Layer 3 LWAPP Discovery also fails, the AP reboots and retries the first step.

Step 2   **Join:** The wireless access point attempts to establish a secured relationship with a controller.

Ctep 0   **Image Data:** The wireless access point downloads code from the WLC when needed.

Step 4   **Config:** The wireless access point receives the configuration from the WLC.

Step 5   **Run:** The wireless access point and the WLC are operating normally, and service data is exchanged.

Step 6   **Reset:** The wireless access point clears the current state, and this process starts over again.

The WLC provides support for radio resource management (RRM). The following are some of the advantages of RRM:

- Continuous analysis of RF environment
- Dynamic channel and power management
- Coverage hole detection and correction
- Coverage resiliency

The WLCs elect a radio frequency (RF) group leader who analyzes RF data and neighbor relationships to make more optimized decisions about the RF environment for wireless infrastructure. Multiple RF domains can coexist within a single RF Group. These RF domains can be intercontroller or intracontroller, as illustrated in Figure 8-22.

Figure 8-22 *Multiple RF Domains*

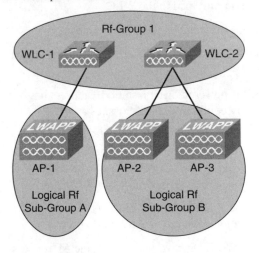
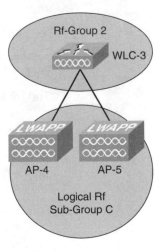

Why is this important to security? A good wireless network design that includes network resiliency is important for the overall security of your wireless network. The WLC has a built-in understanding of the signal strength that exists between lightweight access points within the same network. These controllers can use this information to create a dynamic optimal RF topology for the network. When a Cisco LWAPP-enabled access point boots up, it immediately looks for a wireless LAN controller within the network. After it finds a wireless LAN controller, the LWAPP-enabled access point sends out encrypted "neighbor" messages. These neighbor messages include the MAC address and signal strength of any neighboring access points. In a single wireless LAN controller network, the controller uses this neighbor information to determine the relative spatiality of the access points in the network. The controller then tunes each access point channel and optimal signal strength for optimal coverage and capacity.

When wireless LAN controllers are clustered in the network, a default controller is chosen. All the controllers feed the default controller information to their registered access points. The default controller correlates information for all the access points in the network and then pushes out the optimal channel and power for every access point on the network. The algorithms built into the Cisco Unified Wireless Network architecture prevent the interruption of wireless connectivity.

Wireless Intrusion Prevention System Integration

You can integrate Cisco IPS sensors with the Cisco Unified Wireless Solution. This includes the Cisco IPS sensors, the Cisco Adaptive Security Appliance (ASA), Advanced Inspection and Prevention Security Services Module (AIP-SSM), the Catalyst 6500 Intrusion Detection/Prevention Services Module Version 2 (IDSM-2), and the IPS modules for Cisco IOS routers. When you integrate IPS with the Cisco Unified Wireless Solution, the WLC talks to the Cisco IPS sensor via its management port using the Security Device Event Exchange (SDEE) protocol over TCP port 443. The WLC supports up to five IPS sensors.

NOTE   The WLC also supports the use of a certain limited number of IPS signatures that you can enable to detect security threats within your wireless network. However, the combination of an external IPS device with the WLC provides more granular inspection and detection.

The WLC Software Release Version 4.x and later supports shunning (blocking) from the IPS sensors. A shun request needs to be sent to the WLC from the Cisco IPS device to trigger the client blacklisting or exclusion behavior available on the controller. The WLC queries the Cisco IPS device at a configured query rate to retrieve all the shun events. This is illustrated in Figure 8-23.

Figure 8-23 *IPS Sensor Integration*

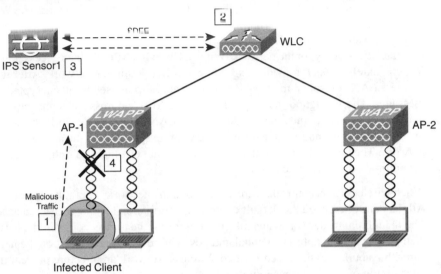

The following steps are illustrated in Figure 8-23:

Step 1 An infected client sends malicious traffic over the wireless network (through access point 1 (AP1)).

Step 2 The WLC sends the traffic to be inspected by the IPS device (IPS Sensor1).

Step 3 The IPS device sends a shun request to the WLC to block the offending client.

Step 4 The client is blocked (shunned).

NOTE The shunned client status is maintained on each controller in the mobility group even if any or all of the controllers are reset. On the controller, clients are disabled based on a MAC address, even though the shun request that the IPS initiates uses the client IP address as its destination. Therefore, although a client remains disabled for the duration of the controller exclusion time and is re-excluded if it reacquires its previous DHCP address, that client is no longer disabled if the IP address of the client that is shunned changes Here is an example. The client connects to the same network, and the DHCP lease timeout has not expired.

Configuring IDS/IPS Sensors in the WLC

You can configure IDS/IPS using the WLC web management console or through the CLI. This section demonstrates how to use the web management console to add IDS/IPS sensors.

Step 1   Connect the Cisco IPS device to the same switch where the WLC resides.

Step 2   Mirror the WLC ports that carry the wireless client traffic to the Cisco IPS device. You do this because the Cisco IPS device must receive a copy of every packet to be inspected on the wireless network. The Cisco IPS device provides a downloadable signature file that you can customize. When a signature is triggered, the Cisco IPS device generates the alarm with a shunning event action. The WLC polls the Cisco IPS device for alarms. When an alarm is detected with the IP address of a wireless client, which is associated to the WLC, the IPS device puts the client into the exclusion list. The WLC generates a trap and notifies the WCS. The WLC removes the user from the exclusion list after the specified period (60 seconds by default).

Step 3   Log in to the WLC as an administrator.

Step 4   To add the Cisco IPS device to the WLC, navigate to the **Security** tab. Under **CIDS**, click **Sensors**.

Step 5   Click **New**.

Step 6   The screen shown in Figure 8-24 is displayed. Enter the sensor IP address. The IP address of the IPS device in this example is **172.18.85.149**. The WLC uses SDEE, and the default port is **443**. Enter the username and password of the Cisco IPS device.

In this example, the query interval is configured for 15 seconds. This query interval is safe to use in most environments. Enter the Cisco IPS device SHA1 fingerprint. You can obtain this by invoking the **show tls fingerprint** command on the Cisco IPS device, as follows:

```
Example 8-1 IPS-sensor# show tls fingerprint
MD5: B8:A7:74:B5:62:AB:C8:15:5C:FE:E6:4C:0C:42:39:CE
SHA1: AC:6A:FA:FC:BE:05:D1:09:31:53:21:DC:36:A0:1A:B6:6A:DA:00:AF
```

The highlighted line shows the fingerprint that is entered into the WLC configuration. You must omit the colons (:) within the hexadecimal fingerprint. The fingerprint must be 40 characters in length.

Figure 8-24 *Adding IPS Sensors*

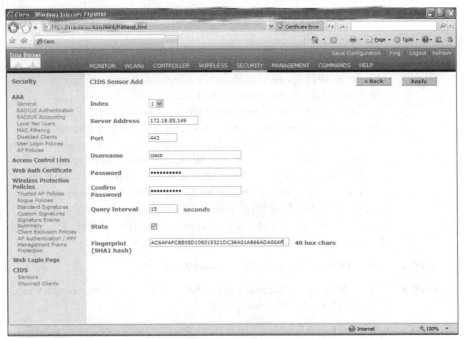

> **Step 1** Click **Apply**.
>
> **Step 1** Navigate to **WLANs** and click **Edit** on the configured WLANs that you want to monitor. Make sure that **Client Exclusion** is enabled. The default client exclusion timeout is 60 seconds. On the other hand, the client exclusion persists as long as the IPS shun (block) remains active. The default block time in the Cisco IPS devices is 30 minutes.

Uploading and Configuring IDS/IPS Signatures

Several signatures come with the WLC by default. You can view the standard signatures by navigating to **Security > Wireless Protection Policies** and then clicking **Standard Signatures**. This is illustrated in Figure 8-25.

You can also upload a signature file from the WLC to customize the signatures. To do this, navigate to **Commands > Upload File > Signature File**. To download the modified signature file, navigate to **Commands > Download File > Signature File**. After you download (or push) the edited signature file to the WLC, all registered wireless access points are refreshed in real time with the new signature configuration.

Figure 8-25 *WLC Standard Signatures*

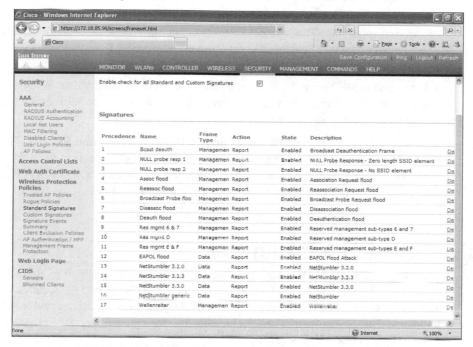

When customizing signatures, you must use the following format:

```
Name = <str>, Ver = <int>, Preced = <int>, FrmType = <frmType-type>, Pattern =
<pattern-format>,
Freq = <int>, Interval = <int>, Quiet = <int>, Action = <action-val>, Desc = <str>
```

NOTE   The maximum length of each line is 1000 characters. The WLC will not correctly parse any lines longer than 1000 characters.

You can view the custom signatures by navigating to **Security > Wireless Protection Policies** and then clicking **Custom Signatures**.

Management Frame Protection (MFP)

Management Frame Protection (MFP) enables authentication of all 802.11 management frames between the WLC and wireless access points. MFP protects against direct and man-in-the-middle attacks. It also detects and reports potential phishing attacks. MFP has three main functions:

- **Frame protection:** This enables the wireless access point to protect the management frames by adding a message integrity check information element (MIC-IE) to each frame.

- **Frame validation:** The wireless access point validates every management frame that it receives from other access points in the network.

- **Event reporting:** The wireless access point notifies the WLC when it detects an anomaly. The WLC can also report these events via SNMP traps to management servers.

You can enable MFP globally. However, you can disable it on individual WLANs and access points. In other words, you can selectively enable or disable MFP on specific wireless access points or WLANs.

To enable MFP globally, navigate to **Security > Wireless Protection Policies**. Then click **AP Authentication/MFP** and choose **Management Frame Protection** from the **Protection Type** pull-down menu. You can view the MFP statistics under **Security > Wireless Protection Policies > Management Frame Protection**.

Precise Location Tracking

The Cisco Wireless Location Appliance uses RF fingerprinting technology to track mobile devices to within a few meters. This allows you to gain visibility into the location of people and assets. In addition, RF fingerprinting technology enables you to respond to security issues and thereby gain insight into the location and movement of people and assets, as well as locating rogue wireless access points.

The Cisco Wireless Location Appliance supports two location tracking options:

- **On-demand location tracking:** The user queries the location of the person or wireless device.

- **Simultaneous location tracking:** This automatically tracks up to thousands of 802.11 wireless devices by adding a Cisco Wireless Location Appliance in conjunction with a Cisco WCS.

TIP   It is recommended that you become familiar with the different methodologies used for location tracking and that you deploy these solutions within your network. Conventionally, many have used three different methods for locating wireless users or devices: closest access point, triangulation, and RF fingerprinting. As previously mentioned, the Cisco Wireless Location Appliance uses RF fingerprinting. A whitepaper explaining each methodology is located at http://www.cisco.com/en/US/products/ps6386/products_white_paper0900aecd80477957.shtml.

Network Admission Control (NAC) in Wireless Networks

Network Admission Control (NAC) was initially designed as two separate solutions: the NAC Framework and NAC Appliance (formerly known as Cisco Clean Access). The most commonly deployed NAC solution for wireless networks is the NAC Appliance. This section covers how to integrate the Cisco NAC Appliance into the Cisco Unified Wireless solution.

As mentioned in previous chapters, the NAC Appliance has three major components:

- Clean Access Server (CAS)
- Clean Access Manager (CAM)
- Clean Access Agent

In the example illustrated in Figure 8-26, the CAS is configured inline and managed by the CAM (172.18.85.181). All wireless traffic will pass through the server before it can reach the corporate network or the Internet. The goal in this example is to separate guest users from employees. The guest users will have only limited access to the Internet via HTTP and HTTPs. The employees will have access to the corporate resources.

Two SSIDs are configured in the Figure 8-26 example:

- **GUESTNET:** Used by guests
- **CORPACCESS:** Used by employees

The WLC is configured to broadcast the GUESTNET SSID, but not the CORPACCESS.

TIP   As a best practice, it is recommended that you use different SSIDs for your employees and guest wireless users. For your employees (internal users), you can also use 802.1X authentication and strong encryption (WPA with TKIP/MIC or WPA2 with AES).

The following sections provide the step-by-step procedures for configuring the NAC Appliance (CAM and CAS), the WLC, and the NAC Agent configuration.

Figure 8-26 *Cisco NAC Appliance Integration to Cisco Unified Wireless Solution*

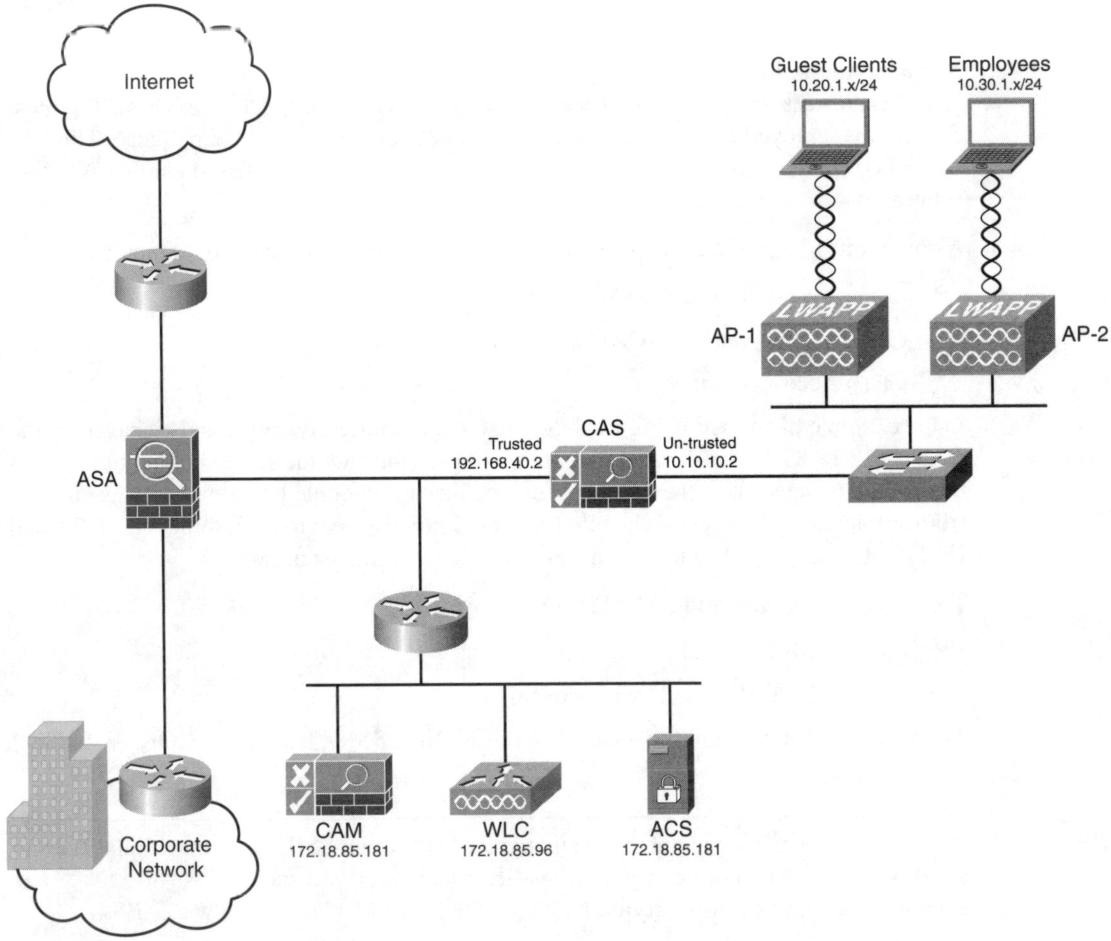

NAC Appliance Configuration

It is recommended that you configure the CAS in the Real-IP gateway mode for wireless network deployments. When the CAS is configured in the Real-IP gateway mode, it handles all routing between the unprotected and protected networks. In this example, the untrusted (unprotected) interface resides in the 10.10.10.0/24 subnet, and the trusted (protected) interface resides in the 192.168.40.0/24 subnet.

Complete the following steps to configure the NAC Appliance solution to protect the corporate resources by performing security posture checks for wireless users. In addition, enforce policy for guest users so that they are only able to access the Internet while employees can access corporate resources. Noncompliant clients will be quarantined and remediated.

Step 1   The CAS is always configured via the CAM. Log in to the CAM with an administrator account.

Step 2   After you are logged in to the CAM, navigate to the **Device Management** section in the menu on the left, and click **CCA Servers**.

Step 3   To add a new CAS, click the **New Server** tab and enter the CAS information, as illustrated in Figure 8-27. In this example, the CAM will access the CAS via the trusted interface (IP address **192.168.40.2**).

Figure 8-27   *Adding a New CAS in the CAM*

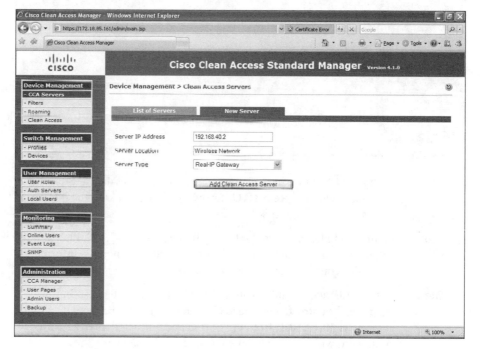

Step 4   Enter a server location description. The description can be any word or phrase that describes the location of the CAS. In this example, the location description is **Wireless Network**.

Step 5   The goal in this example is to configure the CAS in Real-IP gateway mode. Choose **Real-IP Gateway** from the drop-down menu.

Step 6   Click **Add Clean Access Server**.

Step 7   To access the CAS, click the **Manage** icon under **Device Management > CCA Servers**, as illustrated in Figure 8-28.

Figure 8-28 *Accessing the CAS via the CAM*

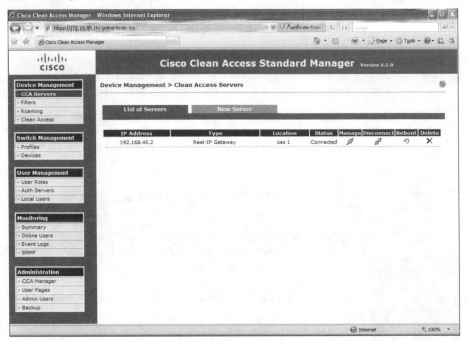

Step 8 Verify the IP addressing information, and verify that the CAS is configured with the **Real-IP Gateway** option by clicking the **Network** tab, as shown in Figure 8-29.

Step 9 In this example, the trusted interface IP address is **192.168.40.2,** and the default gateway is the Cisco ASA (**192.168.40.1**). Enter this information under the Trusted Interface section, as illustrated in Figure 8-29.

Step 10 Enter the IP address information for the untrusted interface. In this example, the untrusted interface IP address is **10.10.10.2,** and the default gateway is **10.10.10.1**. Both the trusted and untrusted interfaces are configured with a 24-bit subnet mask (**255.255.255.0**).

Step 11 Enter your DNS information under the **DNS** section, as illustrated in Figure 8-30. In this example, the CAS name is **cas1**, the domain name is **cisco.com**, and the IP address of the DNS server is **172.18.108.40**.

Step 12 In this example, you will create two users: guest and employee1. To create the local database, navigate to **User Management > Local Users** and enter the user information, as illustrated in Figure 8-31.

Step 13 The next step is to create the user roles. To enter a new user role, go to **User Management > User Roles > New Role** and enter the user role information, as illustrated in Figure 8-32.

Figure 8-29 *Real-IP Gateway Configuration*

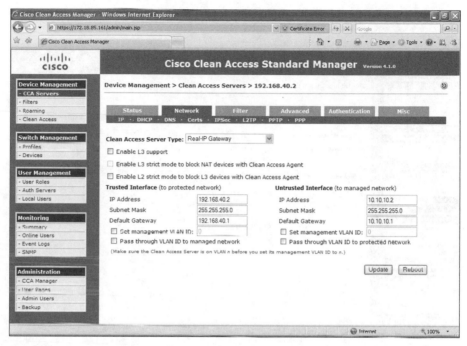

Figure 8-30 *Entering DNS Server Information*

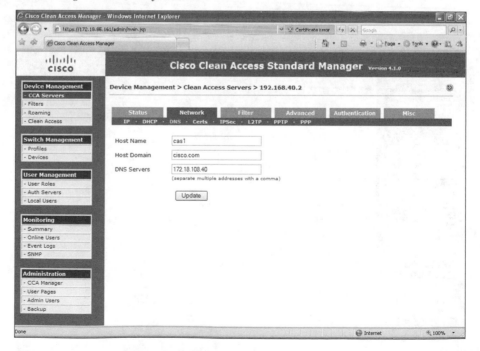

Figure 8-31 *Adding Local Users*

Figure 8-32 *User Roles*

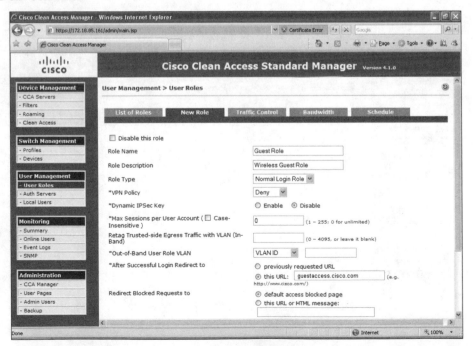

In Figure 8-32, the guest user role is configured. The user role name is **Guest Role**, and the role description is **Wireless Guest Role**. For guest users, at the **After Successful Login Redirect to** field, click to choose this URL, and enter the URL to which you want the guest user redirected. In this case, guest users will be redirected to a site called *guestaccess.cisco.com* with further instructions and disclaimers. All other options are left with default values.

Step 14 You can configure traffic policies to be applied to each user role by clicking the **Policies** icon by the specific role, as illustrated in Figure 8-33.

Figure 8-33 *User Role Policies*

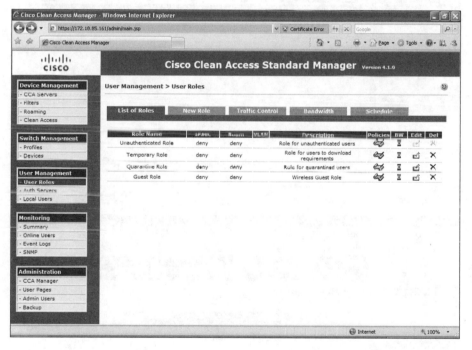

Step 15 By default, all traffic is denied. To enter a new policy, click the **Add Policy** link, as illustrated in Figure 8-34.

Step 16 Enter the policy information. In this example, all guest users are allowed to access the Internet via HTTP (TCP port 80) and HTTPs (TCP port 443). DNS traffic (UDP port 53) also needs to be allowed. Figure 8-35 shows how to configure a new policy to allow HTTP traffic.

Step 17 All internal traffic is denied. In this case, all internal networks can be summarized into two major subnets: 192.168.0.0/16 and 172.18.0.0/16. Figure 8-36 shows how all the guest user policies are configured.

Figure 8-34 *Adding a New Policy*

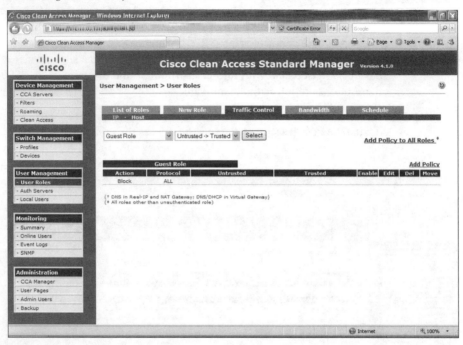

Figure 8-35 *Allowing HTTP for Guest Users*

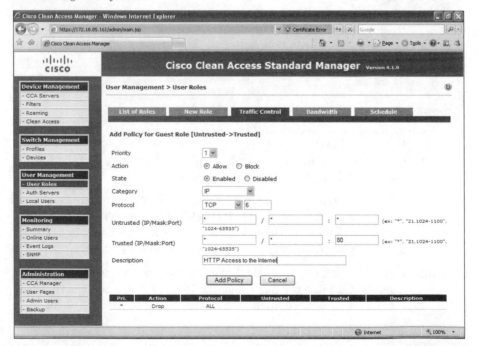

Figure 8-36 *All Guest Users Policies*

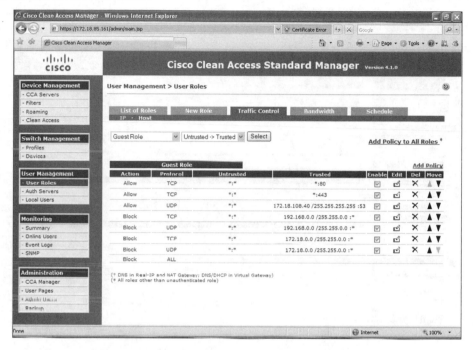

Notice how traffic to HTTP and HTTPS to all destinations is allowed by the first few policy entries. This is done because you cannot map the whole Internet for guest users. However, specific deny statements for all UDP and TCP traffic to internal networks are denied. In addition, a catch-all deny statement is included at the end.

You can assign users to different roles by editing the previously created users.

Step 18 Configure a host-based policy for access to remediation sites when users are quarantined. Navigate to **User Management > User Roles > Traffic Control > Host** and choose **Agent Quarantine Role** in the drop-down menu, as illustrated in Figure 8-37. Then select the sites you want your quarantined clients to be able to access for remediation.

In Figure 8-37, access is allowed to *update.microsoft.com* (the Microsoft update site) and to an internal remediation server.

Step 19 You can create or customize a login page for the wireless users by going to **Administration > User Pages** and choosing **Add** at the **Login Page** tab. You can edit the web login portal page content by going to **Administration > User Pages > Login Page > Edit > Content**.

Figure 8-37 *Host-Based Policy for Remediation Access*

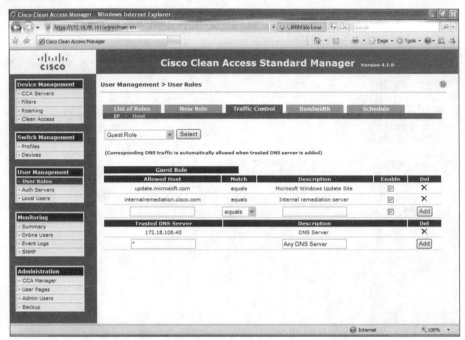

Step 20 To enable basic network scanning for guest user workstations, go to **Network Scanner > Scan Setup** to determine which user role and operating system to use. This is illustrated in Figure 8-38.

Step 21 Select the operating system options under the **Plugins, Options,** and **Vulnerability** tabs.

Step 22 You can also configure a user agreement page for web login users by navigating to the **User Agreement** tab.

Step 23 To establish employee roles for posture assessment, you must create a requirement rules mapping by going to **Device Management > Clean Access > Clean Access Agent > Requirements > Requirement-Rules**. For instance, a user can choose to perform Windows HotFixes checks for Windows-based systems.

Step 24 For employees, you should require the use of the NAC Agent (Clean Access Agent) by clicking **Require use of Clean Access Agent**.

After users are successfully logged in, you will see them under **Monitoring > Online Users**.

Figure 8-38 *Scanner Setup*

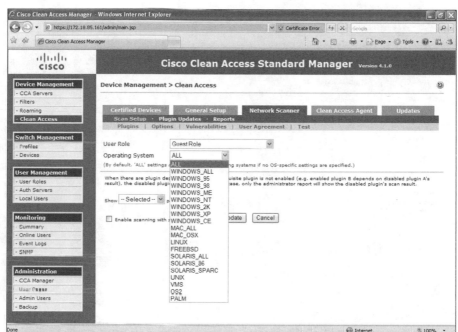

WLC Configuration

This section includes the steps necessary to configure the WLC for the NAC Appliance solution to work. Complete the following steps to configure the WLC.

Step 1 As a best practice, it is recommended that you configure separate VLANs for guest and internal users. To do this, you need to configure two new pseudointerfaces. Log in to the WLC, navigate to **Controller > Interfaces**, and click **New** to add a new interface. Enter the name for the new interface and the VLAN you want to assign. This is illustrated in Figure 8-39. In this example, the interface for guest users is called **guest** and assigned to VLAN Id **123**.

Step 2 The next screen (shown in Figure 8-40) allows you to enter the interface configuration parameters, such as IP address, subnet mask, default gateway, DHCP server information, and others. In this case, the guest interface is configured with the IP address **10.20.1.2** with a 24-bit subnet mask. The default gateway and DHCP server is **10.20.1.1**.

Figure 8-39 *Adding a New Dynamic Guest Interface in the WLC*

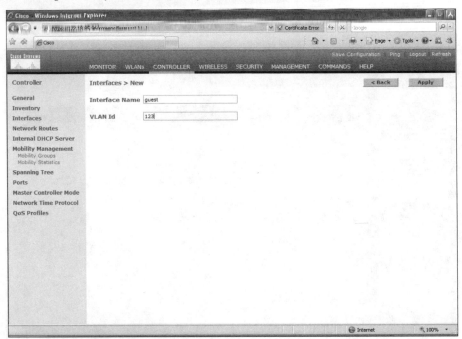

Figure 8-40 *WLC Guest Interface Configuration*

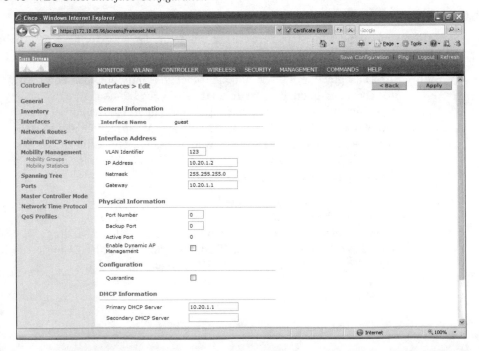

Step 3   Add another interface for employees (internal users).

Step 4   Under **Controller > General,** make sure that **Layer 3** is selected in the
LWAPP Transport Mode drop-down menu, as illustrated in Figure 8-41.

Figure 8-41 *LWAP Setting*

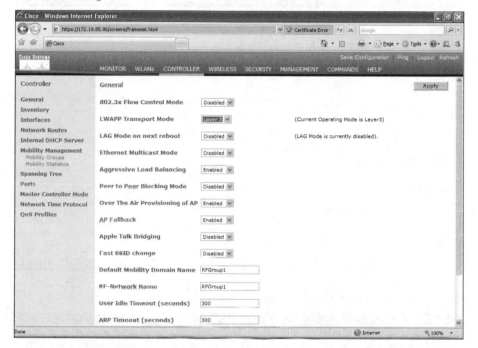

Step 5   In the Default Mobility Domain Name field, enter **RFGroup1**.

Step 6   Create a guest wireless LAN interface named guest and assign an SSID.
(In this example, we also name it **guest**.)

Step 7   Configure the WLAN with open authentication and DHCP address
assignment required. Enter **guest** as the wireless LAN interface **SSID**
under the **WLANs > Edit** window. Click the check box to require **DHCP
Addr. Assignment**, as illustrated in Figure 8-42.

Step 8   Repeat Steps 6 and 7 to create and configure a WLAN for internal users.

Step 9   To add the RADIUS server information for 802.1X authentication, navigate
to **Security > AAA> RADIUS Authentication**. In this case, you use the
same server that you configured previously in this chapter (172.18.85.181).

Step 10 The CAS uses RADIUS accounting packets to trigger the security
posture of wireless users. Configure the CAS as the RADIUS Accounting
server by going to **Security > AAA> RADIUS Accounting > New**. Add
the CAS information, as illustrated in Figure 8-43.

Figure 8-42 *Guest WLAN Configuration*

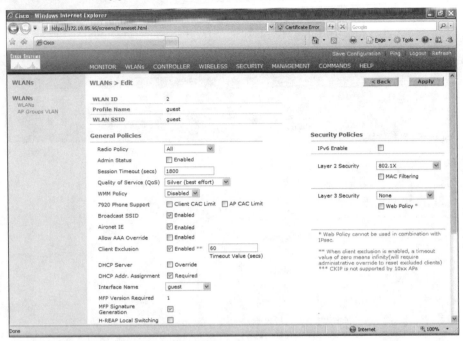

Figure 8-43 *Adding the CAS as a RADIUS Accounting Server*

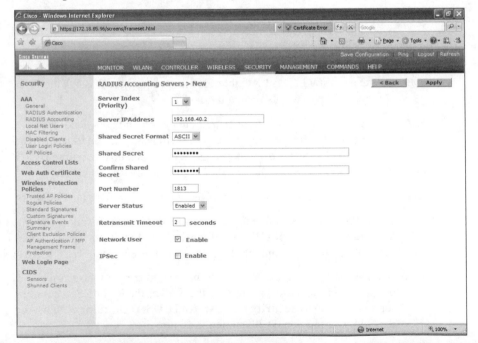

After you complete these steps, you will be able to authenticate using a wireless client. Guest users will be redirected to a web-based login, and regular employees will use the Cisco Clean Access Agent to connect to the network.

Summary

Wireless access is a core part of the infrastructure in most organizations. When developing a wireless implementation, take into consideration the unique security challenges that wireless connectivity brings. Implementing best practice wireless security techniques is a must for any organization. This chapter included best practices when deploying wireless networks. It also covered different types of authentication mechanisms, including 802.1x. In addition, it included an overview of LWAP, location services, MFP, and other wireless features that need to be taken into consideration when designing security within your wireless infrastructure.

This chapter also covered step-by-step configuration examples of the integration of IPS on Cisco wireless networks. In addition, it provided guidance on how to integrate the Cisco NAC Appliance and the Cisco Unified Wireless Network solution.

This chapter covers the following topics:

- Protecting the IP Telephony Infrastructure
- Securing the IP Telephony Applications
- Protecting Against Eavesdropping and Other Attacks

CHAPTER 9

IP Telephony Security

Cisco alone has sold more than 4.5 million IP phones and 3 million Cisco Unity unified messaging licenses. The company has more than 20,000 IP Communications customers. IP telephony or Voice over IP (VoIP) deployments are growing dramatically on a daily basis. Consequently, the need to secure IP telephony networks is also growing by the minute. IP telephony security threats generally fall into one of two categories. The first category includes risks that are aimed to hijack listening or unauthorized listening to voice conversations (phone tapping). The second category includes risks that can compromise IP telephony communications with direct attacks to the network infrastructure, servers, and other systems, such as denial of service (DoS) attacks.

This chapter covers several best practices and strategies for building your infrastructure to successfully identify threats and react to them in a manner that is appropriate to each severity level. It shows how integrated security features must be implemented from end to end across all network elements to increase voice security. IP telephony security has four major elements:

- **Network infrastructure:** Routers, switches, firewalls, and other infrastructure components
- **Call processing systems:** Call management, control, and accounting
- **Endpoints:** IP phones, IP communicator software, video terminals, and so on
- **Applications:** Unified messaging software, conferencing applications, contact, and a custom tool

This chapter offers you different techniques to protect each element.

IP telephony security requires the collaboration of security, network intelligence, and other services to minimize the impact of attacks and risks. With the collaboration of security technologies and network services, you can deploy Defense-in-Depth security that encompasses the entire network, including voice systems.

Protecting the IP Telephony Infrastructure

The first step in IP telephony security is to make sure that you apply the best practices learned in previous chapters to protect the infrastructure as a whole. As previously mentioned, all the infrastructure components are networking devices deployed within your organization, such as:

- Routers
- Switches
- Firewalls
- Voice gateways
- Gatekeepers

Figure 9-1 illustrates a common IP telephony deployment in a medium-to-large enterprise.

In Figure 9-1, several infrastructure components are depicted within a headquarters main office topology, which demonstrates a layered approach. Within the main office segment of the figure, notice the different access, distribution, and core layers. A group of application servers, a Cisco Unified CallManager cluster, and Cisco Unity servers are deployed to provide different VoIP services to the organization. Within the illustrated topology, IP telephony endpoints include both regular IP phones and wireless phones, as well as IP conferencing systems. A voice gateway is deployed to connect to the public switched telephone network (PSTN).

In this figure, voice services are also provided to branch offices, telecommuters, and remote access users. Although Figure 9-1 provides a high-level topology, it represents a highly available, fault-tolerant infrastructure that is based on common infrastructure guidelines. A well-designed infrastructure is essential for easier deployment of IP telephony and its integration with applications such as video streaming and video conferencing. As you learned in previous chapters, resiliency and high availability are crucial for security. As a best practice when designing your network infrastructure, always think about high availability, connectivity options for phones (such as in-line power), and quality of service (QoS) mechanisms. Make sure that you understand the call patterns for your organization.

TIP   You can obtain VoIP provisioning recommendations and best practices listed in the whitepaper at http://www.cisco.com/en/US/products/sw/voicesw/ps556/products_implementation_design_guide_chapter09186a008063743a.html.

Figure 9-1   *Common IP Telephony Deployment*

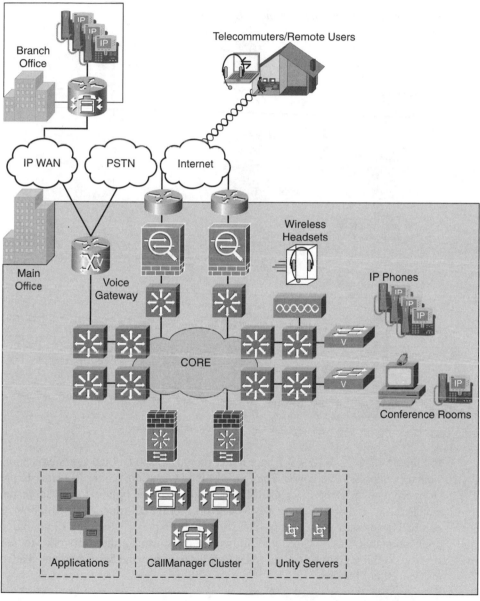

Figure 9-2 illustrates a typical regional site, branch office, or small enterprise deployment.

Figure 9-2 *Branch or Small Enterprise IP Telephony Deployment*

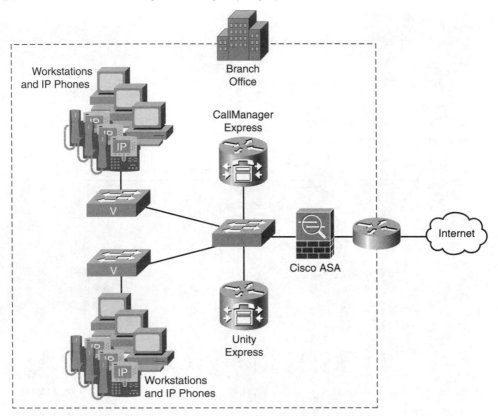

In Figure 9-2, a Cisco IOS Software router running Cisco Unified Communications Manager Express is deployed. The Cisco Unified Communications Manager Express (formerly known as the Cisco CallManager Express) is an optional software feature that enables Cisco routers to deliver Key System or Hybrid PBX functionality for branch offices or small businesses. Also deployed is Cisco Unity Express, which is a Linux-based application that runs on Cisco IOS Software routers, using either Network Module (NM) or Advanced Integration Module (AIM) hardware to provide basic automated attendant and voice mail features.

NOTE

Best practices to secure Cisco Unified CallManager, Cisco Unified Communications Manager Express, Cisco Unity, and Unity Express are covered later in this chapter in the section "Securing the IP Telephony Applications."

All the infrastructure security recommendations you learned in previous chapters (such as Chapter 2, "Preparation Phase") apply to IP telephony networks. It is, therefore, important that you follow those guidelines. For example, disable unnecessary services, implement infrastructure access control lists (ACL), and protect the control plane. This section shows you several other best practices and outline recommendations that are applicable strictly to voice implementations.

You should take a layered approach when securing your IP telephony infrastructure. Build security layer upon layer starting at the ports that your workstations and IP phones connect (access layer), and work your way to the distribution, core, and data center. Figure 9-3 illustrates the different layers within an enterprise network.

The following layers are illustrated in Figure 9-3:

1 **Access layer:** Access switches provide connectivity to user workstations and IP phones. The access layer can also include wireless access points with wireless handsets or workstations with voice software.

2 **Distribution layer:** This is the segment of the network where LAN-based routers and Layer 3 switches reside. These devices ensure that packets are properly routed between subnets and VLANs in your enterprise.

3 **Core:** The core typically consists of two or more high-end Layer 3 switches or routers that glue the network together as a whole.

4 **Data center distribution layer:** The distribution layer at the data center typically includes firewall or other security components (that is, intrusion detection systems [IDS] or intrusion prevention systems [IPS]). In Figure 9-3, two Catalyst 6500 switches with Firewall Services Modules (FWSM) are depicted.

5 **Data center access layer:** This layer includes access switches to which all the servers are connected. Figure 9-3 shows applications, Cisco Unified CallManager, and Cisco Unity servers connected to access switches at the data center.

Figure 9-3 *Layered Approach to Securing IP Telephony Infrastructures*

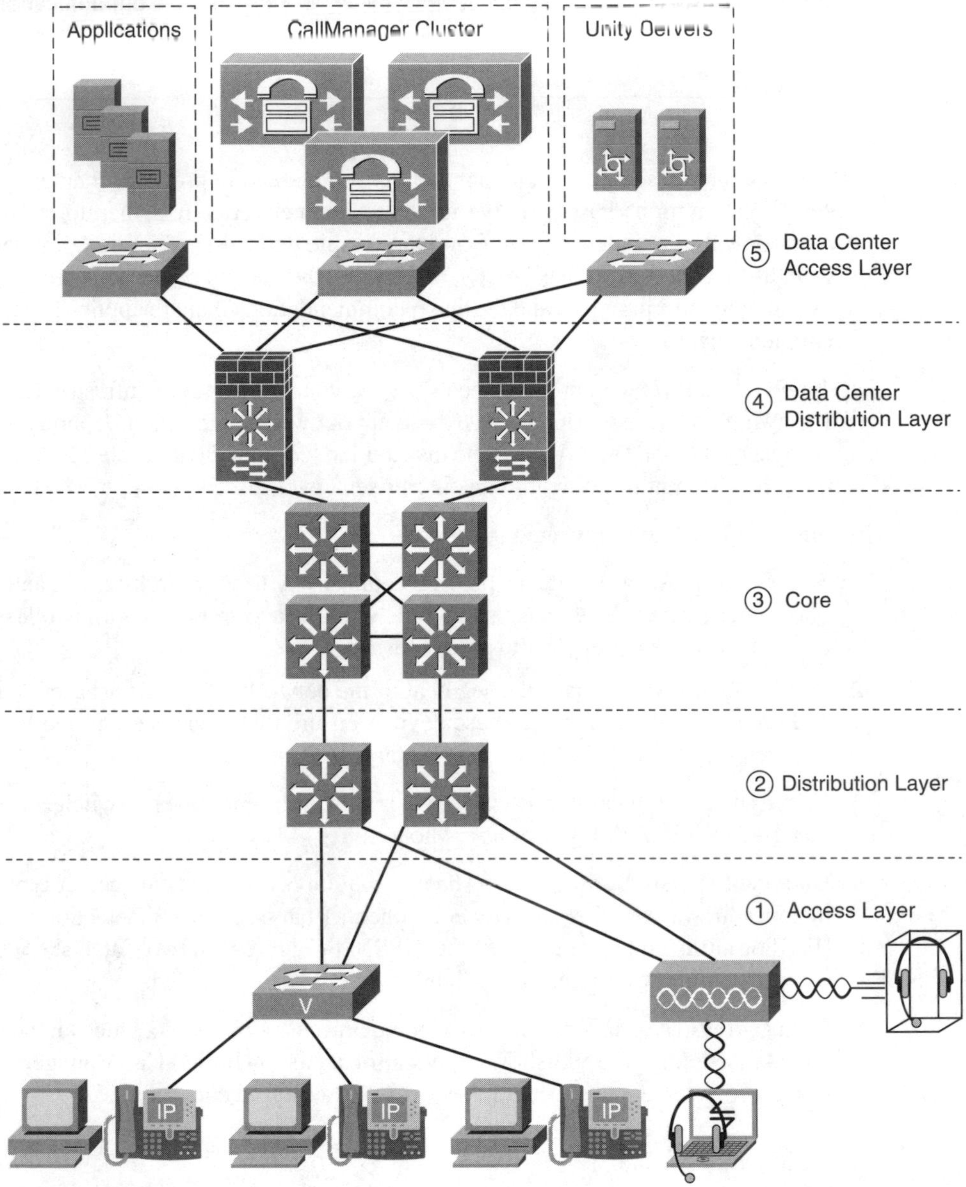

In the following sections, you will learn best practices for securing each infrastructure layer.

Access Layer

The first recommendation, and one of the most important, is that you enable two VLANs at the access layer—one VLAN for data traffic and another VLAN for voice traffic.

The voice VLAN in the Catalyst Switches that are running Catalyst Operating System (CatOS) is also known as an *Auxiliary VLAN*. Figure 9-4 illustrates this recommendation.

Figure 9-4   *Access Layer and VLAN Assignment*

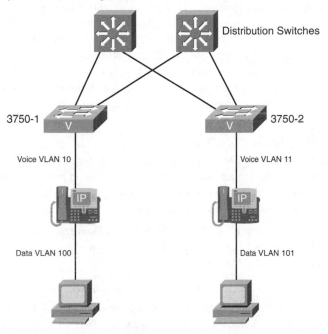

In Figure 9-4, several IP phones are connected to two Cisco Catalyst 3750 switches. User workstations are then connected to the IP phones. The voice VLAN in the 3750-1 switch is VLAN 10, and the data VLAN is VLAN 100. Similarly, the voice VLAN in the 3750-2 switch is VLAN 11, and the data VLAN is VLAN 101.

TIP   When deploying access switches for voice networks, it is recommended that you use switches capable of running the following features:

- Inline power or Power over Ethernet (PoE)

- Multiple queue support

- 802.1p and 802.1Q

- Fast link convergence

The separation of voice and data VLANs is recommended for many reasons. One of the major reasons is for address space conservation as well as for voice device protection from external networks. It is strongly recommended that voice endpoints be addressed using

RFC 1918 private subnet addresses. By separating voice and data VLANs, you can also implement QoS trust boundary configurations that are strictly for voice devices.

In addition, the use of separate voice and data VLANs can help you dramatically when responding to security incidents. This is why previous chapters stressed the importance of good addressing schemes. For example, if you are responding to a security incident such as a worm or a DoS attack, you can easily identify what addresses represent IP phones and what addresses represent user workstations. Subsequently, you can use VLAN access tagging control mechanisms such as VLAN access control lists (VACL), 802.1Q, and 802.1p to provide protection for voice devices from malicious traffic. Last, but not least, are the ease of management and configuration benefits (that is, simplified QoS configuration schemes).

Another recommendation is that you enable root guard or the PortFast bridge protocol data unit (BPDU) guard feature on all access switches. This rules out the possibility of someone introducing a rogue switch that might attempt to become the Spanning Tree root. You can enable PortFast BPDU guard on a global basis on Cisco switches running CatOS, as shown in the following example.

```
Console> (enable) set spantree portfast bpdu-guard enable
```

The next example shows how to enable PortFast BPDU guard on Cisco switches running Cisco IOS Software.

```
myswitch(config)# spanning-tree portfast bpduguard
```

When a switch running BPDU guard disables one of its ports, it remains disabled until it is manually enabled. On the other hand, you can configure a port to re-enable itself automatically from the "errdisable" state on CatOS-enabled switches, as shown in the following example.

```
Console> (enable) set errdisable-timeout interval 450
Console> (enable) set errdisable-timeout enable bpdu-guard
```

The timeout interval in this example is set to 450 seconds. The default timeout interval is 300 seconds and, by default, the timeout feature is disabled. The following example shows how to configure the automatic re-enabling of a disabled port on a switch running Cisco IOS Software.

```
myswitch(config)# errdisable recovery cause bpduguard
myswitch(config)# errdisable recovery interval 450
```

You can also enable port security or dynamic port security to protect against MAC flooding attacks. For instance, if you have an IP phone attached to a switch port and then a workstation connected directly to the IP phone, it is recommended that you limit the number of learned MAC addresses to two: one for the IP phone and one for the workstation behind the phone. Limit the learned MAC addresses to one in case you have only an IP phone connected to the switch port. This configuration is typically used in lobbies, common areas, and conference rooms. Protecting against MAC flooding attacks is important in publicly accessed areas of your organization such as lobbies because you do not want outsiders to be able to plug in laptops to an IP phone or disconnect the IP phone and plug in a laptop. Example 9-1 shows how to configure an access port with dynamic port security for a port on which an IP phone resides and a user workstation is plugged into the data port on the phone.

Example 9-1 *Dynamic Port-Security*

```
myswitch#configure terminal
myswitch(config)#interface GigabitEthernet1/12
myswitch(config-if)# switchport access vlan 100
myswitch(config-if)# switchport mode access
myswitch(config-if)# switchport voice vlan 10
myswitch(config-if)# switchport port-security
myswitch(config-if)# switchport port-security maximum 3
myswitch(config-if)# switchport port-security violation restrict
myswitch(config-if)# switchport port-security aging time 2
myswitch(config-if)# switchport port-security aging type inactivity
```

In the previous example, port security is enabled on the interface GigabitEthernet1/12. Notice the way the VLAN assignment is configured. The voice VLAN is VLAN 10, and the data VLAN is VLAN 100. Port security is configured to restrict learning to a maximum of three MAC addresses—one for the phone itself, another for the integrated PC port on the phone, and the third for a PC connected on the phone.

TIP

The **switchport port-security violation restrict** command enables the switch to learn up to the maximum number of MAC addresses and then stop learning any new MAC addresses. The default setting is to disable the port. If you keep the default setting and the maximum number of MAC addresses is exceeded, the port becomes disabled, and the phone loses power (in case of inline power). In addition, the recommended port security aging time is 2 minutes.

It is also recommended that you enable the DHCP snooping feature to prevent rogue DHCP server attacks and DHCP starvation attacks. Attackers can use different tools to create a DHCP starvation attack (the most common is called Gobbler) by making numerous DHCP requests until you run out of IP addresses. Subsequently, legitimate workstations cannot receive an IP address from your DHCP server successfully. You can enable DHCP snooping globally or on a per-interface basis. The following example shows how to configure DHCP snooping globally on a switch running Cisco IOS Software. An IP phone is connected to the switch, and a user workstation is plugged into the data port on the phone.

```
myswitch(config)#ip dhcp snooping vlan 10, 100
myswitch(config)#ip dhcp snooping
```

In the previous example, DHCP snooping is enabled on VLAN 10 (voice VLAN) and VLAN 100 (data VLAN). The following example shows how DHCP snooping is enabled on a specific port/interface.

```
myswitch(config)#interface GigabitEthernet 1/48
myswitch(config-if)#ip dhcp snooping limit rate 10
myswitch(config-if)#ip dhcp snooping trust
```

DHCP snooping is a DHCP security feature that provides network security by filtering untrusted DHCP messages and by building and maintaining a DHCP snooping binding database (also referred to as a *DHCP snooping binding table*).

DHCP snooping acts like a firewall between untrusted hosts and DHCP servers. You can use DHCP snooping to differentiate between untrusted interfaces connected to the end user and trusted interfaces connected to the DHCP server or another switch. For DHCP snooping to function properly, all DHCP servers must be connected to the switch through trusted interfaces.

Another feature that you can enable to protect the access layer of your voice-enabled network is the Dynamic Address Resolution Protocol (ARP) Inspection (DAI). DAI is commonly used to prevent gratuitous ARP attacks. Workstations bind a MAC address to an IP address in an ARP cache. When the system sends out an ARP request, the device that owns the IP address in that request replies with its IP and MAC address information to the system that originated the request. On the other hand, gratuitous ARP is an unsolicited ARP reply, in which a system tells the rest of the Layer 2 adjacent systems that it owns a specific IP and MAC address. Networking devices commonly use this technique. For example, when the Cisco PIX or the Cisco Adaptive Security Appliances (ASA) fail over, it sends a gratuitous ARP to other devices on the network to advertise the assumed IP addresses. On the other hand, attackers can use gratuitous ARP to spoof the identity of another system. You can use DAI to inspect all ARP requests and replies (gratuitous and nongratuitous) to avoid these types of exploits on untrusted ports.

NOTE   You must enable DHCP snooping to use DAI.

You can enable DAI globally and then on a per-interface basis. The following example shows how to configure DAI globally on a switch running Cisco IOS Software.

```
myswitch#configure terminal
myswitch(config)#ip arp inspection vlan 10,100
myswitch(config)#ip dhcp snooping database tftp://172.18.108.26/dai/dai_db
```

In the previous example, DAI is enabled on VLANs 10 and 100. The switch is configured to save the DHCP snooping database on a TFTP server (172.18.108.26) under a directory called dai and a file called dai_db. You can also enable DAI on a per-interface basis, as shown in the following example:

```
myswitch(config)#interface GigabitEthernet 1/12
myswitch(config-if)#ip arp inspection limit rate 15
```

In the previous example, the **ip arp inspection** command is configured with the **limit rate** option to specify the maximum number of ARP packets per second allowed on the GigabitEthernet 1/12 interface. The switch disables that port when it detects more than 15 ARP packets per second.

NOTE   If you do not want to disable the phone when the port receives more then 15 ARP messages in a second, you can set the rate limit to none which allows the phone to stay up.

Many people are becoming more concerned with unauthorized network access, and potentially, even unauthorized placement of IP phones. More advanced features such as 802.1x and Network Admission Control (NAC) can also be implemented. In 802.1x environments in which user workstations are plugged in to the back of IP phones, the use of automatic port control on Cisco Catalyst switches is recommended. To enable 802.1x automatic port control on switches running Cisco IOS Software, use the **dot1x port-control auto** command. On switches running CatOS, use the **set port dot1x <m/p> port-control auto** command. 802.1x and IP telephony are only supported with the use of Cisco IP phones. You must use multi-VLAN access ports (separate VLANs for voice and data) based on the configurations shown in the previous examples in this chapter.

When you enable 802.1x on a switch port where a Cisco IP phone resides, authentication is done based only on Cisco Discovery Protocol (CDP). It is important to notice that no voice or data packets are allowed before CDP packets are processed. This varies on a per-platform basis. For instance, on a Catalyst 6500 running CatOS, packets other than Extensible Authentication Protocol over LAN (EAPOL) or CDP are dropped by the software at the in-band driver level. The voice VLAN Spanning Tree state is set to "forwarding," and the disabling of learning of other MAC addresses is done on the line cards by setting the appropriate bits in port header control registers. On the other hand, Cisco Catalyst 3750 switches put phones addresses in the TCAM after detecting CDP packets to allow voice traffic through. In addition, an ACL to catch all EAPOL packets is used. The hardware drops any other packets sent from unknown source addresses when they hit the catchall entry in the TCAM, triggering an address learning violation in the switch.

In short, in 802.1x environments, CDP is absolutely necessary for IP phone operation; without it, an IP phone is unusable. In contrast, when you use the Cisco NAC Framework solution in Layer 2 IP (NAC-L2-IP), EAP over UDP (EoU) is used. EOU provides a different type of architecture and access control environment than 802.1x because EoU acts at Layer 3, and 802.1x is strictly Layer 2. In NAC-L2-IP, the security posture check is triggered after an ARP packet is detected or by the use of DHCP snooping. Cisco switches support EoU in an IP telephony environment. In most cases, it is recommended that you use NAC-L2-IP. Based primarily on CDP, you can exempt Cisco IP phones from any EOU rules. An alternative to this approach includes a configured static exception or use of the Generic Authorization Message Exchange (GAME) protocol with an external audit server.

It is recommended that you exempt IP phones from the NAC posture entirely. Example 9-2 demonstrates how to configure an exception policy for Cisco IP phones on a switch running Cisco IOS Software.

Example 9-2 *Exception Policy for Cisco IP Phones*

```
identity profile eapoudp
  device authorize type cisco ip phone policy allow-my-phones
identity policy allow-my-phones
  access-group allow-my-phones
ip access-list extended allow-my-phones
  permit ip any any
```

In the previous example, an identity profile is configured for EoU, and the **device authorize** command is used to "authorize" or exempt all Cisco IP phones from NAC posture checks. This is done by using the CDP information from the Cisco IP phone. The identity policy named **allow-my-phones** is configured with an access list to catch all traffic.

NOTE   Refer to the Cisco Press book *Network Admission Control Volume II* for detailed NAC configuration examples and troubleshooting guides.

You can configure Cisco IP phones to allow an administrator to get statistics and device information through a built-in web server that runs on each phone. Administrators can use this feature for debugging and to obtain the remote status of the phone. This built-in web server is also used to receive application information from the Cisco Unified CallManager. You can enable or disable web access globally or on each phone specifically. It is recommended that you control web access to the phones. If you completely disable web access, troubleshooting voice-related issues can be more difficult to solve. Alternatively, you can restrict access by configuring ACLs or VACLs only, allowing an administrative network or subnet in different parts of the network (in most cases, as close as possible to the phone).

NOTE   As previously mentioned in this book, it is extremely important that you have a separate network segment or subnet dedicated to administrative access and applications.

Distribution Layer

At the distribution layer, you can apply enforcement mechanisms (such as ACLs) based on your security policies for the IP telephony–enabled network. For example, you can configure Layer 3 ACLs so that they do not allow traffic from the nonvoice VLANS to access the voice gateway and voice applications in the network. Typically, voice application servers (such as Cisco Unified CallManager and Cisco Unity) are protected by firewalls in the distribution layer of the data center. On the other hand, you can create ACL templates to strategically deploy within your distribution layer to restrict access from nonvoice VLANs. This method simplifies the ACLs at Layer 3 compared to the ACLs at Layer 2 or VLAN ACLs. Figure 9-5 shows the two access switches you saw in the previous examples, in which IP phones in the 192.168.10.0/24 and 192.168.11.0/24 networks reside (voice VLANs 10 and 11). The user workstations are in VLANs 100 (IP range 192.168.100.0/24) and 101 (IP range 192.168.101.0/24).

The goal is to restrict access from nonvoice segments to the voice gateway (10.10.10.100) and to the CallManager cluster (172.18.124.0/24). You can use a simple ACL in your distribution switches, as demonstrated in Example 9-3.

Example 9-3   *ACL in Distribution Switch*

```
access-list 100 deny ip 192.168.100.0 0.0.0.255 host 10.10.10.100
access-list 100 deny ip 192.168.101.0 0.0.0.255 host 10.10.10.100
! the lines above deny all nonvoice devices to send traffic to the voice
! gateway
access-list 100 deny ip 192.168.100.0 0.0.0.255 172.18.124.0 0.0.0.255
access-list 100 deny ip 192.168.101.0 0.0.0.255 172.18.124.0 0.0.0.255
! the access list entries above deny all nonvoice devices to send
! traffic to the Cisco Unified CallManager servers
access-list 100 permit ip 192.168.100.0 0.0.0.255 any
access-list 100 permit ip 192.168.101.0 0.0.0.255 any
```

Depending on your security policy and your environment, you will allow or restrict access to additional services. Of course, in your data center, you will have more granular ACLs allowing or denying traffic based on your security policy.

High availability is crucial in the distribution layer. Use the Hot Standby Router Protocol (HSRP) at the distribution layer to ensure high availability in the event of a failure.

Figure 9-5 *Distribution Layer Access List*

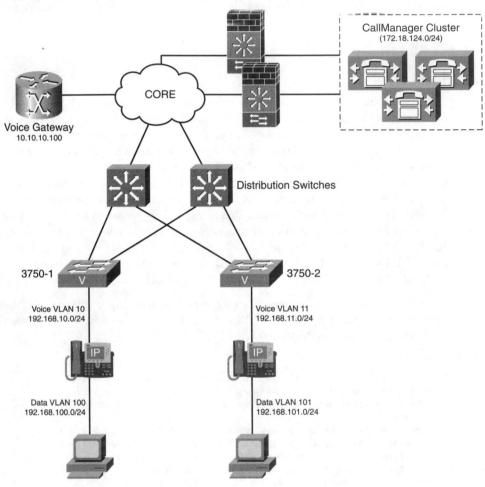

NOTE The following link contains numerous step-by-step examples of methods for configuring HSRP on Cisco Catalyst switches and Cisco IOS Software routers:

http://www.cisco.com/en/US/partner/tech/tk648/tk362/tk321/
tsd_technology_support_sub-protocol_home.html

Gateway Load Balancing Protocol (GLBP) is another redundancy mechanism. GLBP is now Stateful Switchover (SSO) aware. GLBP can detect when a router is failing over to the secondary Route Processor (RP) and continue in its current GLBP group state. Prior to being SSO aware, GLBP was not able to detect that a second RP was installed and configured to take over if the primary RP failed. When the primary failed, the GLBP device would stop participating in the GLBP group and, depending on its role, could trigger another router in the group to take over as the active router. With this enhancement, GLBP detects the failover to the secondary RP, and no change occurs to the GLBP group. If the secondary RP fails and the primary is still not available, the GLBP group detects this and re-elects a new active GLBP router.

At the distribution layer, you can also enable NetFlow to gain complete visibility of what is happening in your network. As you learned in previous chapters, NetFlow brings unmatched telemetry features that allow you to maintain visibility of your network traffic.

Core

A number of books are required to fully cover how to design the core of your network. However, for the purpose of this chapter and this book, the most important thing you need to remember is the need for high availability and the ability to route/switch traffic as fast as possible with little need for traffic filtering in your core. You can use features such as Control Plane Policing (CoPP) to protect the control plane of your core routers. In addition, you should implement the routing protocol security best practices learned in previous chapters and all other Network Foundation Protection (NFP) strategies.

Securing the IP Telephony Applications

In this section, you learn how to protect IP telephony applications such as:

- Cisco Unified CallManager
- Cisco Unified Communications Manager Express
- Cisco Unity
- Cisco Unity Express
- Cisco Personal Assistant

Securing these applications starts with the development of a well-defined application security policy that describes all the processes required to ensure server and application security and assumes that you deployed the recommended network infrastructure best practices described earlier in this chapter. This policy not only includes design guidelines, but also operational practices, such as patch management, antivirus protection, and in-depth protection with the Cisco Security Agent (CSA). In the following sections, you learn best practices for increasing the security of the previously mentioned applications.

Protecting Cisco Unified CallManager

Server and operating system best practices apply when protecting the
Cisco Unified CallManager. Just as with any other critical application, you should make
major configuration changes within a maintenance window to avoid the disruption of voice
services. However, some standard security policies for application servers might not be
adequate for IP telephony servers. For example, on e-mail and web servers, you can
easily resend an e-mail message or refresh a web page. On the other hand, voice
communications are real-time events. Consequently, your user population will quickly
notice any disruption of service.

The first step is to restrict activities on IP telephony servers (such as the
Cisco Unified CallManager) that might be considered normal on application servers within
a network. For instance, you should browse the Internet on CallManager servers. This
sounds obvious, however, many administrators fail to do this.

Patch management is one of the most crucial aspects of application security. Cisco provides
a well-defined patch system for the Cisco Unified CallManager solution. You should
apply only patches that Cisco provides and not patch the system using an operating system
vendor patch (unless Cisco has approved it).

NOTE   You can download all Cisco Unified CallManager patches from
http://www.cisco.com/kobayashi/sw-center/sw-voice.shtml.

Additional information templates show you how to increase the hardening of the operating
system in the Utils\SecurityTemplates directory on your Cisco Unified CallManager
server.

It is important to know that Cisco Unified CallManager 5.x does not support the use of
antivirus software. However, an unmanaged version of the Cisco Security Agent provides
security features above and beyond traditional antivirus solutions. As you learned in
previous chapters, CSA looks at the server traffic and the way the running applications
behave. It then enforces security mechanisms when something is considered abnormal.
For instance, CSA prevents any virus or malware that tries to be installed on the system.
It prevents the infection before it happens. You can also deploy the full version of CSA
to provide granular configuration of security policies within the servers. In addition,
you can monitor all CSA event logs from a centralized location (from the
CSA Management Control, or CSA-MC).

NOTE   Use of CSA is highly recommended not only for Cisco Unified CallManager but to protect
any servers and endpoints within your organization.

In addition, you may want to protect all your servers in your data center with a firewall. The FWSM for the Cisco Catalyst 6500 series switches is typically deployed at the data center. You should configure strict policies on the specific traffic that is allowed to communicate to the Cisco Unified CallManager servers. As a best practice, only allow traffic from your voice VLANs/subnets and traffic from your administrative subnets.

NOTE   Detailed information on how to protect your data center is covered in Chapter 10, "Data Center Security."

Protecting Cisco Unified Communications Manager Express (CME)

As previously discussed in this chapter, the Cisco Unified CME is an entry-level VoIP solution that runs on Cisco IOS Software routers. It is designed for small businesses and autonomous small enterprise branch offices. CME enables you to provide voice, data, and IP telephony services on a single platform. Because it is an integrated solution within Cisco IOS Software routers, all the best practices of router security that you learned in Chapter 2 apply when securing the Cisco Unified CME solution. These best practices include the following:

- Configure enable secret passwords or encrypted passwords within the configuration.
- Configure administrator access privileges within Cisco IOS Software.
- Restrict access to VTY lines for remote administration access.
- Use RADIUS or TACACS+ servers for authentication and authorization of administrative sessions.
- Configure RADIUS or TACACS+ accounting.
- Configure a fallback user account for administrative access when the external authentication server is not available.
- Configure Secure Shell (SSH) access instead of Telnet.
- Control the access of Simple Network Management Protocol (SNMP) sessions.
- Use all other best practices listed in Chapter 2 that protect the control plane and management plane.

In addition to the common infrastructure protection best practices, you should only allow IP phones in the trusted domain for registration. You can use the strict-match option in the **ip source-address** command if your local segment is a trusted domain. This allows only locally attached IP phones to register, as demonstrated in the following example:

```
CME(config-telephony)#ip source-address 192.168.10.1 port 2000
```

Another good practice is to block port 2000 (from external untrusted networks) to prevent unauthorized Skinny Call Control Protocol (SCCP) phones from registering to your Cisco Unified CME. You can use an ACL as demonstrated in the following example:

```
access-list 100 deny tcp any any eq 2000
```

Always use Secure Socket Layer (SSL) and HTTPS to access the web-based admin console, as shown in the following:

```
ip http server
ip http secure-server
```

TIP   You can also use **ip http authentication** to perform external RADIUS or TACACS+ server for HTTPS authentication.

Configure Class of Restrictions (COR) is used to prevent toll fraud. Typically, it is recommended that you configure different classes of service to control the destinations that users can call. For example, you can configure different levels of permissions that allow specific users to dial only local numbers and 911 for any emergencies. In the following example, two different types of users are configured (users and superusers). Superusers are allowed to dial any numbers, and regular users have access to all resources with the exception of toll (1-900 numbers), directory assistance (411), and international calling. This is achieved with the configuration shown in Example 9-4.

Example 9-4 *Protecting Against Toll Fraud Using COR*

```
dial-peer cor custom
name 911
name 1800
name local-call
name ld-call
name 411
name int-call
name 1900
!different dial-peer names are assigned for the different services; additionally,
    different COR
!lists for each service are configured below.
!
dial-peer cor list call911
member 911
!
dial-peer cor list call1800
member 1800
!
dial-peer cor list calllocal
member local-call
!
dial-peer cor list callint
member int-call
```

Example 9-4   *Protecting Against Toll Fraud Using COR (Continued)*

```
!
dial-peer cor list call1d
member ld-call
!
dial-peer cor list call411
member 411
!
dial-peer cor list call1900
member 1900
!
dial-peer cor list user
member 911
member 1800
member local-call
member ld-call
!the previous COR list allows regular users (user) to access/use 911, 1800, local
  calls, and !caller ID services
!
dial-peer cor list superuser
member 911
member 1800
member local-call
member ld-call
member 411
member int-call
member 1900
dial-peer voice 9 pots
corlist outgoing call1d
destination-pattern 91.........
port 1/0
prefix 1
!the previous COR list allows superusers to access/use all available services
!
dial-peer voice 911 pots
corlist outgoing call911
destination-pattern 9911
port 1/0
prefix 911
!
dial-peer voice 11 pots
corlist outgoing callint
destination-pattern 9011T
port 2/0
prefix 011
!
dial-peer voice 732 pots
corlist outgoing calllocal
destination-pattern 9732.......
port 1/0
prefix 732
!
```

continues

Example 9-4   *Protecting Against Toll Fraud Using COR (Continued)*

```
dial-peer voice 800 pots
corlist outgoing call1800
destination-pattern 91800.......
port 1/0
prefix 1800
!
dial-peer voice 802 pots
corlist outgoing call1800
destination-pattern 91877.......
port 1/0
prefix 1877
!
dial-peer voice 805 pots
corlist outgoing call1800
destination-pattern 91888.......
port 1/0
prefix 1888
!
dial-peer voice 411 pots
corlist outgoing call411
destination-pattern 9411
port 1/0
prefix 411
!
dial-peer voice 806 pots
corlist outgoing call1800
destination-pattern 91866.......
port 1/0
prefix 1866
ephone-dn 1
number 2000
cor incoming user
Ephone-dn 2
number 2001
cor incoming superuser
```

You can configure the Cisco IOS Software Firewall on the same router that runs
Cisco Unified CME. On the other hand, you must pay attention to certain requirements needed
for Cisco Unified CME to work in your environment. For example, SCCP support is needed
for locally generated Skinny traffic. SCCP is a Cisco proprietary lite-version of H.323 for
call signaling, control, and media communication. H.323 uses Q.931, H.225, and H.245
for call setup, management, and control. H.323 requires a TCP connection for H.245
signaling that does not have a well-known port associated with it. The H.245 port is
dynamically negotiated. NAT and stateful firewalls can break H.323.

NOTE	Cisco IOS Software supports unidirectional firewall policy configurations between groups of interfaces which have been known as *zones* since Version 12.4(6)T. Previously, all inspect rules had to be applied to specific interfaces on routers running the Cisco IOS Firewall feature set. All inbound and outbound traffic was inspected based on the direction to which the inspect rule was applied.
	Since Version 12.4(11)T, Cisco IOS Software Firewalls have supported H.225 Registration, Admission, and Status (RAS) signaling. H.323 uses the H.225 standard for call setup.

Protecting Cisco Unity

The Cisco Unity solution provides advanced voice mail and messaging features. In this section, you will learn tips for increasing the security of the Cisco Unity solution. Cisco Unity runs over the Microsoft Windows operating system (OS). The first step in protecting the Cisco Unity system is to have a good patch management procedure. Microsoft has different recommendations for installing and securing Windows Server 2003 and Windows 2000 Server systems. For Windows Server 2003, refer to the article "*Checklists; Windows Server 2003, Standard Edition*" at http://technet.microsoft.com/en-us/default.aspx. For the Windows 2000 Server, refer to the article "*Installing and Securing a New Windows 2000 System*," which is available on the same website.

TIP	Make sure that the latest supported Cisco Unity service pack and all updates recommended by Microsoft are installed on the server. All supported service packs and recommended updates are listed at http://www.cisco.com/univercd/cc/td/doc/product/voice/c_unity/cmptblty/msupdate.htm.

You can use security templates to help increase the security of the system. On the other hand, you should always apply all security policies to the Windows server only after the Cisco Unity installation is completed. Some security templates can affect the operation of Cisco Unity. The following Windows 2000 Server settings are recommended to restrict and audit access to the Cisco Unity server. To change these settings, go to **Start > Programs > Administrative Tools > Local Security Policy** on the Windows 2000 server, and perform the following functions:

Step 1   Set the **Audit account login events** option to **Failure**.

Step 2   Set the **Audit account management** option to **Success**, **Failure**.

Step 3 Select **Failure** under **the Audit directory service access** option.

Step 4 Set the **Audit login events** option to **Failure**.

Step 5 Under **Audit object access**, select **No auditing**.

Step 6 Under the **Audit policy change**, select **Success, Failure**.

Step 7 Under the **Audit privilege use** option, select **Failure**.

Step 8 Under **Audit system events**, select **No auditing**.

Step 9 Under the **Act as part of the operating system** option, enter the account used to install Cisco Unity.

Step 10 Under the **Access this computer from the network**, select the following options: **Backup Operators, Power Users, Users, Administrators, servername\IWAM, domainname\ISUR_servername**.

Step 11 Only allow **Backup Operators and Administrators** under the **Shut down the system** option.

It is important that you know the TCP and User Datagram Protocol (UDP) ports used by Cisco Unity. Table 9-1 lists all the TCP and UDP ports and their usage.

Table 9-1 *TCP and UDP Ports Used by Cisco Unity*

Protocols/Ports	Service	Usage
TCP 25	Simple Mail Transfer Protocol (SMTP)	Allowed inbound and outbound by Microsoft Exchange when installed on the Cisco Unity server.
TCP and UDP 53	Domain Name System (DNS)	Allowed outbound for access name resolution. Used inbound if the DNS server is running on the Cisco Unity server. It is recommended that for your DNS server, you use a server other than the system on which Cisco Unity is installed.
UDP 67	DHCP/Bootstrap Protocol (BOOTP)	Allowed outbound if you are using DHCP instead of static IP addresses. It is recommended that you use static addressing for the server.

Table 9-1 *TCP and UDP Ports Used by Cisco Unity (Continued)*

Protocols/Ports	Service	Usage
UDP 68	DHCP/BOOTP	Allowed inbound if you are using DHCP instead of static IP addresses, which is used by the Cisco Unity server to receive DHCP or BOOTP replies.
TCP 80	HTTP	Allowed bidirectional to access the Cisco Unity web console. HTTPS access is recommended.
TCP 135	Microsofts Remote Procedural Call (MS-RPC)	Used to negotiate access to the Media Master, Cisco Unity ViewMail for Microsoft Outlook, the Exchange server, and other Distributed Component Object Model (DCOM) services.
UDP 137	Network Basic Input/Output System (NetBIOS)	NetBIOS Name Service. Used for NetBIOS name resolution or WINS resolution.
UDP 138	NetBIOS	NetBIOS Datagram Service. Used when browsing Windows networks.
TCP 139	NetBIOS	Used to access Windows file shares and perform NetBIOS over TCP/IP connections.
UDP 161	SNMP	Used to send SNMP notifications and to provide SNMP information when the host agent is queried.
UDP 162	SNMP Trap	Used to send SNMP traps.
TCP 389	Lightweight Directory Access Protocol (LDAP) with AD-DC	Allowed outbound to access LDAP directory services.
Configurable (typically it is set to TCP 390 or any unused TCP port)	LDAP with Exchange 5.5	Used to access LDAP directory services.

continues

Table 9-1   *TCP and UDP Ports Used by Cisco Unity (Continued)*

Protocols/Ports	Service	Usage
TCP 443	HTTP/SSL	Used to perform system administration on a remote Cisco Unity server when it is configured for HTTP/SSL.
TCP 445	SMB	Used outbound to access Windows file shares and perform NetBIOS over TCP/IP connections. Used inbound to access Cisco Unity reports and Microsoft Windows file shares.
TCP 636	LDAP/SSL	Used to access LDAP directory services over SSL.
TCP 691	SMTP/link-state advertisement (LSA)	Used when the Exchange server is running on the Cisco Unity server and the Exchange server is accepting SMTP with LSA.
TCP 1432	Telecommunications Development Symposium (TDS) proxy (CiscoUnityTdsProxy)	Used by local processes to access the SQL Server or Microsoft SQL Server Desktop Engine (MSDE) database.
TCP 1433 (default)	MS-SQL-S	Used to access the SQL Server or MSDE database and to perform replication when Cisco Unity failover is configured.
UDP 1434	MS-SQL-M	Used to access the SQL Server or MSDE database.
TCP 2000	Skinny (SCCP)	Used to access Cisco CallManager.
TCP 2443	Secure Skinny (SCCPS)	Used to access Cisco CallManager via an encrypted channel.
TCP 3268	LDAP with AD-GC	Used to access LDAP directory services when the global catalog server is on another server.

Table 9-1   *TCP and UDP Ports Used by Cisco Unity (Continued)*

Protocols/Ports	Service	Usage
TCP 3269	LDAP/SSL with AD-GC	Used to access LDAP directory services over SSL when the global catalog server is on another server.
TCP 3372	Microsoft Distributed Transaction Coordinator (MSDTC)	Used to access the SQL Server or MSDE database when Cisco Unity failover is configured.
TCP 3389	Windows Terminal Services	Used to remotely perform system administration on a Cisco Unity server.
TCP 3653	Node Manager	Used to send manual keepalive packets (or "pings") between the primary and secondary servers when Cisco Unity failover is configured.
TCP 4444	Kerberos authentication	Used to perform Kerberos authentication.
TCP 5060 (default)	Session Initiation Protocol (SIP)	Used when the Cisco Unity server is connecting to SIP endpoints or SIP proxy servers.
TCP 8005	Server Life Cycle (JMX)	Used to access the Tomcat server.
TCP 8009	Apache JServ Protocol (AJP)	Used by Internet Information Server (IIS).
TCP and UDP dynamic (in the range of 1024 through 65535)	DCOM	Used by the Media Master to play and record voice messages, and used when the Cisco Unity server is a domain controller supporting member servers.
Dynamic UDP ports (in the range of 1024 through 65535)	Messaging Application Programming Interface (MAPI) notifications	Used in inbound direction to notify Cisco Unity of changes to subscriber mailboxes when Exchange is the message store.
UDP dynamic (in the range of 22800 through 32767)	Real-Time Protocol (RTP)	Used when sending and receiving VoIP traffic with SCCP or SIP endpoints.

Use the information in Table 9-1 to restrict and allow access to firewalls that protect your Cisco Unity servers.

Cisco Unity uses Microsoft SQL Server. An important recommendation is to make sure that you increase the security of your Microsoft SQL Server 2000 installation. Make sure you select **Windows Authentication Mode** when you install Microsoft SQL Server, as documented in the Cisco Unity installation guide. In addition, make sure that you pay attention to the following guidelines:

- Use a strong password for the SQL administrator (SA) account.

- Restrict client access to Microsoft SQL Server 2000 by only allowing the Cisco Unity service accounts to access the Microsoft SQL Server 2000 directories, folders, and files. You can also grant this access to a highly privileged account designated for use by a system administrator.

- Detach the default Northwind and Pubs databases.

At a minimum, Internet Explorer (IE) 6.0 with Service Pack 1 must be installed on the Cisco Unity server. Use IE on the Cisco Unity server for Cisco Unity administration only. It is not expected that you will use IE on the Cisco Unity server to browse the Internet and other external resources. On the other hand, in some cases, you may have to access the Microsoft or Cisco websites to obtain patches and hotfixes.

TIP As part of securing IE, refer to Microsoft Knowledge Base article 826955 at http://support.microsoft.com/kb/826955. It includes instructions on how to reduce the chance of being exposed to a worm like Blaster or Nachi.

Cisco Unity uses IIS 5.0 and later. Always make sure that you install the latest cumulative update patches for IIS 5.0 on the Cisco Unity server.

TIP You can also use the guidelines specified in the "Secure Internet Information Services 5 Checklist," which is available on the Microsoft TechNet website, with one exception: grant Full Control access to Cisco Unity directories, folders, and files only to Cisco Unity service accounts and the local server administrators group.

In addition, it is recommended that you pay attention to the following best practices:

- Delete all IIS default sample files, folders, and websites.
- Disable all default IIS COM objects.
- Remove unused script mappings. Cisco Unity uses only the ASA and ASP script mappings.
- Do not follow Microsoft recommendations regarding parent paths. The **Parent Paths** option should remain enabled on the Cisco Unity server.

TIP   Cisco Unity uses Microsoft Message Queuing (MSMQ) 2.0. It is recommended that you do not change the default MSMQ setting of **Local Use Only**.

Within Cisco Unity, each application has its own authentication capabilities and mechanisms, and you should become familiar with each of these authentication methods. Cisco has a detailed explanation of each application authentication mechanism at http://www.cisco.com/univercd/cc/td/doc/product/voice/c_unity/unity40/usg/ex/usg006.htm.

Protecting Cisco Unity Express

As mentioned previously in this chapter, Cisco Unity Express is a Linux-based application that runs on Cisco IOS Software routers with either an NM or an AIM. No external interfaces exist on the Cisco Unity Express hardware. In reality, a physical Fast Ethernet interface does exist; however, it is software disabled. All traffic to the Cisco Unity Express hardware must pass through the router. On the other hand, you can access Cisco Unity Express via the router command-line interface (CLI) using the **service-module service-engine x/y session** command in enable mode. The Cisco Unity Express module also has a CLI, but you cannot configure a password on it.

To protect the Cisco Unity Express application, you should first apply all router security best practices that you learned previously in this book to the router itself. In addition, you should only allow SSH access, instead of Telnet, to the router. Cisco Unity Express does not support SSH. However, the communication between the router and Cisco Unity Express is via the router backplane and is not exposed to external interfaces. Therefore, SSH access to the router is sufficient.

The initial versions of Cisco Unity Express did not support HTTPS. However, login to the Cisco Unity Express GUI is password protected. One major limitation is that the login information currently travels in cleartext across the IP network. To provide additional protection, you can use an IP Security (IPsec) tunnel to communicate to the router. However, HTTPS is supported on the Cisco Unified Communications Manager Express and Cisco Unity Express since Cisco IOS Software Version 12.2(15)ZJ2. To enable HTTPS access to the Cisco Unity Express application, you must enable the secure HTTP server on Cisco IOS Software with the following two commands:

```
ip http server
ip http secure-server
```

You should also use ACLs on the router to restrict access to only the protocols and ports that the Cisco Unity Express software uses. The following are the protocols and ports that Cisco Unity Express uses:

- **SSH for administrative access:** TCP port 22
- **DNS:** UDP or TCP port 53
- **TFTP:** UDP port 69
- **FTP:** TCP port 21 for control and TCP port 20 for data (Active FTP only)
- **HTTP:** TCP port 80 for the Cisco IP phones
- **HTTPS:** TCP port 443 for administrative access to the GUI
- **Syslog:** UDP port 514
- **SIP:** UDP port 5060
- **RTP:** UDP port range from port 16384 to port 32767
- **NTP:** UDP port 123

Cisco Unity Express runs on Linux; however, access to the Linux operating system or to the Linux kernel is not direct. The Linux operating system is entirely embedded. Apply only the patches that Cisco provides. The same goes for SQL and LDAP support. Cisco Unity Express includes a SQL server and LDAP directory services; however, direct access does not exist to the SQL server or the LDAP directory.

As with the full version of Cisco Unity, you should also ensure that two servers are configured correctly: first, configuration of authentication to the FTP server that is used for software installation; and second, configuration of the FTP server that is used for backup and restore. Never leave the backup and restore FTP server password configured permanently on the Cisco Unity Express module. In addition, because mailbox PINs do not expire, a best practice is to change all passwords periodically, forcing users to reset their PINs to a new setting.

Protecting Cisco Personal Assistant

This section covers the most common best practices to harden the Cisco Personal Assistant. The recommendations to increase the security of the Cisco Personal Assistant server can be summarized into two major areas:

- Operating environment
- Security policies

NOTE   The Cisco Personal Assistant operating environment is made up of several third-party products. You should follow the security guidelines documented by each of these third-party product vendors. This chapter covers several general guidelines on securing the Cisco Personal Assistant operating environment.

Hardening the Cisco Personal Assistant Operating Environment

The Cisco Personal Assistant operating environment third-party components needed are mainly Microsoft products. Other third-party components, such as Nuance ASR and Real-Speak TTS, are also needed.

NOTE   The following site includes a detailed list of all Cisco Personal Assistant operating environment components:

http://www.cisco.com/en/US/products/sw/voicesw/ps2026/prod_maintenance_guides_list.html

Several of the Cisco Personal Assistant operating environment components are configured by default with minimum security. It is extremely important that customers increase the level of security protection for each of those systems. One of the major flaws is that Microsoft IIS is vulnerable until the Windows 2000 installation on the Cisco Personal Assistant server is complete. You have two options: disable IIS, or wait to install it until after Windows 2000 Service Pack 4 is installed. The recommended method is to install a bundled Windows 2000 installation CD with Service Pack 4.

NOTE	It is recommended that you go query the Microsoft TechNet website (http://technet.microsoft.com/en-us/default.aspx) for IIS vulnerabilities on a periodic basis. Also, you can always go to http://tools.cisco.com/security/center/home.x for a list of the latest (vendor-neutral) vulnerabilities.
	You can apply Microsoft-provided security policies to the Cisco Personal Assistant server; however, you should never apply any of these policies until the Cisco Personal Assistant installation is complete. Some security templates can affect the operation of the Cisco Personal Assistant.

The following are several general guidelines to use when you harden IIS on the Cisco Personal Assistant server:

- Always make sure that the most current cumulative update patches for IIS 5.0 are installed on the server.

- Always remove all IIS sample files, folders, and web applications. This is specified in the complete IIS 5.0 security checklist available on the Microsoft TechNet website.

- Refer to the recommendations described in the complete IIS 5.0 security checklist available on the Microsoft TechNet website to disable all default IIS COM objects. However, do not disable the File System Object (FSO) and Parent Paths. These are enabled by default and are needed for the operation of the Cisco Personal Assistant server.

- You can also use the Microsoft IIS Lockdown and URLScan tools. However, it is extremely important that you not disable support for Active Server Pages (.asp) or the Scripts Virtual directory. You can download these tools from the Microsoft TechNet website.

One of the requirements of the Cisco Personal Assistant is to have IE Version 6.0 with Service Pack 1. However, it is strongly recommended that you use IE on the server for the administration of the Cisco Personal Assistant only.

Microsoft recommends that you subscribe to the Security Notification Service; however, security experts advise against subscribing on the server. To subscribe to that service, drop IE security settings to a lower protection level.

Cisco Personal Assistant Server Security Policies

It is recommended that you change several security policies and server settings from their default values. It is also recommended that you enable auditing to track the way the Cisco Personal Assistant server is being accessed. The following values are recommended for the Audit Policies and User Rights Assignments under the Local Policies:

Step 1   Set **Audit account logon events** to **Failure**.

Step 2   Set **Audit account management** to **Success, failure**.

Step 3   Configure **Audit directory service access** to **Failure**.

Step 4   Set **Audit logon events** to **Failure**.

Step 5   Set **Audit object access** to **No auditing**.

Step 6   Leave **Audit policy change** at its default value (**Success, failure**).

Step 7   Set **Audit privilege use** to **Failure**.

Step 8   Leave **Audit system events** at its default value **No auditing**.

Step 9   Under **Access this computer from the network**, allow only **Backup operators, Power users, Users, Administrators, userservername\IWAM,** and **domainname\ISUR servername**. In other words, leave all default values except **Everyone**.

Step 10   Under **Shut down the system**, only allow **Backup operators and Administrators**.

The following is the recommended list of settings that you can modify by using the Windows Local Security Policy utility on the Cisco Personal Assistant server.

Step 1   Under **Additional restrictions for anonymous connections**, select **Do not allow enumeration of SAM accounts and shares**.

Step 2   Disable the **Allow system to be shut down without having to log on** option.

Step 3   Disable the **Audit use of Backup and Restore privilege** option.

Step 4   Disable the **Clear virtual memory pagefile when system shuts down** option.

Step 5   Under **Digitally sign client communication (always)**, select the default **Disabled** value.

Step 6   Enable the **Digitally sign client communication (when possible)** option.

Step 7   Disable the **Digitally sign server communication (always)** option.

Step 8   Enable the **Digitally sign server communication (when possible)** option.

Step 9   Disable **Ctrl-Alt-Del requirement for login**.

Step 10   Enable the **Do not display last user name in logon screen** option.

Step 11   Under the **LAN manager authentication level** option, select **Send NTLM response only**.

Step 12   Set **Number of previous logons to cache (in case domain controller is not available)** to **5** logons. This is strictly dependent on your security policy and your environment.

Step 13   Enable the **Prevent system maintenance of computer account password** option.

Step 14   Set the **Prompt user to change password before expiration** to **7** days instead of the 14 days default value. This is strictly dependent on your security policy and your environment; however, as a rule of thumb, 7 days is appropriate for most environments.

Step 15   Enable the **Restrict CD-ROM access to locally logged-on users only** option.

Step 16   Enable the **Restrict floppy access to locally logged-on users only** option.

Step 17   Enable the **Secure Channel: Digitally encrypt or sign secure channel data (always)** option.

Step 18   Enable the **Secure Channel: Require strong (Windows 2000 or later) session key** option.

Step 19   Disable the **Send unencrypted password to connect to third-party SMB [small and medium-sized business] servers** option.

Step 20   Set the **Smart card removal behavior** option to **Lock workstation**.

Step 21   Under **Unsigned driver installation behavior**, select the **Do not allow installation** option.

Step 22   Under **Unsigned non-driver installation behavior**, select the **Silently succeed / Warn but allow installation** option.

For any other Windows security–related information, see the Microsoft TechNet site.

Protecting Against Eavesdropping Attacks

Eavesdropping attacks are also known as *phone tapping attacks*. The main goal is for an attacker to listen, copy, or record a conversation. An example of an eavesdropping attack is an incident reported back in 2006. The phones of about 100 Greek politicians and offices (including the U.S. embassy in Athens and the Greek prime minister) were compromised by a malicious code embedded in Vodafone mobile phone software. The attackers tapped into their conference call system. Basically, by using several prepaid mobile phones, the attackers "joined the conference call" and recorded their conversations.

The Cisco ASA, Cisco PIX, and IOS Firewalls provide several features that support the stateful processing of signaling protocols, H.323, and SIP. These devices monitor the specific connection request and required resources and permit only what is specifically necessary for the operation of the system, thereby protecting against session hijacking and spoofing.

The Cisco ASA and Cisco PIX security appliances support H.323 inspection by making sure that only compliant transactions are allowed between IP telephony devices, such as Cisco CallManager and other non-Cisco products. Cisco ASA and Cisco PIX support H.323 Versions 3 and 4. They also support multiple calls on the same call signaling channel. Example 9-5 demonstrates how you can configure an H.323 inspection policy map on a Cisco ASA or Cisco PIX security appliance running Version 7.2 or later.

Example 9-5 *Dynamic Port-Security*

```
my_asa(config)# regex phone1 "5551234567"
my_asa(config)# regex phone2 "5553213212"
my_asa(config)# class-map type inspect h323 match-all voice-traffic
my_asa(config-pmap-c)# match called-party regex phone1
my_asa(config-pmap-c)# match calling-party regex phone2
my_asa(config)# policy-map type inspect h323 h323-policy-map
my_asa(config-pmap)# parameters
my_asa(config-pmap-p)# class voice_traffic
my_asa(config-pmap-p)# rtp-conformance enforce-payloadtype
my_asa(config-pmap-c)# drop
ciscoasa(config)# service-policy h323-policy-map interface inside
```

In Example 9-5, two regular expression entries are configured for two specific phone numbers (5551234567 and 5553213212). This is an optional step, but it gives you the flexibility to inspect traffic based on a specific caller or called party. A class map called **voice-traffic** is configured to inspect all traffic between the two previously defined phone numbers. The class map is applied to a policy map called **h323-policy-map**. All noncompliant traffic is dropped. The **rtp-conformance enforce-payloadtype** parameter is used to ensure that all transit RTP packets comply with protocol specifications. Finally, the policy map is applied to the inside interface using the **service-policy** command.

IPS and IDS devices can also be placed in strategic areas within the network to detect unusual traffic, such as an attempt to execute an unusual command, or a malformed packet indicating some form of protocol manipulation.

A good way to protect your voice traffic in untrusted environments is by the use of the voice- and video-enabled VPN (V3PN) solution. V3PN provides secure site-to-site connectivity to transport voice, video, and data. With V3PN, you can enable remote branch offices and teleworkers to use IP telephony services while reducing business operations costs.

NOTE   The following white paper includes detailed information about V3PN design and implementation:

http://www.cisco.com/application/pdf/en/us/guest/netsol/ns171/c649/ ccmigration_09186a008074f2d8.pdf

---

Media encryption using Secure Real-Time Transport Protocol (SRTP) delivers protection by encrypting the voice conversation, rendering it unintelligible to internal or external eavesdroppers who have gained access to the voice domain. Designed for voice packets, SRTP supports the AES encryption algorithm and is an Internet Engineering Task Force (IETF) RFC 3711 standard. Media encryption on Cisco access routers works with both Cisco CallManager and the media encryption feature on Cisco IP phones, enabling customers to place secure analog phone or fax calls between an IP phone and the PSTN gateway depending on the gateway interface type. The SRTP-encrypted voice packets are almost indistinguishable from RTP voice packets, allowing features like QoS and compression to be implemented without additional development or manipulation. Voice encryption keys derived by Cisco Unified CallManager are securely sent by encrypted signaling path to Cisco Unified IP phones through the use of Transport Layer Security (TLS) and to gateways over IPsec-protected links.

Summary

IP telephony solutions are being deployed at a fast rate in many organizations. The cost savings introduced with VoIP are significant. On the other hand, these benefits can be heavily impacted if you do not have the appropriate security mechanisms in place. This chapter covers several best practices for securing IP telephony networks. It discusses how to protect voice-enabled networks by protecting infrastructure components. It also covered how to secure different IP telephony components, such as the Cisco Unified CallManager, Cisco Unified CME, Cisco Unity, Cisco Unity Express, and Cisco Unified Personal Assistant. Finally, it covered several mechanisms that are used to combat voice eavesdropping and other attacks.

This chapter covers the following topics:

- Protecting the Data Center Against Denial of Service (DoS) Attacks and Worms
- Data Center Segmentation and Tiered Access Control
- Deploying Network Intrusion Detection and Prevention Systems
- Deploying the Cisco Security Agent (CSA) in the Data Center

CHAPTER 10

Data Center Security

Data centers comprise some of the most critical assets within any organization. Typically, applications, databases, and management servers reside in the data center. For this reason, it is extremely important to have the appropriate defense mechanisms in place to protect the data center against security threats. Attacks against data center assets can result in lost business applications and the theft of confidential information. This chapter covers several best practices and recommendations used to increase the security of your data center. These topics include protecting against denial of service (DoS) attacks, worms, information theft, and other security threats. The recommendations in earlier chapters are put into action in this chapter to provide an in-depth defense mechanism against existing and new threats.

Protecting the Data Center Against Denial of Service (DoS) Attacks and Worms

You can implement different mechanisms and technologies on infrastructure components to help mitigate the effects of DoS and worms on your network. The following are some examples:

- SYN cookies in firewalls and load balancers
- Intrusion Prevention Systems (IPSs) and Intrusion Detection Systems (IDSs)
- Cisco NetFlow in the data center
- Cisco Guard
- Data center infrastructure protection

SYN Cookies in Firewalls and Load Balancers

A commonly used distributed denial of service (DDoS) attack is known as *SYN-flooding*. In this type of attack, the attacker sends a series of TCP SYN packets that typically originate from spoofed IP addresses. The constant flood of SYN packets can prevent servers within the data center from handling legitimate connection requests. You can use firewalls and security appliances such as the Cisco ASA and the Cisco PIX enabled with the SYN cookies algorithm to combat SYN flood attacks. In large data centers, the Cisco Firewall Services Module (FWSM), for the Catalyst 6500 series switches, is typically used for this same purpose. Figure 10-1 demonstrates how TCP synchronization message (SYN) cookies work in the Cisco Adaptive Security Appliance (ASA), the Cisco PIX, and the FWSM for the Cisco Catalyst 6500 switches. In this example, a Cisco FWSM is used.

Figure 10-1 *SYN Cookies in FWSM*

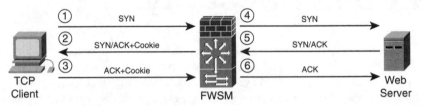

The following steps are illustrated in Figure 10-1:

1 A client machine attempts a TCP connection to a web server behind the FWSM and sends the initial SYN packet to the firewall.

2 When the embryonic (half-open) connection limit is reached, the Cisco ASA, Cisco PIX, or Cisco FWSM can act as a proxy for the server and generate a SYN-ACK response to the client SYN request. The SYN-ACK reply has a "cookie" in the sequence (SEQ) field of the TCP header. The cookie is a message digest 5 algorithm (MD5) authentication of the source and destination IP addresses and port numbers. All the connection requests are rebuilt from these cookies.

3 The acknowledgement (ACK) packet SEQ field has the value of the cookie+1. In this case, when the FWSM receives an ACK from the client, it "authenticates" the client and allows the connection to the server.

4 The FWSM sends its own SYN packet to the server.

5 The server replies with an ACK.

6 The FWSM sends its SYN-ACK to the server, and the connection is built.

On the Cisco FWSM, you can use the **show np** command to view SYN cookie statistics. Example 10-1 shows the output of the **show np 2 syn** command on an FWSM.

Example 10-1 *Output of* **show np 2 syn** *Command*

```
FWSM# show np 2 syn
------------------------------------------------------------------
            Fast Path Syn Cookie Statistics Counters (NP-2)
------------------------------------------------------------------
SYN_COOKIE: Syn cookie secret wheel index              : 16
SYN_COOKIE: Total number of SYNs intercepted           : 231356987
SYN_COOKIE: Total number of ACKs intercepted           : 204
SYN_COOKIE: Total number of ACKs dropped after lookup  : 0
```

Example 10-1 *Output of* **show np 2 syn** *Command (Continued)*

```
SYN_COOKIE: Total number of ACKs successfully validated        : 193
SYN_COOKIE: Total number of ACKs Dropped: Secret Expired        : 11
SYN_COOKIE: Total number of ACKs Dropped: Invalid Sequence      : 0
SYN_COOKIE: Total number of Syn Cookie Entries inserted by NP3  : 12
SYN_COOKIE: ACKs dropped: Syn cookie ses not yet established     : 0
SYN_COOKIE: Leaf allocation failed                              : 0
SYN_COOKIE: Leaf insertion failed                               : 2088
```

In the highlighted line in Example 10-1, you can see that the total number of intercepted SYN packets is 231356987. This is most definitely indicative of a SYN flood.

Load-balancing solutions such as the Cisco Content Switching Module (CSM) also support SYN cookies. You can deploy the CSM in inline mode or one-arm mode. Figure 10-2 illustrates a CSM configured in inline mode. Traffic from certain applications cannot be load-balanced because of the nature of those applications. In Figure 10-2, the traffic that cannot be load-balanced is labeled as direct traffic.

Figure 10-2 *CSM in Inline Mode*

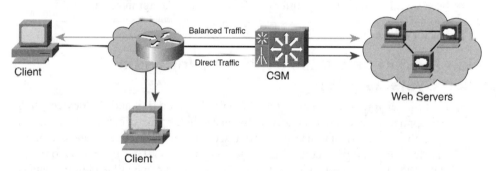

In Figure 10-2, the CSM is configured with both physical interfaces that are connected to the network with all traffic passing through the CSM. Figure 10-3 illustrates the one-arm CSM design.

The CSM uses a virtual IP address. In a "one-arm" design, you can combine it with a Cisco FWSM. One of the major benefits of using a CSM one-arm design in combination with the Cisco FWSM is that the CSM protects against DoS attacks directed at its virtual IP address, and the Cisco FWSM protects against attacks directed at non-load-balanced servers.

The use of SYN cookies has certain limitations. For example, SYN cookies cannot carry TCP options that are set up in SYN packets; SYN cookies can carry only an encoding of the maximum segment size (MSS) value of the server. Some TCP options are used for performance and scalability (for example, large windows, selective acknowledgement, and so on). Another limitation of SYN cookies is that they do not protect against established connection attacks.

Figure 10-3 *CSM in One-Arm Mode*

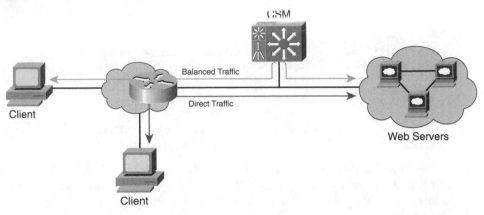

NOTE   Established connection attacks are attacks that exploit vulnerabilities after a connection has been established such as a buffer overflow to a specific application.

Intrusion Prevention Systems (IPS) and Intrusion Detection Systems (IDS)

In earlier chapters, you learned the difference between IDS and IPS devices. IDS and IPS appliances and modules are usually placed in the data center distribution center not only to alert an administrator when a security threat has been detected, but also to take action and protect the data center assets. In small environments, one or more IDS/IPS appliances (such as the Cisco 4200 sensors) can be placed in the data center. The Cisco Catalyst 6500 IDS/IPS module (IDSM) is used in larger environments.

The Cisco Security Agent (CSA) provides host-based prevention services that help you protect the servers in the data center from attacks that exploit OS and application vulnerabilities. These two technology solutions (network and host-based) complement each other. Despite the fact that both solutions provide intrusion prevention mechanisms that guard against direct attacks, the technologies are different in numerous ways. Later sections in this chapter cover the deployment of both network and host-based IPS solutions. The benefits and limitations of each solution are discussed in their respective sections.

Cisco NetFlow in the Data Center

Cisco NetFlow provides network traffic visibility that can help in identifying and classifying potential DDoS attempts and other security threats. In addition, it provides valuable information about application usage that can be beneficial for network planning and traffic engineering. You can enable NetFlow in data center infrastructure devices, such as your distribution switches or routers. A new version of NetFlow called *Flexible* NetFlow is now available on Cisco IOS routers starting with IOS Version 12.4(9)T. Cisco is working to provide this functionality in other platforms such as the Catalyst 6500 series switches.

NOTE   You can use the Cisco Feature Navigator tool to find information about platform support. To access this tool, go to http://tools.cisco.com/ITDIT/CFN/jsp/index.jsp.

With Flexible NetFlow, you can configure a range of parameters for traffic analysis and data export on a networking device. For instance, you can define your own records by specifying the key and nonkey fields to customize the data collection to your specific requirements. In previous versions of NetFlow, a flow was based on a set of seven IP packet attributes:

- Source IP
- Destination IP
- Source port
- Destination port
- Layer 3 Protocol
- Type of Service (ToS) byte
- Input interface

Flexible NetFlow adds the ability to check other information, such as the number of bytes and packets in a flow. You can also create custom records for functions like quality of service (QoS), bandwidth monitoring, application and end user traffic profiling, and security monitoring.

The main limitation is that, currently, Flexible NetFlow is not supported in the Cisco Catalyst 6500. In most cases, it is recommended that you enable NetFlow at the data center distribution switches. In large data centers, Cisco Catalyst 6500 switches are used as distribution switches. However, the benefits of NetFlow Versions 5 and 9 are still extremely valuable, because NetFlow is one of the most helpful tools for identifying and classifying security threats. In addition, you can use network monitoring tools such as the Cisco Security Monitoring, Analysis, and Response System (CS-MARS) to analyze NetFlow and other telemetry data from many different network devices.

Cisco Guard

The Cisco Detector and Cisco Guard provide anomaly detection and attack mitigation features. You can place them in large data centers to divert traffic directed at the target host for analysis and filtering, so that legitimate transactions can still be processed while illegitimate traffic is dropped. On the other hand, in most cases small, medium, and large enterprises place their Cisco Guard at their Internet edge or subscribe to managed services provided by service providers.

NOTE   The managed service solution is called Clean Pipes. Cisco has detailed information about the Clean Pipes solution at http://www.cisco.com/en/US/netsol/ns615/ networking_solutions_sub_solution.html.

Data Center Infrastructure Protection

The infrastructure protection best practices that you learned in Chapter 2, "Preparation Phase," also apply in the data center. For example, you should harden control protocols as a basic security precaution on all applicable devices in the data center. In addition, you should disable unnecessary services on infrastructure components and implement device protection mechanisms, such as infrastructure access control lists (iACLs) and Control Plane Policing (CoPP). These device protection mechanisms will help you greatly in case of worm outbreaks, DDoS, or even in case of an anomaly other than a security threat (that is, a misconfigured application).

TIP   Remember to implement basic best-practice recommendations such as hardening device authentication, hardening Simple Network Management Protocol (SNMP), using Network Time Protocol (NTP), and all others that you learned in Chapter 2.

You can also develop configuration templates for data center access switch ports where servers reside. Basic Layer 2 security mechanisms, such as limits on the number of MAC addresses that the server can originate on a port, can be included in the configuration template. You can also disable the Cisco Discovery Protocol (CDP) when it is not needed; be careful, however, because certain applications use CDP for legitimate transactions. Example 10-2 shows a basic template.

Example 10-2 *Data Center Access Switch Port Template*

```
interface GigabitEthernet2/4
 no ip address
 switchport
 switchport access vlan 100
```

Example 10-2 *Data Center Access Switch Port Template (Continued)*

```
switchport mode access
spanning-tree portfast
switchport port-security maximum 2
switchport port-security violation shutdown
spanning-tree bpduguard enable
no cdp enable
```

The highlighted commands in Example 10-2 enable port security and BPDU guard and disable CDP.

NOTE   An important point about port security is that it does not interoperate well with virtual servers because they may carry multiple MAC addresses of virtual hosts. You should also be careful when implementing port security with certain server failover mechanisms. In some environments, servers with multiple network interface cards (NIC) may share the same MAC address between interfaces when a failover occurs.

For antispoofing protection, you can also enable Unicast Reverse Path Forwarding (Unicast RPF) in routers, security appliances such as the Cisco ASA, or in the Cisco FWSM. In the data center, it is most common to deploy Unicast RPF on the firewalls (Cisco ASA or FWSM). With Unicast RPF, if traffic enters the outside or untrusted interface from an address that is known to the routing table, but it resides on the inside interface, the firewall drops the packet. Similarly, if traffic enters the inside interface from an unknown source address, the firewall drops the packet to prevent spoofed attacks. You can enable Unicast RPF on the Cisco ASA, Cisco PIX, or Cisco FWSM with the **ip verify reverse-path** command, as shown in the following example:

```
FWSM(config)#ip verify reverse-path interface outside
FWSM(config)#ip verify reverse-path interface inside
```

In the previous example, Unicast RPF is enabled in the outside and inside interfaces. Because firewalls require traffic path symmetry, in most cases, Unicast RPF can provide great benefits without impacting traffic flow.

Data Center Segmentation and Tiered Access Control

By isolating different types of servers and services, you can use segmentation and tiered access control in your data center to provide a multilayered architecture while adding security. The easiest way to segment your data center is to configure different Layer 2 domains or VLANs. In addition, you can use firewalls for policy enforcement between each segment. By using private VLANs, you can also use segmentation that is local to the VLAN. This helps in preventing a compromised or infected server from affecting adjacent systems. In a multitier architecture, you separate systems based on the different functions they handle. For example, you can separate the presentation, business logic, and database layers, as illustrated in Figure 10-4.

Figure 10-4 *Multitier Server Segmentation Example*

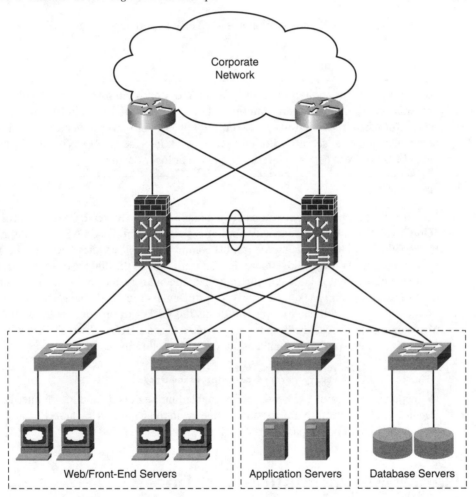

In Figure 10-4, a web server farm is separated from the application and the database servers. This is done to protect the application and the database in case the web servers are compromised.

You can also segment the data center by separating other types of application servers and devices. It is a best practice to separate all your management servers. For example, your management segment can include your TACACS+, RADIUS, SNMP, and any configuration management servers such as CiscoWorks, Cisco Security Manager, CS-MARS, and others.

Figure 10-5 shows how management servers can also be separated from the rest of the data center.

Figure 10-5 *Management Servers Segmented*

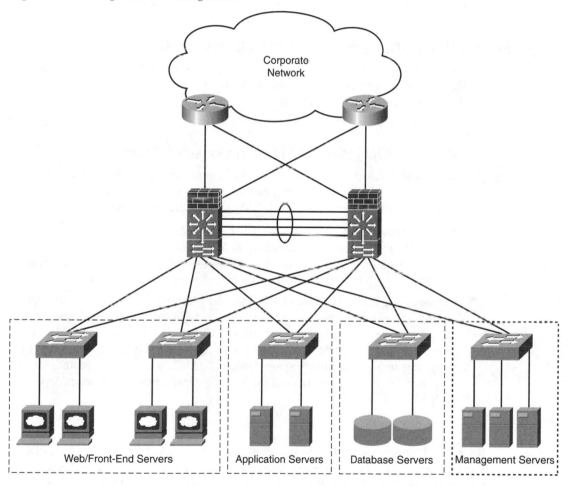

As previously mentioned, you can segment your data center simply by configuring separate VLANs; however, this does not truly provide a complete solution that allows you to enforce your security policies between each boundary. Therefore, you can configure firewalls to provide additional security while allowing the necessary traffic to pass between segments.

NOTE You can also segment your data center by configuring Virtual Routing and Forwarding (VRF) interfaces with Multiprotocol Label Switching (MPLS) or by using VRF-Lite. This is more suitable for large environments and requires your staff to be familiar with more advanced routing features such as MPLS. The next section explains how to achieve segmentation using separate VLANs and the Cisco FWSM for policy enforcement and additional protection.

Segmenting the Data Center with the Cisco FWSM

In this section, you will learn how to take advantage of some of the Cisco FWSM features to segment your data center. It covers the modes of operation of the FWSM, design considerations, and configuration steps.

Cisco FWSM Modes of Operation and Design Considerations

You can use the Cisco FWSM not only to segment your data center, but also to enforce policy and to provide additional security benefits such as stateful and deep packet inspection. You can configure the Cisco FWSM in two different modes:

- **Routed mode:** The default behavior. The Cisco FWSM in routed mode acts as a Layer 3 device supporting features such as Network Address Translation (NAT) and routing protocols. In most cases, when a Cisco FWSM is deployed in routed mode in the data center, it becomes the default gateway for a majority of the servers.

- **Transparent mode:** The Cisco FWSM acts as a Layer 2 device. One of the major benefits of transparent mode is that you do not have to worry about readdressing your infrastructure when deploying a new firewall within your data center, because the firewall acts as a bridge between the external and internal network. On the other hand, when you are operating in transparent mode, the FWSM does not support features such as NAT routing protocols and some specific inspections engines that depend on NAT.

NOTE   Routed and transparent modes are also supported in the Cisco ASA and the Cisco PIX security appliances. In smaller environments, you can deploy the Cisco ASA at the data center. The configuration is identical except that the Cisco FWSM runs in the Catalyst 6500 series switches or in the Cisco 7600 series routers; therefore, specific configuration steps are needed in the switch or the router. This subject is covered later in this section.

Figure 10-6 shows a Cisco FWSM configured in transparent mode.

Figure 10-6 *Cisco FWSM in Transparent Mode*

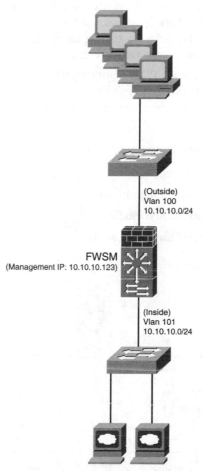

In Figure 10-6, the Cisco FWSM outside interface resides on VLAN 100, and the inside interface resides on VLAN 101. Both interfaces belong to the same network subnet (10.10.10.0/24). The Cisco FWSM must have a management IP address configured for traffic to pass through it when configured in transparent mode. In this example, the management IP address is 10.10.10.123.

You can take advantage of the virtualization capabilities of the Cisco FWSM to segment your data center. You can partition the Cisco FWSM into multiple virtual firewalls, known as *security contexts*. Each of these virtual firewalls has its own configuration enforcing separate security policies to each segment in the data center.

NOTE	When you have multiple virtual security contexts configured, it is similar to having multiple standalone firewalls. Many features are supported when you configure the Cisco FWSM with multiple contexts, including routing tables, firewall features, and management. However, certain features are not supported, including dynamic routing protocols.
	The Cisco ASA and Cisco PIX security appliances also support virtual firewalls. Their behavior is similar to the Cisco FWSM.

Figure 10-7 illustrates the four modes of operations of the Cisco FWSM:

- Single context routed mode
- Single context transparent mode
- Multiple context routed mode
- Multiple context transparent mode

Figure 10-7 *Cisco FWSM Modes of Operation*

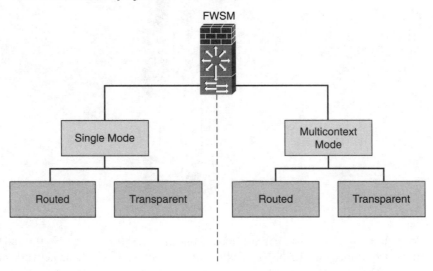

Figure 10-8 shows a Cisco FWSM configured with three different contexts. Each context includes its own configuration to protect each data center segment.

Figure 10-8 *Cisco FWSM Contexts*

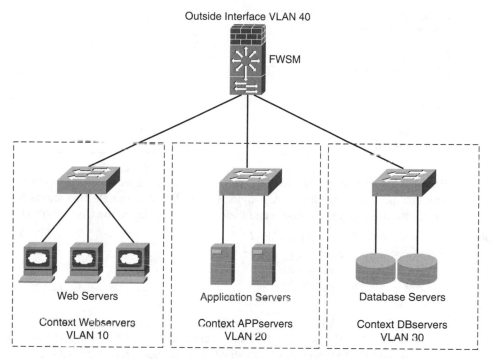

In Figure 10-8, the Cisco FWSM contexts separate the web servers, applications servers, and database servers. The following are the context names:

- Webservers
- APPservers
- DBservers

The inside interface of context Webservers resides in VLAN 10. The inside interface of context APPservers is in VLAN 20, and the context DBserver inside interface is in VLAN 30.

Configuring the Cisco Catalyst Switch

In the Cisco Catalyst switch, you must create the necessary VLANs and assign those to the Cisco FWSM. Example 10-3 shows the commands used to create VLANs 10, 20, 30, and 40 in the Cisco Catalyst 6500 switch.

Example 10-3 *Creating the VLANs in the Switch*

```
vlan 10
name webservers
!
vlan 20
name appservers
!
vlan 30
name dbservers
!
vlan 40
name tocorpnetwork
```

Each VLAN entry is configured with a descriptive name based on the data center segment. You then have to assign the VLANs to the Cisco FWSM. Example 10-4 shows how you can create firewall VLAN groups and then assign the group to the Cisco FWSM.

Example 10-4 *Assigning the VLANs to the Cisco FWSM*

```
firewall multiple-vlan-interfaces
firewall module 2 vlan-group 1
firewall vlan-group 1 10,20,30,40
```

In Example 10-4, a VLAN group with ID of 1 is configured. This VLAN group includes VLANs 10, 20, 30, and 40 and is applied to the Cisco FWSM with the **firewall module 2 vlan-group 1** command. The number 2 indicates that the Cisco FWSM resides on the second slot in the Cisco Catalyst 6500 switch.

TIP For security reasons, by default, only one switch virtual interface (SVI) can exist between the switch and the Cisco FWSM. You might also choose to use multiple SVIs in routed mode so that you do not have to share a single VLAN for the outside interface. You can use the **firewall multiple-vlan-interfaces** command to allow you to add more than one SVI to the Cisco FWSM. In this example, the outside interfaces of each context reside on VLAN 40.

Creating Security Contexts in the Cisco FWSM

When you configure the Cisco FWSM in multiple context modes, you add and manage all security contexts in the system space or system configuration mode. By default, a context named *admin* is created. The admin context is just like any other context, except that when a user logs into the admin context, that user has system administrator rights and can access the system and all other contexts. The admin context is not restricted in any way and can be used as a regular context. However, because logging into the admin context grants you administrator privileges over all contexts, you might need to restrict access to the admin context for appropriate users.

TIP   The admin context configuration must reside on flash memory and not on a remote system. If your system is already in multiple context mode, or if you convert from single mode, the admin context is created automatically as a file on the internal flash memory called "admin.cfg." This context is named "admin." If you do not want to use admin.cfg as the admin context, you can change the admin context.

Because the default mode in the Cisco FWSM is single routed mode, to start creating security context, you need to change the FWSM to multiple mode. You can use the **mode multiple** command from configuration mode to enable multiple mode, as shown here:

```
FWSM(config)# mode multiple
```

NOTE   After you enter the **mode multiple** command, you are prompted to reboot the Cisco FWSM.

Example 10-5 shows the context configuration on the Cisco FWSM that was pictured in the previous example.

Example 10-5 *Creating the Security Contexts*

```
context webservers
  description Webserver segment
  allocate-interface vlan40 int1
  allocate-interface vlan10 int2
  config-url disk:/webservers.cfg
!
context appservers
  description Application server segment
  allocate-interface vlan50 int1
  allocate-interface vlan20 int2
  config-url disk:/appservers.cfg
!
context dbservers
  description Database servers segment
  allocate-interface vlan60 int1
  allocate-interface vlan30 int2
  config-url disk:/dbservers.cfg
```

The contexts webservers, appservers, and dbservers are defined in Example 10-5. Each security context or virtual firewall has two interfaces.

In this example, the configuration of each security context is stored locally and not on an external server. After the contexts have been created, you can change to any of them by using the **changeto context** command, as shown here:

```
FWSM(config)# changeto context webservers
FWSM/webservers(config)#
```

Notice that the prompt changes with the hostname followed by the context name you are currently configuring.

Configuring the Interfaces on Each Security Context

The interface identifiers on each security context that were previously created were int1 for the outside interface and int 2 for the inside interface. Figure 10-9 shows the IP address configuration of the interfaces on each security context (virtual firewall).

Figure 10-9 *IP Address Configuration on Each Virtual Firewall*

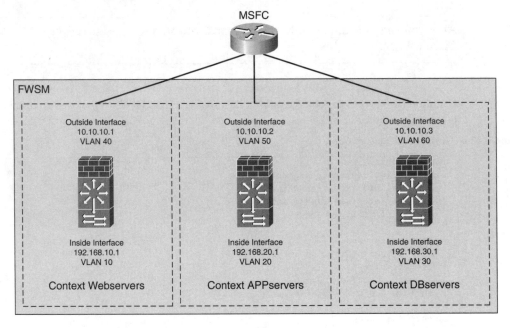

Example 10-6 shows the configuration of the interfaces on the Webservers security context.

Example 10-6 *webservers Security Context IP Address Configuration*

```
interface int1
 nameif outside
 security-level 0
 ip address 10.10.10.1 255.255.255.0
!
interface int2
 nameif inside
 security-level 100
 ip address 192.168.10.1 255.255.255.0
```

Example 10-7 shows the configuration of the interfaces on the APPservers security context.

Example 10-7 *appservers Security Context IP Address Configuration*

```
interface int1
 nameif outside
 security-level 0
 ip address 10.10.10.2 255.255.255.0
!
interface int2
 nameif inside
 security-level 100
 ip address 192.168.20.1 255.255.255.0
```

Example 10-8 shows the configuration of the interfaces on the DBservers security context.

Example 10-8 *dbservers Security Context IP Address Configuration*

```
interface int1
 nameif outside
 security-level 0
 ip address 10.10.10.3 255.255.255.0
!
interface int2
 nameif inside
 security-level 100
 ip address 192.168.30.1 255.255.255.0
```

Configuring Network Address Translation

The goal is to configure static NAT for each server residing on each security context. Three systems reside in the web server segment (context webservers). This is illustrated in Figure 10-10.

Figure 10-10 *webserver IP Address Configuration*

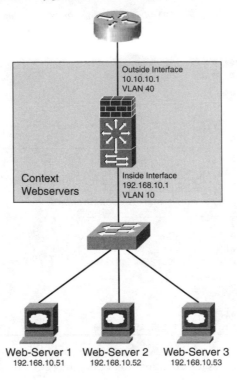

Table 10-1 lists the physical IP addresses of each web server with the statically translated address.

Table 10-1 *Web Servers NAT Mapping*

Web Server Name	Translated IP Address	Physical IP Address
Web-Server 1	10.10.10.51	192.168.10.51
Web-Server 2	10.10.10.52	192.168.10.52
Web-Server 3	10.10.10.53	192.168.10.53

Example 10-9 shows the static NAT configuration for each server on the webservers security context.

Example 10-9 *webservers Context NAT Configuration*

```
static (inside,outside) 10.10.10.51 192.168.10.51 netmask 255.255.255.255
static (inside,outside) 10.10.10.52 192.168.10.52 netmask 255.255.255.255
static (inside,outside) 10.10.10.53 192.168.10.53 netmask 255.255.255.255
```

Two application servers are in the data center as illustrated in Figure 10-11. They are protected by the virtual firewall (context) called APPservers.

Figure 10-11 *Application Servers IP Address Configuration*

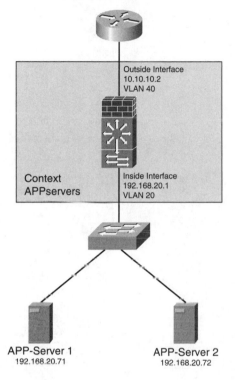

Table 10-2 lists the physical IP addresses of each application server along with the statically translated address.

Table 10-2 *Application Servers NAT Mapping*

Server Name	Translated IP Address	Physical IP Address
APP-Server 1	10.10.20.71	192.168.20.71
APP-Server 2	10.10.20.72	192.168.20.72

Example 10-10 shows the static NAT configuration for each server on the appservers security context.

Example 10-10 *appservers Context NAT Configuration*

```
static (inside,outside) 10.10.20.71 192.168.20.71 netmask 255.255.255.255
static (inside,outside) 10.10.20.72 192.168.20.72 netmask 255.255.255.255
```

The data center has two database servers, as illustrated in Figure 10-12. They are protected by the virtual firewall (context) called DBservers.

Figure 10-12 *Database Servers IP Address Configuration*

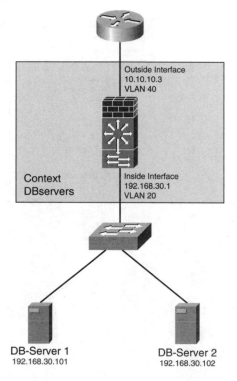

Outside Interface
10.10.10.3
VLAN 40

Context
DBservers

Inside Interface
192.168.30.1
VLAN 20

DB-Server 1
192.168.30.101

DB-Server 2
192.168.30.102

Table 10-3 lists the physical IP addresses of each application server along with the statically translated address.

Table 10-3 *Database Servers NAT Mapping*

Server Name	Translated IP Address	Physical IP Address
DB-Server 1	10.10.30.101	192.168.30.101
DB-Server 2	10.10.30.102	192.168.30.102

Example 10-11 shows the static NAT configuration for each server on the DBservers security context.

Example 10-11 *dbservers Context NAT Configuration*

```
static (inside,outside) 10.10.30.101 192.168.30.101 netmask 255.255.255.255
static (inside,outside) 10.10.30.102 192.168.30.102 netmask 255.255.255.255
```

Controlling Access with ACLs

It is recommended that you configure ACLs on both interfaces of each security context for more granular security policy enforcement. You can tune the ACLs based on your security policies and application usage. The ACLs that are configured on each of the security contexts in this example only allow the necessary traffic for each server and application.

Table 10-4 lists the protocols and ports that need to be allowed on the webservers security context.

Table 10-4 *Protocols and Ports Used by the webservers*

Usage/Application	Protocol or Port	Allowed by ACL
HTTP	TCP 80	inbound-traffic
HTTPS	TCP 443	inbound-traffic
SSH[1]/SCP[2]	TCP 22	inbound-traffic
Mgmt-App	TCP 890	inbound-traffic
App-X	TCP 987	outbound-traffic
DNS[3]	UDP[4] 53	outbound-traffic
SYSLOG	UDP 514	outbound-traffic

1 SSH = Secure Shell

2 SCP = Secure Copy Protocol

3 DNS = Domain Name System

4 UDP = User Datagram Protocol

Users connect to the web servers via HTTP and HTTPS; therefore, this traffic is allowed on the outside interface in the webservers context. The web servers are Linux-based machines. The administrator transfers files over SCP and connects to the server command-line interface (CLI) via SSH. In addition, the administrator uses a custom management application to install software and patches on the systems (Mgmt-App). This traffic from the management network (10.10.100.0/24) needs to be allowed.

The web servers themselves need to access an application called App-X running on the servers in the APPservers context over TCP port 987. DNS resolution and SYSLOG must also be allowed to external servers. Example 10-12 shows the ACLs configured in the Webservers context allowing the previously mentioned ports and protocols.

Example 10-12 *webservers Context ACL Configuration*

```
access-list inbound-traffic remark INBOUND TRAFFIC TO WEBSERVERS
access-list inbound-traffic extended permit tcp any host 10.10.10.51 eq www
access-list inbound-traffic extended permit tcp any host 10.10.10.51 eq https
```
continues

Example 10-12 *webservers Context ACL Configuration (Continued)*

```
access-list inbound-traffic extended permit tcp 10.10.100.0 255.255.255.0 host
    10.10.10.51 eq ssh
access-list inbound-traffic extended permit tcp 10.10.100.0 255.255.255.0 host
    10.10.10.51 eq 890
access-list inbound-traffic extended permit tcp any host 10.10.10.52 eq www
access-list inbound-traffic extended permit tcp any host 10.10.10.52 eq https
access-list inbound-traffic extended permit tcp 10.10.100.0 255.255.255.0 host
    10.10.10.52 eq ssh
access-list inbound-traffic extended permit tcp 10.10.100.0 255.255.255.0 host
    10.10.10.52 eq 890
access-list inbound-traffic extended permit tcp any host 10.10.10.53 eq www
access-list inbound-traffic extended permit tcp any host 10.10.10.53 eq https
access-list inbound-traffic extended permit tcp 10.10.100.0 255.255.255.0 host
    10.10.10.53 eq ssh
access-list inbound-traffic extended permit tcp 10.10.100.0 255.255.255.0 host
    10.10.10.53 eq 890
access-group inbound-traffic in interface outside
!
access-list outbound-traffic remark OUTBOUND TRAFFIC FROM WEBSERVERS
access-list outbound-traffic extended permit tcp  host 192.168.10.51 host
    10.10.20.71 eq 987
access-list outbound-traffic extended permit tcp  host 192.168.10.51 host
    10.10.20.72 eq 987
access-list outbound-traffic extended permit udp  host 192.168.10.51 host
    10.10.111.11 eq 53
access-list outbound-traffic extended permit udp  host 192.168.10.51 host
    10.10.111.12 eq 53
access-list outbound-traffic extended permit udp  host 192.168.10.51 host
    10.10.100.100 eq 514
access-list outbound-traffic extended permit tcp  host 192.168.10.52 host
    10.10.20.71 eq 987
access-list outbound-traffic extended permit tcp  host 192.168.10.52 host
    10.10.20.72 eq 987
access-list outbound-traffic extended permit udp  host 192.168.10.52 host
    10.10.111.11 eq 53
access-list outbound-traffic extended permit udp  host 192.168.10.52 host
    10.10.111.12 eq 53
access-list outbound-traffic extended permit udp  host 192.168.10.52 host
    10.10.100.100 eq 514

access-list outbound-traffic extended permit tcp  host 192.168.10.53 host
    10.10.20.71 eq 987
access-list outbound-traffic extended permit tcp  host 192.168.10.53 host
    10.10.20.72 eq 987
access-list outbound-traffic extended permit udp  host 192.168.10.53 host
    10.10.111.11 eq 53
access-list outbound-traffic extended permit udp  host 192.168.10.53 host
    10.10.111.12 eq 53
access-list outbound-traffic extended permit udp  host 192.168.10.53 host
    10.10.100.100 eq 514
access-group outbound-traffic in interface inside
```

In Example 10-12, ACLs are configured to allow the traffic specified in Table 10-4. The ACL named **inbound-traffic** is applied to the outside interface, and the ACL named

outbound-traffic is applied to the inside interface. Notice that the web server IP addresses in the **inbound-traffic** ACL are the translated addresses. However, because the **outbound-traffic** ACL is applied to the inside interface, the physical IP addresses are used as the source. The web servers must access two DNS servers. The primary DNS server is 10.10.111.11, and the secondary is 10.10.111.12. The IP address of the SYSLOG server is 10.10.100.100.

Table 10-5 lists the necessary protocols and ports that need to be allowed on the appservers security context.

Table 10-5 *Protocols and Ports Used by the appservers*

Usage/Application	Protocol and/or port	Allowed by ACL
App-X	TCP 987	inbound-traffic
SSH/SCP	TCP 22	inbound-traffic
Mgmt-App	TCP 890	inbound-traffic
MySQL	TCP 3306	outbound-traffic
DNS	UDP 53	outbound-traffic
SYSLOG	UDP 514	outbound-traffic

The web servers communicate with the application (App-X) running on the servers in the APPservers context over TCP port 987. Similar to the web servers, the administrator transfers files over SCP and connects to the server CLI via SSH. In addition, the administrator uses a custom management application to install software and patches on the systems (Mgmt-App). This management traffic from the management network (10.10.100.0/24) needs to be allowed. The application servers connect to the database servers running MySQL over TCP port 3306. DNS resolution and SYSLOG must also be allowed to external servers.

Example 10-13 shows the ACLs configured in the appservers context allowing the ports and protocols listed in Table 10-6.

Example 10-13 *appservers Context ACL Configuration*

```
access-list inbound-traffic remark INBOUND TRAFFIC TO APPSERVERS
access-list inbound-traffic extended permit tcp host 10.10.10.51 host 10.10.20.71
  eq 987
access-list inbound-traffic extended permit tcp host 10.10.10.52 host 10.10.20.71
  eq 987
access-list inbound-traffic extended permit tcp host 10.10.10.53 host 10.10.20.71
  eq 987
access-list inbound-traffic extended permit tcp host 10.10.10.51 host 10.10.20.72
  eq 987
access-list inbound-traffic extended permit tcp host 10.10.10.52 host 10.10.20.72
  eq 987
access-list inbound-traffic extended permit tcp host 10.10.10.53 host 10.10.20.72
  eq 987
```

continues

Example 10-13 *appservers Context ACL Configuration (Continued)*

```
access-list inbound-traffic extended permit tcp 10.10.100.0 255.255.255.0 host
   10.10.20.71 eq 22
access-list inbound-traffic extended permit tcp 10.10.100.0 255.255.255.0 host
   10.10.20.72 eq 22
access-list inbound-traffic extended permit tcp 10.10.100.0 255.255.255.0 host
   10.10.20.71 eq 890
access-list inbound-traffic extended permit tcp 10.10.100.0 255.255.255.0 host
   10.10.20.72 eq 890
access-group inbound-traffic in interface outside
!
access-list outbound-traffic remark OUTBOUND TRAFFIC FROM APPSERVERS
access-list outbound-traffic extended permit tcp  host 192.168.20.71 host
   10.10.30.101 eq 3306
access-list outbound-traffic extended permit tcp  host 192.168.20.72 host
   10.10.30.101 eq 3306
access-list outbound-traffic extended permit tcp  host 192.168.20.71 host
   10.10.30.102 eq 3306
access-list outbound-traffic extended permit tcp  host 192.168.20.72 host
   10.10.30.102 eq 3306
access-list outbound-traffic extended permit udp  host 192.168.20.71 host
   10.10.111.11 eq 53
access-list outbound-traffic extended permit udp  host 192.168.20.72 host
   10.10.111.11 eq 53
access-list outbound-traffic extended permit udp  host 192.168.20.71 host
   10.10.111.12 eq 53
access-list outbound-traffic extended permit udp  host 192.168.20.72 host
   10.10.111.12 eq 53
access-list outbound-traffic extended permit tcp  host 192.168.20.71 host
   10.10.100.100 eq 514
access-list outbound-traffic extended permit tcp  host 192.168.20.72 host
   10.10.100.100 eq 514
access-group outbound-traffic in interface inside
```

In Example 10-13, ACLs are configured to allow the traffic specified in Table 10-5. The ACL named **inbound-traffic** is applied to the outside interface, and the ACL named **outbound-traffic** is applied to the inside interface.

Table 10-6 lists the necessary protocols and ports that need to be allowed on the DBservers security context.

Table 10-6 *Protocols and Ports Used by the dbservers*

Usage/Application	Protocol and/or port	Allowed by ACL
MySQL	TCP 3306	inbound-traffic
SSH)/SCP	TCP 22	inbound-traffic
Mgmt-App	TCP 890	inbound-traffic
DNS	UDP 53	outbound-traffic
SYSLOG	UDP 514	outbound-traffic

The application servers communicate with the MySQL database running on the servers in the DBservers context over TCP port 3306. Linux-based servers also exist, and the administrator transfers files over SCP and connects to the server CLI via SSH. As with the other servers, the administrator uses the custom management application to install software and patches on the systems (Mgmt-App). This management traffic from the management network (10.10.100.0/24) needs to be allowed. DNS resolution and SYSLOG must also be allowed to external servers.

Example 10-14 shows the ACLs configured in the APPservers context allowing the ports and protocols listed in Table 10-6.

Example 10-14 *dbservers Context ACL Configuration*

```
access-list inbound-traffic remark INBOUND TRAFFIC TO DATABASE SERVERS
access-list inbound-traffic extended permit tcp host 10.10.20.71 host 10.10.30.101
  eq 3306
access-list inbound-traffic extended permit tcp host 10.10.20.72 host 10.10.30.101
  eq 3306
access-list inbound-traffic extended permit tcp host 10.10.20.71 host 10.10.30.102
  eq 3306
access-list inbound-traffic extended permit tcp host 10.10.20.72 host 10.10.30.102
  eq 3306
access-list inbound-traffic extended permit tcp 10.10.100.0 255.255.255.0 host
  10.10.30.101 eq 22
access-list inbound-traffic extended permit tcp 10.10.100.0 255.255.255.0 host
  10.10.30.102 eq 22
access-list inbound-traffic extended permit tcp 10.10.100.0 255.255.255.0 host
  10.10.30.101
eq 890
access-list inbound-traffic extended permit tcp 10.10.100.0 255.255.255.0 host
  10.10.30.102
eq 890
access-group inbound-traffic in interface outside
!
access-list outbound-traffic remark OUTBOUND TRAFFIC FROM DATABASE SERVERS
access-list outbound-traffic extended permit udp  host 192.168.30.101 host
  10.10.111.11 eq 53
access-list outbound-traffic extended permit udp  host 192.168.30.102 host
  10.10.111.11 eq 53
access-list outbound-traffic extended permit udp  host 192.168.30.101 host
  10.10.111.12 eq 53
access-list outbound-traffic extended permit udp  host 192.168.30.102 host
  10.10.111.12 eq 53
access-list outbound-traffic extended permit tcp  host 192.168.30.101 host
  10.10.100.100 eq 514
access-list outbound-traffic extended permit tcp  host 192.168.30.102 host
  10.10.100.100 eq 514
access-group outbound-traffic in interface inside
```

In Example 10-14, ACLs are configured to allow the traffic specified in Table 10-6. The ACL named **inbound-traffic** is applied to the outside interface, and the ACL named **outbound-traffic** is applied to the inside interface.

Virtual Fragment Reassembly

The Cisco FWSM, Cisco ASA, and Cisco PIX security appliances drop fragments. However, many different applications generate fragments. If you enable fragment forwarding, you open yourself to fragment attacks (like the ones defined in RFC 1858). You can use the Virtual Fragment Reassembly feature to protect against this type of attack. You enable Virtual Fragment Reassembly with the **fragment** command. In the following example, the Cisco FWSM is limiting its fragment buffer size to 200 packets on its outside and inside interfaces.

```
fragment size 200 outside
fragment size 200 inside
```

TIP   By using the **chain** and **timeout** options in the **fragment** command, you can also define the maximum number of fragments to be chained together and the length of time the Cisco FWSM waits for the fragments to arrive before discarding them.

Deploying Network Intrusion Detection and Prevention Systems

You can use network IDS/IPS appliances in small-to-medium organizations or the Cisco IDSM-2 for the Cisco Catalyst 6500 series switches in larger organizations. The implementation of each solution depends on the size of your data center and its requirements. When designing a network IDS/IPS solution for the data center, for both scalability and manageability, you should reduce the amount of traffic that is sent to the sensor. You should also avoid sending duplicate frames to the IDS/IPS sensors or modules. At the same time, you should avoid the situation in which you must change existing ACLs or VACLs before being able to implement an IDS/IPS solution. In most cases, you want to create several SPAN sessions to be able to send the traffic to multiple IDS/IPS devices. This section includes several best practices to use when you deploy an IDS/IPS solution in your data center.

Sending Selective Traffic to the IDS/IPS Devices

Depending on the size of your data center, you may use one or more IPS/IDS devices. In large data centers, you can use several IDSMs to monitor the activity within your server farms. Figure 10-13 illustrates a data center with three different IDSMs installed on each Cisco Catalyst 6500 along with the Cisco FWSM.

Figure 10-13 *IDSMs Deployed in the Data Center*

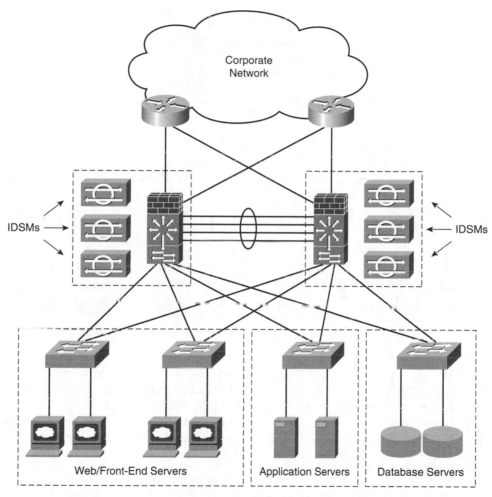

In some cases, exposing IPS/IDS sensors to all the traffic that flows within a data center can oversubscribe the IPS/IDS devices. To avoid performance problems in the data center, some administrators prefer to use only IDS features (promiscuous inspection) instead of inline IPS services. Others prefer to limit the number of protocols or the type of traffic to which a sensor is assigned. For example, in the high-level data center topology illustrated in Figure 10-13, you can selectively send traffic from each data center segment to specific IDSMs. For instance, you may want to send all web-related traffic on the webservers segment to the first IDSM. Similarly, you may want to send all traffic that traverses the application server segment to the second IDSM, and traffic destined and originated by the database servers to the third IDSM. This is illustrated in Figure 10-14.

Figure 10-14 *Sending Selective Traffic to the IDS/IPS Devices*

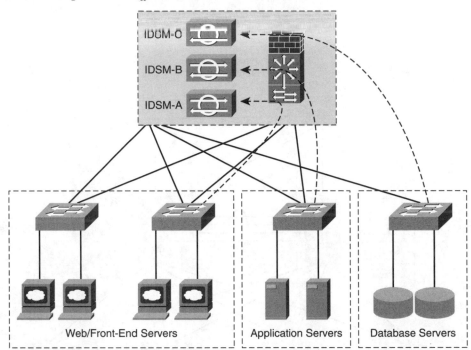

Based on VLAN information, you can use a SPAN session to differentiate traffic on multiple ports. This is supported on the Cisco Catalyst 6500 starting from Cisco IOS Versions 12.2(18)SXD and 12.1(24)E. You can configure a single SPAN session to capture traffic from the three VLANs and send traffic from each VLAN to a specific IDSM or external sensor. With this configuration, the IDS/IPS devices can inspect client-to-server traffic, locally switched traffic, and server-to-server routed traffic.

Alternatively, you can use VACL capture. You do this by simply configuring three VACLs with the **forward capture** action and assigning them to the three different segments. You assign IDSM-A to the web servers segment, IDSM-B to the application servers segment, and IDSM-C to the database segment.

In certain trunk environments, the use of VACLs achieves half the goal of this design. The IDSMs may still experience substantial noise traffic. In addition to this, you have to modify the security VACLs that might already be in place in the data center to include the capture action for the traffic that you want to monitor. To address this problem, you can use RSPAN and VACL redirect together. You can configure RSPAN to create a copy of the traffic from all the ports connecting the Catalyst 6500 to the core and to the server farms. All these frames are locally copied onto an RSPAN VLAN which is a special VLAN that is equally visible to three IDSMs. Then you configure VACL redirection. This does not permit or deny the traffic, it simply redirects the traffic to the desired IDSM. One VACL entry specifies that traffic to the web servers on the RSPAN VLAN be redirected to IDSM-1; another VACL entry specifies that traffic destined to the application servers on the RSPAN VLAN be redirected to IDSM-2; the same applies for the database server traffic to IDSM-3.

NOTE	You can find a detailed white paper on how to use RSPAN with VACLs for granular traffic analysis at http://www.cisco.com/warp/public/cc/pd/si/casi/ca6000/prodlit/rspan_wp.pdf.

Monitoring and Tuning

Monitoring tools such as CS-MARS help not only to identify and detect security threads, but also to reduce steps in the tuning process. *Tuning* is the process of managing and minimizing the number of false positives and false negatives that the network IDS/IPS device reports. As you learned in previous chapters, a *false positive* is a benign network activity mistakenly identified as malicious by the sensor. A *false negative* is malicious network activity mistakenly identified as benign or not detected by the sensor. To tune sensors, you enable, disable, or modify the signatures used in the network. The tuning process is one of the most crucial operational tasks that you perform when increasing the security of your data center. In Chapter 3, "Identifying and Classifying Security Threats," you learned best practices to use when deploying IDS/IPS devices. These same best practices apply in the data center.

Deploying the Cisco Security Agent (CSA) in the Data Center

CSA provides several security features that are more robust than a traditional antivirus or a personal firewall. CSA not only protects against viruses, worms, and direct attacks, but it also protects against day-zero threats. CSA plays an important role in data center security.

CSA Architecture

In the CSA solution architecture, a central management center maintains a database of policies and information about the workstations and servers on which the CSA software is installed. Agents register with the Cisco Security Agent Management Center (CSA-MC). Subsequently, the CSA-MC checks its configuration database and deploys a configured policy for that particular system.

NOTE	Starting with CSA Version 5.1, the CSA-MC is a standalone system. Prior to Version 5.1, CSA-MC was part of the Cisco Works VPN and Security Management System (VMS).

The CSA software constantly monitors all activity on the end host and polls to the CSA-MC at configurable intervals for policy updates. The agent sends events and alerts to the global event manager of the CS-AMC. The global event manager inspects the event logs and then alerts the administrator or triggers the agent to take action based on the specific alert.

NOTE   All the communication between the agents and the CSA-MC is via Secure Socket Layer (SSL). The administrator also connects to the CSA-MC via SSL to manage and monitor the agents.

Configuring Agent Kits

As previously mentioned, CSA-MC comes with preconfigured agent kits that can be used to fulfill initial security needs. However, CSA-MC allows you to create custom agent kits to fit your specific requirements. For example, you can create different agent kits for the various servers within your data center. To create a new agent kit, complete the following steps:

Step 1   Choose **Systems** > **Agent Kits** from the CSA-MC console.

Step 2   Click **New** at the bottom of the page displayed. A dialog box appears asking you to specify the operating system on which the agent kit will be applied.

Step 3   Enter a name and description for the new agent kit. For example, you can create agent kits for the web servers, application, and database servers in the examples in the previous sections.

Step 4   Select the groups that will be associated with this agent kit. You can select from predefined groups designed for different type of servers.

Step 5   Optionally, you can select to reboot the system after the CSA installation is complete. You can also select a quiet install to avoid end-user interaction.

Step 6   Click **Make Kit** to create the new agent kit.

Step 7   Click **Generate Rules** to generate all pending rules. A new window appears with information about the rule generation. After you have made the appropriate selections, click **Generate**.

Step 8   All rules and configuration changes are applied at this point. A summary window appears if the rule generation completes successfully.

Phased Deployment

When you start your CSA deployment, select the initial hosts on which CSA will be installed based on the following guidelines:

- Select at least one host per each distinct application or server environment.

- During the pilot, make the test host a mirror sample of the production systems.

- When installing CSA on servers, use a test machine for each server type to ensure that there is no negative impact from the CSA agent software installation.

- Create a group for each type of application environment to be protected.

Building and tuning of CSA policies is a continuous task. You need to have the proper staff and procedures to minimize the administrative burden. The security staff is responsible not only for maintaining the CSAMC policies, but also for creating and organizing appropriate exception rules and for monitoring user activity. You can organize the exception rules as follows:

- Create a global exception policy to allow legitimate traffic and application behavior that is required on all the systems within the organization. Subsequently, add these global exception rules to this exception policy.

- Create one exception policy for each group.

- Apply these policies to their respective groups and collect all necessary data to complete any additional tuning.

The following summarizes the steps that your security staff should use when deploying the agent kits throughout the organization:

Step 1   Deploy the CSA agents in test mode throughout your organization.

Step 2   Collect and analyze results. Subsequently, start policy tuning (as needed).

Step 3   Enable protection mode.

Step 4   Make sure that your security, operations, and engineering staff members are comfortable with the support of your deployment.

Summary

In most cases, data centers are equipped with surveillance cameras, biometric locks, authorization-based access policies, strict security personnel, and other physical security options. However, data centers that use such precautions, and are therefore prepared for physical intrusions, often do not deploy the necessary technologies and tools to combat cyberattacks. A good balance between physical and network security is crucial.

This chapter covered several best practices to use when deploying Defense-in-Depth strategies to secure the data center. It discussed several tools and mechanisms to help you protect the data center against DoS, worms, and other security outbreaks. You learned several tips for segmenting your data center in a multilayered architecture. This chapter also covered some tips for deploying network IDS/IPS solutions and CSA in the data center.

This chapter covers the following topics:

- Reconnaissance
- Filtering in IPv6
- Spoofing
- Header Manipulation and Fragmentation
- Broadcast Amplification or Smurf Attacks
- IPv6 Routing Security
- IPsec in IPv6

CHAPTER 11

IPv6 Security

Internet Protocol Version 6 (IPv6) is often called the next generation protocol and is designed to replace the widely deployed Internet Protocol Version 4 (IPv4). Despite that, IPv6 has only been implemented in a few places, but it is expected to grow over time. For example, Microsoft Windows Vista includes support for IPv6.

IPv6 enables easier support and maintenance of service provider networks than previous versions. The large address space improves the usage of online support systems and enables the inexpensive provision of address space to end users. Many service providers in Europe, Asia, and the United States are currently working on providing IPv6 services to enterprises and small businesses. This chapter includes several IPv6 security topics. It also provides a comparison with IPv4 from a threat and mitigation perspective.

NOTE   This chapter requires a basic knowledge of the IPv6 protocol.

IPv6 is defined in RFC 2460, "Internet Protocol, Version 6 (IPv6) Specification." The following are some of the main differences between IPv6 and IPv4:

- **Expanded addressing:** The IP address size is increased in IPv6 to 128 bits from the 32 bits supported in IPv4. This introduces considerable flexibility while supporting more levels of addressing hierarchy. Multicast routing scalability is also improved by the addition of a "scope" field to multicast addresses.

- **Simplified header format:** Several of the header fields used in IPv4 are not used in IPv6. These fields include check sum, Internet header length (IHL), identification flag, and fragment offset.

- **Improved support for extensions and options:** IPv6 encodes information into separate headers.

- **Fragmentation performed at the end hosts:** Unlike IPv4 packets, routers do not perform packet fragmentation on IPv6 packets. IPv6 supports payloads that are longer than 64 Kilobytes (KB).

- **Authentication:** IPv6 supports built-in authentication and confidentiality.

TIP Several sites include good information about IPv6, including the following:

- **Cisco IPv6 Information on IOS:** http://www.cisco.com/go/ipv6

- **IPv6 Forum:** http://www.ipv6forum.com

- **6Net IPv6 International Research:** http://www.6net.org

- **Internet2 IPv6 Working Group:** http://ipv6.internet2.edu

The first thing you need to learn about IPv6 security is the different types of security threats that may affect your IPv6 deployment. This chapter covers the most common types of threats in IPv6 and other security topics, such as:

- Reconnaissance
- Filtering in IPv6
- Spoofing
- Header manipulation and fragmentation
- Broadcast amplification or smurf attacks
- IPv6 routing security
- IPsec and IPv6

Reconnaissance

Reconnaissance in IPv6 is not as easy to perform as in IPv4 networks. Do not forget that IPv6 has many more addresses than IPv4 (2^{64} to be exact, or 128-bit addresses). Performing a network scan for that many addresses is not feasible for an attacker because it takes a considerable amount of time to scan millions of addresses.

Attackers use different techniques to gain more visibility of your network. Inevitably, many network administrators may adopt addresses that are easy to remember to assign to network devices (for example, ::10, ::20, ::F00D). Attackers may use these types of addresses in specific scans or reconnaissance methodologies. Instead of standardizing on host addresses, try something that is more difficult for attackers to guess. For example, you may want to use something like ::DEE1 for default gateways. Some people refer to this technique as *security through obscurity.* That technique can be beneficial, because it does not require administrative complications. Standardizing on a short, fixed pattern for interfaces that should not be directly accessed from the outside allows for a short filter list at the border routers.

Because Domain Name System (DNS) is still used to map systems to IPv6 addresses on external and internal networks, an attacker can obtain information on your IPv6 network addresses if he compromises the DNS infrastructure/application.

Just as for IPv4, it is recommended that you filter all IPv6 services at the perimeter router or firewall in an effort to protect the internal networks.

Privacy becomes a problem when you use DHCPv6 on an IPv6 network. An IPv6 address has two parts. The first part is the subnet prefix, and the second part is a local identifier. This identifier is typically derived from your MAC address. The subnet prefix is a fixed 64-bit length for all current definitions. DHCP is not suitable for some IPv6 environments because you can technically get an IPv6 address via DHCPv6 in your corporate network and then get the same address when you are at home or at a hotel. Attackers can track you down with the use of web cookies that can retain your address information. That is why it is recommended that you use IPv6 Privacy Extensions for external communication. RFC 3041 defines the use of IPv6 Privacy Extensions.

Filtering in IPv6

Filtering of unauthorized access in IPv6 is similar to IPv4. This section includes examples of IPv6 access control lists (ACL), in addition to best practices when filtering ICMPv6 unnecessary packets and extension headers.

Filtering Access Control Lists (ACL)

You can configure the filters or ACLs using Layer 3 and Layer 4 information. You can configure an IPv6 ACL in a Cisco IOS router using the **ipv6 access-list** command. The command uses the permit and deny subcommands with the following options:

```
ipv6 access-list command and its subcommands
permit protocol {source-ipv6-prefix/prefix-length | any | host source-ipv6-address}
[operator [port-number]] {destination-ipv6-prefix/prefix-length | any | host
destination-ipv6-address} [operator [port-number]] [dest-option-type [doh-number |
doh-type]] [dscp value] [flow-label value] [fragments] [log] [log-input] [mobility]
[mobility-type [mh-number | mh-type]] [reflect name [timeout value]] [routing]
[routing-type routing-number] [sequence value] [time-range name]
deny protocol {source-ipv6-prefix/prefix-length | any | host source-ipv6-address}
[operator [port-number]] {destination-ipv6-prefix/prefix-length | any | host
destination-ipv6-address} [operator [port-number]] [dest-option-type [doh-number |
doh-type]] [dscp value] [flow-label value] [fragments] [log] [log-input] [mobility]
[mobility-type [mh-number | mh-type]] [routing] [routing-type routing-number]
[sequence value] [time-range name] [undetermined-transport]
```

Example 11-1 shows an ACL in a Cisco IOS router allowing HTTP traffic (TCP port 80) from a trusted IPv6 host and denying all other traffic.

Example 11-1 *IPv6 Access Control List*

```
ipv6 access-list outside_acl
 permit tcp 2001:1234:0300:0101::/32 any eq 80
interface FastEthernet 0/0
 ipv6 traffic-filter outside_acl in
```

In the previous example, the ACL name is **outside_acl**, and it is applied inbound to the FastEthernet 0/0 interface.

| NOTE | Standard IPv6 ACLs are supported starting with Cisco IOS Version 12.2(2)T and 12.0(21)ST and later. |

In the Cisco ASA and Cisco PIX security appliances, the IPv6 ACLs are similar to IOS. To create an IPv6 ACL to allow the same host to pass HTTP traffic on the Cisco ASA or Cisco PIX, use the **ipv6 access-list** command, as shown in the following example:

```
ipv6 access-list asa_outside_acl permit tcp 2001:1234:0300:0101::/32 any eq www -
access-group asa_outside_acl in interface outside
```

Notice that the IPv6 access list is applied to the outside interface using the **access-group** command just as for IPv4 access lists.

| NOTE | IPv6 has been supported on the Cisco PIX since Version 7.0. The Cisco ASA supports IPv6 in all versions, because the first version of Cisco ASA software is 7.0. |

ICMP Filtering

You may also want to filter unnecessary ICMPv6 messages, just as with ICMPv4. It is recommended that you configure your ICMPv6 filters and policies in a manner that is similar to your ICMPv4 policies, with the following additions:

- **ICMPv6 Type 2:** Packet too big
- **ICMPv6 Type 4:** Parameter problem
- **ICMPv6 Type 130-132:** Multicast listener
- **ICMPv6 Type 133/134:** Router solicitation and router advertisement
- **ICMPv6 Type 135/136:** Neighbor solicitation and neighbor advertisement

Make sure that, if you need to allow these options, you only allow trusted sources and deny everything else.

Extension Headers in IPv6

In IPv6, IP options are replaced with extension headers. An attacker may use these extension headers to evade your security configuration. All devices running IPv6 must accept packets with a routing header. In some cases, it may be possible for end-host devices to also process routing headers and forward the packet somewhere else. Attackers can take advantage of this and use routing headers to evade the ACLs configured on your routers and firewalls.

As a best practice, you should designate specific devices that are allowed to act as Mobile IPv6 (MIPv6) home agents. MIPv6 is a protocol developed as a subset of IPv6 to support mobile connections. You should typically only assign the default router for a specific subnet to act as an MIPv6 home agent. If MIPv6 is not needed, packets with the routing header can easily be dropped at your firewalls and routers without relying on the end host not to forward the packets.

Spoofing

One of the most common techniques that attackers use is spoofing. *Spoofing* is the technique of modifying your source IP address or the ports to appear as your packets are initiated from another location. From a Layer 3 spoofing perspective, IPv6 presents a huge benefit because the allocations of IPv6 addresses are designed to easily be summarized allowing service providers to at least ensure that their own customers are not using addresses outside their allocated range. You can use filtering techniques such as those defined in RFC 2827.

The following are the most common best practices suggested to protect against IPv6 Layer 3 and Layer 4 spoofing:

- Implement filtering techniques as defined in RFC 2827. In Chapter 2, "Preparation Phase," you learned how to create antispoofing ACLs for your IPv4. You should do the same for your IPv6 addresses by denying all traffic from your own network range to be sourced from outside your networks.

- In an IPv6 subnet, an attacker has numerous options to select an IP address to spoof. It is critical to have tools to determine the true physical source of the traffic within your network. This generally entails some combination of Layer 2 and Layer 3 information gleaned from switches and routers.

Header Manipulation and Fragmentation

IPv6 is susceptible to fragmentation and other header manipulation attacks. With these types of attacks, the attacker uses fragmentation to evade network intrusion detection systems (IDS), intrusion prevention systems (IPS), and firewalls.

An attacker can also use out-of-order fragments to try to avoid an IDS/IPS device that is deployed to detect attacks based on the enabled signatures on the system. RFC 2460 prohibits fragmentation of IPv6 packets by intermediary network devices.

As is the case with IPv4, you should always deny IPv6 fragments destined to an internetworking device whenever possible. On the other hand, you should test this in the lab and make sure that this does not cause problems with specific applications in your particular network environment.

The combination of multiple extension headers and fragmentation in IPv6 creates the potential that the Layer 4 protocol will not be included in the first packet of a fragment set. Make sure that your IDS/IPS system or any other security monitoring device accounts for this possibility and reassembles fragments. Today, Cisco IPS/IDS devices support multiple extension headers and fragmentation.

Broadcast Amplification or Smurf Attacks

Broadcast amplification attacks are typically referred to as *smurf attacks*. These are denial of service (DoS) attacks where the attacker sends an echo-request message with a destination address of a subnet broadcast and a spoofed source address using the host IP address of the victim. This causes all the devices on the subnet to respond to the spoofed source IP address and flood the victim with echo-reply messages. RFC 2463 prohibits IP-directed broadcasts within IPv6. In addition, it states that an ICMPv6 message should not be generated as a response to a packet with an IPv6 multicast destination address, a link-layer multicast address, or a link-layer broadcast address.

Smurf attacks should not be a threat if all the devices within your network are compliant with RFC 2463. On the other hand, you should always implement ingress filtering of packets with IPv6 multicast source addresses.

IPv6 Routing Security

Some routing protocols change in respect to security in IPv6; however; others do not. This section lists the routing protocols that change as well as those that remain the same.

Border Gateway Protocol (BGP) continues to have authentication mechanisms such as MD5 authentication but what, if anything, changes with IPv6? The Intermediate System-to-Intermediate System (IS-IS) protocol was extended in a draft specification to support IPv6. In IPv4, the simple password authentication of IS-IS was not encrypted. However, RFC 3567 defines the IS-IS cryptographic authentication. IS-IS in IPv6 also supports this cryptographic authentication mechanism.

The Open Shortest Path First Version 3 (OSPFv3) protocol changed to support IPv6. The authentication fields were removed from the header of OSPF messages/packets. Another protocol that removed authentication capabilities was the Routing Information Protocol Next-Generation (RIPng). For this reason, it is recommended that you use traditional authentication mechanisms for BGP and IS-IS. OSPF for IPv6 requires the use of IPsec to enable authentication. It is always a best practice to use OSPF in conjunction with IPsec to secure routing protocol updates in OSPF for IPv6.

NOTE	Cisco IOS routers support the use of IPv6 IPsec to authenticate OSPFv3 starting with Versions 12.3(4)T, 12.4, and later.

IPsec and IPv6

IPsec is available with IPv6. IPv6 headers have no security mechanisms themselves, just as in IPv4. Administrators rely on the IPsec protocol suite for security. The same security risks for man-in-the-middle attacks in Internet Key Exchange (IKE) in IPv4 are present in IPv6. Most people recommend using IKE main mode negotiations when the use of preshared keys is required. On the other hand, IKE Version 2 (IKEv2) is expected to address this issue in the future. IKEv2 supports different peer authentication options with built-in support for asymmetric user authentication through the Extensible Authentication Protocol (EAP).

The IPv6 IPsec packet format is basically the same as in IPv4. Figure 11-1 illustrates an IPv6 packet where Authentication Header (AH) and Encapsulation Security Payload (ESP) protocols are used. IPv6 AH and ESP extension headers are used to provide authentication and confidentiality to IPv6 packets.

Figure 11-1 *IPv6 IPsec Packet*

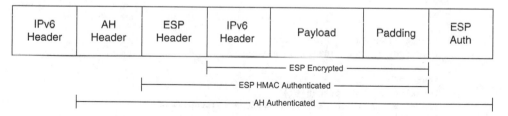

Cisco IOS supports IPv6 IPsec for VPN tunnels starting with IOS Version 12.4(4)T. Figure 11-2 illustrates a topology where two Cisco IOS routers are configured to terminate a site-to-site IPv6 IPsec tunnel. The IPv6 address of the router in New York is 2EEE:1001::DCBA:BBAA:DDCC:4321, and the IPv6 address of the router in London is 2EEE:2002::ABCD:AABB:CCDD:1234.

Figure 11-2 *IPv6 IPsec Configuration Example*

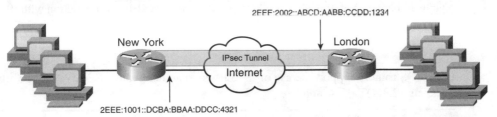

Virtual tunnel interfaces (VTI) are configured on each router in this example.
Example 11-2 shows the configuration of the router in New York. Notice that the
configuration is almost identical to the IPv4 VTI implementation. In this example, routers
use preshared keys with SHA for hashing, and Diffie-Hellman group 1 for Phase 1.
AH-SHA-HMAC and ESP-3DES are used for Phase 2.

Example 11-2 *New York Router Configuration*

```
crypto isakmp policy 1
  authentication pre-share
!
crypto isakmp key 1qaz2wsx address ipv6 2EEE:2002::ABCD:AABB:CCDD:1234/128
!
crypto ipsec transform-set 3des ah-sha-hmac esp-3des
!
!
crypto ipsec profile myprofile
  set transform-set 3des
!
ipv6 cef
!
interface Tunnel0
  ipv6 address 2EEE:1001::/64 eui-64
  ipv6 enable
  ipv6 cef
  tunnel source FastEthernet0
  tunnel destination 2EEE:2002::ABCD:AABB:CCDD:1234
  tunnel mode ipsec ipv6
  tunnel protection ipsec profile myprofile
```

Example 11-3 shows the configuration of the router in London. Notice that the
configuration is almost identical for the exception of the IP addresses.

Example 11-3 *London Router Configuration*

```
crypto isakmp policy 1
  authentication pre-share
!
!
crypto isakmp key 1qaz2wsx address ipv6 2EEE:1001::DCBA:BBAA:DDCC:4321/128
!
crypto ipsec transform-set 3des ah-sha-hmac esp-3des
!
crypto ipsec profile myprofile
  set transform-set 3des
!
ipv6 cef
!
interface Tunnel0
  ipv6 address 2EEE:2002::/64 eui-64 -
  ipv6 enable
  ipv6 cef
  tunnel source FastEthernet0
  tunnel destination 2EEE:1001::DCBA:BBAA:DDCC:4321
  tunnel mode ipsec ipv6
  tunnel protection ipsec profile myprofile
```

The IKE and IPsec Security Associations (SA) are negotiated and established before the line protocol for the tunnel interface is changed to the UP state. The remote IKE peer is the same as the tunnel destination address; the local IKE peer will be the address picked from the tunnel source interface, which has the same IPv6 address scope as the tunnel destination address.

Summary

This chapter introduced security topics in IPv6. Although it is assumed that you already have a basic understanding on IPv6, this chapter covered fundamental topics of IPv6 including how to filter IPv6 traffic in infrastructure devices such as the Cisco ASA and Cisco IOS routers. When deploying IPv6 on your network, you should pay attention to several security considerations. These considerations include the use of authorization for automatically assigned addresses and configurations, protection of IP packets, host protection from scanning and attacks, and control of traffic that is exchanged with the Internet. In many cases, these security considerations also exist for IPv4 traffic. Understanding the IPv6 security threats is a must for every security professional. This chapter included the most common IPv6 security threats and the best practices adopted by many organizations to protect their IPv6 infrastructure.

Many IPv6-enabled devices also support IPsec. This chapter covered how to configure Cisco IOS routers to terminate IPsec in IPv6 networks. It provided sample configurations to enhance the learning.

Case Studies

This chapter covers the following topics:

- Case Study of a Small Business
- Case Study of a Medium-Sized Enterprise
- Case Study of a Large Enterprise

CHAPTER 12

Case Studies

Having Defense-in-Depth mechanisms and tools in place is important to any organization regardless of its size. This chapter includes three different case studies explaining how a small (Company-A), medium (Company-B), and large enterprise (Company-C) apply the best practices learned in all previous chapters. These case studies provide you with an in-depth and objective analysis of security technologies and techniques applied in different environments. The intent is to help you identify and implement practical security strategies that are both flexible and scalable.

Case Study of a Small Business

This section uses Company-A as an example. Company-A is a small web development company based in Raleigh, North Carolina. Its office in Raleigh hosts 35 employees. The user population is composed of sales, marketing, finance personnel, and several web developers. Figure 12-1 illustrates the network architecture and topology of the Raleigh office of Company-A.

The Raleigh office has a simple network architecture. Client workstations are connected to an access switch and then connected to the Cisco Adaptive Security Appliance (ASA) inside interface. The Cisco ASA outside interface connects directly to a router provided by the Internet service provider (ISP) of Company-A. The ISP completely manages this router; Company-A has no control over it. A third interface on the Cisco ASA hosts a demilitarized zone (DMZ) hosting several servers. These servers include web, e-mail, and FTP applications.

Figure 12-1 *Raleigh Office of Company-A*

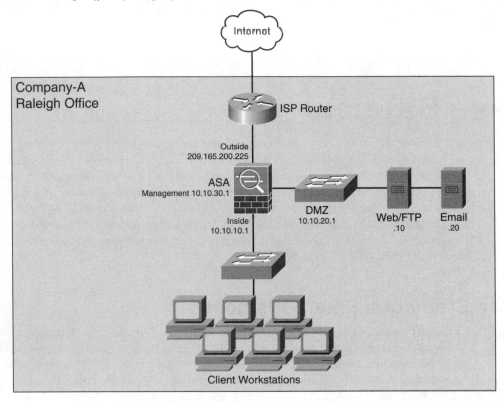

Because this is a simple topology, all security policies are enforced in the Cisco ASA. The goal is to protect the internal and DMZ hosts from external threats, while allowing the following:

- Client workstations must be able to access the web server at the DMZ (10.10.20.10) over HTTP and HTTPS. Clients should also be able to put and get files via FTP to the same server at 10.10.20.10.

- Client workstations must be able to access the Internet over HTTP and HTTPS. No other protocol access is allowed to the Internet.

- Client workstations must be able to check their e-mail on the e-mail server at the DMZ (10.10.20.20).

- The web server should be reachable from outside Internet clients over HTTP and HTTPS only. The Cisco ASA should do static Network Address Translation (NAT) for the web server to be reachable via a public IP address from the Internet.

- The e-mail server should be able to receive e-mail from external hosts over the Simple Mail Transfer Protocol (SMTP). The Cisco ASA should do static NAT for the e-mail server to be reachable via a public IP address from the Internet.

- The client workstations will be translated to the external public IP address of the Cisco ASA using Port Address Translation (PAT).

Raleigh Office Cisco ASA Configuration

The following sections cover the steps necessary to complete the goals listed earlier.

Configuring IP Addressing and Routing

This section demonstrates how to configure the interfaces and default gateway on the Cisco ASA using the Adaptive Security Device Manager (ASDM). The following are the configuration steps:

Step 1 Working with a new Cisco ASA installation, the administrator logs in via the command-line interface (CLI) and sets the management interface IP address (10.10.30.1) and other interface configuration with the following commands.

```
Co-A-ASA1# configure terminal
Co-A-ASA1(config)# interface Management0/0
Co-A-ASA1(config-if)# nameif management
Co-A-ASA1(config-if)# security-level 80
Co-A-ASA1(config-if)# ip address 10.10.30.1 255.255.255.0
Co-A-ASA1(config-if)# no shutdown
Co-A-ASA1(config-if)# exit
Co-A-ASA1(config)#
```

Step 2 The administrator enables ASDM access only from machines on the management network with the following commands:

```
Co-A-ASA1(config)# http server enable
Co-A-ASA1(config)# http 10.10.30.0 255.255.255.0 management
Co-A-ASA1(config)# asdm location 10.10.30.0 255.255.255.0 management
```

Step 3 The next step is to configure the outside, inside, and DMZ interfaces. The administrator connects to the Cisco ASA via ASDM and clicks **Configuration > Device Setup > Interfaces**, as illustrated on Figure 12-2.

Step 4 The administrator selects the **GigabitEthernet0/0** interface and clicks the **Edit** button. The screen illustrated in Figure 12-3 is shown. The administrator enters the interface name (**outside**), the IP address configuration (**209.165.200.225**), subnet mask (**255.255.255.0**), and a description for the outside interface.

Figure 12-2 *Configuring the Cisco ASA Interfaces on ASDM*

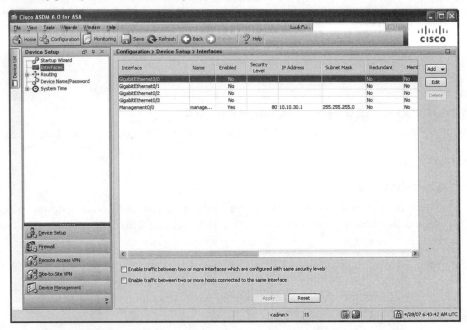

Figure 12-3 *Outside Interface Configuration*

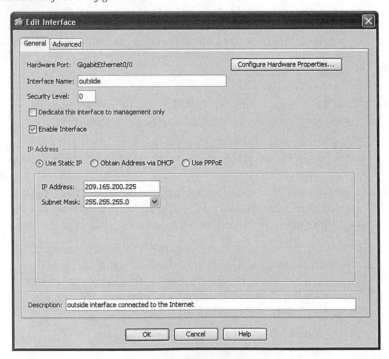

Step 5 Similarly, the **GigabitEthernet0/1** interface is configured as the inside
interface, as shown in Figure 12-4. The security level for the inside
interface is set to **100**.

Figure 12-4 *Inside Interface Configuration*

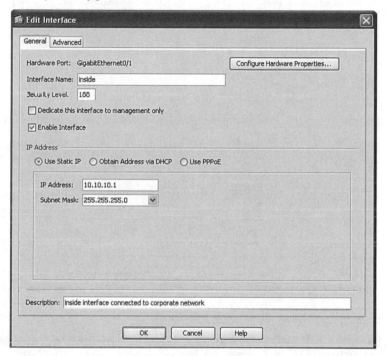

Step 6 The **GigabitEthernet0/2** interface is configured as the **dmz** interface, as
shown in Figure 12-5. The security level of the **dmz** interface is set to **50**.

Step 7 The next step is to configure the default route of the Cisco ASA to point
to the ISP router (**209.165.200.226**). To configure the default route,
navigate to **Configuration > Device Setup > Routing > Static Routes**
and click **Add**. The screen shown in Figure 12-6 is displayed. Choose the
outside interface from the drop-down menu, and enter **0.0.0.0** for the IP
address and **0.0.0.0** for the Mask. The Gateway IP is **209.165.200.226**,
and the metric is **1**. Leave all the other options with their default value.

Figure 12-5 *DMZ Interface Configuration*

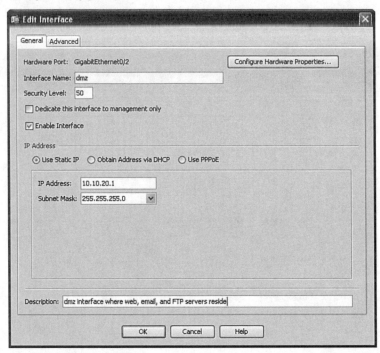

Figure 12-6 *Inside Interface Configuration*

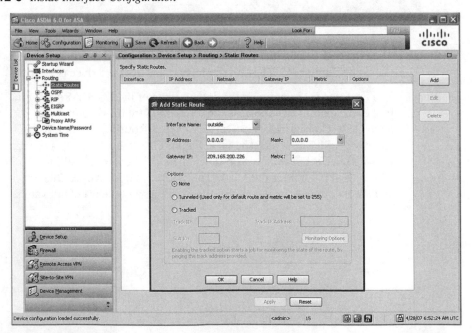

Configuring PAT on the Cisco ASA

The next step is to configure PAT for internal users to be able to communicate to the Internet. Complete the following steps to configure PAT on the Cisco ASA.

Step 1   To configure PAT, go to **Configuration > Firewall > NAT Rules**, click **Add**, and choose **Add Dynamic NAT Rule** from the drop-down menu, as illustrated in Figure 12-7.

Figure 12-7 *Configuring PAT for Internal Users*

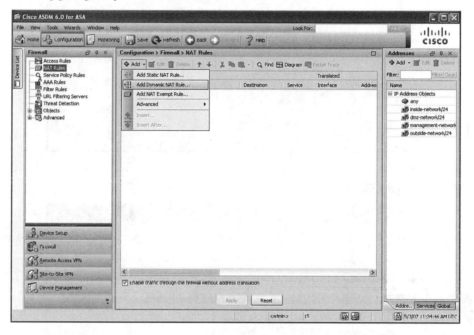

Step 2   The screen shown in Figure 12-8 is displayed. Under the **Original** section, choose the **inside** interface from the drop-down menu.

Step 3   Expand the Source option to select the inside source address space. This is illustrated in Figure 12-9. Select the **inside network (10.10.10.0/24)** and click **OK**.

Figure 12-8 *Adding a Dynamic NAT Rule*

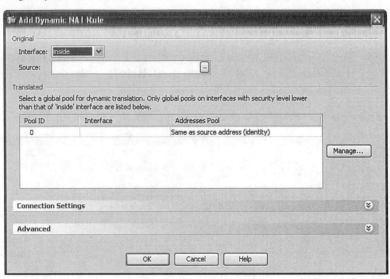

Figure 12-9 *Selecting the Source*

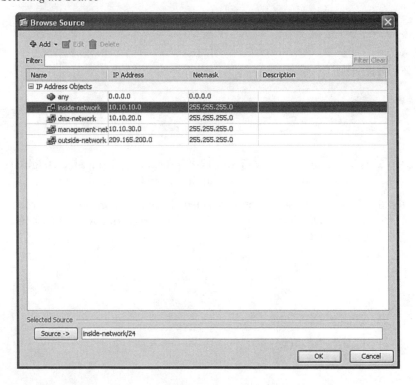

Step 4 Under the **Translated** section, click the **Manage** button to add a global address pool.

Step 5 The screen shown in Figure 12-10 is displayed. Under the **IP Addresses to Add** section, click **Port Address Translation (PAT) using IP Address of the interface** and click the **Add** button to include it under the **Address pools**, as shown in Figure 12-10.

Figure 12-10 *Configuring PAT to Use the Outside Interface Address*

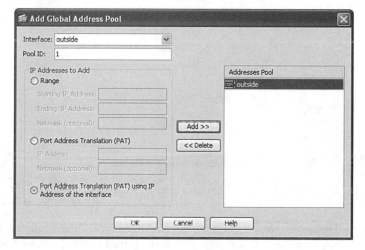

Step 6 Click **OK** and apply your changes to the Cisco ASA.

Configuring Static NAT for the DMZ Servers

The DMZ servers must be statically translated with a public IP address. Table 12-1 lists the IP address mapping of the DMZ servers.

Table 12-1 *IP Address Mapping of DMZ Servers*

Server	Inside IP Address	Translated Address
Web server	10.10.20.10	209.165.200.227
E-mail server	10.10.20.20	209.165.200.228

Complete the following steps to configure static NAT for the DMZ web and e-mail servers.

Step 1 Navigate to **Configuration > Firewall > NAT Rules**, click **Add**, and choose **Add Static NAT Rule** from the drop-down menu, as illustrated in Figure 12-11.

Figure 12-11 *Adding a Static NAT Rule*

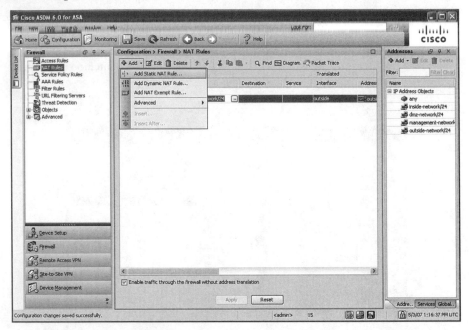

Step 2 The screen shown in Figure 12-12 is displayed. First configure static NAT for the web server. Under the **Original** section, choose the **dmz** interface from the drop-down menu, and enter the web server physical IP address (**10.10.20.10**) as the source.

Figure 12-12 *Adding a Static NAT Rule*

Step 3 Under the **Translated** section, choose the **outside** interface from the drop-down menu.

Step 4 Click the **Use IP address** option, and enter the public address to which the web server will be translated (**209.165.200.227**).

Step 5 Click **OK**.

Step 6 Repeat the same procedure for the e-mail server.

Configuring Identity NAT for Inside Users

The inside users must be able to communicate with the DMZ servers. The goal is to configure identity NAT for inside users when communicating to the DMZ servers. Complete the following steps to configure identity NAT for inside users.

Step 1 Navigate to **Configuration > Firewall > NAT Rules**, click **Add**, as illustrated in Figure 12-13.

Figure 12-13 *Configuring Identity NAT for the Inside Network on the DMZ*

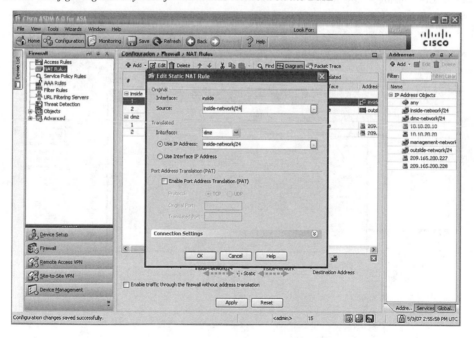

Step 2 Under the **Original** section, choose the **inside** interface from the drop-down menu, and the inside network as the source (**10.10.10.0/24**).

Step 3 Under the Translated section, choose the **dmz** interface from the drop-down menu, and select the same inside network (**10.10.10.0/24**) as the translated IP address, as shown in Figure 12-13.

Step 4 Click **OK**.

Step 5 Apply the changes to the Cisco ASA.

Controlling Access

Next, you need to configure policies on the Cisco ASA to control access and achieve the following goals.

- The web server should be reachable from outside Internet clients over the HTTP and HTTPS protocols only.

- The e-mail server should be able to receive e-mail from external hosts over the SMTP only.

Complete the following steps to configure access rules on the Cisco ASA.

Step 1 Navigate to **Configuration > Firewall > Access Rules**, click **Add**. In Figure 12-14 the Access Rule configuration is displayed.

Figure 12-14 *Configuring Access Rules*

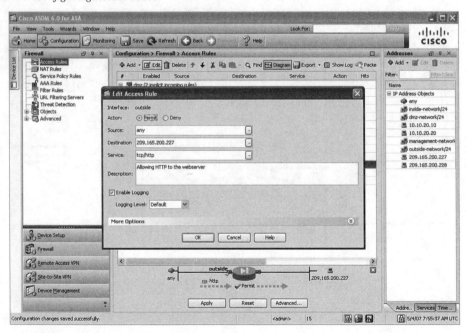

Step 2 First, the access rule to allow Internet users to reach the web server at the DMZ is configured. Under **Action**, click **Permit**.

Step 3 Under source, select **any**.

Step 4   Under destination, enter the IP address of the web server
209.165.200.227.

Step 5   Select HTTP (**TCP/HTTP**) under the service.

Step 6   Optionally, you can enter a description for this access rule, as illustrated
in Figure 12-14.

Step 7   Click **OK**.

Step 8   Repeat the same steps to allow HTTPS (TCP port 443) access to the web
server and SMTP (TCP port 25) access to the e-mail server.

Cisco ASA Antispoofing Configuration

The Company-A security administrator wants to protect the infrastructure from spoofed
sources. The administrator enables Unicast Reverse Path Forwarding (Unicast RPF) to
protect against IP spoofing attacks by ensuring that all packets have a source IP address that
matches the correct source interface according to the routing table. To enable Unicast RPF,
navigate to **Configuration > Firewall > Advanced > Anti-spoofing**. Select the desired
interface, and click **Enable**, as illustrated in Figure 12-15.

Figure 12-15 *Configuring Unicast RPF*

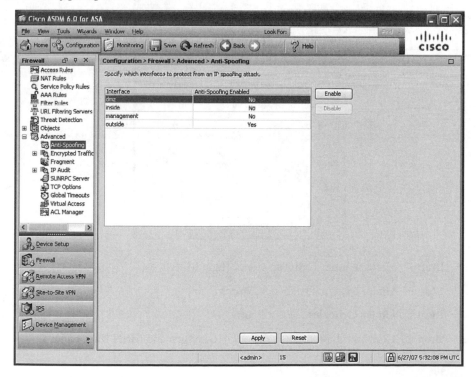

Blocking Instant Messaging

The security administrator is now tasked by his management to come up with a solution to prevent internal users from using Yahoo! and MSN instant messaging (IM) programs. The solution is to configure the Cisco ASA to block this traffic and log it. The security administrator completes the following steps to achieve this goal.

Step 1   The first step is to configure an inspect map on the Cisco ASA. To do this, navigate to **Configuration > Firewall > Objects > Inspect Maps > Instant Messaging (IM)**.

Step 2   Click **Add**.

Step 3   The **Add Instant Messaging (IM) Inspect** screen is displayed.

Step 4   Enter a name and an optional description for the new inspect map configuration. In this example, the inspect map name is **IM**.

Step 5   Click **Add** to add a new inspection criterion.

Step 6   The screen is shown in Figure 12-16 is displayed.

Figure 12-16 *Adding an Instant Messaging Inspect Map*

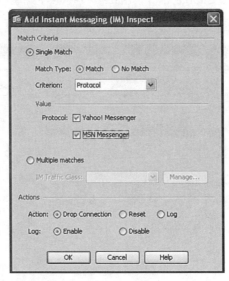

Step 7   Under **Match Criteria**, click **Single Match**.

Step 8   Under **Match Type**, click **Match**.

Step 9   Under **Criterion**, select **Protocol**.

Step 10 Check both protocols (**Yahoo! Messenger** and **MSN Messenger**).

Step 11 Under the **Actions** sections, leave the default of **Drop Connection and Log** enabled.

Step 12 Click **OK**.

Step 13 Navigate to **Configuration > Firewall > Service Policy Rules** and click **Add**. The first screen of the Configuration Wizard is displayed, as illustrated in Figure 12-17.

Figure 12-17 *Adding a New Service Policy Rule*

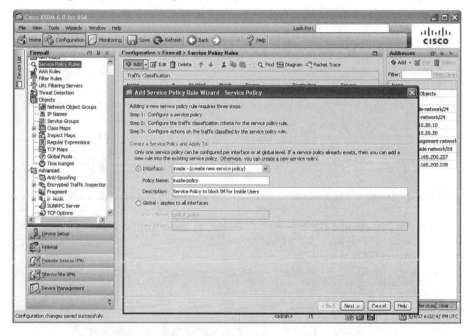

Step 14 In this example, the service policy will be applied only to the inside interface. To do this, click **Interface** under the **Create a Service Policy and Apply To** section.

Step 15 Select the **inside** interface, and enter a name, as shown in Figure 12-17.

Step 16 Click **Next**.

Step 17 The **Traffic Classification Criteria** screen is displayed, as shown in Figure 12-18. Click **Use class-default as the traffic class**.

Step 18 Click **Next**.

Figure 12-18 *Traffic Classification Criteria Screen*

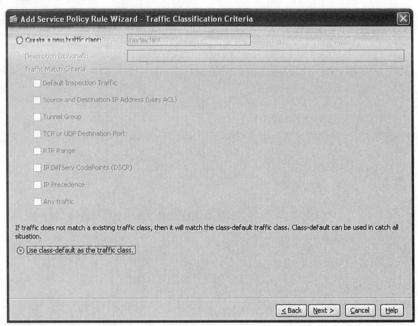

Step 19 The **Rule Actions** screen is shown, as illustrated in Figure 12-19.

Figure 12-19 *Rule Actions Screen*

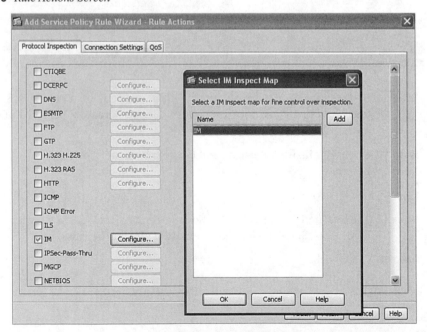

Step 20 Under the Protocol Inspection tab, check **IM** and click **Configure**.

Step 21 Select the previously configured inspection map (**IM**).

Step 22 Click **OK** on the **Select IM Inspect Map** screen.

Step 23 Click **Finish** to end the wizard.

Step 24 Apply the configuration to the Cisco ASA.

Example 12-1 shows the Cisco ASA CLI configuration for Company-A.

Example 12-1 *CLI Configuration of the Cisco ASA at the Raleigh Office*

```
Co-A-ASA1# show running-config
: Saved
:
ASA Version 8.0(1)
!
hostname Co-A-ASA1
enable password 8Ry2YjIyt7RRXU24 encrypted
names
!
!outside interface configuration
interface GigabitEthernet0/0
 description outside interface connected to the Internet
 nameif outside
 security-level 0
 ip address 209.165.200.225 255.255.255.0
!
!inside interface configuration
interface GigabitEthernet0/1
 description inside interface connected to corporate network
 nameif inside
 security-level 100
 ip address 10.10.10.1 255.255.255.0
!
!dmz interface configuration
interface GigabitEthernet0/2
 description dmz interface where web, email, and FTP servers reside
 nameif dmz
 security-level 50
 ip address 10.10.20.1 255.255.255.0
!
interface GigabitEthernet0/3
 shutdown
 no nameif
 no security-level
 no ip address
!
!management interface configuration
interface Management0/0
 nameif management
 security-level 80
```

continues

Example 12-1 *CLI Configuration of the Cisco ASA at the Raleigh Office (Continued)*

```
 ip address 10.10.30.1 255.255.255.0
 !
 !ACL controlling access to the web and e-mail server
access-list outside_access_in extended permit tcp any host 209.165.200.228 eq smtp
access-list outside_access_in_ remark Allowing HTTP to the webserver
access-list outside_access_in_ extended permit tcp any host 209.165.200.227 eq www
access-list outside_access_in_ remark Allowing HTTPS to the webserver
access-list outside_access_in_ extended permit tcp any host 209.165.200.227 eq https
access-list outside_access_in_ remark Allowing SMTP to the email server
access-list outside_access_in_1 extended permit tcp any host 209.165.200.228 eq smtp
 !
pager lines 24
mtu outside 1500
mtu inside 1500
mtu dmz 1500
mtu management 1500
 !
!Unicast RPF Configuration
ip verify reverse-path interface outside
ip verify reverse-path interface inside
ip verify reverse-path interface dmz
 !
no failover
icmp unreachable rate-limit 1 burst-size 1
no asdm history enable
arp timeout 14400
 !
!PAT Configuration for inside users
nat-control
global (outside) 1 interface
nat (inside) 1 10.10.10.0 255.255.255.0
 !
!Static NAT configuration for web and e-mail servers
static (dmz,outside) 209.165.200.227 10.10.20.10 netmask 255.255.255.255
static (dmz,outside) 209.165.200.228 10.10.20.20 netmask 255.255.255.255
 !
!Static identity NAT configuration for inside network at the DMZ
static (inside,dmz) 10.10.10.0 10.10.10.0 netmask 255.255.255.0
 !
!ACL is applied to the outside interface
access-group outside_access_in_1 in interface outside
route outside 0.0.0.0 0.0.0.0 209.165.200.226 1
timeout xlate 3:00:00
timeout conn 1:00:00 half-closed 0:10:00 udp 0:02:00 icmp 0:00:02
timeout sunrpc 0:10:00 h323 0:05:00 h225 1:00:00 mgcp 0:05:00 mgcp-pat 0:05:00
timeout sip 0:30:00 sip_media 0:02:00 sip-invite 0:03:00 sip-disconnect 0:02:00
timeout uauth 0:05:00 absolute
dynamic-access-policy-record DfltAccessPolicy
http server enable
http 10.10.30.0 255.255.255.0 management
no snmp-server location
no snmp-server contact
```

Example 12-1 *CLI Configuration of the Cisco ASA at the Raleigh Office (Continued)*

```
snmp-server enable traps snmp authentication linkup linkdown coldstart
no crypto isakmp nat-traversal
telnet timeout 5
ssh 10.10.30.0 255.255.255.0 management
ssh timeout 5
console timeout 0
threat-detection basic-threat
threat-detection statistics access-list
!
class-map inspection_default
 match default-inspection-traffic
!
!
policy-map type inspect dns preset_dns_map
 parameters
   message-length maximum 512
!
!policy map to block Yahoo! and MSN IM.
policy-map type inspect im IM
 description Blocking Instant Messanging
 parameters
 match protocol msn-im yahoo-im
   drop-connection log
policy-map global_policy
 class inspection_default
  inspect dns preset_dns_map
  inspect ftp
  inspect h323 h225
  inspect h323 ras
  inspect netbios
  inspect rsh
  inspect rtsp
  inspect skinny
  inspect esmtp
  inspect sqlnet
  inspect sunrpc
  inspect tftp
  inspect sip
  inspect xdmcp
!
!Service policy map to block IM
policy-map inside-policy
 description Service Policy to block IM for Inside Users
 class class-default
   inspect im IM
!
!global service policy
service-policy global_policy global
!
!service policy for IM applied to the inside interface only
service-policy inside-policy interface inside
```

Atlanta Office Cisco IOS Configuration

Company-A opened a small branch office in Atlanta, Georgia. This new office has only 4 salesmen and 12 web developers. The Atlanta office network topology is simple. A Cisco IOS Software router with the IOS Firewall features can be configured to protect the internal network. This is illustrated in Figure 12-20.

Figure 12-20 *Atlanta Office Network Topology*

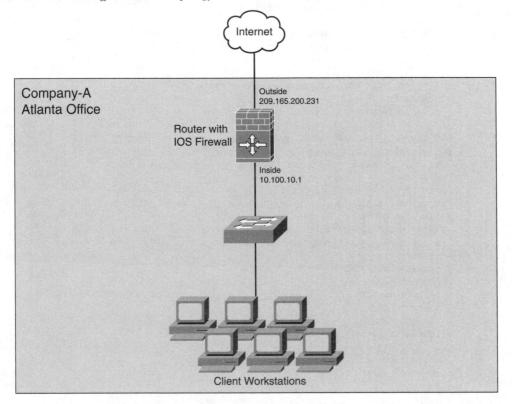

The router has only two interfaces enabled. The inside interface resides on the 10.100.10.0/24 network, and the outside interface faces the Internet.

Locking Down the Cisco IOS Router

The security administrator at Company-A must configure the router appropriately to increase the security of the Atlanta office network. The administrator uses the Security Device Manager (SDM) to configure the router and perform a security audit. Using SDM, the administrator can configure the router quickly using the best practices recommended in Chapter 2, "Preparation Phase."

You can complete the following steps to perform a security audit and fix any discrepancies found on the Cisco IOS router.

Step 1   Log in to the Cisco IOS router using SDM.

Step 2   Navigate to **Configure > Security Audit**, and click the **Perform security audit** button, as illustrated in Figure 12-21. Alternatively, you can perform a one-step lockdown to configure default recommendations by clicking the **One-step lockdown** button. In this example, the step-by-step option is selected, which allows you to customize your configuration.

Figure 12-21   *Performing a Security Audit with SDM*

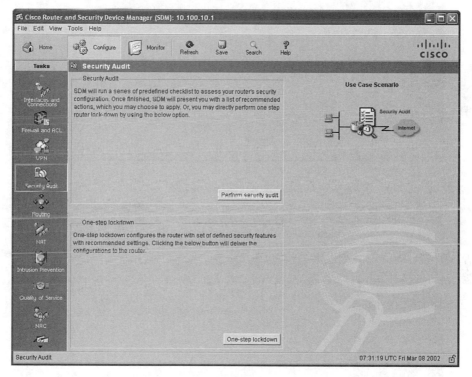

Step 3   The **Security Audit Wizard** welcome screen shown in Figure 12-22 is displayed.

Step 4   Click **Next**.

Step 5   The Security Audit Interface Configuration screen shown in Figure 12-23 is displayed. In this example, a Cisco 871 router is used. The outside interface is **FastEthernet4**, and the inside interface is **Vlan 1**.

Figure 12-22 *Security Audit Wizard Welcome Screen*

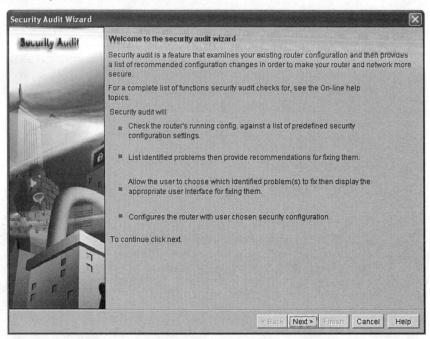

Figure 12-23 *Security Audit Wizard Interface Configuration Screen*

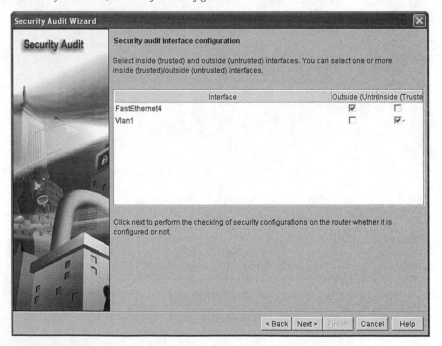

Step 6   Click **Next**.

Step 7   SDM performs the audit to make sure that the recommended settings are configured on the router. As illustrated in Figure 12-24, the router fails on numerous items.

Figure 12-24   *Security Audit Wizard Interface Configuration Screen*

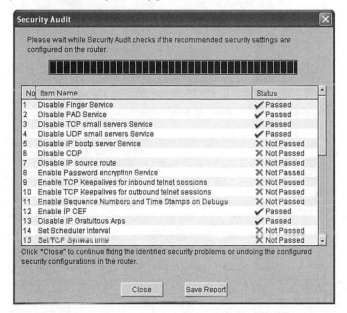

SDM allows you to save a report that lists all the configuration checks that have passed or failed. The report is illustrated in Figure 12-25.

Figure 12-25 *Security Audit Report*

Hostname	company-A-ios-fw	

Report Summary

No	Item Name	Status
1	Disable Finger Service	✓ Passed
2	Disable PAD Service	✓ Passed
3	Disable TCP small servers Service	✓ Passed
4	Disable UDP small servers Service	✓ Passed
5	Disable IP bootp server Service	✗ Not Passed
6	Disable CDP	✗ Not Passed
7	Disable IP source route	✗ Not Passed
8	Enable Password encryption Service	✗ Not Passed
9	Enable TCP Keepalives for inbound telnet sessions	✗ Not Passed
10	Enable TCP Keepalives for outbound telnet sessions	✗ Not Passed
11	Enable Sequence Numbers and Time Stamps on Debugs	✗ Not Passed
12	Enable IP CEF	✓ Passed
13	Disable IP Gratuitous Arps	✓ Passed
14	Set Scheduler Interval	✗ Not Passed
15	Set TCP Synwait time	✗ Not Passed
16	Set Banner	✗ Not Passed
17	Enable Logging	✗ Not Passed
18	Set Enable Secret Password	✗ Not Passed
19	Disable SNMP	✓ Passed
20	Set Scheduler Allocate	✗ Not Passed
21	Set Users	✗ Not Passed
22	Enable Telnet settings	✗ Not Passed
23	Enable NetFlow Monitoring	✗ Not Passed
24	Disable IP Redirects	✗ Not Passed
25	Disable IP Proxy Arp	✗ Not Passed
26	Disable IP Directed Broadcast	✓ Passed
27	Disable IP Unreachables	✗ Not Passed
28	Disable IP Mask Reply	✓ Passed
29	Disable IP Unreachables on Null interface	✗ Not Passed
30	Enable Unicast RPF on all outside interfaces	✗ Not Passed
31	Enable Firewall on all outside interfaces	✗ Not Passed
32	Set Access class on HTTP server service	✗ Not Passed
33	Set Access class on VTY lines	✗ Not Passed
34	Enable SSH for access to the router	✗ Not Passed
35	Enable AAA	✗ Not Passed

Step 8 SDM asks you to enter a new enable secret password and to configure a login banner, as illustrated in Figure 12-26.

Step 9 After you enter the new enable secret password and login banner, click **Next**.

Step 10 SDM allows you to configure an administrative account, as shown in Figure 12-27. To configure a new account, click **Add**.

Figure 12-26 *Configuring a New Enable Secret Password and Login Banner*

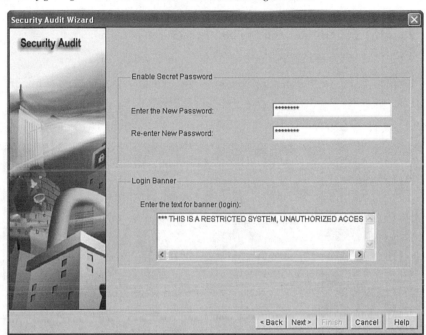

Figure 12-27 *Creating an Administrative Account*

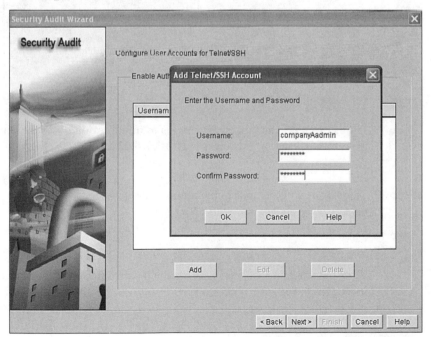

Step 11 Enter the username and password, as shown in Figure 12-27. In this
example, a user named **companyAadmin** is created.

Step 12 Click **OK** after entering the username and password.

Step 13 Click **Next** to continue with the Security Audit Wizard.

Step 14 In the next screen, SDM allows you to enable logging and configure a
system log (SYSLOG) server, as illustrated in Figure 12-28.

Figure 12-28 *Configuring Logging*

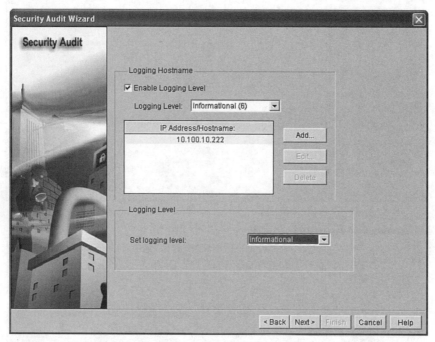

Step 15 In this example, the logging level is set to **informational (level 6)**, and
the SYSLOG server IP address is **10.100.10.222**.

Step 16 Click **Next**.

Step 17 The Advanced Firewall Configuration Wizard welcome screen is
displayed, as shown in Figure 12-29.

Step 18 Click **Next**.

Step 19 Check the inside and outside interfaces. In this example, **FastEthernet4**
is the outside interface, and **Vlan1** is the inside interface. This is
illustrated in Figure 12-30.

Figure 12-29 *Advanced Firewall Configuration Wizard Welcome Screen*

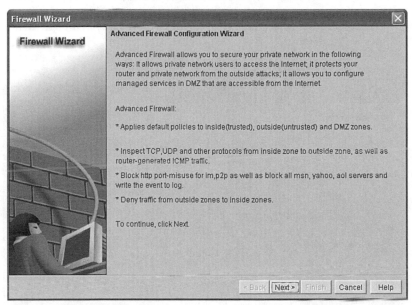

Figure 12-30 *IOS Firewall Inside and Outside Interface Selection*

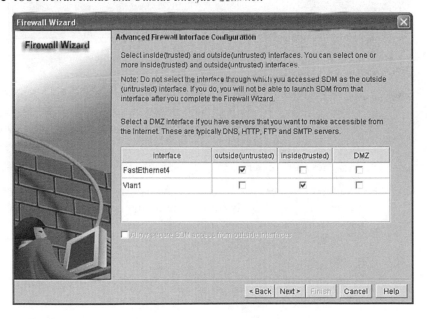

Step 20 Click **Next**.

Step 21 The screen shown in Figure 12-31 is displayed. In this screen, SDM allows you to enable predefined application security policies. You can use the slider to select the security level. In this example, the security level is set to **High**.

Figure 12-31 *Application Security Policies*

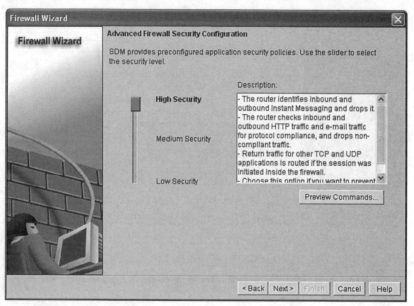

Step 22 Click **Next**.

Step 23 The SDM Wizard allows you enter the primary and secondary DNS servers for name resolution, as illustrated in Figure 12-32. In this example, the primary DNS server is **10.100.10.21**, and the secondary DNS server is **10.100.10.22**.

Step 24 Click **Next** after entering the DNS server information.

Step 25 A summary screen lists the configuration changes, as illustrated in Figure 12-33. Click **Finish** to send the configuration changes to the Cisco IOS router.

Figure 12-32 *DNS Server Configuration*

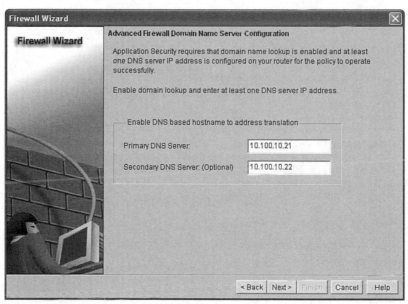

Figure 12-33 *Security Audit Wizard Summary Screen*

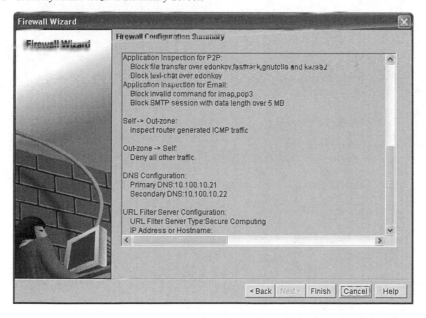

Example 12-2 shows the CLI configuration of the router at the Atlanta office after completing the previous steps.

Example 12-2 *CLI Configuration of the Cisco IOS Router at the Atlanta Office*

```
company-A-ios-fw#show running-config
Building configuration...
Current configuration : 8080 bytes
!
version 12.4
no service pad
service tcp-keepalives-in
service tcp-keepalives-out
service timestamps debug datetime msec localtime show-timezone
service timestamps log datetime msec localtime show-timezone
service password-encryption
service sequence-numbers
!
hostname company-A-ios-fw
!
boot-start-marker
boot-end-marker
!
no logging buffered
logging console critical
enable secret 5 $1$XlSV$Pa0oIYeuSY5CZOGXXOJjF/
!
aaa new-model
!
aaa authentication login local_authen local
aaa authorization exec local_author local
!
aaa session-id common
no ip source-route
ip cef
!
!
ip tcp synwait-time 10
no ip bootp server
ip name-server 10.100.10.21
ip name-server 10.100.10.22
ip ssh time-out 60
ip ssh authentication-retries 2
!
parameter-map type protocol-info msn-servers
 server name messenger.hotmail.com
 server name gateway.messenger.hotmail.com
 server name webmessenger.msn.com
!
parameter-map type protocol-info aol-servers
 server name login.oscar.aol.com
 server name toc.oscar.aol.com
 server name oam-d09a.blue.aol.com
!
```

Example 12-2 *CLI Configuration of the Cisco IOS Router at the Atlanta Office (Continued)*

```
parameter-map type protocol-info yahoo-servers
 server name scs.msg.yahoo.com
 server name scsa.msg.yahoo.com
 server name scsb.msg.yahoo.com
 server name scsc.msg.yahoo.com
 server name scsd.msg.yahoo.com
 server name cs16.msg.dcn.yahoo.com
 server name cs19.msg.dcn.yahoo.com
 server name cs42.msg.dcn.yahoo.com
 server name cs53.msg.dcn.yahoo.com
 server name cs54.msg.dcn.yahoo.com
 server name ads1.vip.scd.yahoo.com
 server name radio1.launch.vip.dal.yahoo.com
 server name in1.msg.vip.re2.yahoo.com
 server name data1.my.vip.sc5.yahoo.com
 server name address1.pim.vip.mud.yahoo.com
 server name edit.messenger.yahoo.com
 server name messenger.yahoo.com
 server name http.pager.yahoo.com
 server name privacy.yahoo.com
 server name csa.yahoo.com
 server name csb.yahoo.com
 server name csc.yahoo.com
!
parameter-map type regex sdm-regex-nonascii
 pattern ["\x00-\x80]
!
!
!
!
username companyAadmin password 7 02050D4808095E731F
!
!
class-map type inspect smtp match-any sdm-app-smtp
 match  data-length gt 5000000
class-map type inspect http match-any sdm-app-nonascii
 match  req-resp header regex sdm-regex-nonascii
class-map type inspect imap match-any sdm-app-imap
 match  invalid-command
class-map type inspect match-any sdm-cls-insp-traffic
 match protocol dns
 match protocol https
 match protocol icmp
 match protocol imap
 match protocol pop3
 match protocol tcp
 match protocol udp
class-map type inspect match-all sdm-insp-traffic
 match class-map sdm-cls-insp-traffic
class-map type inspect match-all sdm-protocol-pop3
 match protocol pop3
```

continues

Example 12-2   *CLI Configuration of the Cisco IOS Router at the Atlanta Office (Continued)*

```
class-map type inspect match-any sdm-cls-icmp-access
 match protocol icmp
 match protocol tcp
 match protocol udp
class-map type inspect match-any sdm-cls-protocol-im
 match protocol ymsgr yahoo-servers
 match protocol msnmsgr msn-servers
 match protocol aol aol-servers
class-map type inspect pop3 match-any sdm-app-pop3
 match  invalid-command
class-map type inspect http match-any sdm-http-blockparam
 match  request port-misuse im
 match  request port-misuse p2p
 match  request port-misuse tunneling
 match  req-resp protocol-violation
class-map type inspect match-all sdm-protocol-im
 match class-map sdm-cls-protocol-im
class-map type inspect match-all sdm-icmp-access
 match class-map sdm-cls-icmp-access
class-map type inspect match-all sdm-invalid-src
 match access-group 100
class-map type inspect http match-any sdm-app-httpmethods
 match  request method bcopy
 match  request method bdelete
 match  request method bmove
 match  request method bpropfind
 match  request method bproppatch
 match  request method connect
 match  request method copy
 match  request method delete
 match  request method edit
 match  request method getattribute
 match  request method getattributenames
 match  request method getproperties
 match  request method index
 match  request method lock
 match  request method mkcol
 match  request method mkdir
 match  request method move
 match  request method notify
 match  request method options
 match  request method poll
 match  request method post
 match  request method propfind
 match  request method proppatch
 match  request method put
 match  request method revadd
 match  request method revlabel
 match  request method revlog
 match  request method revnum
 match  request method save
 match  request method search
```

Example 12-2 *CLI Configuration of the Cisco IOS Router at the Atlanta Office (Continued)*

```
 match  request method setattribute
 match  request method startrev
 match  request method stoprev
 match  request method subscribe
 match  request method trace
 match  request method unedit
 match  request method unlock
 match  request method unsubscribe
class-map type inspect match-all sdm-protocol-http
 match protocol http
class-map type inspect match-all sdm-protocol-smtp
 match protocol smtp
class-map type inspect match-all sdm-protocol-imap
 match protocol imap
!
!
policy-map type inspect sdm-permit-icmpreply
 class type inspect sdm-icmp-access
  inspect
 class class-default
  pass
policy-map type inspect http sdm-action-app-http
 class type inspect http sdm-http-blockparam
  log
  reset
 class type inspect http sdm-app-httpmethods
  log
  reset
 class type inspect http sdm-app-nonascii
  log
  reset
 class class-default
policy-map type inspect smtp sdm-action-smtp
 class type inspect smtp sdm-app-smtp
  reset
 class class-default
policy-map type inspect imap sdm-action-imap
 class type inspect imap sdm-app-imap
  log
  reset
 class class-default
policy-map type inspect pop3 sdm-action-pop3
 class type inspect pop3 sdm-app-pop3
  log
  reset
 class class-default
policy-map type inspect sdm-inspect
 class type inspect sdm-invalid-src
  drop log
 class type inspect sdm-protocol-http
  inspect
  service-policy http sdm-action-app-http
```

continues

Example 12-2 *CLI Configuration of the Cisco IOS Router at the Atlanta Office (Continued)*

```
 class type inspect sdm-protocol-smtp
  inspect
  service-policy smtp sdm-action-smtp
 class type inspect sdm-protocol-imap
  inspect
  service-policy imap sdm-action-imap
 class type inspect sdm-protocol-pop3
  inspect
  service-policy pop3 sdm-action-pop3
 class type inspect sdm-protocol-im
  drop log
 class type inspect sdm-insp-traffic
  inspect
 class class-default
policy-map type inspect sdm-permit
 class class-default
!
zone security out-zone
zone security in-zone
zone-pair security sdm-zp-self-out source self destination out-zone
 service-policy type inspect sdm-permit-icmpreply
zone-pair security sdm-zp-out-self source out-zone destination self
 service-policy type inspect sdm-permit
zone-pair security sdm-zp-in-out source in-zone destination out-zone
 service-policy type inspect sdm-inspect
 !
 !
 !
 !
 !
interface Null0
 no ip unreachables
!
interface FastEthernet0
!
interface FastEthernet1
!
interface FastEthernet2
!
interface FastEthernet3
!
interface FastEthernet4
 description $FW_OUTSIDE$
 ip address 209.165.200.231 255.255.255.0
 no ip redirects
 no ip unreachables
 no ip proxy-arp
 zone-member security out-zone
 ip route-cache flow
 duplex auto
```

Example 12-2 *CLI Configuration of the Cisco IOS Router at the Atlanta Office (Continued)*

```
 speed auto
 !
interface Vlan1
 description $FW_INSIDE$
 ip address 10.100.10.1 255.255.255.0
 no ip redirects
 no ip unreachables
 no ip proxy-arp
 zone-member security in-zone
 ip route-cache flow
 !
ip route 0.0.0.0 0.0.0.0 209.165.200.225
 !
ip http server
no ip http secure-server
 !
logging trap informational
logging 10.100.10.222
access-list 100 remark SDM_ACL Category=128
access-list 100 permit ip host 255.255.255.255 any
access-list 100 permit ip 127.0.0.0 0.255.255.255 any
access-list 100 permit ip 209.165.200.0 0.0.0.255 any
access-list 101 remark VTY Access-class list
access-list 101 remark SDM_ACL Category=1
access-list 101 permit ip 10.100.10.0 0 0.0.255 any
access-list 101 deny   ip any any
no cdp run
 !
 !
 !
control-plane
 !
banner login ^C*** THIS IS A RESTRICTED SYSTEM, UNAUTHORIZED ACCESS^C
 !
line con 0
 login authentication local_authen
 no modem enable
 transport output telnet
line aux 0
 login authentication local_authen
 transport output telnet
line vty 0 4
 access-class 101 in
 authorization exec local_author
 login authentication local_authen
 transport input telnet ssh
 !
scheduler max-task-time 5000
scheduler allocate 4000 1000
scheduler interval 500
end
```

Configuring Basic Network Address Translation (NAT)

The router administrator needs to configure basic NAT for internal users to access the Internet. The following steps are completed to enable basic NAT on the Cisco IOS router.

Step 1 Log in to the router using SDM.

Step 2 Navigate to **Configure > NAT** and click **Basic NAT**, as illustrated in Figure 12-34.

Figure 12-34 *Configuring Basic NAT*

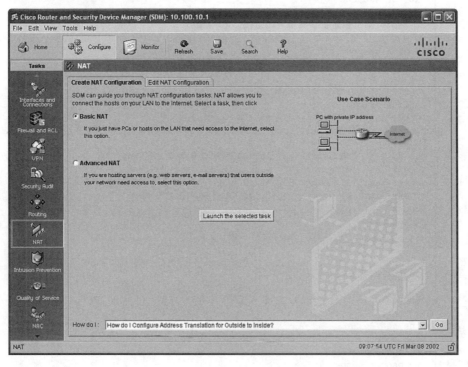

Step 3 Click the **Launch the selected task** button to start the NAT Configuration Wizard.

Step 4 The NAT Configuration Wizard welcome screen appears. Click **Next**.

Step 5 The screen shown in Figure 12-35 is displayed.

Figure 12-35 *Basic NAT Configuration Wizard*

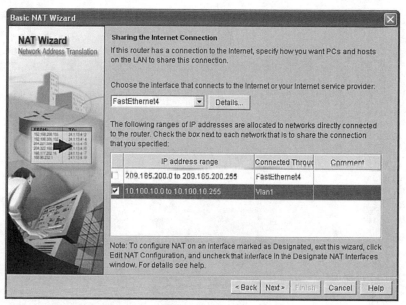

Step 6 Choose the interface that connects to the Internet from the drop-down menu. **FastEthernet4** is selected in this example.

Step 7 In this example, the inside network will be translated to the public IP address of the outside interface.

Step 8 Click **Next**.

Step 9 The wizard displays a summary screen listing the configuration changes. Click **Finish**.

Configuring Site-to-Site VPN

Users at the office in Atlanta need to securely access resources in the Raleigh office. The security administrator configures a site-to-site IPsec tunnel between the Cisco ASA in Raleigh and the Cisco IOS router in Atlanta.

The following are the steps that need to be completed to configure the Cisco IOS router in Atlanta to terminate a site-to-site IPsec tunnel with the Cisco ASA in Raleigh.

Step 1 Log in to the router using SDM.

Step 2 Navigate to **Configure > VPN** and choose **Site-to-Site VPN**, as illustrated in Figure 12-36.

Figure 12-36 *Configuring a Site-to-Site VPN Using SDM*

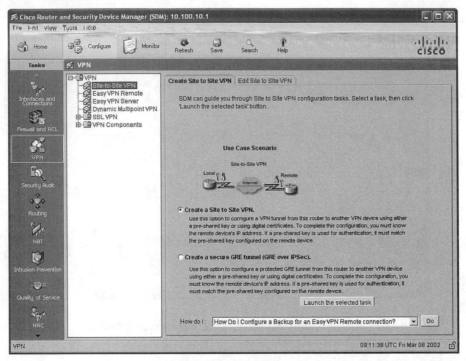

Step 3 Click **Create a Site to Site VPN** and click the **Launch the selected task** button.

Step 4 The **Site-to-Site VPN Wizard** welcome screen is displayed, as illustrated in Figure 12-37. The **Quick setup** option allows you to easily configure a site-to-site VPN tunnel to another Cisco router with minimal interaction. In this case, the router will be creating a site-to-site VPN tunnel to a Cisco ASA, then the **Step by step wizard** is selected. This option lets you customize the configuration.

Step 5 Click **Next**.

Step 6 The screen shown in Figure 12-38 is displayed. Select the interface that will terminate the VPN tunnel. In this example, **FastEthernet4** (the outside interface of the router) is selected.

Figure 12-37 *SDM Site-to-Site VPN Wizard Welcome Screen*

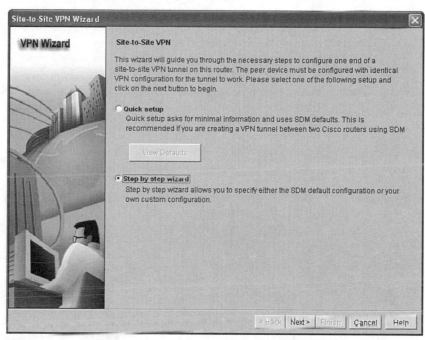

Figure 12-38 *Configuring the VPN Interface, Remote Peer, and Preshared Keys*

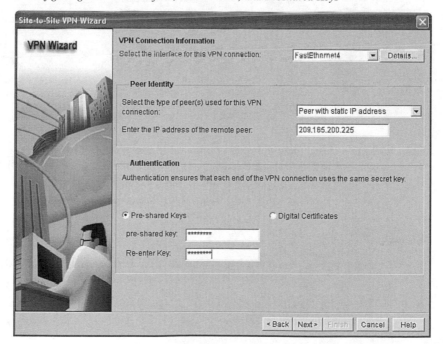

Step 7 In this case, the VPN peer (Cisco ASA) is configured with a static IP address. Choose **Peer with static IP address** from the drop-down menu and enter the IP address of the peer (**209.165.200.225**). Preshared keys are used in this example for tunnel authentication.

Step 8 Click **Next**.

Step 9 The next screen allows you to configure an Internet Key Exchange (IKE) (as illustrated in Figure 12-39). This policy must match the IKE policy on the Cisco ASA. Click **Add** to enter a new IKE policy.

Figure 12-39 *Configuring the IKE Policy with SDM*

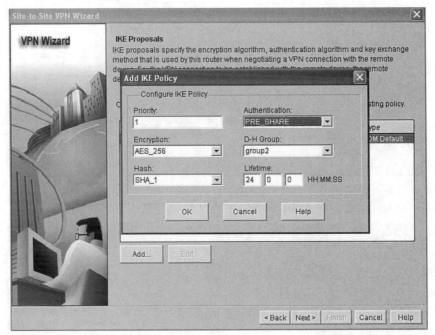

Step 10 In this case, a new policy is configured to use preshared keys for authentication. The selected encryption protocol is Advanced Encryption Standard **AES_256**. Diffie-Hellman (DH) **Group 2** is used. The IKE hashing algorithm is Secure Hash Algorithm **SHA_1**. The default 24-hour lifetime for IKE is selected.

Step 11 Click **Next**.

Step 12 The next screen enables you to configure the IPsec policies. Click **Add** to add a new transform-set (IPsec phase two policies).

Step 13 The dialog box illustrated in Figure 12-40 appears allowing you to configure the IPsec policies.

Figure 12-40 *Configuring the IPsec Phase Two Policies with SDM*

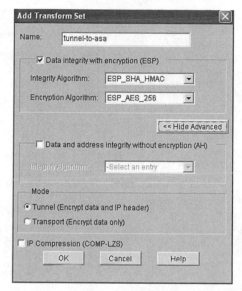

Step 14 Enter a name for the new transform set. In this case, the name is
tunnel-to-asa.

Step 15 The Encapsulatation Security Payload (ESP) protocol is used in
this example. The integrity algorithm used in this example is
ESP_SHA_HMAC, and the encryption algorithm is **ESP_AES_256**.
The Cisco ASA configuration must match these settings to establish the
site-to-site IPsec VPN tunnel.

Step 16 Tunnel mode is used in this example to encrypt both the payload (data)
and IP header.

Step 17 Click **OK** to add the new transform-set.

Step 18 Click **Next**.

Step 19 The screen shown in Figure 12-41 is displayed. It allows you to select the
traffic you would like to protect.

Step 20 Click **Protect all traffic between the following subnets**.

Step 21 Configure the local and remote networks (the networks that will be able
to communicate over the VPN tunnel). In this case, the local network
is **10.100.10.0/24**, and the remote network is **10.10.10.0/24**.

Step 22 Click **Next**.

Figure 12-41 *Traffic to Protect*

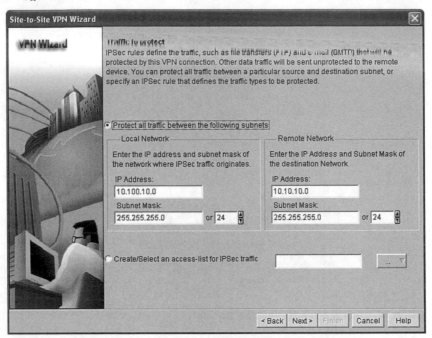

Step 23 A summary screen listing the configuration changes is displayed. Click **Finish** to apply the changes.

Step 24 Because NAT/PAT was configured on the router, SDM shows a warning message asking you if you would like to bypass NAT for the traffic over the VPN tunnel. The warning screen is shown in Figure 12-42.

Figure 12-42 *SDM Warning Screen*

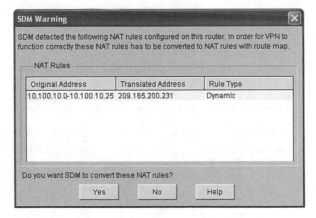

Step 25 Click **Yes** to bypass NAT for the tunnel traffic.

Example 12-3 shows the CLI VPN configuration of the router.

Example 12-3 *CLI VPN Configuration of the Router*

```
!Phase 1 IKE policy
crypto isakmp policy 2
 encr aes 256
 authentication pre-share
 group 2
crypto isakmp key cisco123 address 209.165.200.225
!
!Phase 2 policy
crypto ipsec transform-set tunnel-to-asa esp-aes 256 esp-sha-hmac
!
!crypto-map configuration for the Tunnel to the Cisco ASA
crypto map SDM_CMAP_1 1 ipsec isakmp
 description Tunnel to209.165.200.225
 set peer 209.165.200.225
 set transform-set tunnel-to-asa
 match address 102
!
!ACL defining tunnel traffic
access-list 102 remark SDM_ACL Category=4
access-list 102 remark IPSec Rule
access-list 102 permit ip 10.100.10.0 0.0.0.255 10.10.10.0 0.0.0.255
!
!Outside Interface Configuration
interface FastEthernet4
 description $FW_OUTSIDE$
 ip address 209.165.200.231 255.255.255.0
ip nat outside
crypto map SDM_CMAP_1
!
!NAT Configuration - bypassing NAT for tunnel traffic
ip nat inside source route-map SDM_RMAP_1 interface FastEthernet4 overload
!
route-map SDM_RMAP_1 permit 1
 match ip address 105
access-list 105 remark SDM_ACL Category=2
access-list 105 remark IPSec Rule
access-list 105 deny   ip 10.100.10.0 0.0.0.255 10.10.10.0 0.0.0.255
access-list 105 permit ip 10.100.10.0 0.0.0.255 any
```

The next task is to configure the Cisco ASA in the Raleigh office to terminate the site-to-site VPN tunnel. Complete the following steps to complete this task.

Step 1 Log in to the Cisco ASA using ASDM.

Step 2 From the main ASDM menu, choose **Wizards > IPsec VPN Wizard**, as shown in Figure 12-43.

Step 3 The VPN Wizard starts by allowing you to select the tunnel type, as illustrated in Figure 12-44. Click **Site-to-Site**.

Step 4 Choose the **outside** interface as the VPN tunnel interface from the drop-down menu.

Figure 12-43 *Launching the ASDM IPsec VPN Wizard*

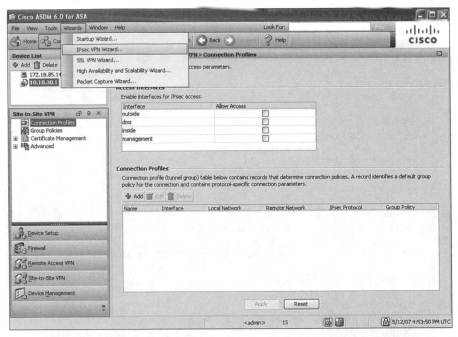

Figure 12-44 *ASDM VPN Wizard—VPN Tunnel Type*

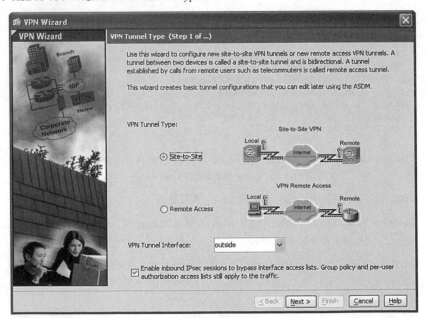

Step 5 In this example, the Cisco ASA will be configured to allow inbound IPsec sessions to bypass all configured access control lists (ACL).

Step 6 Click **Next**.

Step 7 The screen shown in Figure 12-45 is displayed. Here you can enter the remote site peer information.

Figure 12-45 *ASDM VPN Wizard—Remote Peer Information*

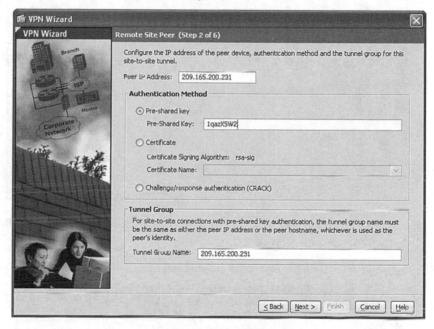

Step 8 Enter the peer IP address (**209.165.200.231** in this example).

Step 9 Under **Authentication Method**, click **Pre-shared key** and enter the preshared key. In this example, the preshared key is **1qazXSW2**.

Step 10 By default, the IP address of the remote peer is used as the tunnel group name. Leave the default configuration.

Step 11 Click **Next**.

Step 12 The screen shown in Figure 12-46 is displayed. Here you can enter the IKE policy information.

Step 13 The IKE policy parameters must match those configured in the router. In this case, the same encryption protocol, authentication hashing algorithm, and DH group are configured.

Step 14 Click **Next**.

Figure 12-46 *ASDM VPN Wizard—IKE Policy*

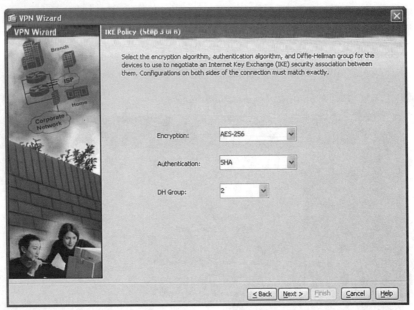

Step 15 The screen shown in Figure 12-47 is displayed. Here you can enter the IPsec phase 2 information.

Figure 12-47 *ASDM VPN Wizard—IPsec Encryption and Authentication*

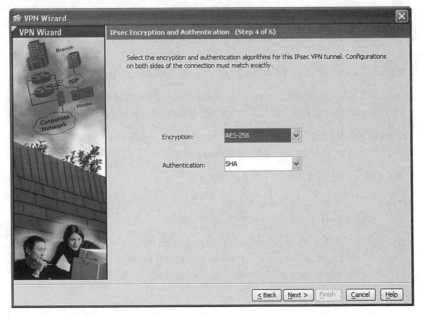

Step 16 The IPsec encryption and authentication protocol parameters must match those configured in the router, as shown in Figure 12-47.

Step 17 Click **Next**.

Step 18 The screen shown in Figure 12-48 is displayed. This screen allows you to enter the local and remote networks that will communicate over the IPsec site-to-site VPN tunnel.

Figure 12-48 *ASDM VPN Wizard—Hosts and Networks*

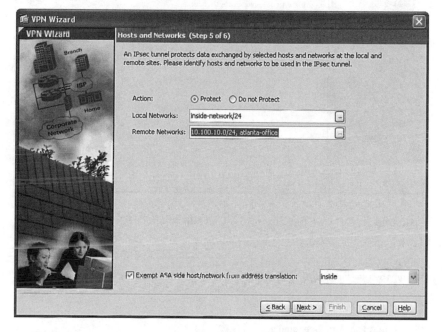

Step 19 Under **Action**, click **Protect**.

Step 20 Enter the local network information. In this case, the **inside-network/24** is selected.

Step 21 Enter the remote network information. The **10.100.10.0/24, atlanta-office** remote network is selected in this example.

Step 22 Check the **Exempt ASA side host/network from address translation** option and choose the **inside** interface from the drop-down menu to bypass NAT for tunnel traffic.

Step 23 Click **Next**.

Step 24 The summary screen shown in Figure 12-49 is displayed.

Step 25 Click **Finish** to apply the changes to the Cisco ASA.

Figure 12-49 *ASDM VPN Wizard—Summary Screen*

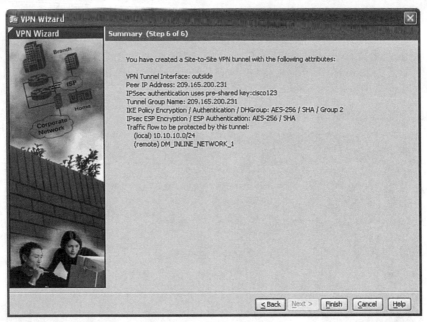

Example 12-4 shows the Cisco ASA CLI site-to-site VPN configuration.

Example 12-4 *Cisco ASA CLI Site-to-Site VPN Configuration*

```
!IKE Enabled on the outside interface
crypto isakmp enable outside
!
!IKE Policy (phase one policy)
crypto isakmp policy 10
 authentication pre-share
 encryption aes-256
 hash sha
 group 2
 lifetime 86400
!
!Phase 2 policy and crypto map configuration
crypto ipsec transform-set ESP-AES-256-SHA esp-aes-256 esp-sha-hmac
crypto map outside_map 20 match address outside_20_cryptomap
crypto map outside_map 20 set peer 209.165.200.231
crypto map outside_map 20 set transform-set ESP-AES-256-SHA
!
!Crypto map is applied to the outside interface
crypto map outside_map interface outside
```

Example 12-4   *Cisco ASA CLI Site-to-Site VPN Configuration (Continued)*

```
!
!ACL used by the crypto map to define the traffic that will be encrypted
access-list outside_20_cryptomap extended permit ip 10.10.10.0 255.255.255.0
  object-group atlanta-office
!
!Tunnel group configuration for the site-to-site tunnel
tunnel-group 209.165.200.231 type ipsec-l2l
tunnel-group 209.165.200.231 ipsec-attributes
 pre-shared-key *
!
!Bypassing NAT for the VPN tunnel traffic
nat (inside) 0 access-list inside_nat0_outbound
access-list inside_nat0_outbound extended permit ip 10.10.10.0 255.255.255.0
  object-group atlanta-office
!
!Object Group defining the Atlanta office remote network
object-group network atlanta-office
 network-object 10.100.10.0 255.255.255.0
```

Case Study of a Medium-Sized Enterprise

Company-B is a medium-sized software development company based in Chicago, Illinois. This organization has 1200 employees and 75 contractors at a call center in a partner office (Partner-A). Figure 12-50 illustrates a high-level overview of the Chicago office for Company-B.

Two routers (R1 and R2) reside at the Internet Edge followed by two Cisco ASAs with the Advanced Inspection and Prevention Security Services Module (AIP-SSM). The AIP-SSM provides intrusion prevention system (IPS) functionality. Web, e-mail, and DNS servers reside at a DMZ network. A Cisco Secure Monitoring, Analysis, and Response System (CS-MARS), a Cisco Secure Access Control Server (ACS), and a Simple Network Management Protocol (SNMP) server reside in the management network.

Company-B has three major user groups in the Chicago office:

- Sales
- Engineering
- Finance

Company-B's security manager has learned the techniques and methodologies discussed earlier on this book. The security manager develops a strategic plan to implement best practices to increase the security of their network infrastructure. The following sections include several tasks that the security manager of Company-B completes to increase the security of the network and its components.

Figure 12-50 *High-Level Overview of Company-B Chicago Office*

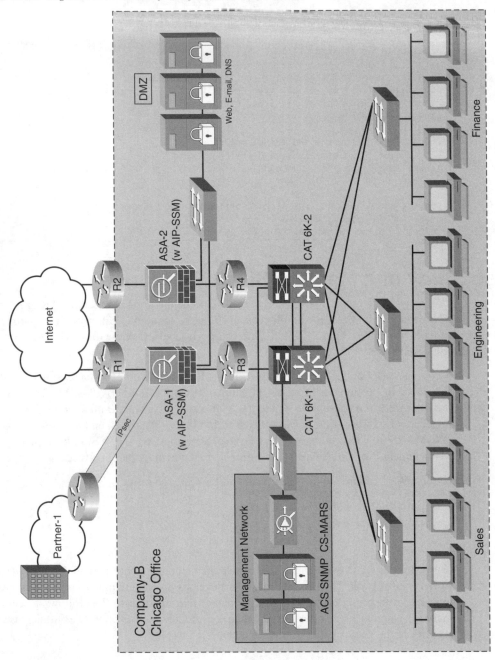

Protecting the Internet Edge Routers

On the Internet edge routers (R1 and R2), the administrator configures an ACL to deny packets from illegal sources (RFC 1918 and RFC 3330 addresses). In addition, this ACL denies traffic with source addresses belonging within the internal address space of Company-B (that is, 209.165.201.0/24) that is entering from an external source. Example 12-5 shows the ACL configuration.

Example 12-5 *Antispoofing ACL*

```
access-list 100 deny ip host 0.0.0.0 any
access-list 100 deny ip 127.0.0.0 0.255.255.255 any
access-list 100 deny ip 192.0.2.0 0.0.0.255 any
access-list 100 deny ip 224.0.0.0 31.255.255.255 any
access-list 100 deny ip 10.0.0.0 0.255.255.255 any
access-list 100 deny ip 172.16.0.0 0.15.255.255 any
access-list 100 deny ip 192.168.0.0 0.0.255.255 any
access-list 100 deny ip any 209.165.201.0 0.0.0.255
access-list 100 permit ip any any
```

NOTE   In addition, the administrator performs a security audit using SDM and makes the necessary changes, as the Company-A administrator.

Configuring the AIP-SSM on the Cisco ASA

Two Cisco ASAs protect the Chicago office internal network. The IP address configuration of both Cisco ASAs is illustrated in Figure 12-51.

Figure 12-51 *Cisco ASAs at the Chicago Office*

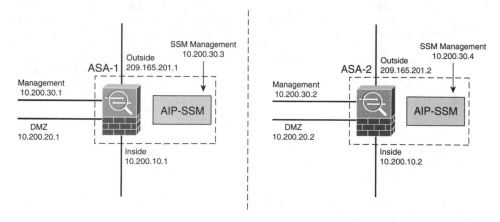

The following are the IP addresses of each of the interfaces of the primary Cisco ASA (ASA-1):

- **Outside:** 209.165.201.1
- **Inside:** 10.200.10.1
- **DMZ:** 10.200.20.1
- **Management:** 10.200.30.1
- **AIP-SSM Management interface:** 10.200.30.3

The following are the IP addresses of each of the interfaces of the secondary Cisco ASA (ASA-2):

- **Outside:** 209.165.201.2
- **Inside:** 10.200.10.2
- **DMZ:** 10.200.20.2
- **Management:** 10.200.30.2
- **AIP-SSM management interface:** 10.200.30.4

The administrator configures the necessary access and address translation for internal services in a procedure that is similar to the steps you learned previously in this chapter. After performing these basic configuration steps, the security administrator initializes the AIP-SSM. To verify that the ASA-1 recognizes the AIP-SSM, the administrator uses the **show module** command, as shown in Example 12-6.

Example 12-6 *Output of the* **show module** *Command*

```
companyB-ASA1# show module
Mod Card Type                                       Model              Serial No.
--- -------------------------------------------- ------------------ -----------
  0 ASA 5520 Adaptive Security Appliance          ASA5520-K8         JMX1113L0Y4
  1 ASA 5500 Series Security Services Module-10   ASA-SSM-10         JAB101502D9
Mod MAC Address Range                    Hw Version  Fw Version  Sw Version
--- ----------------------------------- ----------- ----------- -----------
  0 001a.6d7c.8c95 to 001a.6d7c.8c99     2.0         1.0(11)2    8.0(2)
  1 0016.c79f.78c1 to 0016.c79f.78c1     1.0         1.0(10)0    6.0(2)E1
Mod SSM Application Name         Status          SSM Application Version
--- ----------------------- ----------------- --------------------------
  1 IPS                         Up              6.0(2)E1
Mod Status              Data Plane Status     Compatibility
--- ------------------- --------------------- -------------
  0 Up Sys              Not Applicable
  1 Up                  Up
```

The highlighted lines show that the module is running IPS Software Version 6.0(2)E1 and that it is operational.

The administrator logs into ASA-1 via the CLI and connects to the AIP-SSM using the **session 1** command. This puts him on the AIP-SSM CLI. To initialize the AIP-SSM, the administrator uses the **setup** command, as demonstrated in Example 12-7.

Example 12-7 *Initializing ASA-1 AIP-SSM*

```
sensor# setup
     --- System Configuration Dialog ---
At any point you may enter a question mark '?' for help.
Use ctrl-c to abort configuration dialog at any prompt.
Default settings are in square brackets '[]'.
Current Configuration:
service host
network-settings
host-ip 10.1.9.201/24,10.1.9.1
host-name sensor
telnet-option disabled
ftp-timeout 300
login-banner-text
exit
time-zone-settings
offset 0
standard-time-zone-name UTC
exit
summertime-option disabled
ntp-option disabled
exit
service web-server
port 443
exit
Current time: Mon May 14 18:26:51 2007
Setup Configuration last modified: Mon May 14 17:45:30 2007
Continue with configuration dialog?[yes]: yes
Enter host name[sensor]: companyB-AIP-SSM1
Enter IP interface[10.1.9.201/24,10.1.9.1]: 10.200.30.3/24,10.200.30.1
Enter telnet-server status[disabled]:
Enter web-server port[443]:
Modify current access list?[no]: yes
Current access list entries:
  No entries
Permit: 10.200.30.0/24
Permit:
Modify system clock settings?[no]: no
Modify virtual sensor "vs0" configuration?[no]: yes
Current interface configuration
  Command control: GigabitEthernet0/0
  Unused:
    GigabitEthernet0/1
  Monitored:
    None
Add Monitored interfaces?[no]: yes
Interface[]: GigabitEthernet0/1
Interface[]:
The following configuration was entered.
service host
network-settings
```

continues

Example 12-7 *Initializing ASA-1 AIP-SSM (Continued)*

```
host-ip 10.200.30.3/24,10.200.30.1
host-name companyB-AIP-SSM1
telnet-option disabled
access-list 10.200.30.0/24
ftp-timeout 300
no login-banner-text
exit
time-zone-settings
offset 0
standard-time-zone-name UTC
exit
summertime-option disabled
ntp-option disabled
exit
service web-server
port 443
exit
service analysis-engine
virtual-sensor vs0
physical-interface GigabitEthernet0/1
exit
exit
[0] Go to the command prompt without saving this config.
[1] Return back to the setup without saving this config.
[2] Save this configuration and exit setup.
Enter your selection[2]: 2
Configuration Saved.
```

In Example 12-7, the administrator configures the AIP-SSM hostname, IP address, and
subnet mask of the management interface, in addition to the default gateway. The
administrator allows management access only from machines in the 10.200.30.0/24
management network. Also, the GigabitEthernet0/1 interface is enabled for traffic
inspection. Finally, the administrator saves the configuration and exits the interactive
setup session.

Configuring Active-Standby Failover on the Cisco ASA

Maintaining appropriate redundancy mechanisms within infrastructure devices is
extremely important for any organization. The Cisco ASA supports active-active and
active-standby failover.

NOTE   When the active unit fails, it changes to the standby state while the standby unit changes
to the active state. The unit that becomes active takes ownership of the IP addresses and
MAC addresses of the failed unit. The unit that is now in standby state takes over the
standby IP addresses and MAC addresses. Because network devices see no change in the
MAC-to-IP address pairing, no ARP entries change or time out anywhere on the network.

When a pair of Cisco ASAs is configured in active-active failover mode, both appliances are actively passing traffic at the same time. In contrast, when configured in active-standby mode, the primary appliance is the active one and the secondary appliance is in standby and does not pass traffic. After the primary fails, the secondary takes over and begins to pass traffic.

The network security team of Company-B evaluates both options. They decide to implement active-standby failover because, for active-active to work, the appliances must be configured in multicontext mode. Active-active requires a minimum of two security contexts on each appliance. Company-B has a site-to-site VPN tunnel to a business partner (Partner-A). The Cisco ASA does not support VPN when configured in multicontext mode.

The following are the steps taken to configure active-standby failover on the Cisco ASAs.

Step 1   Log in to the Cisco ASA using ASDM.

Step 2   On the main toolbar, click **Wizards** and choose **High Availability and Scalability Wizard**, as illustrated in Figure 12-52.

Figure 12-52 *Launching the High Availability and Scalability Wizard*

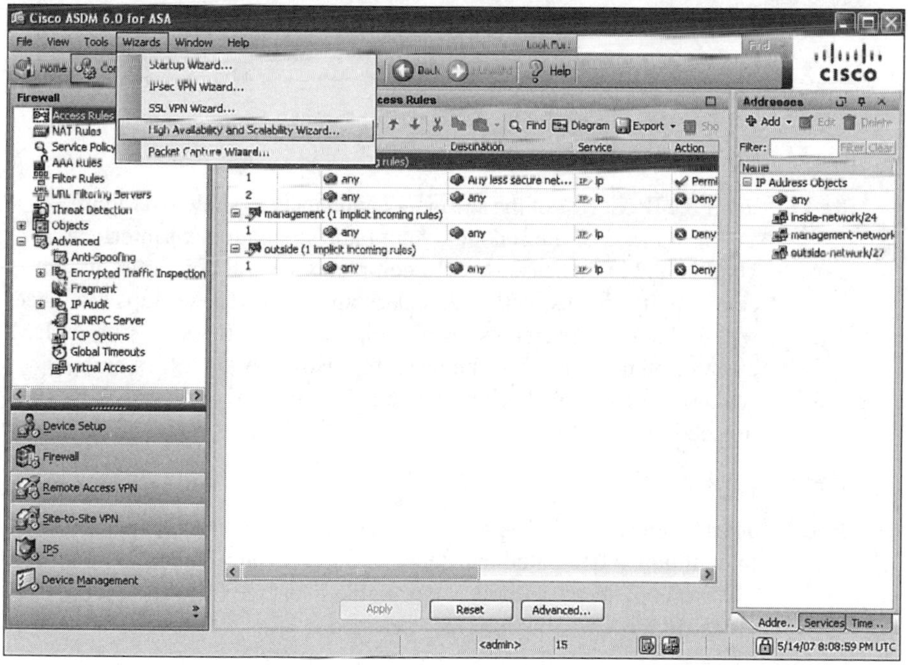

Step 3   The screen shown in Figure 12-53 is displayed. Click **Configure Active/Standby failover**.

Figure 12-53 *Configuring Active/Standby Failover*

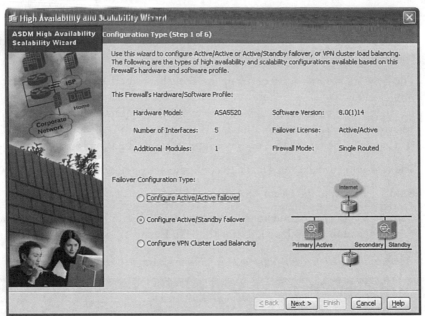

Step 4   Click **Next**.

Step 5   Enter the IP address of the secondary appliance, as shown in Figure 12-54. The IP address of the secondary appliance management interface is **10.200.30.2** in this case. ASDM completes several compatibility and connectivity checks on the secondary appliance. These steps are listed within the ASDM screen shown in Figure 12-54. If successful, ASDM allows you to proceed to the next step. However, if issues exist, ASDM marks each check that failed. You must fix any errors before proceeding further.

Step 6   Click **Next**.

Step 7   The screen shown in Figure 12-55 is displayed. This screen allows you to configure a dedicated interface for failover communication between the two appliances. Choose an available interface from the drop-down menu. In this case, the interface selected is **GigabitEthernet0/3**.

Step 8   Enter a name for the failover interface. In this example, the interface is called **failover** for simplicity. This is an arbitrarily name.

Figure 12-54 *Failover Peer Connectivity and Compatibility Check*

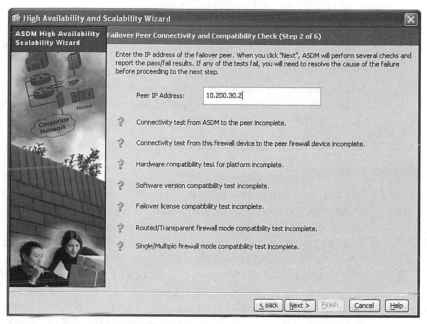

Figure 12-55 *Configuring the Failover LAN Link*

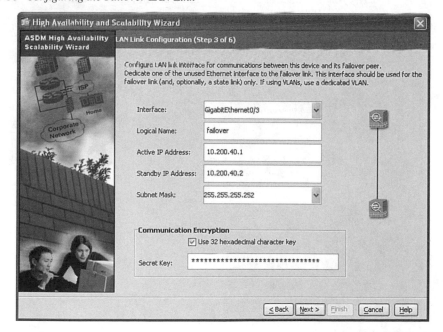

Step 9 Assign an IP address for this interface, in addition to a standby IP address, as shown in Figure 12-55. In this example, the active IP address is **10.200.40.1**, and the secondary is **10.200.40.2**.

Step 10 Configure a subnet mask for this interface. A 30-bit (**255.255.255.252**) subnet mask is configured in this example.

Step 11 You can optionally encrypt the failover communication data exchanged by both appliances. To enable encryption, select the **Use 32 hexadecimal character key** option under **Communication Encryption**.

Step 12 Enter a 32 hexadecimal character key.

Step 13 Click **Next**.

Step 14 You can configure stateful failover to maintain connection status, translation, and other information on the standby appliance to avoid interruption of services when a failover occurs. You can configure a dedicated interface or use the previously configured failover interface for this communication. On busy networks where numerous connections are built and torn down at a fast pace, a dedicated interface is suggested. In this case, all other interfaces on the Cisco ASAs are used for other purposes, and the stateful failover traffic of Company-B does not present an oversubscription risk based on tests that the administrator performed in the lab prior to deployment. The administrator configures the failover LAN link interface as the stateful failover link, as shown in Figure 12-56.

Figure 12-56 *Configuring the Stateful Failover Link*

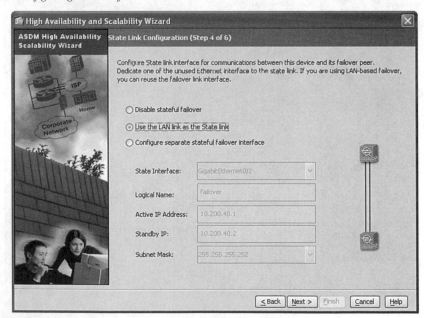

Step 15 You must configure a standby IP address for each interface that is enabled on the Cisco ASA. The standby appliance uses these IP addresses. The screen shown in Figure 12-57 allows you to configure the standby IP address for each interface.

Figure 12-57 *Configuring the Standby IP Addresses*

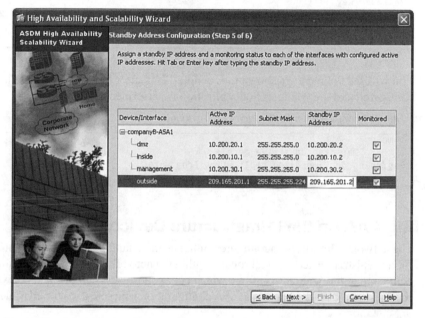

Step 16 Click **Next**.

Step 17 A summary screen showing the configuration items to be sent to the security appliance is displayed. Click **Finish** to apply the changes.

Example 12-8 includes the CLI commands sent to the primary appliance.

Example 12-8 *Failover Configuration on the Primary ASA*

```
failover
failover lan unit primary
failover lan interface failover GigabitEthernet0/3
failover key *****
failover link failover GigabitEthernet0/3
failover interface ip failover 10.200.40.1 255.255.255.252 standby 10.200.40.2
interface GigabitEthernet0/3
 description LAN/STATE Failover Interface
monitor-interface dmz
monitor-interface inside
monitor-interface outside
monitor-interface management
```

Example 12-9 includes the CLI commands sent to the secondary appliance.

Example 12-9 *Failover Configuration on the Secondary ASA*

```
failover
failover lan unit secondary
failover lan interface failover GigabitEthernet0/3
failover key *****
failover interface ip failover 10.200.40.1 255.255.255.252 standby 10.200.40.2
interface GigabitEthernet0/3
no shutdown
```

You will see the message shown in Example 12-10 after the secondary appliance is configured and the configuration replication is performed.

Example 12-10 *Failover Configuration Replication Confirmation*

```
companyB-ASA1#..
        Detected an Active mate
Beginning configuration replication from mate.
companyB-ASA1# End configuration replication from mate.
```

Configuring AAA on the Infrastructure Devices

The network administrator configures authentication, authorization, and accounting (AAA) for administrative access to all routers within the network. The network administrator uses command authorization to enforce which commands users can invoke and execute in the routers. Example 12-11 shows a AAA configuration template used for all routers within the organization:

Example 12-11 *AAA Configuration on Routers*

```
aaa new-model
aaa authentication login default group tacacs+ local
tacacs-server host 172.18.85.181
tacacs-server key 1qaz2wsx
```

The **aaa new-model** command enables the AAA security services. The **aaa authentication** command defines the default method list. Incoming logins on all interfaces (by default) use TACACS+ for authentication. If no TACACS+ server responds, the network access server uses the information contained in the local username database for authentication. The **tacacs-server host** command identifies the TACACS+ server as having an IP address of **172.18.85.181**. The **tacacs-server** key command defines the shared encryption key to be **1qaz2wsx**.

The administrator also configures AAA on the Cisco ASAs for Telnet, Secure Shell (SSH), HTTPS, and serial console access. The commands used are shown in Example 12-12.

In this example, authentication is performed using an external TACACS+ server (that is, Cisco Secure ACS).

Example 12-12 *Cisco ASA AAA Configuration*

```
!The following commands define a TACACS+ server and limit the number of failed
  attempts to 4.The server group name is svrgrp
!
aaa-server svrgrp protocol tacacs+
 max-failed-attempts 4
!
!The TACACS+ server (172.18.85.101) and a shared secret (1qaz2wsx) are defined. The
  timeout is set to 5 seconds.
aaa-server svrgrp host 172.18.85.101 1qaz2wsx timeout 5
!
!Telnet authentication
aaa authentication telnet console svrgrp
!
!Serial console port authentication
aaa authentication serial console svrgrp
!
!HTTPS authentication for ASDM connections
aaa authentication secure-http-client
```

Cisco Secure ACS is used as the TACACS+ server. The following steps are taken to add the routers and the Cisco ASAs as authentication clients on Cisco Secure ACS:

Step 1 Log in to the Cisco Secure ACS web admin console.

Step 2 Choose **Network Configuration** on the left, and click **Add Entry** to add an entry for the Cisco ASAs or routers in either the TACACS+ or RADIUS server database.

Step 3 Choose the server database according to the routers and Cisco ASA configurations. Because TACACS+ is used in this example, choose **TACACS+ (Cisco IOS)** under the **Authenticate Using** drop-down menu.

Step 4 Configure the shared key. This key is used for authentication between the authentication client (router or Cisco ASA) and Cisco Secure ACS.

Case Study of a Large Enterprise

Company-C is a large enterprise that offers numerous information technology products and services. Over the past few years, this company has been growing at a fast pace. Recently, Company-C acquired Company-A and Company-B. The Raleigh and Atlanta offices of Company-A became branch offices, and the Chicago office of Company-B became a regional office, as illustrated in Figure 12-58. The headquarters is located in New York City.

Figure 12-58 *Company-C High-Level Network Topology*

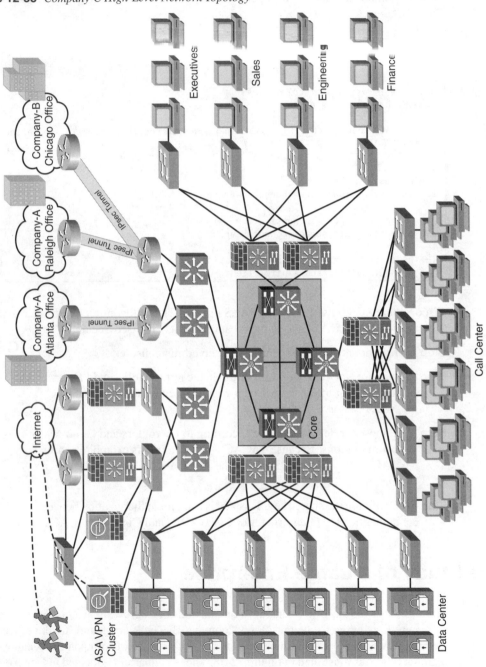

The following is a high-level explanation of the New York office topology:

- At the Internet edge, a pair of Cisco Catalyst 6500 switches is deployed with FWSMs.
- A cluster of Cisco ASAs is configured for IPsec- and SSL-based remote access VPN.
- Cisco routers are configured to terminate IPsec site-to-site VPN tunnels to the branch offices and the regional office.
- The user population includes the following:
  - A call center of more than 100 customer service representatives
  - The executive floor
  - Sales representatives
  - Engineering
  - Finance
- A large data center is also located at the New York office.

With the dramatic growth, Company-C staff members initiate several corporate initiatives and projects to increase the security of the network. The following sections include information about different techniques and methodologies that Company-C staff members use.

Creating a New Computer Security Incident Response Team (CSIRT)

Company-C management starts the process to create a Computer Security Incident Response Team (CSIRT). The CSIRT will comprise staff members from different departments within an organization:

- Global information technology (IT)
- Information Security (InfoSec)
- Operation Security (OpSec)
- Business analysis team

TIP   In some large organizations, the CSIRT may be a full-time staff. Deciding whether the staff members should be full-time or not depends on your organizational needs and budget. What is important is to clearly identify who needs to be involved at each level of the CSIRT planning, implementation, and operation. For instance, one of the most challenging tasks is the process of identifying the staff members who will be performing security incident response functions.

In addition, you must identify which internal and external organizations will interface with the CSIRT. Evangelize and communicate the CSIRT responsibilities accordingly with these entities.

The new CSIRT team develops and documents roles and responsibilities for all CSIRT members and their functions. Each member has a different background and qualifications. These roles and responsibilities are assigned based on the experience and strengths of each member.

Creating New Security Policies

The executive team of Company-C also delegates the tasks of creating new security policies within the organization. Since Company-C acquired Company-A and Company-B new policies need to be defined and followed. The following are the new policies that are created:

- Physical security
- Perimeter security
- Device security
- Remote access VPN
- Patch management
- Change management
- Internet access policy

Physical Security Policy

The physical security policy is created to protect and preserve information, physical assets, and human assets by reducing the exposure to various physical threats. A new employee badge system is deployed to deny unauthorized access and to track authorized entry. Card access and monitoring devices will be used to ensure that sensitive information is not compromised and access to control office work areas is monitored. The building facility manager will ensure that appropriate monitoring devices allow monitoring of primary accesses and that each individual is screened for access. In addition, a video surveillance system must be implanted and appropriately managed. This video system should function with an existing Ethernet switched environment, and it should reduce the complexity while lowering the cost of deploying video surveillance. It also provides video surveillance system owners with the flexibility to design solutions tailored to their unique requirements.

Perimeter Security Policy

The company already has perimeter configuration guidelines that are implemented within the organization. However, these guidelines were never documented in an organized fashion. The staff members at Company-C create a detailed perimeter security policy.

Device Security Policy

Just as with perimeter security, the company already has device configuration guidelines that are implemented within the organization. However, these guidelines were never documented in an organized fashion. The staff members at Company-C create a detailed device security policy. These devices include infrastructure devices such as routers, switches, and other equipment.

Remote Access VPN Policy

The remote access VPN policy defines the appropriate use of remote access VPN (including IPsec and SSL-based remote access VPNs). The policies include the process of how employees request remote access VPN and how administrators create, modify, and delete remote access accounts. In this case, Company-C uses generic token cards with one-time passwords (OTP) for remote access. When Company-C staff members start developing the remote access VPN policy, they are trying to clarify answers to the following questions:

- Does a remote access security policy exist?

- Is the security policy frequently reviewed and revised to reflect technology changes, outmoded approaches, or new product or service offerings affecting company/ customer relationships and system interaction?

- Does the remote access policy specify guidelines for the selection and implementation mechanisms that control access among authorized users and corporate computers and networks?

- Does the remote access policy conform to all existing corporate communications guidelines?

- Does the remote access policy address the physical protection of the communications medium, devices, computers, and data storage at the remote site?

- Does the security policy require the classification of the functions, applications, and data to determine the levels of security needed to protect the asset?

- Does a policy exist to obtain access to important proprietary information at remote sites?

- Does a policy exist for reporting unauthorized activity?

- Does a policy exist that defines appropriate personal use of company equipment?

- Do remote access users have to sign a form stating they know and understand the remote access policies?

- Is there a formal, complete, and tested disaster recovery plan in place for the remote sites?

Patch Management Policy

The patch management policy establishes requirements for a secure patch management program for all Company-C networks to prevent disruption of service and unauthorized use because of vulnerabilities in unpatched systems. The patch management program shall be used to create a consistently configured environment that ensures security against known vulnerabilities in operating systems and application software. A key component of patch management is the intake and selection of information regarding both security issues and patch release. The patch cycle shall be used to facilitate the application of standard patch releases and updates. This cycle can be time or event based. For example, the schedule can mandate that system updates occur quarterly, or a cycle may be driven by the release of service packs or maintenance releases. Testing of software patches is crucial. Company-C creates a patch test process within this policy. After a patch has been determined valid, it shall be placed in a test environment that closely mirrors the production environment. Critical applications and supported operating platforms must be fully accounted for while testing the patch infrastructure.

Change Management Policy

Change management practices are applied to the patch management process and any other configuration or system changes within the whole infrastructure. After a configuration or a system has been identified for change, a request-for-change must be submitted, and the configuration should be modified according to the procedures that the change management process has established.

Internet Usage Policy

The Internet usage policy allows for reasonable use of the Internet by outlining the permitted and prohibited behaviors and defining violations. This policy should apply to all Internet users who access the Internet through the computing or networking resources. This includes permanent, full-time, and part-time employees; contract workers; temporary agency workers; business partners; and vendors. The Internet users of your organization are expected to be familiar with and to comply with this policy, which should also require the use of common sense and good judgment while using Internet services.

Deploying IPsec Remote Access VPN

Company-C deploys a cluster of Cisco ASAs to provide IPsec remote access VPN services. Figure 12-59 illustrates the topology listing the Cisco ASAs and their corresponding IP addresses.

Figure 12-59 *Remote Access VPN Cisco ASAs*

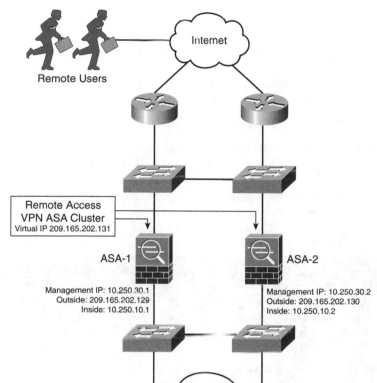

The following are the IP addresses of each interface on the first Cisco ASA (ASA-1):

- **Management interface:** 10.250.30.1
- **Inside interface:** 10.250.10.1
- **Outside interface:** 209.165.202.129

The following are the IP addresses of each interface on the second Cisco ASA (ASA-2):

- **Management interface:** 10.250.30.2
- **Inside interface:** 10.250.10.2
- **Outside interface:** 209.165.202.130

The following sections demonstrate how the Cisco ASAs are configured for IPsec and SSL remote access VPN.

Configuring IPsec Remote Access VPN

The administrator completes the following steps to configure IPsec remote access VPN on the Cisco ASAs:

Step 1 Log in to the Cisco ASA using ASDM.

Step 2 On the main menu, choose **Wizards**.

Step 3 Select the **IPsec VPN Wizard**.

Step 4 The IPsec VPN Wizard starts. Specify the tunnel type as shown in Figure 12-60.

Figure 12-60 *Configuring the Tunnel Type*

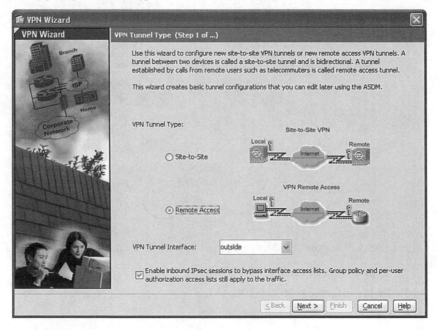

Step 5 All remote access VPN clients will be connecting to the outside interface. Choose the **outside** interface from the **VPN Tunnel Interface** drop-down menu, as shown in Figure 12-60.

Step 6 Enable inbound IPsec sessions to bypass all configured ACLs, as shown in Figure 12-60.

Step 7 Click **Next**.

Step 8 The screen shown in Figure 12-61 is displayed. Under **VPN Client Type**, click **Cisco VPN Client, Release 3.x or higher, or other Easy VPN Remote product**.

Figure 12-61 *Remote Access VPN Client Type*

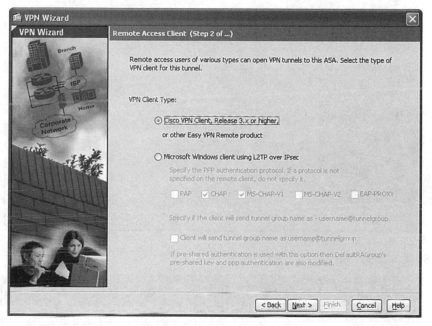

Step 9 Click **Next**.

Step 10 The screen shown in Figure 12-62 is displayed. Configure a preshared key and a VPN tunnel group, as shown in Figure 12-62. In this example, the preshared key is **1qaz2wsx**, and the tunnel group is **IPSEC-RA-GROUP**.

Step 11 Click **Next**.

Step 12 The screen shown in Figure 12-63 is displayed. In this example, the Cisco ASAs are configured for external authentication to a RADIUS server. The AAA server group name is **RADIUS-Server**, as shown in Figure 12-63.

Figure 12-62 *VPN Client Authentication Method and Tunnel Group Name*

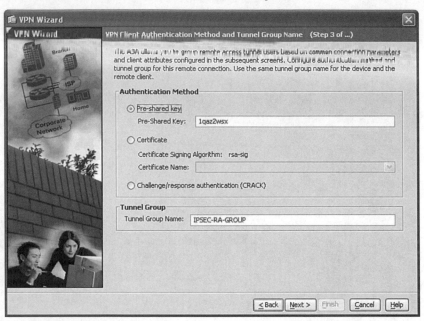

Figure 12-63 *Client Authentication*

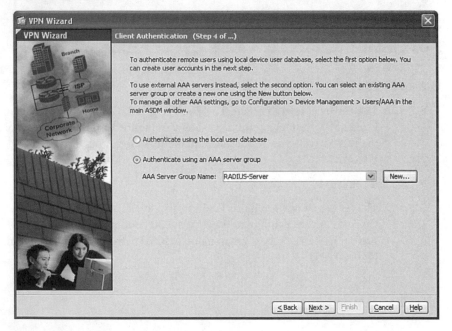

Step 13 Click **Next**.

Step 14 The screen shown in Figure 12-64 is displayed. This screen allows you to configure an IP address pool used for remote access VPN connections. Click **New** to add a new pool.

Figure 12-64 *IPsec Remote Access VPN IP Address Pool*

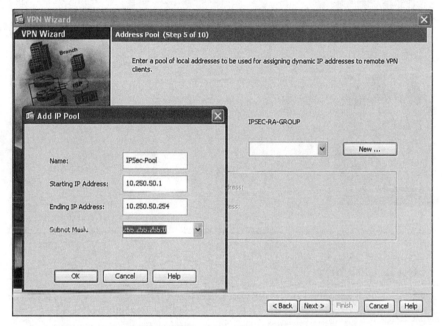

Step 15 Specify a name for the IP address pool. In this example, the name of the pool is **IPSec-Pool**.

Step 16 Configure the starting and ending IP addresses, in addition to a subnet mask. In this example, the address range in the pool is from **10.250.50.1** to **10.250.50.254**, with a 24-bit subnet mask (**255.255.255.0**).

Step 17 Click **Next**.

Step 18 The screen shown in Figure 12-65 is displayed. This screen allows you to configure the primary and secondary DNS and WINS servers, in addition to the domain name. In this example, the primary DNS server is **172.18.124.12**; the secondary DNS server is **172.18.124.13**; the primary WINS server is **172.18.124.14**; and the secondary WINS server is **172.18.124.15**. The domain name is **companyc.com**.

Figure 12-65 *DNS and WINS Server Configuration*

Step 19 Click **Next**.

Step 20 The screen shown in Figure 12-66 is displayed. This screen allows
you to configure the IKE policy used by remote access VPN
connections. In this example, the encryption algorithm used is
AES-256. **SHA** is used for authentication, and the Diffie-Hellman
(DH) group used is **5**.

Step 21 Click **Next**.

Step 22 The screen shown in Figure 12-67 is displayed. This screen allows you
to configure the IPsec encryption and authentication parameters. In this
example, the encryption protocol used is **AES-256**, and **SHA** is used for
IPsec Phase 2 authentication.

Figure 12-66 *Remote Access VPN IKE Policy*

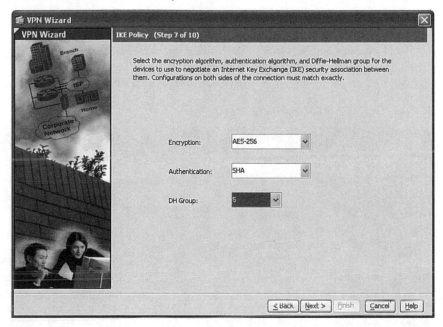

Figure 12-67 *Remote Access VPN IPsec Encryption and Authentication*

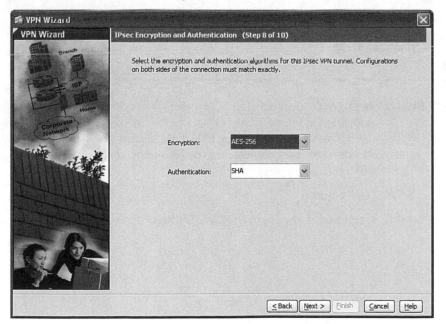

Step 23 Click **Next**.

Step 24 The screen shown in Figure 12-68 is displayed. This screen allows you
to configure the Cisco ASA to bypass NAT for remote access VPN
connections. In this case, the inside network is selected (**10.250.10.0/24**).
The inside 10.250.10.0/24 network will not be translated
when communicating with remote access VPN clients.

Figure 12-68 *Bypassing NAT and Configuring Split Tunneling*

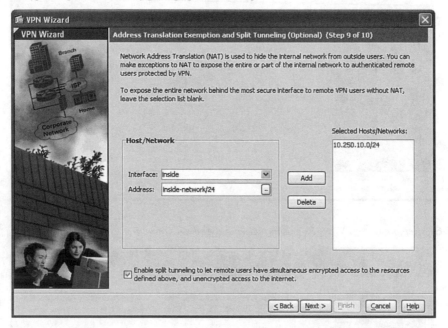

Step 25 The screen shown in Figure 12-68 also allows you to configure split
tunneling for remote access VPN connections. To enable split tunneling,
select **Enable split tunneling** to let remote users have simultaneous
encrypted access to the resources defined earlier, and unencrypted access
to the Internet option.

Step 26 Click **Next**.

Step 27 A summary screen appears. Click **Finish** to apply the changes to the
Cisco ASA.

Configuring Load-Balancing

The administrator configures load-balancing on each security appliance. The following are the steps to configure load-balancing for remote access VPN.

Step 1 Log in to the Cisco ASA using ASDM.

Step 2 On the main menu, choose **Wizards**.

Step 3 Choose the **High Availability and Scalability Wizard**.

Step 4 The High Availability and Scalability Wizard starts. The screen shown in Figure 12-69 is displayed. Click **Configure VPN Cluster Load Balancing,** as shown in Figure 12-69.

Figure 12-69 *High Availability and Scalability Wizard*

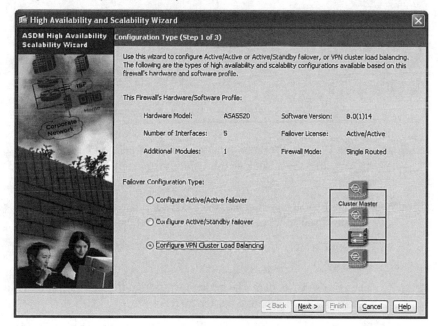

Step 5 Click **Next**.

Step 6 The screen shown in Figure 12-70 is displayed. Enter the cluster IP address. The cluster IP address is the virtual address that VPN clients will use to connect to the cluster. In this example, the cluster IP address is **209.165.202.131**.

Figure 12-70 *VPN Cluster Load-Balancing Configuration*

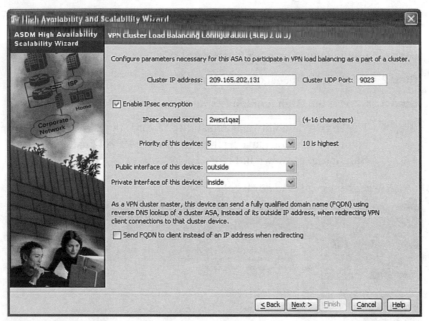

Step 7 Enter a UDP port for load-balancing communication between all Cisco ASAs within the cluster. In this example, the default UDP port (**9023**) is used.

Step 8 Optionally, you can encrypt all VPN load-balancing traffic. Check the **Enable IPsec encryption** option to enable encryption.

Step 9 Configure a preshared secret. In this example, the preshared secret is **2wsx1qaz**.

Step 10 The priority is set to **5**. The higher the priority, the more commonly that this ASA will become the master of the cluster.

Step 11 The public interface is the **outside** interface in this example. The private interface is the **inside** interface, as shown in Figure 12-70.

Step 12 Click **Next**.

Step 13 A summary screen is displayed.

Step 14 Click **Finish** to apply the configuration to the Cisco ASA.

Example 12-13 shows the Cisco ASA remote access VPN and load-balancing CLI configuration.

Example 12-13 *Cisco ASA Remote Access VPN and Load-Balancing Configuration*

```
hostname asa-1
!
interface GigabitEthernet0/0
 description Outside interface connected to the Internet
 nameif outside
 security-level 0
 ip address 209.165.202.129 255.255.255.0
!
interface GigabitEthernet0/1
 description Inside interface connected to corporate network
 nameif inside
 security-level 100
 ip address 10.250.10.1 255.255.255.0
!
interface Management0/0
 nameif management
 security-level 0
 ip address 10.250.30.1 255.255.255.0
 management-only
!
!Split tunneling ACL
access-list IPSEC-RA-GROUP_splitTunnelAcl standard permit 10.250.10.0 255.255.255.0
!ACL to bypass NAT for remote access VPN connections
access-list inside_nat0_outbound extended permit ip 10.250.10.0 255.255.255.0
  10.250.50.0 255.255.255.0
 !
 !IP address pool for remote access VPN clients
ip local pool IPSec-Pool 10.250.50.1-10.250.50.254 mask 255.255.255.0
!
!NAT configuration
nat (inside) 0 access-list inside_nat0_outbound
!
!RADIUS Configuration for remote access VPN authentication
aaa-server RADIUS-Server protocol radius
aaa-server RADIUS-Server (management) host 172.18.85.181
 timeout 5
 key cisco123
!
!Crypto map configuration
crypto ipsec transform-set ESP-AES-256-SHA esp-aes-256 esp-sha-hmac
crypto dynamic-map SYSTEM_DEFAULT_CRYPTO_MAP 65535 set transform-set ESP-AES-256-
  SHA
crypto map outside_map 65535 ipsec-isakmp dynamic SYSTEM_DEFAULT_CRYPTO_MAP
crypto map outside_map interface outside
```

continues

Example 12-13 *Cisco ASA Remote Access VPN and Load-Balancing Configuration (Continued)*

```
!
!IOAKMP enabled on the outside interface
crypto isakmp enable outside
!ISAKMP policy for Remote Access VPN
crypto isakmp policy 10
 authentication pre-share
 encryption aes-256
 hash sha
 group 5
 lifetime 86400
!
!Load-balancing Configuration
vpn load-balancing
 cluster key 2wsx1qaz
 cluster ip address 209.165.202.131
 cluster encryption
 participate
!
!Remote Access Group Configuration
group-policy IPSEC-RA-GROUP internal
group-policy IPSEC-RA-GROUP attributes
 wins-server value 172.18.124.14 172.18.124.15
 dns-server value 172.18.124.12 172.18.124.13
 vpn-tunnel-protocol IPSec
 split-tunnel-policy tunnelspecified
 split-tunnel-network-list value IPSEC-RA-GROUP_splitTunnelAcl
 default-domain value companyc.com
tunnel-group IPSEC-RA-GROUP type remote-access
tunnel-group IPSEC-RA-GROUP general-attributes
 address-pool IPSec-Pool
 authentication-server-group RADIUS-Server
 default-group-policy IPSEC-RA-GROUP
tunnel-group IPSEC-RA-GROUP ipsec-attributes
 pre-shared-key *
```

Reacting to a Security Incident

It is 4:00 a.m. (0400) on Christmas day, and the CSIRT team hotline rings with a call from one of the database administrators. The network is congested, and no transactions are possible to the most critical application in the organization from different sections of the organization. The CSIRT collects all available information from the database administrator and completes the steps described in the following sections.

Identifying, Classifying, and Tracking the Security Incident or Attack

One of the members of the CSIRT collects NetFlow data from the data center distribution switch and correlates this data with CS-MARS. He notices that most of the traffic is HTTP (TCP port 80). This traffic is originating from known sources in the sales department (floor) in the New York office and from unknown sources. The CSIRT team works with a network administrator and discovers that the unknown sources are IP addresses belonging to the Atlanta branch office network. However, this process took almost an hour.

Reacting to the Incident

The CSIRT team works with the network administrators in the Atlanta and New York offices to configure an ACL on the router in the Atlanta office and a VACL on the access switch in the sales floor. This ACL only blocks HTTP traffic from the offending machines. The malicious traffic has been contained, but it is possible that other machines have been infected.

The CSIRT team works with the desktop support group and server administrators. After doing research and forensics on the traffic, they discover that the traffic pattern is similar to a published vulnerability on security intelligence sites such as Cisco Security Center and US-CERT. However, their network IPS and other mechanisms were not able to detect the threat because the necessary signatures were not installed.

The server administrators and desktop support representatives download a security patch from the operating system vendor. Subsequently, they install this operating system patch on the affected machines. They also push this update via their patch management system to all machines within the organization. In addition, the correct signatures are installed on the IPS systems within the organization.

Postmortem

The CSIRT creates a postmortem including the following information:

- Total amount of labor spent working on the incident
- Elapsed time from the beginning of the incident to its resolution
- Elapsed time for each stage of the incident-handling process
- Time it took the incident response team to respond to the initial report of the incident
- Estimated monetary damage from the incident
- Lessons learned
- Action plan

The lessons learned section in the postmortem is documented, including all items that will improve the incident response process and the proactive preparation of resources and processes to better defend against new threats. In this example, the following are areas that should be improved and are taken into an action plan:

- The incident identification process was successful because the correct tools and mechanisms were in place. However, the identification of the Atlanta office IP address space was not obvious, and the process was delayed for more than an hour. Better documentation and diagrams should be prepared to avoid this in the future. The CSIRT team, in addition to network administrators, should have this information accessible when responding to an attack.

- IPS signatures were not upgraded because of a bad tuning and update process. A new process is developed to address this caveat.

- ACLs were deployed manually to contain and mitigate the attack. The network engineering teams will evaluate and create other tools and technologies, such as remotely triggered black holes (RTBH) or more appropriate mechanisms, to quarantine infected sources in a more effective fashion.

Each item on this action plan is assigned an owner and a due date.

Summary

This chapter covered three case studies: a small business, a medium-sized enterprise, and a large enterprise. It demonstrated some of the most common applications and procedures discussed within this book. However, each of the previous chapters presented detailed instructions on how to proactively and reactively defend against security threats.

Various configuration examples were included in this chapter. The examples included infrastructure protection mechanisms and practices, basic firewall configuration, site-to-site and remote access VPNs, and a basic example of a CSIRT responding to a security incident. Security threats such as distributed denial of service (DDoS) attacks, worms, and others can result in significant loss of time and money for many organizations. It is highly recommended that you consider the extent to which the organization could afford a significant service outage and take steps commensurate with the risk.

The network security lifecycle requires specialized support and a commitment to best practice standards. In this book, you learned best practices drawn upon disciplined processes, frameworks, expert advice, and proven technologies that will help you protect your infrastructure and organization. You learned the complete security lifecycle of a network, from strategy development to operations and optimization. You must take a proactive approach to security, an approach that starts with an assessment to identify and categorize your risks. In addition, you need to understand the network security technical details relating to security policy and incident response procedures. This book covered numerous best practices that will help you orchestrate a long-term strategy for your organization.

INDEX

Numerics

802.1x, 219
    access layer (IP telephony), 271
    authentication negotiation schemes, 220
    authenticators, 26
    components of, 219
    configuring Secure ACS Servers, 229, 232–233
    configuring with EAP-FAST in Unified
        Wireless Solutions, 226
    EAP methods, 220–221
    IEEE 802.1x, 26
    supplicants, 26

A

AAA
    identity and trust (SAVE framework), 183–184
    infrastructure devices, configuring
        medium-sized business case studies,
            400–401
**AAA (Authentication, Authorization,
Accounting), 23**
    identity management solutions/systems, 26
        IBNS, 26
        IEEE 802.1x, 26
    RADIUS, 23, 25
    TACACS+, 25
aaa authorization command, 65
aaa new-model command, 65
access control
    small business case study, 352
access layer (IP telephony), 265, 272
    802.1x, 271
    ARP, 270
    BPDU, 268
    DAI, 270
    DHCP snooping, 269–270
    NAC, 271
    port security, 268–269
    root guards, 268
    VLAN assignment, 267

access-class command
    interactive access control (infrastructure
        security), 62
accounting, 23
ACL
    blocking unauthorized hosts/users from routers,
        6
    exception ACL, configuring, 64
ACL (Access Control Lists), 157
    controlling FWSM access via, 317–321
    iACL (infrastructure Access Control Lists)
        infrastructure security policy enforcement,
          82
    IPv6 filtering, 331–332
    rACL (receive Access Control Lists)
        infrastructure security, 78–80
    VACL, 157
action plans, building, 173–174
active-standby failovers
    ASA, configuring on
        medium-sized business case studies,
          394–396, 398–399
**AES (Advanced Encryption Standard)
encryption protocol**
    WEP, 218
AIP-SSM
    ASA, configuring on
        medium-sized business case studies,
          391–394
Aironet AP (Access Points)
    managing, 216
analyzing data
    postmortems, 169
anomaly detection
    IPS devices, 137–138
    visibility (SAVE framework), 190
anomaly detection systems, 22
anomaly detection zones
    isolation and virtualization (SAVE framework),
        198
anomaly/telemetry detection
    CS-MARS, 121–122, 125
    Guard XT, 127, 129–131
    IPS, 137–138
    NAM, 125–126

D

E

SEARCH THOUSANDS OF BOOKS FROM LEADING PUBLISHERS

Safari® Bookshelf is a searchable electronic reference library for IT professionals that features more than 2,000 titles from technical publishers, including Cisco Press.

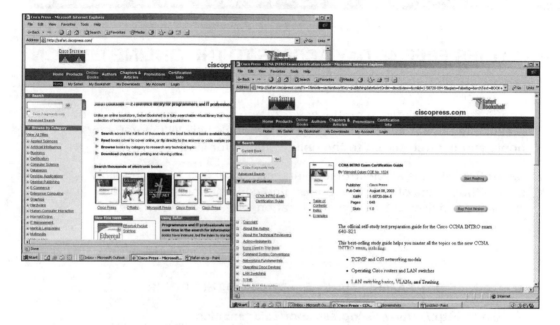

With Safari Bookshelf you can

- **Search** the full text of thousands of technical books, including more than 70 Cisco Press titles from authors such as Wendell Odom, Jeff Doyle, Bill Parkhurst, Sam Halabi, and Karl Solie.

- **Read** the books on My Bookshelf from cover to cover, or just flip to the information you need.

- **Browse** books by category to research any technical topic.

- **Download** chapters for printing and viewing offline.

With a customized library, you'll have access to your books when and where you need them—and all you need is a user name and password.

TRY SAFARI BOOKSHELF FREE FOR 14 DAYS!

You can sign up to get a 10-slot Bookshelf free for the first 14 days.
Visit **http://safari.ciscopress.com** to register.

BOOKS ONLINE

ENABLED

THIS BOOK IS SAFARI ENABLED

INCLUDES FREE 45-DAY ACCESS TO THE ONLINE EDITION

The Safari® Enabled icon on the cover of your favorite technology book means the book is available through Safari Bookshelf. When you buy this book, you get free access to the online edition for 45 days.

Safari Bookshelf is an electronic reference library that lets you easily search thousands of technical books, find code samples, download chapters, and access technical information whenever and wherever you need it.

TO GAIN 45-DAY SAFARI ENABLED ACCESS TO THIS BOOK:

- Go to **http://www.ciscopress.com/safarienabled**

- Complete the brief registration form

- Enter the coupon code found in the front of this book before the "Contents at a Glance" page

If you have difficulty registering on Safari Bookshelf or accessing the online edition, please e-mail customer-service@safaribooksonline.com.

CISCO SYSTEMS

Cisco Press

3 STEPS TO LEARNING

STEP 1

First-Step

STEP 2

Fundamentals

STEP 3

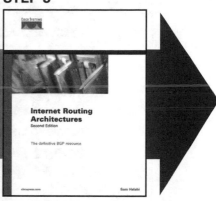

**Networking
Technology Guides**

STEP 1 **First-Step**—Benefit from easy-to-grasp explanations.
No experience required!

STEP 2 **Fundamentals**—Understand the purpose, application,
and management of technology.

STEP 3 **Networking Technology Guides**—Gain the knowledge
to master the challenge of the network.

NETWORK BUSINESS SERIES

The Network Business series helps professionals tackle the
business issues surrounding the network. Whether you are a
seasoned IT professional or a business manager with minimal
technical expertise, this series will help you understand the
business case for technologies.

Justify Your Network Investment.

Look for Cisco Press titles at your favorite bookseller today.

Visit **www.ciscopress.com/series** for details on each of these book series.

CISCO SYSTEMS

Cisco Press

SAVE UP TO 30%

Become a member and save at **ciscopress.com**!

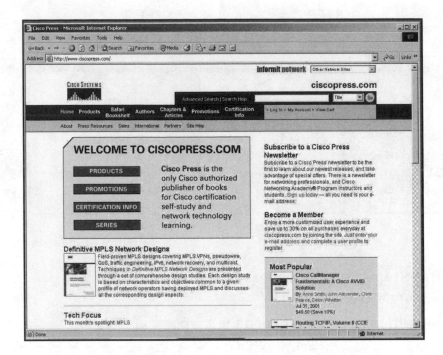

Complete a **user profile** at ciscopress.com today to become a member and benefit from **discounts up to 30% on every purchase** at ciscopress.com, as well as a more customized user experience. Your membership will also allow you access to the entire Informit network of sites.

Don't forget to subscribe to the monthly Cisco Press newsletter to be the first to learn about new releases and special promotions. You can also sign up to get your first **30 days FREE on Safari Bookshelf** and preview Cisco Press content. Safari Bookshelf lets you access Cisco Press books online and build your own customized, searchable electronic reference library.

Visit **www.ciscopress.com/register** to sign up and start saving today!

The profile information we collect is used in aggregate to provide us with better insight into your technology interests and to create a better user experience for you. You must be logged into ciscopress.com to receive your discount. Discount is on Cisco Press products only; shipping and handling are not included.

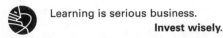

Learning is serious business.
Invest wisely.